The Rhetorics of Life-Writing in Early Modern Europe

STUDIES IN MEDIEVAL AND EARLY MODERN CIVILIZATION
Marvin B. Becker, General Editor

Charity and Children in Renaissance Florence:
The Ospedale degli Innocenti, 1410–1536
  Philip Gavitt

Humanism in Crisis: The Decline of the French Renaissance
  Philippe Desan, editor

Upon My Husband's Death: Widows in the Literature
and Histories of Medieval Europe
  Louise Mirrer, editor

The Crannied Wall: Women, Religion, and the Arts
in Early Modern Europe
  Craig A. Monson, editor

The Rhetorics of Life-Writing in Early Modern Europe:
Forms of Biography from Cassandra Fedele to Louis XIV
  Thomas F. Mayer and D. R. Woolf, editors

The Rhetorics of Life-Writing in Early Modern Europe

*Forms of Biography
from Cassandra Fedele to Louis XIV*

edited by
THOMAS F. MAYER
AND
D. R. WOOLF

Ann Arbor
THE UNIVERSITY OF MICHIGAN PRESS

Copyright © by the University of Michigan 1995
All rights reserved
Published in the United States of America by
The University of Michigan Press
Manufactured in the United States of America
⊗ Printed on acid-free paper

1998 1997 1996 1995   4 3 2 1

A CIP catalogue record for this book is available from the British Library.

Library of Congress Cataloging-in-Publication Data

The rhetorics of life—writing in early modern Europe : forms of
  biography from Cassandra Fedele to Louis XIV / edited by Thomas F.
  Mayer and D. R. Woolf.
    p. cm. — (Studies in medieval and early modern civilization)
  Includes bibliographical references and index.
  ISBN 0-472-10591-4 (alk. paper)
  1. Biography as a literary form. 2. Europe—Biography—History
and criticism. I. Mayer, Thomas F. (Thomas Frederick), 1951– .
II. Woolf, D. R. (Daniel R.) III. Series.
CT21.R52 1995
808'.06692—dc20   95-1859
                                                              CIP

Preface

The idea for this volume arose while Thomas Mayer was visiting the Dalhousie University Late Medieval and Early Modern Studies Colloquium in January 1990, and the first draft of the introduction was written during Daniel Woolf's tenure as the Humanities Fund Visiting Professor at Augustana College in January 1992. The editors would like to thank the Humanities Fund and Faculty Research Fund of Augustana College, the Faculty of Arts and Social Sciences Travel Fund of Dalhousie University, and the Social Sciences and Humanities Research Council of Canada for their material support of this project. We are also grateful to the Sixteenth Century Studies Conference and to its 1990–91 president Brian G. Armstrong for offering us a venue at which earlier versions of most of these chapters could be aired. The comments and encouragement received there, especially from James Michael Weiss, Charles Nauert, Robert Schnucker, and other members of the audiences have greatly strengthened the collection. Critical readings of the introduction by the various contributors were very helpful, and we would also like to thank, in this connection, Albert R. Ascoli, William J. Connell, John E. Crowley, Ronald Huebert, Cynthia Neville, and Patricia M. Rubin. Gregory Bak, a doctoral candidate at Dalhousie, assisted in the task of compiling the index. Finally, we wish to thank our respective secretaries, Maria Diaz and Jane Tiedge at Augustana and Mary Wyman-Leblanc and Tina Jones at Dalhousie, for assistance in the non-free-trade zone of word processing. The editors and contributors are also extremely grateful for close and critical readings of the manuscript by Arthur J. Slavin and Leonard Barkan; to Joyce Harrison and her successor, Ellen Bauerle, of the University of Michigan Press for encouraging the project at successive stages; to Nancy Vlahakis, also of the Press, for overseeing the production with care and patience; and to Professors Marvin Becker and Michael MacDonald of the University of Michigan for their continued interest in the book. All the above are exculpated from responsibility for any errors that may remain.

Insofar as this book is ours to dedicate, we assign our shares to our families: TFM to Jan Popehn and Molly Mayer-Popehn and DRW to Jane Arscott and Sarah, Samuel, and David Woolf.

Contents

Introduction 1
   Thomas F. Mayer and D. R. Woolf

1. Paolo Giovio and the Rhetoric of Individuality 39
   T. C. Price Zimmermann

2. Giorgio Vasari's *Vita di Michelangelo Buonarroti*
and the Shade of Donatello 63
   Barbara J. Watts

3. Burying the Brethren: Lutheran Funeral Sermons
as Life-Writing 97
   Robert Kolb

4. "With Friends Like This...": The Biography of
Philip Melanchthon by Joachim Camerarius 115
   Timothy J. Wengert

5. Manipulating Reputations: Sir Thomas More, Sir
Thomas Elyot, and the Conclusion of William
Roper's *Lyfe of Sir Thomas Moore, Knighte* 133
   F. W. Conrad

6. Characterizations of the "Obscure Men" of
Cologne: A Study in Pre-Reformation
Collective Authorship 163
   James V. Mehl

7. Cassandra Fedele's *Epistolae* (1488–1521):
Biography as Ef-facement 187
   Diana Robin

viii   Contents

8. A Sticking-Plaster Saint? Autobiography and
   Hagiography in the Making of Reginald Pole 205
   Thomas F. Mayer

9. A Protestant Poetics of Process:
   Reformation Rhetorics of the Self in Sponde,
   de Bèze, and d'Aubigné 223
   Catharine Randall

10. The Rhetoric of Martyrdom: Generic
    Contradiction and Narrative Strategy in
    John Foxe's *Acts and Monuments* 243
    D. R. Woolf

11. Montaigne's *Essais:* The Literary and Literal
    Digesting of a Life 283
    William E. Engel

12. Whose Life Is It, Anyway? Subject and Subjection
    in Fulke Greville's *Life Of Sidney* 299
    Adriana McCrea

13. Exemplarity and Gender: Three Lives of Queen
    Catherine de' Medici 321
    Sheila ffolliott

14. The Politics and Poetics of the Mancini
    Romance: Visions and Revisions of the Life
    of Louis XIV 341
    Elizabeth C. Goldsmith and Abby E. Zanger

Contributors 373

Index 377

Introduction

Thomas F. Mayer and D. R. Woolf

Perfect history is of three kinds, according to the object which it propounds for representation. For it either represents a portion of time, or a person worthy of mention, or an action or exploit of the nobler sort. The first we call Chronicles or Annals; the second, Lives; the third, Narrations or Relations.... Lives, if they be well and carefully written (for I do not speak of elegies and barren commemorations of that sort), propounding to themselves a single person as their subject, in whom actions both trifling and important, great and small, public and private, must needs be united and mingled, certainly contain a more lively and faithful representation of things [than in chronicles], and one which you may more safely and happily take for example in another case. (Francis Bacon, *De augmentis scientiarum*)

In treating life-writing as a subgenre of history, Francis Bacon was at one with most of his contemporaries and most life-writers and historians before him.[1] In stressing that a life had to be well written (and in distinguishing it from elegy and commemorative addresses), Bacon emphasized the rhetorical dimension of life-writing, again in common with historians and biographers before him. Finally, by putting a "lively and faithful representation" of a life to the service of example, he assigned life-writing its traditional moral and didactic function. For all this, Bacon distanced himself from most previous life-writing when he noted later that all history dealt with men's actions, not their words, even though these might sometimes be included in order to "contribute to the perspicuity and weight of the narrative." Bacon's own biography of Henry VII, however, has not enjoyed the esteem of many subsequent historians, often for not being factual ("perspicuous and weighty," we might say) enough.

Thus, Bacon balanced his assessment and practice of life-writing on an edge between earlier writers who easily assumed both the value and the place of the genre, to speak a little loosely for the moment, and the more modern assessment of it as, at best, a stepchild of real history or, in the case of literature, real criticism. As history and literature have increasingly parted company since the Enlightenment, they have left life-writing suspended between them, a bastard child that neither wishes to claim. (Art history, the third discipline represented in this collection, poses an exception to this generalization, since it has been organized from its inception in terms of "lives of the artists.")[2]

To judge from two recent National Endowment for the Humanities summer seminars and two discussions of teaching biography in the American Historical Association's *Perspectives,* this situation has begun to change as, on the one hand, interest in individual lives and their description picks up among historians, and, on the other, literary critics give increasing attention to ways in which life-writing is organized and how its texts function. Even prominent Annalistes, whose commitment to the *longue durée* once automatically ruled single human lifespans out of consideration, have begun to reconsider.[3] Recently, theorists have applied techniques developed for reading literary texts to life-writing, with promising results.[4] For us, we wish to sit firmly between these two stools, emphasizing the permanently problematic dynamic in life-writing of the fit between real (that is, extratextual) lives and their representation in texts of various kinds. The difficulties along this face of life-writing, of sorting out fact and fiction, largely account for historians' reluctance to mine it. That literary biographers have usually weighed in on the fact side of the balance has probably only served to reinforce historians' prejudices. More recent critics' attention to the surfaces of life-writing may well smack so much of the dreaded deconstruction as to reinforce the lack of interest displayed both by historians and by conservative-minded life-writers in other disciplines.

Yet these surfaces ought to be the crucial locus of attention, as they were for Bacon, as they were for all writers trained in rhetoric.[5] Depths there might well be, lives outside texts there certainly were, but the object of interest remained the text, together with its persuasive impact on its readers. Thus, any attempt to test the reality of any particular representation had to take account of the form in which it was cast. Probably, as Thomas Heffernan suggests in the case of medieval "sacred biography," many readers unconsciously performed this correction, acting on shared cultural perceptions that bridged the gap between text and world.[6] Undoubtedly, keeping the web seamless became steadily more difficult in the Renaissance, as writers became adept at (and aware of) more self-consciously rhetorical forms of constructing texts. Thus, the taken-for-granted purpose of most life-writing, exemplarity, became increasingly problematic as later humanism began to appreciate that ancient examples could, in fact, be "less than exemplary," either frustratingly inapplicable or embarrassingly inappropriate.[7] Rhetoric itself appeared to lose its power to persuade as the community of readers, which Heffernan—following Hans-Georg Gadamer—posits as crucial to the interpretation of texts, became ever more divided.[8]

The consequences of this development for historians and critics on this side of the great divide have been frequently observed.[9] Put most bluntly, rhetoric gets in the way of the "real" story. This is somewhat less true for scholars of the Renaissance and seventeenth century who can scarcely ignore the fact that, in their period, rhetoric *was* the way, but it is still largely the case. One need only think of one of the most compelling and subtle recent analyses of some of the central problems of identity and hence of life-writing, Stephen Greenblatt's construct of "self-fashioning," which depends on looking past the surfaces. The same is true of similarly sophisticated and influential efforts by historians, for example, Natalie Zemon Davis's *The Return of Martin Guerre* or, even more clearly, Carlo Ginzburg's *The Cheese and the Worms*.[10] (In fairness, the microhistory [*microstoria*] both Davis and Ginzburg practice has served as a major catalyst for the return to individual lives, albeit exotic ones; by the same token, the recent reaction, triggered in some instances by this same "school," against history written exclusively from nonliterary sources also helps to renew interest in the highly literary forms of life-writing.)[11] In all these cases, the contained, the life, is infinitely more significant than the container, the life-writing. This approach, especially among students of literature, descends in large measure from the work of Kenneth Burke, for whom rhetoric was of the essence, but the essence (or substance) was still what counted most.[12]

Among historians, and to some extent literary critics, placing the rhetoric of historical texts in high relief conjures up the names of Hayden White and Dominick LaCapra. Of late, White's formulation of how historical texts work has poked its nose under the tent of biographical theory. According to White and now to Ira Nadel, any historical or biographical text depends on what Burke called "four master tropes": metaphor, metonymy, synecdoche, and irony. No text can work without them, and, White would say, no historian can do *anything*—inside a text or out—without them. Any object of investigation is always already constituted by the linguistic preconceptions a historian shares with his or her culture. Events in themselves, whether of a single life or of a collection of them, have no meaning. (This is a possibility Burke excludes by definition.) They acquire it only through being cast into the form of a story, after the fact. Such is history. White is ambivalent about this state of affairs, but Nadel embraces it, claiming that these tropes provide the coherence necessary to make a life or lives into a story.[13]

Although Nadel's book marks a large advance on most previous theory, it still tends in the direction of the life itself rather than treating the text itself as an object worthy of independent investigation. This is assuredly the way that historians have traditionally treated life-writing, that is, in terms of the correspondence between it and the life. We, by contrast, are concerned less with the accuracy of any biographical or autobiographical representation than with the manner of its presentation—with some of the ways, as one recent writer has put it, that "culture ... intervenes between the writer and the text."[14] Historiographers have long concentrated on the early modern contribution to historical scholarship and, in particular, to the use of documents. This positivist understanding of the advance of historiography, which animates most general works on the subject, including those of Arnaldo Momigliano, also informs accounts such as Eric Cochrane's or the seminal books on sixteenth-century French historical thought by Donald R. Kelley, Julian Franklin, and George Huppert.[15] In this volume, it is the rhetoric of life-writing, rather than its research, that stands central: not so much how and with what materials authors and artists constructed lives, but why and in what shapes.[16] As will become clear from many of the essays, the gulf between the life as lived and the life as depicted in text or image can often be great. Early modern life-writers were not engaged in the study of past and present persons for the sake of advancing "pure" historical scholarship and its methods, nor were they intent on establishing biography as a kind of master genre. In virtually every case, the artist or author came to his or her subject with a mind far from neutral or uncommitted, with some fixed ideas both as to what should be written about the subject and the points to be derived therein by the reader or spectator.

A few of us, in common with White and LaCapra, may sometimes appear to threaten the life in the name of the text; any critic of normal historical practice is probably fated to be thus perceived. Yet neither White nor LaCapra loses sight of the dialectic between text and life.[17] Privileging the text works especially clearly in LaCapra's case in order to challenge the easy acceptance of any kind of equivalence between text, document, and extratextual reality. His argument that context is constructed to the same degree as is a text has direct relevance to how life-writing establishes coherence (and to the problem of whether it must).[18] More urgently, LaCapra proposes to restore rhetoric to historiography, but with some notable cautions about how history must move between the two ends of the rhetorical spectrum.[19] These are of vital importance here. First, historians must recognize that "scientific" or "empirical" history (about which Peter Novick has many wise things to say in *That Noble Dream*) depends on a very narrowly conceived kind of rhetoric, but rhetoric nonetheless. This point is now fairly openly acknowledged.[20] LaCapra's second point is less often frankly stated, but it accounts for a good deal of historians' resistance to rhetoric: at the other end of the spectrum, rhetoric cannot be conceived in a narrowly technical sense as an arsenal of purely persuasive techniques, object propaganda.[21] As Paolo Giovio put a similar point in 1534, history and encomium are two different things.[22]

LaCapra offers an extended discussion of the ways in which rhetoric functions in history, all of them instructive. Two are particularly so in the case of life-writing. Rhetoric cannot be reduced to "utilitarian, workaday, and instrumental" language. Hence epideictic rhetoric—the rhetoric of praise and blame to which Giovio was referring and the bread and butter of any Renaissance rhetorician—always puts pressure on any attempt to read texts only as information containers.[23] But rather than abandon the attempt to make sense of such texts, as was the traditional response to this problem, LaCapra posits a "contestation" between the "playful" (to impose on him a term borrowed from Richard Lanham) language of epideictic and "serious" forms of argument. These were customarily and automatically combined in the Renaissance. Further, in common with White, LaCapra urges more attention to rhetoric as a means of making manifest historians' ideology, rather than as a means of masking it. This, unlike the first point, might well mean reversing usual early modern practice.

Taking full account of LaCapra's second point also means that we intend neither to harness one or the other of two powerful motors behind the current interest in lives, both of which explicitly construct their objects for ideological reasons, nor to enter directly the debate about the nature of Renaissance selves or identity.[24] Although several of our contributors raise anew the old question of Renaissance "individualism," they also show, unlike Burckhardt—for whom that construct carried a heavy ideological freight—that it must be treated in rhetorical terms.[25] Among Burckhardt's theses, the one connected with the place of the individual within the cosmos, as subsequently taken up by countless scholars from Ernst Cassirer and Alfred von Martin to Agnes Heller and, most recently, William Kerrigan and Gordon Braden, has proved perhaps the most controversial, yet also the most durable.[26]

Much of this work, as in Burckhardt's original, is unclear about its presuppositions, above all individualism itself. Some of our essays put forward reservations about this concept, which seems particularly ill suited to the representation of early modern women.[27] At the same time as we raise such problems, and as virtually all of our essays explore ways in which texts create coherence, we assume no particular ideological reason why either the specific form of coherence associated with individualism or coherence of a more general kind might be necessary. A renewed emphasis on lives as coherences happens to fit especially closely both the agenda of the so-called new communitarians and those who would restore individualism to historical practice.[28] That two such ideologically nearly opposite movements as Burckhardtian cultural (and political) conservatism and the vaguely leftist new communitarians should display strong interest in individual lives suggests that the texts that represent them should have a virtually limitless plasticity. This, if nothing else, our essays demonstrate.[29]

This volume moves between LaCapra's two poles. Some essayists pay detailed attention to the technical rhetorical strategies by which Renaissance and Reformation writers constructed their texts (Zimmermann, Kolb, Wengert, Conrad, Mehl). Others take a large view of rhetoric as coming close to what has come to be called "poetics," that is, all the principles by which a text might be organized (one or two essayists play so much with this notion as to introduce other kinds of life-writing than the purely literary). We deploy a similar range of understandings of the probably unavoidable category of genre, at the same time as we offer a demonstration that it, like rhetoric, has little interpretive power if narrowly conceived.[30] Analysis in terms of fairly traditional generic labels, comedy and tragedy, for example, sheds much light in two of our essays on martyrology (Randall, Woolf), even if the period witnessed the blending of these two into one of the most notoriously unreadable genres, tragicomedy.[31] We also bring out the degree to which the late Renaissance experimented with genres *avant la lettre;* their formalization was a long, painfully combative process, and not just in the case of epic poetry or dialogue.[32] Our essays further describe the wide-open climate of experimentation in yet another realm of early modern literature. And as Robert Kolb's essay on Lutheran funeral orations implies, that process depended on larger social and political processes.[33]

Lack of terms is no certain proof of the absence of things, but the fact that no society prior to the middle of the seventeenth century developed a word for "biography" supports our argument about the instability of genre. Despite the existence of the hellenistic term *bios* to describe life-focused historical writing, *biografia, biographie,* and such are later additions to the Italian and French vocabulary, just as *biography* appears only in eighteenth-century English. Bacon, who perhaps came closest to formalizing generic rules, called his third domain merely "lives." This bespeaks fuzziness of thinking less than it suggests that humanist life-writing was not sufficiently formalized to be considered under the rubric of a single genre, hence Bacon's strong feeling that the bounds needed to be beaten between life-writing and other varieties of historical narrative. For that reason alone, any attempt to understand the nature of life-writing during and after the Renaissance must steer clear of generic prisons while nonetheless remaining cognizant of certain constrictions of form, in part descended from ancient models.

Eric Cochrane, following in the footsteps of Eduard Fueter, recognized the overlap between biography and history in his magisterial survey of Renaissance Italian historiography, published little over a decade ago; yet both Fueter and Cochrane elected to regard biography, with antiquities, as a "lateral" (and implicitly less important) genre.[34] There is unquestionably much "history," in the sense of concern with deeds beyond the immediate biographical subject, in Antonio Beccadelli's (better known as Il Panormita) *De dictis et factis Alphonsi regis Aragonum et Neapolis* (Sayings and deeds of Alfonso, king of the Aragonese and Neapolitans) written in 1455 and modeled either on Xenophon or Valerius Maximus; and even more in a rival history, written at about the same time and in a form approved by the subject himself, Bartolomeo Facio's *De rebus gestis ab Alphonso primo Neapolitanorum rege commentariorum libri decem* (Ten books of commentaries on the acts of

Alfonso the first, king of the Neapolitans).³⁵ Conversely, one can find little gems of "biography" lurking in such wider-ranging books as Machiavelli's *Istorie fiorentine*. Machiavelli's sketch of Cosimo il Vecchio's life and character both drew on and made more famous Cosimo's witty remarks, immortalizing the speaker more than his subject.³⁶ One of the goals of the present volume is to challenge, without utterly discarding, formalist and generic distinctions, and to show the great variety of ways in which not simply prose biographers or historians, but also painters, poets, dramatists, preachers, and martyrologists took lives, individual and collective, as their concern.

One major generic distinction we work to subvert is the hoary one between biography and autobiography, life-writing by someone other than the subject as distinct from a recreation by the subject's own hand.³⁷ For one thing, as Judith H. Anderson pointed out in the case of Thomas More, his biographers readily adopted his own image of himself, however they might have rearranged its presentation to suit their purposes.³⁸ This was also true of a biographer of More whom Anderson does not consider, Reginald Pole. It might therefore be best to speak in terms of collective authorship in both the first (autobiographical) and the second (biographical) instance. For another, since Pole deliberately fed his biographers his view of himself, this raises the problem of intention, an issue also raised in connection with Lorenzo de' Medici.³⁹ This is also central to the study of the explicitly collective authorship—in comic rather than tragic mode—of the *Letters of Obscure Men*. We thus go a long way toward endorsing Jonathan Crewe's insistence that Michel Foucault's criticism of the idea of an "author" marks "an irrevocable critical advance," as well as toward bringing Philippe Lejeune's conceptions of more modern autobiography back to the Renaissance.⁴⁰ Not only does Lejeune specifically use the case of "collaborative autobiography" to raise questions of author/ity, but he argues that autobiography, as a form of discourse, is historically variable. We also, in a small way, imitate Lejeune's vast project to survey the forms of autobiography in the nineteenth century, offering several studies of its variability in the Renaissance (Mayer, Robin).⁴¹

How ever we may deform the notion of genre, we certainly consider a number of *modes* of representation, including the visual and plastic arts. The question of their relation in eighteenth-century life-writing has recently been elegantly put by Richard Wendorf, and much of his interpretation could strike sparks in earlier periods: it is worth recalling that

Petrarch composed the final version of his *De viris illustribus,* the earliest humanist effort at collective biography, on behalf of a despot, Francesco da Carrara, who planned to surround himself with portraits of the famous immortalized in Petrarch's work.[42] The relation of literature (including history) and the sister arts certainly consumed a good deal of theoretical discussion from the Renaissance to the eighteenth century.[43] Giovio, creator of both universal history and individual biographies (free-standing and collected) as well as one of the first celebrated museums of portraits of famous persons, again provides a perfect instance.[44]

In terms of both method and content, our essays are deliberately eclectic. In the first place, given its relative neglect in the recent past, we have attempted merely to survey some of the many forms of life-writing. Second, that survey has led us to realize how central life-writing was as a mode of organizing experience, and we redoubled our resolve to be as inclusive as possible. Casting our net broadly also reveals the vital importance of a comparative approach, across national lines (as is increasingly usual in studies of this period), across generic boundaries, and across disciplinary frontiers. We sketch some of the results of overstepping all three.

We hope to make contributions in three major areas. Above all, our essays ought to direct attention to the problematic dialectic between container and contained (to use Burke's language): neither is simply and uncomplicatedly a synecdoche (or a metonymy, to state the worst case) for the other, as most life-writers and many students of the form are guilty of believing. Thus, a major question of the relation between text and life arises, as well as the subsidiary problem of which came first. Once the dialectic between text and life comes to be seen as not automatically reversible, as it was for Burke, then questions about the relation of individual events to overall plot may be profitably raised.[45]

Second, we suggest that the surfaces of texts, their rhetoric and form, provide information as valuable as the extratextual reality life-writing is often supposed to represent. That is, the mode of perception reflected in the organization of information may have as much value as the information organized, particularly to the study of early modern culture.[46] Thus, by examining surfaces both in their own right and as a representation of something beyond them, we can more than double the amount of information we can get from and about the texts of life-writing.

This latter problem of cultural perception raises yet a third of periodization. We have referred to the era covered by our essays under the colorless but inclusive rubric "early modern," rather than Renaissance, because most deal with the tail end of the Renaissance and with its Reformation and Counter-Reformation aftermaths rather than with its classical period (from, say, 1300 to 1500). Several essays, Catharine Randall's in particular, explicitly raise further questions of periodization. We would argue that although we may appear to have played fast and loose with established labels, we have not grossly misused them; many of the hallmarks of both the Renaissance and the Reformation we find to be present at later times. Then, too, all historical periods are hopelessly inadequate. As Burke pointed out, that may be because they have been misconceived. Instead of thinking of them as totalizing entities, all the elements of which must be subsumed into a unity with a beginning and an end, it might prove more useful to substitute for periods what Burke called "historical characters," which "never... begin or end, but rather... change in intensity or poignancy."[47] This recipe for ironic history is not quite what we have in mind, but, rather, the strong possibility (raised but not explored by Novick) that what changes over history is cognitive styles, the way humans process and interpret information.[48] That life-writers in the late seventeenth century should approach their materials in much the fashion of their predecessors two hundred years earlier, in an allegedly different epoch, makes a plausible case for this proposition. It also depends on a more manageable unit of historical analysis, individual humans, which, not by coincidence, are the usual frame of reference of life-writing. The past is a distant mirror?

Early modern life-writers, in common with most other historians, certainly believed that it was, at the same time as they were highly uncertain about how exactly mirrors worked, how much they reflected and how much they distorted. We hope to offer a few suggestions toward sorting out this ancient conundrum.

Life-writing came to early modern Europe via a variety of channels. The ancients had written lives of great men and, to a lesser extent, women. Although the Greeks were, as John Garraty once suggested, more interested in the lives of collectives—peoples, armies, fleets—than of any single person, a tradition of Greek biography can nevertheless be traced back to Hellenic times.[49] There are scraps of memoirs such as those of the poet Ion of Chios surviving from the fifth century B.C., and parts of Herodotus and Thucydides have the look of biography, including Pericles's funeral oration. The most commonly cited example of a classical Greek biographer, Xenophon, wrote lives in a variety of forms. In the *Cyropaedia,* he created a semifanciful portrait of the young Cyrus, largely for instructive purposes.[50] His continuation of Thucydides, the *Hellenica,* contains what amounts to a biographical appendix on the Athenian Thirty, and he represented the life and thoughts of Socrates in a number of different tracts that add up to a fragmentary biography (especially in the *Memorabilia*). Finally, Xenophon's *Agesilaus,* perhaps his most rhetorically loaded work, is essentially an encomium of the great Spartan king, composed shortly after its subject's death in 360 B.C.

But ancient biography did not become a major enterprise until the Hellenistic and Roman eras, and then principally in the various collections of biographies by authors such as Suetonius, Cornelius Nepos, and Plutarch.[51] Roman biography in a sense picked up where Greek biography left off, while also building on its own more ancient tradition—also important to the Renaissance—of the *laudatio funebris* in honor of a deceased person, designed to encapsulate his or her character for his survivors and posterity.

Late antiquity, as Patricia Cox suggests, had already happened upon the problem of defining genres, and she notes that the principal task of patristic-age biographers was the adaptation of biographic forms to a new purpose, the commemoration and sanctification of the holy.[52] Despite the obvious shift of interest in the direction of the holy man, the Middle Ages nevertheless remained in possession of several ancient biographical writers: Suetonius and Plutarch, in particular, were well suited to the medieval life-writer. Beginning with Einhard's admiring but not uncritical *Life of Charlemagne,* a genre of "lives of emperors" grew up. More common, and constituting the Middle Ages' most distinctive form of life-writing, was sacred biography, including hagiography (which Heffernan suggests be discarded as a label because of its negative associations) but also the lives of celebrated clergy and even pious members of the laity, many of which were as concerned with their subjects' earthly deeds as much as with their godliness or evidence of the miraculous.[53]

The accounts of the holy in many medieval chronicles, for instance that of Bede (who also wrote an important and, according to Anderson, paradigmatic, *Life of Saint Cuthbert*), were supplemented by occasional gems such as Eadmer's twelfth-century *Life of Anselm.*[54] Popes in particular, as the personifications of the continuity of the church, lent themselves to collective biographical efforts such as the *Gesta,* which began in the Carolingian period, largely dying out by the twelfth century, and the biographically organized chronicles that succeeded it, such as William of Malmesbury's early twelfth-century compositions, the *Gesta Regum Anglorum* and *Gesta Pontificum Anglorum*. Pure hagiography, with its stress on the supernatural, on the signs of divine favor meted out to hermits and clergy and demonstrated by irreproachable lives, by conversion experiences, and by miracles testifed to by "credible persons," was certainly the most influential and popular of all medieval biographical genres. It would come in for sharp criticism at the Renaissance. Erasmus, who contributed much to the discussion of both rhetoric and life-writing, found the criteria for saintliness applied inconsistently and doubted the veracity of much that was contained in some of the more popular collections of saints' lives, such as the *Legenda aurea* (Golden legend), Jacobus de Voragine's notorious compilation.[55] But it survived despite, and perhaps in part because of, humanist skepticism; and humanist philology would in time be applied to hagiography in the work of the Bollandists and Maurists, beginning in the mid-seventeenth century.[56]

Meanwhile, humanist and Reformation historiographers continued to immortalize the lives, as well as the images, of their most heroic exemplars. But, in many cases, such lives as these were intended to do more than merely immortalize the subject: they became polemics in confessional or intraconfessional disputes over theology and ecclesiology. Timothy Wengert's essay on the often-reprinted 1566 *narratio* of the life of Melanchthon by Joachim Camerarius—significantly a leading German authority on rhetoric—demonstrates the importance of rhetorical techniques in the construction of a life designed to make a point. Wengert aptly calls this "narration for the sake of rhetoric."

That other writers, like Camerarius, would build on their ancient and medieval heritage in producing a large corpus of life-writing is not surprising. Classifying that body of materials without employing at least a provisional taxonomy (which may resemble a generic classification) has proved difficult. Thus, we shall return for a moment to the gross division between "biography" and "autobiography," strictly for analytical reasons.

Cochrane distinguished between two streams of influence when discussing humanist biography, one springing from Saint Jerome, the other from Diogenes Laertius.[57] While useful as a place to begin, this binary categorization leaves much out of account, in particular, the biography written as part of a larger work. Broadly speaking, one can define several

Introduction   13

distinct, though often overlapping, types of biographical life-writing in the early modern period, only a few of which will be represented in the present volume.

1. The Plutarchan exemplary life, designed to immortalize the character, rather more than the deeds, of either individuals or groups of individuals.
2. The Suetonian courtly tradition. This did not necessarily, as in the case of Einhard, bind the author to the critical attitude to his subject which is such an obvious feature of Suetonius, but Einhard and others still conformed to Suetonius's arrangement of his material in the sequence deeds, *then* character.
3. The humanist *vita,* or life of a celebrated individual, which, as Price Zimmermann shows in the case of Giovio, must be treated as a new form because of the slippage between it and its alleged classical models. Boccaccio's life of Dante is an example, as are Bruni's *vite* of Dante and Petrarch (written in the vernacular in part because Bruni considered them of less importance than his Latin works, especially his famous *Historiarum Florentini populi libri XII*); Machiavelli's *La vita di Castruccio Castracani* would also figure here, like Bruni's (and unlike one of Machiavelli's principal sources, the Latin life of Castruccio by Niccolò Tegrimi), composed in Italian.[58]
4. The humanist collection of lives, or sketches of several individuals, a very diverse category (and one which stretched far beyond the humanists, so-called).[59] Petrarch may be said to have initiated this in his *De viris illustribus,* and Boccaccio, once again, popularized the genre in his *De casibus virorum illustrium* and *De mulieribus claris,* which invested the collective *vitae* with the added point of cautionary tales. The *De casibus virorum illustrium* would enjoy a large popularity outside Italy, particularly in England, where John Lydgate translated it in the fifteenth century, and the authors of the successful *Mirror for Magistrates* re-adapted it into verse prosopopeia a century later.[60] *De mulieribus claris* was similarly widely read, especially in France. Christine de Pizan's adaptation, *Le livre de la cité des dames,* was read mainly as a straight translation.[61] The more straightforward "lives," didactic in a general sense but without explicit cautionary purpose (even when discussing infamous tyrants or criminals like

Dionysius of Syracuse or Ezzelino da Romano), continued to prosper in Enea Silvio Piccolomini's *De viris aetate sua claris*, in its successor, Facio's *De viris illustribus* (dedicated to Piccolomini as Pope Pius II), and, above all, in Giovio's celebrated *Vitae*.[62]

Aside from these, and the "fall of princes" subgenre, the collected lives approach also appeared in nontraditional areas: when applied to the rebirth of classical art in the Renaissance and conceptualized as a story of innovation and improvement by Giorgio Vasari in his justly famous *Vite de' più eccellenti pittori, scultori, e architettori*, the *vite* could shed their Plutarchan-Suetonian and Plinian limits, as studied here by Barbara J. Watts and also recently by Paul Barolsky.[63] (Since we have stressed the difficulties of genre, it is worth observing that Barolsky treats Vasari's life of Michelangelo in terms of all of our first four forms, plus hagiography.) Vasari's collection was the most famous, but by no means the only, instance of lives of artists: it remained a particularly vibrant mode in the Netherlands, often written by practicing artists.[64] In Italy it virtually died out by 1642, when Giovanni Baglione published his continuation of Vasari to that year.[65]

A type of humanist collective life-writing that endured rather longer was the "lives of scholars," sometimes cloaked as the study of the "origins of letters" or of poesy. This was, in a sense, biography turned back on its own practitioners, as well as historians and philologists. A vogue for this continued into the seventeenth century, ultimately giving way to the biographical dictionary tradition represented most notably by Pierre Bayle; as Cochrane suggested, once the moral and educational purpose of biography, inherited from antiquity, had been lost, as appears to have happened by the mid-seventeenth century, there were a limited number of directions in which to go.[66]

5. Insofar as it lacked any specific classical model (though its writers were often admirers of humanists and sought to imitate their style), one can distinguish a nonhumanist tradition of collective life-writing roughly corresponding to (4), such as Filippo Villani's lives of illustrious Florentines, written at the end of the fourteenth century. One of the best, and best-known, specimens is the set of short biographies written by the bookseller Vespasiano da Bisticci in the later fifteenth century, in which the lives are organized

according to profession or calling: churchmen, statesmen, writers.⁶⁷

6. The "life and times" of a great person, generally a ruler. This genre would prove highly durable outside Italy and would be imitated by authors such as the English "politic historians" Sir John Hayward, William Camden, Edward Lord Herbert of Cherbury, and Bacon himself.⁶⁸

7. A continuation of the medieval hagiographic tradition, modified and given stronger scholarly underpinnings by Tridentine reform, and leading, by way of seventeenth-century scholarship, to the sort of calendar of saints' lives later perfected by the Bollandists; a neglected subgenre here is the numerous lives of *Beati*—those "blessed," many of whom would be subsequent candidates for canonization—that would appear in sixteenth- and seventeenth-century Italy.

8. A type of ecclesiastical biography owing something to hagiography but, as with medieval ecclesiastical history, concerned with institutional and this-worldly greatness as much as with the divine. Often written as collective biography, this tradition embraces Platina's fifteenth-century *Lives of the Popes* (its Latin and Italian titles vary widely) and its sixteenth-century successor, the history of the popes by Onofrio Panvinio (who was also an expert in portraiture).⁶⁹

9. Protestant sacred biography, which again borrows superficially from the hagiographic in terms of its emphasis on the spiritual, but which departs from it radically in ignoring, as superstitious, the miraculous and in imputing holiness less to outward miracles and deeds than to divine inspiration and aid, signs of an individual's grace and election. This tradition begins with the sort of elaborate funeral orations as that performed for Luther by Melanchthon, and discussed by James Michael Weiss in a useful essay of a few years ago, and those examined here by Kolb.⁷⁰

10. Writing that does not amount to biographies in any formal sense, but which nevertheless encapsulates the lives of famous men and women: prefaces, a favored humanist form throughout the period, are one example, but celebrations of the famous can also be found hiding around even more unexpected corners, in dedications of works, in letters, in political tracts such as Machiavelli's *Il principe,* even in chorographies like Giovio's *Descriptio Britan-*

niae, or in works of religious controversy that are not explicitly biographical or hagiographical.[71] Humanist collections of letters, in particular, offered an almost infinitely flexible form, which could range from the nearly biographical to the more-or-less explicitly autobiographical, depending on the degree of authorial and/or editorial intervention and on the mode of publication.[72]

The other grand category of early modern life-writing, autobiography, borrowed less than biography from ancient sources and is perhaps partly in consequence even harder to classify. This schema is thus even more provisional than that offered for biography.

1. The most influential ancient work was the most impersonal, Caesar's *Commentaries,* which was written in the third person and did not provide an ideal model. Nevertheless, after its rediscovery by Petrarch in the fourteenth century, the *Commentaries* quickly became highly influential and was imitated by memoir writers from Philippe de Commynes to the sixteenth-century French soldier Blaise de Monluc, as well as by Martin du Bellay in his 1559 *Mémoires*. It also influenced many of the political life-writers mentioned earlier, for instance, those discussed by Gary Ianziti.[73] Via Jacques-Auguste de Thou the commentary evolved into the political memoir and *Historia sui temporum* of the seventeenth century and later.
2. In the Christian era, the shapes of autobiography began to crystallize, with the addition of the "confession," as written by church fathers like Augustine.[74] From such works, which parallel Cox's description of the quest for holiness in biographical writing of late antiquity, one gets a much more personalized vision of self, albeit one still driven, in spite of its various authors' protestations to the contrary, by the rules and tricks of rhetoric. The Renaissance early took up this specific form in Dante's *La vita nuova*.
3. The number of Augustinian-style "confessions" remained small, but the model was nonetheless significant in other ways: such largely nonautobiographical works as Calvin's *Institutes* and many of Luther's writings contain lengthy passages of self-analysis which owe much to the Augustinian model.
4. The Augustinian model also lay behind the spiritual autobiography and its close cousin, the diary, which became popular among the

godly in all parts of Europe in the late sixteenth and seventeenth centuries.[75]

5. Other writers added a wide range of autobiographical forms, both formal autobiography such as Cellini's exaggerated and colorful life of himself, and other genres not explicitly designed as formal lives. This included, especially during the later seventeenth century, the writings of a number of female autobiographers.[76] It also embraced autobiographical drama, a genre not directly considered here but one that deserves more attention in view of the dramatic quality of much autobiography: here again, the generic boundaries are highly permeable.[77]

6. One of the most popular (and easily identified) forms was the humanist collection of *epistolae,* which could be adapted to virtually any autobiographical purposes, as in the cases of Cassandra Fedele and Laura Cereta, compared here by Diana Robin, or the writings of the Venetian courtesan Veronica Franco.[78]

7. "Table talk" was a form of life-writing that would assume large proportions beginning at least with Luther's virtually paradigmatic multiple-recorder remarks and sayings.[79] The seventeenth-century successor to such works, for instance the series of "ana" published from remarks of French, Dutch, and Italian luminaries (including Joseph Justus Scaliger and his English counterpart, John Selden) in effect constructed lives of the great reformers and scholars of the age while making them appear more immediate (and less formidable) than would either their own writings or any simple biography.

In addition to these literary genres of life-writing, there is a final grand category of nonliterary forms. These have, if anything, received even less attention from modern scholars, certainly from mainstream historians. If one leaves out the *laudatio* and various forms of panegyric such as the *encomium,* many of which began as verbal oratory rather than as published text, then one can still look to a whole range of visual representations of lives. The printing press, when combined with new artistic techniques, allowed for a wide variety of ways in which individual lives could be told, or at least embodied, in images.[80] These included the woodcut, as used by martyrologists such as John Foxe and Jean Crespin later in the sixteenth century, together with engraving (most famous perhaps in Albrecht Dürer's self-portraits) and drypoint and etching (both well represented in Rembrandt's numerous self-representations a century later). Most of these also contributed a great deal to the humanist and reformed emblem book, which certainly deserves to be considered as a type of life-writing, for example, the great French Calvinist Théodore de Bèze's 1580 compilation, the *Icones,* with portraits of the famous attached to textual descriptions (here explored briefly by Catharine Randall).[81] Creative litterateurs such as Nicolas Houel could even manipulate historical imagery into a type of contemporary biography, using the life of an ancient figure such as Artemisia to represent a contemporary personage, unconcerned as to whether the contemporary and the ancient resembled each other, as Sheila ffolliott demonstrates in her essay. As with Robin's essay on Fedele, the gendered character of early modern exemplarity emerges from the reluctance of Houel, and other biographers of regnant queens, to treat their subjects in anything other than masculine colors; such writings conformed to social practice that placed men and women on different tracks.

Houel and his illustrators dealt with an individual subject, but the collection of portraits of individuals also flourished. It was greatly encouraged by Giovio, for example, in his *invenzioni* for Vasari's frescoes in the Sala dei Cento Giorni in the Cancellaria, and then in his books of *Elogiae,* illustrated with portraits. A constant from at least the late fifteenth century, collective portraiture reached a high degree of development in the late Renaissance, for example, at the Villa Farnese at Caprarola where history, painting, and lives were all rolled together into one grand celebration of the Farnese.[82] It appeared in a humbler—but reproducible—form in collections of portrait busts on roll-stamps, used in Regensburg (and elsewhere) to decorate book bindings.[83] Other artists experimented with yet other forms, including autobiography "written" in still life.[84]

Vicino Orsini's garden at Bomarzo represents one of the more peculiar directions in which life-writing veered once its didactic purpose began to be lost. A phantasmagorical psychogogia, in part modeled on Ariosto's *Orlando Furioso* (itself a mammoth world without coherence), Bomarzo was also in part Orsini's autobiography. Its sculptures, its locus, and the wide circle of Vicino's friends suggest that this mode of life-writing deserves more study than it has yet received.[85] We could find no more appropriate example of the breadth of the phenomenon we have only begun to study.

The goals of the editors in assembling this volume may be summarized as follows.

1. To broaden understanding of what constitutes a "life" beyond traditional biography, while not neglecting the centrality of that form;
2. To subject the notion of biography, and other generic distinctions, to rigorous scrutiny and to challenge many of them;
3. To explore the overlaps and mixtures in life-writing, as life-writers borrowed from, or in some instances reacted against, a variety of ancient and medieval models to construct often radically innovative genres of their own, or how they used unconventional media, from funeral sermons to personal writings to commemorate lives, including their own;
4. To provide a series of studies that examine a number of contexts, political and religious, within which lives were written, and elucidate the rhetorical process of constructing them.

In short, the volume arises from an effort to understand the place of the "life" in early modern culture, and the various ways in which lives were "written." The contributors come from history, art history, and literature, and they meet on the common ground of both subject and method—all the pieces are seriously interdisciplinary.

T. C. Price Zimmermann's essay on Giovio denotes many of the limitations of two often-used classical models, Plutarch and Suetonius, and suggests that the claim of Renaissance biographers like Giovio to be imitating them was often in itself a rhetorical assertion. As Zimmermann shows, Giovio's own 1549 *Vitae* ill fit either the Suetonian or Plutarchan model, being more concerned with drawing character from history than the other way around (as in Plutarch) and scarcely having Suetonius's liberty to comment freely on all his subjects. Zimmermann also treats Giovio's experimentation with alternative forms of life-representation, one of the most successful of which was the *Imprese*.

As images, so their creators. Barbara J. Watts analyzes how Vasari established the biographical framework of the future discipline of art history in his famous *Vite*, as he, like Giovio, experimented with various previous forms of life-writing. These included both classical and medieval models, above all, Dante's famously autobiographical *Commedia*, as Barolsky has recently emphasized. According to both Watts and Barolsky, Vasari organized the first (1550) edition of his lives as a progression to the divine Michelangelo. As Watts shows, a detailed doubling of episodes between the lives of Donatello and Michelangelo served as a major structural principle of the work. The point was thus frequently repeated that Michelangelo had surpassed Donatello on all scales; this would become even clearer were *Le Vite* to be read diachronically, as Dante's poem was meant to be. Whereas Donatello was a craftsman, Michelangelo was a humanist who admired, but did not stoop to practice, craftwork; whereas Donatello's imagination remained painterly, Michelangelo's was fully sculptural; and so on.

As Watts observes, Vasari concluded his life of Michelangelo with a commonplace of medieval hagiography, the lack of decay of Michelangelo's corpse twenty-five days after his death. Michelangelo was as exemplary in death as in life. But in Vasari's writings, a good example almost had to be dead. This crucial point of Timothy Hampton's about Renaissance exemplarity in general emerges with particular force from Robert Kolb's exploration of a hitherto neglected genre of life-writing, the Lutheran funeral sermon.[86] Unlike their humanist predecessors or Catholic and reformed contemporaries, Lutherans did not engage in more formal varieties of life-writing, despite their "rich historical tradition." Depending on Melanchthon's loci method and their related rhetorical training, the authors of *Leichenpredigten* stressed the minister's calling—a sign of the working of providence—and virtues, despite the difficulty of using clergy as models for the laity.[87] The emphasis on the "Hauskreuz" borne by many clergy may have been an attempt to remedy this second lack, as the need to represent champions of the faith meant major transformations in the topoi of classical rhetoric, akin to those in Giovio's reworking of his models. In any event, the pressures of confessional defense and lay instruction led writers of funeral sermons to tailor their material, rigorously excluding anything that weakened the heroic image of their subjects.

One topos frequently employed was that of friendship with other pastors, but as Robin has recently stressed, *amicitia* could mask asymmetrical patronage relations as well as other less-pleasing facets of Renaissance intellectuals' lives.[88] On Timothy J. Wengert's showing, this is also true of Camerarius's *Narratio* for Melanchthon. Drawing on the resources of classical *progymnastica*, Camerarius perpetuated Melanchthon's own rhetorically constructed persona as a Stoic hero, a commonplace of early modern biography, no matter what its confessional (or temporal) alignment.[89] Its reception provides a typical case of how humanist rhetoric could be received as positivist historiography.

F. W. Conrad's discussion of the political and diplomatic context of William Roper's reconstruction of More's life, and especially of his death, provides a similar warning against taking even the most silken-tongued biographer at face value. Without actually deceiving us, Roper, whether accidentally or—as Conrad suspects—through artifice, so shaped his narrative and telescoped time as to conflate two discrete events: the Emperor Charles V's reception of Thomas More's announcement of his intention to surrender the Great Seal, and the news, three years later, of More's execution. Conrad demonstrates not simply that the interview between Sir Thomas Elyot and Charles must be fabrication, or at least part invention, but also how endorsement from a well-respected humanist and diplomat such as Elyot enhanced the authority of Roper's account, and the public stature of its subject. At the same time, he places Roper's art within the contexts of continental and Tudor *artes rhetoricae,* and of ancient canons of history writing. We have here, and in several other essays, further explorations of what Judith Anderson described a decade ago as "biographical truth" in her book of that title.

All the essays so far have dealt with life-writing about real persons and real events, but the field was not so delimited in the sixteenth century. James V. Mehl demonstrates how the triumvirate of Crotus Rubeanus, Ulrich von Hutten, and the previously overlooked Hermann von dem Busche assembled the highly influential *Letters of Obscure Men* in an openly satirical mode designed to recast historical characters in an increasingly violent polemic against scholasticism, especially as represented by their erstwhile colleague in the university of Cologne, Ortwin Gratius. (In an operation a little like that proposed by Wengert for Melanchthon, Mehl has been working over the last several years to recover a less polemically grounded Gratius.) Drawing on the work of Reinhart Becker and others, Mehl places the epistolary deformation of Gratius and his allies into a long tradition of university satire, fed by attacks on the scholastics' abuses of language and form, all of which made them obstacles to the religious, social, and political reform of the empire, forwarded by Hutten. Mehl's careful treatment of the dynamics of this act of collective authorship reveals a phenomenon quite common during the Renaissance and Reformation, and, if we are right, especially in life-writing, in which autobiographer and biographer or biographer and subject combine to produce a single text, if not always in the same hostile relationship Mehl describes.

Diana Robin, who provides perhaps the boldest challenge here to the traditional division of text and life, employs some of Mehl's techniques of analysis in her subtle exploration of the way in which Cassandra Fedele denatured the language of her letters to make her selves, both textual and lived, "proto-male." Through her *epistolario,* Fedele constructed an identity that was literally a removal of face, rather than its making, as was the usual function of male humanist letterbooks (and as Robin herself shows in her recent *Filelfo in Milan*). Through steady employment of diminutive language and demeaning comparisons between herself and her male patrons, Fedele "put under erasure" the standard feminine virtues. Julius Caesar Scaliger would endorse that strategy in a poem later affixed to the printed seventeenth-century edition of Fedele's letterbook, simply calling her a man, but she had already made herself "a *figura*" for the combination of "virginity and eloquence" and "youth and transsexual virtue."

Cardinal Pole, the subject of Thomas F. Mayer's essay, also constructed an extensive *epistolario* as part of a vast autobiographical project. To judge from the multitude of hands in the surviving versions of Pole's letter collections (whether *raccolta* or *epistolario* seems a moot question in his case),[90] that autobiographical project was a collective effort. Certainly that was true of the creation of Pole's image through other means. As Mayer shows, Pole first assembled a retrospective image of himself as principled opponent of Henry VIII and then handed that image to his first two biographers, probably by supplying them with copies of several letters, as well as his "table talk." From them, as in the case of Camerarius's life of Melanchthon, Pole's "myth of sanctity" passed almost directly via the transformations of salvation history into positivist historiography.[91]

Catharine Randall's study of d'Aubigné's martyrological narrative, which places its subject in the context of meditational works by fellow Calvinists Théodore de Bèze and Jean de Sponde, reveals a collective biography in which the disordered body becomes central, tying Reformation martyrology to current critical concerns about the relations between textual and fleshly bodies. Literature, we learn here, is composed of "lives and corpses," and a "martyrological narrative" is accordingly made up of clusters of descriptions of martyrdoms, painted in excruciating detail. The body is no longer the thing of beauty valorized in Renaissance representations of the microcosm; it is a "mishmash" of parts with no closure. If the body, indeed, is only knowable, only meaningful, not through its twisted and charred limbs, but through the confessional language being expelled along with the soul, then the early "word balloons" used in the woodcuts to Foxe's text and those of other martyrologists assume a highly significant role: they, and they alone, can serve to distinguish among groups of martyrs who physically may be indistinguishable, given the proclivity of printers to recycle and adapt woodcuts several times within a text. D'Aubigné's language in *Les tragiques* is the critical device that mediates here between the event and our reception of it, making sense of the martyrdoms both singly and as a group. Randall's suggestion that Reformation martyrology is more than a simple adaptation of hagiography to confessional ends, and in fact constitutes an entirely different genre brought into existence, or at least revived, by religious persecution, deserves further attention. So does her argument in favor of a sharp disjuncture, not between medieval and Renaissance, but between Renaissance and Reformation modes of life-writing. The coincidence in time between this change and that observed by Sheila ffolliott in her essay, with special reference to Catherine de' Medici, raises further doubts about conventional understandings of the "modernity" of the Renaissance and Reformation.

The transformations of medieval hagiography and perhaps martyrology considered by Randall also figure in Woolf's essay on John Foxe, as do the questions of genre and model raised earlier in this introduction. Commentators have often noted the untidiness or disorganization of Foxe's *Acts and Monuments*. Woolf attributes this to a plurality of models and genres at play in the work, and to the tensions between conflicting authorial purposes. Woolf argues that Foxe borrowed from medieval chronicles not simply material, but a narrative structure that resembles Northrop Frye's mythos of romance, upon which Foxe superimposed hagiographic and comic elements as he sought to reconcile his need to relate the history of the True Church with a compelling urge to memorialize the life of every martyr for whom he could find material, written or oral.

William E. Engel's essay paints a Proustian image of the contemplative Montaigne, sitting solitary in his study, refashioning his life not directly from the massive shelves of books that surrounded and soothed him, but from his own recollections. Engel documents the ways in which that most personal of sixteenth-century contributions to genre, the *essai*, amounted to an innovative form of life-writing, in this instance one which allowed its author the opportunity to "digest" as much as to spew forth his sense of self. Moreover, Engel demonstrates the profound importance of memory, not merely as the most accessible source of exempla, but also as a critical force intervening between the author's life as lived and as written; the quality of "stoic" resignation and common sense that is so much a part of the *Essais* is tempered by the essayist-autobiographer's awareness of the frailty, and painfulness, of his being.

Stoicism was indeed a stream of influence on life-writing, the full importance of which has not been fully appreciated. In Adriana McCrea's essay, the influence of the particular late Renaissance formulation of the Stoic inheritance, the neostoicism of Justus Lipsius, played a crucial role in Fulke Greville's writing of a life of his friend Sir Philip Sidney. Greville had a closer relationship to Sidney than many biographers did to their subject: this is not the portrayal of an admired superior, but of an equal; it is certainly far from Roper's pious panegyric on a humanist saint who was close to being a father figure. Instead, it is a retrospective on a man who was both Greville's exact contemporary and a friend whom he had known since that October day in 1564 when the two ten-year-old boys entered Shrewsbury school. If Sidney's "end," in the sense of purpose, was "not in writing" but, as Greville would have us believe, on the battlefield, then it equally appears to have been Greville's own purpose not simply to shape his friend for posterity, but also to provide another type of end, the terminating kind, to replace in textual, immortal form that lingering and untidy conclusion at Zutphen, an end that was not particularly satisfactory to Sidney's admirers and perhaps did not square very well with Sidney's "real" end. Perhaps even more significantly, McCrea—echoing both Engel's depiction of Montaigne's bodily musings and Wengert's essay on Camerarius's reconstruction of Melanchthon—demonstrates that Greville was in fact displacing a few guiltier aspects of his own post-Sidneian career into the incomplete portrayal of his dead hero's life and premature death. By placing at the center of her discussion not only the subjectivity, but the *subjection,* of the depicted life to the authorial life, McCrea points out another fissure between biography and history, while at the same time further undermining the barrier between biography and autobiography.

Sheila ffolliott's study of the attempt to represent Catherine, the queen regent, as the ancient Queen Artemisia ruling after the death of her husband raises some similar questions because of the evident lack of an exact fit between Catherine and her legendary counterpart. This is an instance in which the artist stretched the notion of types to a considerable degree in response to political and social constraint: it is one thing to have compared Catherine to Artemisia in a Plutarchan sense, in language; it is quite another to represent the French regent as an Other to whom she bears virtually no resemblance. ffolliott focuses on some of the principal problems of historical personation, the reinvention of a contemporary through the construction of a heroic, or at least exemplary, personality derived from historical or mythical sources. For the obscure apothecary Houel, operating in a tradition that prized males as exemplary and females as merely complementary, the description of a regent who was not merely female but foreign (even worse, Florentine) presented a real challenge, a point made even easier to appreciate when one compares Houel's text with the unabashedly negative assessment of the near-contemporary *Discours merveilleux* attributed to Estienne. Houel's challenge was greater than that faced by English contemporaries in representing Queen Elizabeth as Astraea, Belphoebe, or Cynthia. If such a queen was to be praised for her statecraft at all, it is clear that this must be as "one of the boys."

Elizabeth C. Goldsmith's and Abby E. Zanger's chapter, which delimits the chronological extent of this volume, probes the subject of life-writing and politics in the context of a famous political scandal, the romance of Louis XIV and Marie Mancini. In this case, the rewriting of recent history by various agents of Cardinal Mazarin can be thoroughly documented. This is no longer the war-ravaged France of the late Valois kings, with its recurrently weak monarchy, but the absolutist state of Louis XIV, which, as work by scholars such as William Church, Orest Ranum, Jean-Marie Apostolidès, and Louis Marin has demonstrated, was possessed of the ways and means not simply to restrict writing from the center, but to use the public press and literary hired guns to create images of glory and potency for the monarchy, probably to a greater degree than any regime before its time.[92] This essay traces the reporting of an episode, at government behest, as a type of "damage control," shaping an unworthy event in a particular way to turn a royal liability into an asset: amorous and virile young kings fight good wars and produce strong heirs.

Yet the essay goes beyond this testimony to absolutist literary potency to examine unintended consequences, well after the event. These include numerous rival accounts of the same events in which, as Goldsmith and

Zanger note, multiple voices are brought to bear, thereby reinventing the king once more. For all the earlier talk of a transition between the sixteenth and seventeenth centuries in the rhetorics of life-writing, we seem here to be still, in the 1660s and 1670s, very close to the kind of invention employed in Reformation and Counter-Reformation martyrology and biography. Even if the rhetoric had changed, life-writing had not become a one-way conversation emanating from Versailles; it remained, in the authors' terms, "dialogic," an ongoing conversation between the subject and various texts that it inspires. Goldsmith and Zanger also return to the question of genre in their consideration of the multivalent senses that the word *romance* had come to bear in the mid-1700s.

NOTES

1. A word about our usage of *life-writing*. We agree with Judith H. Anderson, *Biographical Truth: The Representation of Historical Persons in Tudor-Stuart Writing* (New Haven, CT: Yale University Press, 1984), 2, that this term is more historically accurate than is *biography*, and we also prefer it because we treat a much broader range of forms than even an elastic meaning of biography can easily stretch around.

2. Colin Eisler offers some reflections on this anomalous state of affairs in "'Every Artist Paints Himself': Art History as Biography and Autobiography," *Social Research* 54 (1987): 73–99. For an early exploration of the Renaissance treatment of the relations between biography and history, see Albert H. Buford, "History and Biography, the Renaissance Distinction," in A. Williams, ed., *A Tribute to George Coffin Taylor* (Chapel Hill, NC: University of North Carolina Press, 1953), 100–112.

3. Jacques Le Goff, "The Whys and Ways of Writing a Biography: The Case of St. Louis," *Exemplaria* 1 (1989): 207–23.

4. For two recent collections of brief studies, see Susan G. Bell and Marilyn Yalom, eds., *Revealing Lives: Autobiography, Biography, and Gender* (Albany: SUNY Press, 1990); and Marlene Kadar, ed., *Essays on Life Writing: From Genre to Critical Practice* (Toronto: University of Toronto Press, 1992), esp. 3–16, 83–127.

5. For a sustained argument on this score, see William H. Epstein, *Recognizing Biography* (Philadelphia: University of Pennsylvania Press, 1987).

6. Thomas J. Heffernan, *Sacred Biography: Saints and Their Biographers in the Middle Ages* (New York: Oxford University Press, 1988), 18–22.

7. This point has been made frequently of late in connection with Machia-

velli. See Albert R. Ascoli, "Machiavelli's Gift of Counsel," in Albert R. Ascoli and Victoria Kahn, eds., *Machiavelli and the Discourse of Literature* (Ithaca, NY: Cornell University Press, 1993), 219–57 (we are indebted to Professor Ascoli for showing us his essay before publication); cf. Victoria Kahn, "Virtù and the Example of Agathocles," *Representations* 13 (1986): 63–83; Barbara Spackman, "Machiavelli and Maxims," *Yale French Studies* 77 (1989): 137–55; Jeffrey T. Schnapp, "Machiavellian Foundlings: Castruccio Castracani and the Aphorism," *Renaissance Quarterly* 45 (1992): 653–76. Study of exemplarity must now take note of two major works: John D. Lyons, *Exemplum: The Rhetoric of Example in Early Modern France and Italy* (Princeton: Princeton University Press, 1990); and, especially useful to us, Timothy Hampton, *Writing from History: The Rhetoric of Exemplarity in Renaissance Literature* (Ithaca, NY: Cornell University Press, 1990), 18, 62, and passim. But see also Victoria Kahn, *Rhetoric, Prudence, and Skepticism in the Renaissance* (Ithaca, NY: Cornell University Press, 1985), 20ff.; David Quint, *Origin and Originality in Renaissance Literature: Versions of the Source* (New Haven, CT: Yale University Press, 1983), chap. 1; D. R. Woolf, *The Idea of History in Early Stuart England: Erudition, Ideology, and "The Light of Truth" from the Accession of James I to the Civil War* (Toronto: University of Toronto Press, 1990), 50–51 for Sir Walter Ralegh's rejection of ancient exempla.

8. Cf. Hampton, *Writing from History*, 18.

9. Walter J. Ong, *Ramus, Method and the Decay of Dialogue: From the Art of Discourse to the Art of Reason* (Cambridge, MA: Harvard University Press, 1958), 98–130, and "The Orality of Language," in *Orality and Literacy: The Technologizing of the Word* (London: Methuen, 1982), chap. 1; and Hans Kellner, *Language and Historical Representation: Getting the Story Crooked* (Madison: University of Wisconsin Press, 1989), esp. chap. 2.

10. Stephen Greenblatt, *Renaissance Self-fashioning, from More to Shakespeare* (Chicago: University of Chicago Press, 1980); Natalie Zemon Davis, *The Return of Martin Guerre* (Cambridge, MA: Harvard University Press, 1983); Carlo Ginzburg, *The Cheese and the Worms: The Cosmos of a Sixteenth-Century Miller*, trans. John and Anne Tedeschi (Baltimore: Johns Hopkins University Press, 1980). Various aspects of the Self are handled in *Imaging the Self in Renaissance Italy*, special issue of *Fenway Court* (1990–91). See especially John W. O'Malley, "Imaging the Self: The Religious and Rhetorical Framework," 61–69; Michael Baxandall, "Alberti's Self," 31–36; and Christiane Klapisch-Zuber, "Images without Memory: Women's Identity and Family Consciousness in Renaissance Florence," 37–43.

11. Ginzburg's call for "intuitive" reading of surfaces might also contribute, were it not for his further insistence that those surfaces are really depths ("Morelli, Freud and Sherlock Holmes: Clues and Scientific Method," trans. Anna Davin, *History Workshop* 9 [1980]: 5–36). Michael MacDonald suggests

that social historians should treat the stories of biographical narrative as a vital source in "*The Fearfull Estate of Francis Spira:* Narrative, Identity, and Emotion in Early Modern England," *Journal of British Studies* 31 (1992): 32–61.

12. Kenneth Burke, *A Grammar of Motives* (Berkeley: University of California Press, 1969), chap. 1 and passim.

13. Hayden White, "Interpretation in History" and "The Historical Text as Literary Artifact," both in *Tropics of Discourse: Essays in Cultural Criticism* (Baltimore: Johns Hopkins University Press, 1978), 80, and *The Content of the Form* (Baltimore: Johns Hopkins University Press, 1987), together with his classic *Metahistory: The Historical Imagination in Nineteenth-Century Europe* (Baltimore: Johns Hopkins University Press, 1973); Ira Bruce Nadel, *Biography: Fiction, Fact & Form* (New York: Macmillan, 1984). Cf. Anne Rigney, "Narrative Discourse and Historical Representation," *Poetics Today* 12 (1991): 591–605.

14. Elizabeth S. Cohen, "Court Testimony from the Past: Self and Culture in the Making of Text," in Marlene Kadar, ed., *Essays on Life Writing: From Genre to Critical Practice* (Toronto: University of Toronto Press, 1992), 86.

15. Arnaldo Momigliano, *The Classical Foundations of Modern Historiography* (Berkeley and Los Angeles: University of California Press, 1991), the last of numerous important works by this author on various aspects of ancient, medieval, and early modern historical writing; Donald R. Kelley, *Foundations of Modern Historical Scholarship: Language, Law, and History in the French Renaissance* (New York: Columbia University Press, 1970); Julian Franklin, *Jean Bodin and the Sixteenth-Century Revolution in the Methodology of Law and History* (New York: Columbia University Press, 1963); George Huppert, *The Idea of Perfect History* (Urbana: University of Illinois Press, 1970). Zachary Sayre Schiffman criticizes the French literature for its reading back of modern historicism into the sixteenth century: see most recently "The Order of the Self," in his *On the Threshold of Modernity: Relativism in the French Renaissance* (Baltimore: Johns Hopkins University Press, 1991), 53–77.

16. As Paul Barolsky and William E. Wallace have pointed out, "Although we know that Renaissance history is rhetorical, we nevertheless lapse, despite ourselves, into accepting as fact many of its exemplary fictions, taking them too literally.... It is one thing to regard such texts as 'primary sources.' It is another to know how to read them." "The Myth of Michelangelo and Il Magnifico," *Source: Notes in the History of Art* 12 (1993): 16–21.

17. White, "Historical Text," 85 and 99. Dominick LaCapra, "Rhetoric and History," in *History and Criticism* (Ithaca, NY: Cornell University Press, 1985), 21, 35, and passim, and *Soundings in Critical Theory* (Ithaca, NY: Cornell University Press, 1989), 5.

18. LaCapra, "Rethinking Intellectual History and Reading Texts," in *Rethinking Intellectual History: Texts, Contexts, Language* (Ithaca, NY, and Lon-

don: Cornell University Press, 1983), 35ff., and "Reading Exemplars: Wittgenstein's *Vienna* and Wittgenstein's *Tractatus,*" ibid., 95ff.

19. LaCapra, "Rhetoric and History," 35ff.

20. See, e.g., John S. Nelson, Allan Megill, and Donald N. McCloskey, eds., *The Rhetoric of the Human Sciences: Language and Argument in Scholarship and Public Affairs* (Madison: University of Wisconsin Press, 1987).

21. Two good surveys of rhetoric as a collection of techniques are Brian Vickers, *In Defence of Rhetoric* (Oxford: Clarendon Press, 1988) and George A. Kennedy, *Classical Rhetoric and its Christian and Secular Tradition from Ancient to Modern Times* (Chapel Hill: University of North Carolina Press, 1980).

22. Paolo Giovio, *Lettere,* ed. G. G. Ferrero, 2 vols. (Rome: Istituto poligrafico dello stato, 1956–58), 1:174.

23. For an excellent study of why this is the case, in the context of Roman curial politics, see John W. O'Malley, *Praise and Blame in Renaissance Rome: Rhetoric, Doctrine, and Reform in the Sacred Orators of the Papal Court, c. 1450–1521* (Durham, NC: Duke University Press, 1979), 36–76.

24. George Lincoln Burr in 1903 explicitly associated biographical history with at least historiographical conservatism. See Peter Novick, *That Noble Dream: The "Objectivity Question" and the American Historical Profession* (Cambridge and New York: Cambridge University Press, 1988), 90.

25. Jacob Burckhardt, *The Civilization of the Renaissance in Italy,* trans. S. G. C. Middlemore, 2 vols. (New York: Harper and Row, 1958), 2:324ff. Elizabeth Eisenstein offers a particularly trenchant criticism of Burckhardt's rhetorical method in "The Advent of Printing and the Problem of the Renaissance," *Past and Present* 45 (1969): 19–89, at 57.

26. Ernst Cassirer, *The Individual and the Cosmos in Renaissance Philosophy,* trans. Mario Domandi, 3d ed. (Philadelphia: University of Pennsylvania Press, 1983); Alfred von Martin, *The Sociology of the Renaissance,* trans. W. L. Luetkens, ed. Wallace K. Ferguson (New York: Harper & Row, 1963); Ralph Roeder, *The Man of the Renaissance* (New York: Meridian, 1958 [1933]); Agnes Heller, *Renaissance Man,* trans. Richard E. Allen (London: Routledge and Kegan Paul, 1978), 197–245; and William Kerrigan and Gordon Braden, *The Idea of the Renaissance* (Baltimore: Johns Hopkins University Press, 1989), which explicitly dusts off Burckhardt.

27. For a recent survey of both female life-writing and portraiture, see Romeo De Maio, *Donna e Rinascimento* (Milan: Mondadori, 1987), 147–211, which paints a bleak picture; the construction of Renaissance femininity is well handled by Pamela Joseph Benson in *The Invention of the Renaissance Woman: The Challenge of Female Independence in the Literature and Thought of Italy and England* (University Park: Pennsylvania State University Press, 1992), esp. 9–31 on Boccaccio's *De mulieribus claris.*

28. Cf. the new communitarians in "The Virtues, the Unity of a Human Life and the Concept of a Tradition," in Alasdair MacIntyre, *After Virtue,* 2d ed. (Notre Dame: University of Notre Dame Press, 1984), chap. 15, or Charles Taylor, *Sources of the Self: The Making of the Modern Identity* (Cambridge, MA: Harvard University Press, 1989), and for individualism, the essays by Greenblatt and Davis in Thomas C. Heller, Morton Sosna, and David E. Wellbery, eds., *Reconstructing Individualism: Autonomy, Individuality, and the Self in Western Thought* (Stanford, CA: Stanford University Press, 1986).

29. The nearly opposite ideological valences assigned to the term *lived experience,* depending upon whether it comes from Wilhelm Dilthey or Jean-Paul Sartre, illustrate a similar elasticity.

30. For another argument about genre as necessary but most valuable as a provisional construct, see Fredric Jameson, "Magical Narratives: On the Dialectical Use of Genre Criticism," in *The Political Unconscious: Narrative as a Socially Symbolic Act* (Ithaca, NY: Cornell University Press, 1981), chap. 2. Cf. also Richard A. Lanham, *The Motives of Eloquence: Literary Rhetoric in the Renaissance* (New Haven, CT: Yale University Press, 1976), 16, for the interaction between rhetoric and genre.

31. Nancy Klein Maguire, ed., *Renaissance Tragicomedy: Explorations in Genre and Politics* (New York: AMS Press, 1987).

32. The often fierce debates over the status of *Orlando Furioso,* charted by Daniel Javitch in *Proclaiming a Classic: The Canonization of Orlando Furioso* (Princeton: Princeton University Press, 1991), can serve as a marker for more general discussions of genre. Cf. also the tergiversations of writers and theorists of dialogue, a perhaps even murkier domain. For a brief summary, see Thomas F. Mayer, *Thomas Starkey and the Commonweal: Humanist Politics and Religion in the Reign of Henry VIII* (Cambridge: Cambridge University Press, 1989), 63–64 and 106.

33. Cf. also David D'Avray, "The Comparative Study of Memorial Preaching," *Transactions of the Royal Historical Society,* fifth series, 40 (1990): 25–42, at 41. D'Avray suggests that funeral sermons can be used to track the development of concepts of the individual.

34. Eric Cochrane, *Historians and Historiography in the Italian Renaissance* (Chicago: University of Chicago Press, 1981), 393ff.; Eduard Fueter, *Geschichte der Neueren Historiographie* (Munich and Berlin: R. Oldenbourg, 1911).

35. Jerry H. Bentley, *Politics and Culture in Renaissance Naples* (Princeton: Princeton University Press, 1987), especially 224ff., and for them in the context of Alfonso's historical tastes, see Alan Ryder, *Alfonso the Magnanimous* (Oxford: Clarendon Press, 1990), 307; cf. Cochrane, *Historians and Historiography,* 146–48, who points to the existence of similar works from the Neapolitan court, including Gaspare Pellegrino's unpublished manuscript of Alfonso's "Gesta," written in 1443.

36. Niccolò Machiavelli, *Florentine Histories,* trans. Laura F. Banfield and Harvey C. Mansfield, Jr. (Princeton: Princeton University Press, 1988), 328–30; Alison Brown, "Cosimo de' Medici's Wit and Wisdom," in F. Ames-Lewis, ed., *Cosimo "il Vecchio" de' Medici, 1389–1464* (Oxford: Clarendon Press, 1992), 95–113, at 96. As Patricia L. Rubin has pointed out to us, Machiavelli considered the *vita* to be a literary form distinct from history, and the Florentine secretary did, late in life, offer a short life of the Lucchese tyrant Castruccio Castracani; for his pillaging of history for aphorisms and exempla to illustrate lives—and make points—see Lyons, *Exemplum,* 71ff; Schnapp, "Machiavellian Foundlings," 655ff.

37. For recent work on autobiography, see James Olney, ed., *Autobiography: Essays Theoretical and Critical* (Princeton: Princeton University Press, 1980), in particular Georges Gusdorf, "Conditions and Limits of Autobiography," 28–48; Paul John Eakin, *Fictions in Autobiography: Studies in the Art of Self-Invention* (Princeton: Princeton University Press, 1985); Nicholas Spadaccini and Jenaro Talens, eds., *Autobiography in Early Modern Spain* (Minneapolis: University of Minnesota Press, 1988), and above all Philippe Lejeune, *On Autobiography,* ed. and intro. Paul John Eakin, trans. Katherine Leary (Minneapolis: University of Minnesota Press, 1989), esp. Eakin's intro., x and xvii for "collaborative autobiography." Useful comments on autobiography and Renaissance consciousness can be found in Agnes Heller, "Individuality, Knowledge of Men, Self-knowledge, Autobiography," in *Renaissance Man,* chap. 7.

38. Anderson, *Biographical Truth,* 41.

39. Melissa M. Bullard, "Lorenzo de' Medici: Anxiety, Image Making, and Political Reality in the Renaissance," in Gian Carlo Garfagnini, ed., *Lorenzo de' Medici Studi* (Florence: Olschki, 1992), 3–40.

40. Jonathan Crewe, *Trials of Authorship, Anterior Forms and Poetic Reconstruction from Wyatt to Shakespeare* (Berkeley and Los Angeles: University of California Press, 1990), 14; Michel Foucault, "What is an Author?" in Paul Rabinow, ed. *The Foucault Reader* (New York: Pantheon, 1984), 101–20.

41. Natalie Zemon Davis has drawn attention to another variety in "Fame and Secrecy: Leon Modena's *Life* as an Early Modern Autobiography," in *The Autobiography of a Seventeenth-Century Venetian Rabbi: Leon Modena's Life of Judah,* ed. and trans. Mark R. Cohen (Princeton: Princeton University Press, 1988).

42. Richard Wendorf, *The Elements of Life: Biography and Portrait-Painting in Stuart and Georgian England* (Oxford: Clarendon Press, 1990); Myron P. Gilmore, "The Renaissance Conception of the Lessons of History," in Gilmore, *Humanists and Jurists: Six Studies in the Renaissance* (Cambridge, MA: Harvard University Press, 1963), 15.

43. Leonard Barkan, *The Gods Made Flesh: Metamorphosis and the Pursuit of Paganism* (New Haven, CT: Yale University Press, 1986), 175ff.

44. Paul Ortwin Rave, "Paolo Giovio und die Bildnisvitenbücher des Humanismus," *Jahrbuch der Berliner Museen* 1 (1959): 119–54. See most recently the exhaustive study of Linda S. Klinger, "The Portrait Collection of Paolo Giovio," Ph.D. dissertation, Princeton University, 1991. On the more general use of collections of portraits as a mode of life-writing, see Francis Haskell, "Portraits from the Past," in *History and its Images: Art and the Interpretation of the Past* (New Haven, CT: Yale University Press, 1993), chap. 2.

45. See LaCapra's stimulating discussions, especially in "Sartre and the Question of Biography," in *Rethinking Intellectual History,* 184–233, and "Reading Exemplars," passim.

46. Randolph Starn calls this double emphasis the "characteristic mode of cultural history" ("Seeing Culture in a Room for a Renaissance Prince," in Lynn Hunt, ed., *The New Cultural History* [Berkeley and Los Angeles: University of California Press, 1989], 206). Starn, like Jameson (*Political Unconscious,* 56, 76, 99), treats form as a function of power, a move that could well prove productive in the treatment of life-writing.

47. Burke, *Grammar of Motives,* 513. Cf. also Jameson, *Political Unconscious,* 275ff. and passim, and Dominick LaCapra, "The Temporality of Rhetoric," in *Soundings,* 91.

48. Novick, *That Noble Dream,* 274.

49. John A. Garraty, *The Nature of Biography* (New York: Knopf, 1957), 31–53; Momigliano, *The Development of Greek Biography* (Cambridge, MA: Harvard University Press, 1971), which though only a brief survey, contains a good bibliography of ancient and modern writings on biography.

50. Momigliano, *Greek Biography,* 50–55.

51. Although not in themselves a variety of life-writing, the *Characters* of Theophrastus deserve mention among related ancient literary forms, since they would have an enormous vogue in the later Renaissance: Benjamin Boyce, *The Theophrastan Character in England to 1642* (Cambridge, MA: Harvard University Press, 1947) and Charles B. Schmitt, "Theophrastus," in *Catalogus Translationum et Commentariorum: Medieval and Renaissance Latin Translations and Commentaries,* II, ed. P. O. Kristeller (Washington, D.C., 1971), 239–322. The popularity of the *Characters* is especially noteworthy because of their stereotypicality, which suggests that whatever connection existed between life-writing and individualism in the earlier Renaissance had become a debatable (or at least much more problematic) phenomenon by the seventeenth century.

52. Patricia Cox, *Biography in Late Antiquity: A Quest for the Holy Man* (Berkeley and Los Angeles: University of California Press, 1983), esp. chap. 3; cf. ibid., 42 for Cox's useful discussion of the formation of hagiographic subgenres. She points out that greater attention is needed to the style and form of presentation rather than exclusively to factual aspects like the subject's ability to produce miracles.

53. Heffernan, *Sacred Biography*, 15.
54. Anderson, *Biographical Truth*, 20–26.
55. Peter G. Bietenholz, *History and Biography in the Work of Erasmus of Rotterdam* (Geneva: Droz, 1966), 23, 51. Bietenholz's brief book is essential to the understanding of the humanist problem in dealing with the medieval sacred biographical heritage, but much remains to be done on Erasmus's notion of *fides historica;* in the meantime, see Myron P. Gilmore's important essay, "*Fides et Eruditio:* Erasmus and the Study of History," in *Humanists and Jurists,* 87–114. For Erasmus as biographer, see, most recently, John B. Gleason, *John Colet* (Berkeley and Los Angeles: University of California Press, 1989), passim.
56. David Knowles, *Great Historical Enterprises* (London: Nelson, 1963).
57. Cochrane, *Historians and Historiography,* 393–5.
58. Giovanni Boccaccio, *De casibus virorum illustrium, Opere in versi, Corbaccio, Trattatello in Laude di Dante, Prose Latine, Epistole,* ed. G. Ricci (Milan and Naples, n.d.), 786–891; *De mulieribus claris,* in ibid., 706–83. Cf. Bruni's comment, "Avendo in questi giorni posto fine a un' opera assai lunga, mi venne appetito di volere, per ristoro dello affaticato ingegno, leggere alcuna cosa volgare" [Having recently finished a rather long work, I felt like reading something in the vernacular in order to restore my tired spirit]. *Le vite di Dante e di Petrarca (1436),* in *Leonardo Bruni Aretino Humanistisch-Philosophische Schriften,* ed. Hans Baron (Wiesbaden: M. Sändig, 1969), 50. On the other hand, when, much earlier in his career, Bruni had written the life of an ancient, he felt no compulsion to use the vernacular and instead wrote his short biography of Aristotle in Latin (1429; ibid., 41–49), as also his even earlier (1405–6) preface, dedicated to Salutati, to Plutarch's life of Mark Antony (ibid., 102–4). For Machiavelli's use of Tegrimi's *Vita Castrucci Antelminelli Castracani Lucensis ducis* (Modena, 1486), see Cochrane, *Historians and Historiography,* 267.
59. For the popularity of collective exemplary lives among the Modern Devotion in the fifteenth century, see Heiko A. Oberman, "*Die Gelehrten die Verkehrten:* Popular Response to Learned Culture in the Renaissance and Reformation," in Steven Ozment, ed., *Religion and Culture in the Renaissance and Reformation* (Kirksville, MO: Sixteenth Century Essays and Studies, 1989), 52 ff., and *Devotio Moderna: Basic Writings,* ed. John Van Engen (New York: Paulist Press, 1988), 45–46.
60. Donald A. Stauffer, *English Biography before 1700* (Cambridge, MA: Harvard University Press, 1930), 31–63; Harold Nicolson, *The Development of English Biography* (London: Harcourt, Brace, 1928), 7–64.
61. Christine de Pizan, *The Book of the City of Ladies,* trans. and ed. Earl Jeffrey Richards (New York: Persea Books, 1982), 266–7. For Boccaccio and Pizan, see Margaret L. King, *Women of the Renaissance* (Chicago: University of Chicago Press, 1991), 219–32; and Constance Jordan, *Renaissance Feminism:*

Literary Texts and Political Models (Ithaca, NY: Cornell University Press, 1990), 34ff.

62. See Michael Baxandall, *Giotto and the Orators: Humanist Observers of Painting in Italy and the Discovery of Pictorial Composition 1350-1450* (Oxford: Clarendon Press, 1971), 99ff., for Facio's work written between literary and artistic stools.

63. Paul Barolsky, *Michelangelo's Nose: A Myth and its Maker* (University Park: Pennsylvania State University Press, 1990) and *Giotto's Father and the Family of Vasari's Lives* (University Park: Pennsylvania State University Press, 1992). See also Catherine M. Sousloff, "*Lives* of Poets and Painters in the Renaissance," *Word & Image* 6 (1990): 154-62. For a comprehensive study of the workings of Vasari's classic, see Patricia L. Rubin, *Giorgio Vasari: Art and History* (New Haven, CT: Yale University Press, 1994).

64. For example, the sometime painter and bureaucrat Dominic Lampson, who had been in contact with Vasari and sent him information about Flemish painters for the second edition of his *Vite,* wrote a *Vita Lamberti Lombardi,* while Karel van Mander imitated Vasari more directly in the form of the collected lives in his *Het Schilder-Boeck* (Haarlem: Pasquier van Wesbach, 1604). On Lampson, see Jean Puraye, *Dominique Lampson, Humaniste 1532-1599* (Brussels: Desclée de Brouwer, 1950); "Dominique Lampson. Lamberti Lombardi... Vita," *Revue belge d'Archeologie et d'histoire de l'Art* 18 (1949): 53-77; and Simon A. Vosters, "Lampsonio, Vasari, van Mander y Pacheco," *Goya: Revista de Arte* (November-December, 1985): 130-39. For van Mander, see especially the work of Walter S. Melion, including "Karel van Mander's 'Life of Goltzius': Defining the Paradigm of Protean Virtuosity in Haarlem around 1600," *Studies in the History of Art* 27 (1989): 113-33 and his *Karel van Mander's "Schilder-Boeck": Shaping the Netherlandish Canon* (Chicago: University of Chicago Press, 1992).

65. For the flourishing of the medieval tradition of *uomini illustri* just before that point, see Susan J. Barnes, "The *Uomini Illustri,* Humanist Culture, and the Development of a Portrait Tradition in Early Seventeenth-Century Italy," *Studies in the History of Art* 27 (1989): 81-92, and for its roots, M. M. Donato, "Gli eroi romani tra storia ed 'exemplum': I primi cicli umanistici di 'Uomini famosi,' " in S. Settis, ed., *Memoria dell'antico nell'arte italiana,* 3 vols. (Turin: G. Einaudi, 1984-86), 2:97-152.

66. Cochrane, *Historians and Historiography,* 420-22.

67. Vespasiano, *Vite di uomini illustri del Secolo XV,* trans. W. George and Emily Waters as *Renaissance Princes, Popes, and Prelates: The Vespasiano Memoirs,* ed. Myron P. Gilmore (New York: Harper and Row, 1963).

68. F. J. Levy, *Tudor Historical Thought* (San Marino, CA: Huntington Library, 1967), 237-85; Woolf, *Idea of History,* chaps. 4 and 5.

69. Cochrane, *Historians and Historiography,* 106–8, 398; Stauffer, *English Biography before 1700,* 64–90.

70. James Michael Weiss, "Erasmus at Luther's Funeral: Melanchthon's Commemorations of Luther in 1546," *Sixteenth Century Journal* 16 (1985): 91–114.

71. For Giovio, see Thomas F. Mayer, "Reginald Pole in Paolo Giovio's *Descriptio:* A Strategy for Reconversion," *Sixteenth Century Journal* 16 (1985): 431–50.

72. See, e.g.: Gigliola Fragnito, "Per lo studio dell'epistografia volgare del Cinquecento: Le lettere di Ludovico Beccadelli," *Bibliothèque d'humanisme et renaissance* 43 (1981): 61–87; numerous works of Cecil H. Clough, especially "The Cult of Antiquity: Letters and Letter Collections," in C. H. Clough, ed., *Cultural Aspects of the Italian Renaissance: Essays in Honour of Paul Oskar Kristeller* (Manchester: Manchester University Press, 1976), 33–67; and the overview in Claudio Guillen, "Notes Toward the Study of the Renaissance Letter," in Barbara Kiefer Lewalski, ed., *Renaissance Genres: Essays on Theory, History, and Interpretation* (Cambridge, MA: Harvard University Press, 1986), 70–101.

73. Gary Ianziti, *Humanistic Historiography Under the Sforzas: Politics and Propaganda in Fifteenth-Century Milan* (Oxford: Clarendon Press, 1988), 175–76.

74. William C. Spengemann, *The Forms of Autobiography: Episodes in the History of a Literary Genre* (New Haven and London: Yale University Press, 1980), 1–44.

75. Kaspar von Greyerz, "Religion in the Life of German and Swiss Autobiographers (Sixteenth and Early Seventeenth Centuries)," in Kaspar von Greyerz, ed., *Religion and Society in Early Modern Europe 1500–1800* (London: German Historical Institute/Allen and Unwin, 1984), 223–41; Paul Delany, *British Autobiography in the Seventeenth Century* (London: Routledge and Kegan Paul, 1969).

76. See, e.g., Anne Jacobson Schutte, "Irene di Spilimbergo: The Image of a Creative Woman in Late Renaissance Italy," *Renaissance Quarterly* 44 (1991): 42–61, and Retha M. Warnicke, "Lady Mildmay's Journal: A Study in Autobiography and Meditation in Reformation England," *Sixteenth Century Journal* 20 (1989): 55–68.

77. Nancy Klein Maguire, "Regicide and Reparation: The Autobiographical Drama of Roger Boyle, Earl of Orrery," *English Literary Renaissance* 21 (1991): 257–82; Evelyn Hinz, "Mimesis: the Dramatic Lineage of Auto/Biography," in Marlene Kadar, ed., *Essays on Life Writing: From Genre to Critical Practice* (Toronto: University of Toronto Press, 1992), 196–212.

78. Margaret F. Rosenthal, "A Courtesan's Voice: Epistolary Self-Portraiture

in Veronica Franco's *Terze Rime*," in Elizabeth C. Goldsmith, ed., *Writing the Female Voice: Essays on Epistolary Literature* (Boston: Northeastern, 1989), 3–24, together with the rest of the volume. On the lack of formal autobiography among, for instance, fifteenth-century Florentine women, see Klapisch-Zuber, "Images without Memory," 37–43.

79. Luther, *Table Talk,* trans. T. G. Tappert, in *Luther's Works,* ed. H. T. Lehmann, American edition, ed. J. Pelikan, 55 vols. (St. Louis: Concordia Publishing House, 1955–86), vol. 54 (1967).

80. T. K. Rabb and Jonathan Brown, "The Evidence of Art: Images and Meaning in History," in T. K. Rabb and Jonathan Brown, eds., *Art and History: Images and their Meaning* (Cambridge and New York: Cambridge University Press, 1988), 1–6.

81. We no more than touch on the emblem, which has a vast literature and is becoming an increasingly contested area. See, most recently, Ellen Caldwell, "Discursive Figures: Emblem Theory in the Renaissance," unpublished essay, and Karen E. Pinkus, "The 'Symbolicae Quaestiones' of Achille Bocchi: Humanist Emblems and Counter-Reformation Communication," Ph.D. diss., City University of New York, 1990.

82. Loren W. Partridge, "Divinity and Dynasty at Caprarola: Perfect History in the Room of Farnese Deeds," *Art Bulletin* (1978): 494–530; see also Clare Robertson, *'Il Gran Cardinale': Alessandro Farnese, Patron of the Arts* (New Haven, CT: Yale University Press, 1992), 88–124, who criticizes some of Partridge's more ingenious interpretations. There is a similar cycle of frescoes—now considerably reduced in scale and much damaged—in the Palazzo Vitelli in Città di Castello; for them, see Julian Kliemann, "Prospero Fontana und Mitarbeiter im Palazzo Vitelli a S. Egidio in Città di Castello: Dokumente und Zeichnungen," *Mitteilungen des Kunsthistorisches Institut in Florenz* 31 (1987): 177–94.

83. Kristin E. S. Zapalac, *"In His Image and Likeness": Political Iconography and Religious Change in Regensburg, 1500–1600* (Ithaca, NY: Cornell University Press, 1990), 108ff.

84. Celeste Brusati, "Stilled Lives: Self-Portraiture and Self-Reflection in Seventeenth-Century Netherlandish Still-Life Painting," *Simiolus* 20 (1990/1991): 168–82. We are indebted to Professor Brusati for much help with Netherlandish portraiture and life-writing.

85. Josephine von Henneberg, "Bomarzo: nuovi dati e un'interpretazione," *Storia dell'Arte,* 13 (1972), 43–55 treats the garden as autobiography, while M. J. Darnall and M. S. Weil in "Il sacro Bosco di Bomarzo: Its Sixteenth-Century Literary and Antiquarian Context," *Journal of Garden History* 4 (1984): 1–94 explore its roots in Ariosto's poem. See also the exhaustive but tendentious treatment of H. Bredekamp, *Vicino Orsini und der heilige Wald von Bomarzo: Ein Furst als Kunstler und Anarchist,* 2 vols. (Rome: Edizioni dell' Elefante, 1985).

86. Hampton, *Writing from History*, 27.

87. For one of the best treatments of Melanchthon's method, see Uwe Schnell, *Die homiletische Theorie Philipp Melancthons* (Berlin and Hamburg: Lutherisches Verlagshaus, 1968), 17–53, together with Cesare Vasoli, "L'insegnamento logico del Melantone," in *La dialettica e la retorica dell'Umanesimo: "Invenzione" e "Metodo" nella cultura del XV e XVI secolo* (Milan: Feltrinelli, 1968), 278–309.

88. Diana Robin, *Filelfo in Milan* (Princeton: Princeton University Press, 1991), 5–6.

89. See the treatment of De Maio, "L'ideale eroico nei processi di canonizzazione della Controriforma," in *Riforme e miti nella Chiesa del Cinquecento* (Naples: Guida, 1973), 257–78.

90. See the distinction drawn in Marcantonio Flaminio, *Lettere*, ed. Alessandro Pastore (Rome: Edizioni dell'Ateneo, 1978), 4.

91. Paolo Simoncelli, *Il caso Reginald Pole: eresia e santitá nelle polemiche religiose del Cinquecento* (Rome: Edizioni di storia e letteratura, 1977) investigates the origins of Pole's "mito."

92. William F. Church, *Richelieu and Reason of State* (Princeton: Princeton University Press, 1972); Orest Ranum, *Artisans of Glory* (Chapel Hill: University of North Carolina Press, 1980); Jean-Marie Apostolidès, *Le Roi-machine* (Paris: Minuit, 1981); and Louis Marin, *Le Portrait du Roi* (Paris: Minuit, 1981).

1
Paolo Giovio and the Rhetoric of Individuality

T. C. Price Zimmermann

> The same Platina and Giovio, whose great histories we only read because and so far as we must, suddenly come forward as masters in the biographical style.
>
> Jacob Burckhardt

In dedicating the first edition of his *Lives of Illustrious Men* to Cosimo I de' Medici, Paolo Giovio averred that he had written them "in imitation of Plutarch, a philosopher of supreme gravity, although in a somewhat freer style."[1] The key phrase was "a somewhat freer style." Giovio's major biographies were not so much revivals of Plutarch as extensions of a tradition of Renaissance humanism, historical biography or, as it is sometimes called, biographical history.[2] In listing his sources for his life of Muzio Attendolo Sforza, Giovio indicated some of the major exemplars of the tradition he was following, among them Platina's lives of the popes, Giovannantonio Campano's life of the Perugian condottiere Braccio da Montone, Pier Candido Decembrio's life of Filippo Maria Visconti, and Lodrisio Crivelli's life of Francesco Sforza.[3]

Instead of creating a coherent interpretation of an individual's life based on a central core of internal characteristics—the Plutarchan model—humanist biography let subjects be defined by the history in which they had been involved, with a resume of personal characteristics and traits subjoined. In Plutarch, character was typically delineated toward the beginning of a biography on the basis of early signs and developed through events of the subject's maturity. By the time of death, it was already fully clarified. While the Plutarchan model contained much history, the history was carefully selected and ordered to reveal the character. It was his design, Plutarch reminded his readers in the life of Alexander, to write not histories, but lives. In Plutarch, narrative revealed character much as plot reveals character in fiction.

Humanist biography, on the other hand, left the reader to adduce the character from the history, a subtle but important difference which had the effect of making the history paramount.[4] The humanists saw biography as a natural outgrowth of history, making a sharp distinction only between biography and encomium.[5] Even where the history was carefully selected according to the aims of the biographer, as, for example, with Giovanni Simonetta's commentaries on the career of Francesco Sforza, the focus was still on history rather than on character.[6]

A better prototype for humanist biography than Plutarch might have been Suetonius, whose lives normally elaborated on character only after the subject's public career had been delineated, but few humanists were in a position to explore character with Suetonian license.[7] Indeed, historical biography, or biographical history, was eminently suited to the humanists, for whom, in most instances, a frank analysis of the moral dimensions of their princely subjects would not have been convenient. In general, humanist biography relied only vaguely on classical precedents.[8]

All Giovio's major biographies were historical in format.[9] The life of Muzio Attendolo, the first to be published (Rome: Blado, 1539), was written in particularly close conformity with the humanist tradition. Indeed, it was almost a commentary on earlier accounts: the life of Sforza by Crivelli, the prior parts of the *res gestae* of Francesco Sforza by Simonetta and the latter portions of Merula's history of the Visconti.[10] Fifty-seven concise chapters on Sforza's birth, life, and deeds were followed by chapters on subjects such as his liberality (58), his concubines (59), his three wives (60–62), his clemency and severity (65–71), the nature of his mind (72), his domestic and military habits (73–74), his piety (75), devotion to his patria (76), prudence (79), straightforwardness (80), stoicism (83), witticisms (84–86), stature (87), agility (88), and gallant death (89), including a rehearsal of the various portents (91). Plutarchan, perhaps, but if so, crudely so.

Giovio's lengthy biographies of Gonzalo de Córdoba and Fernando d'Avalos (Florence: Torrentino, 1549) were intensely historical in nature. They not only contained valuable material for the history of the respective epochs, particularly in regard to warfare, but also were based on conceptual structures that were themselves historical. Compared to the narrative elements, the sections dealing with character were relatively brief. Aside from a few conventional pieties, the biography of Gonzalo was virtually all history. The ferocity of d'Avalos was more than evident from the accounts of his campaigns, but there was no real probing of character.

Although they contained more overt analysis of character, Giovio's lives of Leo X and Adrian VI (Florence: Torrentino, 1548), like Platina's *Lives of the Popes,* were likewise historical in conception and formed the basis for much subsequent history of the two pontificates. In fact, Giovio's structuring of the history of Leo X's papacy was so historiographically appropriate that it was closely followed by Guicciardini in his *Storia d'Italia.*[11] Giovio's last biography, that of Alfonso d'Este, was virtually all political. A few brief paragraphs on Alfonso's habits and character were followed by a long synopsis of his role in the political complexities of the Italian wars. Yet once again, in writing of the life to Ercole II d'Este, Giovio claimed that it had been "dexterously composed in imitation of Plutarch."[12]

What probably justified in Giovio's mind the appropriation of a Plutarchan precedent was not so much his delineation of character as his willingness to chronicle bad deeds as well as good. Among humanists, it was fashionable to perpetuate the ancient classification of history as didactic rhetoric, as moral philosophy teaching by example.[13] Like the late trecento humanist Pier Paolo Vergerio, whose *De ingenuis moribus* formed a text of his boyhood education, Giovio believed that history was the source of examples of conduct, both good and bad, which served the reader as guides in what to imitate and what to avoid.[14] For a time Giovio taught moral philosophy at Rome, and in a sketch for a work never written, he proposed to write a treatise illustrating Aristotle's theories of ethics with ancient and modern examples drawn from history.[15] It must have been this rhetorical view of history (and biography) that made him call Plutarch "a philosopher of the greatest gravity." Victoria Kahn has stressed that in humanist practice, the intellectual virtue of right judgment about actions applied to the acts of interpretation made by both authors and readers.[16] In this sense, both the writing and the reading of history became an exercise in moral philosophy. In a recent and suggestive study on "the rhetoric of exemplarity" in the Renaissance, Timothy Hampton has called attention to the delicate interface between the hermeneutical procedures by which early modern culture appropriated ancient texts and figures and the rhetorical procedures through which the figures and texts were used to fashion the responses of contemporary readers.[17] A simplified analogue existed in the interface between the procedures by which biographers appropriated texts and figures from contemporary history and the rhetoric by which they presented them to contemporary readers.

The implicit presumption of humanist historical biography (however unwarranted) was of an identity between text and life.[18] Because early modern biographers considered life-writing a branch of history, historical truth became a bond between life and text. Life was text and text life. The fact that the term *biography* was coined only in a later age, as Mayer and Woolf point out in the introduction to this volume, underscores the fusion of life and text in early modern usage. There being no cultural gap to bridge for biographers of Renaissance personalities, no problem of anachronism, hermeneutics was reduced to the canons of history and rhetoric to the canons of historical style—*res et verbum,* as the late quattrocento theorist Giovanni Pontano categorized them.[19]

Cicero's definition of history in the *De oratore* (2.62–64) formed the paradigm for humanist historiography, and his challenge to tell not only the truth, but all the truth, was part of the formal convention of historical writing, however violated it may have been in actuality. Composition was presumed to be essentially a matter of condensing events, following the canons of *dignitas* and *brevitas,* and, above all, a matter of style, in which vivid narrative displayed the truth of historical events.[20] In historical biography, the "rhetoric of exemplarity" thus consisted in vivid presentation of the lived text.[21] Overt judgment as to which deeds were good, which bad, could be left to the reader. The only conceptual difference between historical biography and history lay in the dispensation given the biographer from the second half of the Ciceronian injunction; that is, the biographer was freed from the obligation of telling all the truth and licensed to delete unfavorable materials. Even this conceptual accommodation was unnecessary for some historical theorists, such as Bartolomeo Facio, who thought "ignoble" actions should be deleted anyway as unworthy of the "dignity" of history.[22]

In a letter to the humanist Girolamo Scannapeco, Giovio outlined the prevailing cinquecento theories of encomium, history, and biography. Scannapeco had complained that in a short biography of the Neapolitan humanist Pietro Gravina, Giovio had said unflattering things needlessly.[23] Giovio's response to Scannapeco's reproach was first to distinguish between history, which is based on truth and therefore rightly termed *magister vitae,* and encomium, "which praises people with all banners spread, without any fear of falling into the mud of lies, and which is silent regarding all the vices which often accompany even the most distinguished virtues, as with Alexander, Hannibal, Caesar and many others." As examples of encomium, Giovio gave Pliny's *Panegyric on Trajan* and Ausonius's eulogy of Gratian, the *Gratiarum actio.* Here and elsewhere, Giovio revealed his familiarity with the Roman rhetorical practices of praise and blame as codified by Quintilian in his *Institutio oratoria.*[24]

"Now history," Giovio continued, delineating the theory of historical biography, "has a branch which is writing the lives of excellent men whom Fortune has made important whether in politics or arms ... or ... letters and sciences...."[25] But whereas the historian must follow the Ciceronian imperative of telling not only the truth, but all of the truth (*De oratore,* 2.62), the biographer, while likewise committed to truth, is free to make convenient omissions. To illustrate this point, Giovio retold a story derived from Pliny of the three disciples of Apelles faced with the problem of painting a portrait of the tyrant Antigonus, who had lost his right eye. Polygnotus painted him exactly as he was, missing eye and all. Scopa, on the other hand, painted him as if he had not lost the eye. The astute Diocles simply painted him in profile, neither flattering nor offending the royal dignity (the solution used by Piero della Francesca in his portrait of Federigo da Montefeltro). A "Plutarchan" biography, it may be inferred, would be one that did tell the whole truth, bad deeds as well as good.[26]

Despite the imputed license of the biographer, Giovio's major biographies were remarkably forthright in addressing bad qualities in his subjects as well as good. The remainder of his letter to Scannapeco, in fact, defended the frankness he had used in noting Gravina's vices along with his virtues and argued the ultimate folly of adulation. Giovio's only concession to Diocles was his protest to Scannapeco that he had sketched in the vices of Gravina with a very light brush. Since no human was without vices, he warned, to ignore them was to run the risk of adulation.

To emphasize his point, Giovio retold the tale of the poet Philoxenus of Cythera, whose critical honesty finally won the respect of the tyrant Dionysius of Syracuse. Recently liberated from the prisons where he had been sent for his criticisms of the tyrant's verses, Philoxenus had been summoned with other men of letters to hear the tyrant's new tragedy. At the conclusion of the reading, while the others were praising Dionysius as another Euripides, Philoxenus got up and moved toward the door. "Where are you going, Philoxenus?" asked the tyrant. "To the prisons," he replied, "to spare myself being dragged there by your henchmen." This time even Dionysius could not forbear laughing.[27] Giovio's fundamental belief was that the flattered great would ultimately see the self-defeating nature of adulation, which invites not admiration but, rather, ridicule.[28] "Let us write of virtues and vices," he concluded, "although with tempered humanity, not angry satire, so that the thoughtful can take the virtues like ports at sea and flee the shoals to avoid shipwreck."[29]

From the standpoint of frankness, the most remarkable of Giovio's biographies was the life of Leo X. Although commissioned and published by members of the Medici family, the *Vita Leonis Decimi* concealed none of Leo X's vices: his extravagance, his unanticipated cruelty, his brazen aggrandizement of his family, even the "infamy" of his "dishonest" loves for handsome noble youths.[30] Giovio's other biographies followed suit to a greater or lesser degree. The life of Adrian VI was highly critical, that of Gonsalo de Córdoba largely laudatory.[31] The life of Alfonso d'Este left the duke's character to be drawn almost entirely from the account of his warfare and diplomacy, a narrative of expedience navigating the treacherous waters of the Italian wars, tacking this way and that for the interests, not of Italy, but of Ferrara and the Este family. In an epoch in which, as Giovio himself complained, "to have praised sparingly is tantamount to having spoken ill," his historical biographies might well have seemed to him "Plutarchan."[32] His famous *Elogia*, however, were to become even more authentically Plutarchan.

Giovio's most enduring contribution to Renaissance culture was his portrait museum and collection of capsule lives, respectively the *Elogia* of writers (*Elogia veris clarorum virorum imaginibus apposita quae in Musaeo Joviano Comi spectantur* [Venice: Tramezzino, 1546]) and of rulers, statesmen, and generals (*Elogia virorum bellica virtute illustrium veris imaginibus supposita quae apud Musaeum spectantur* [Florence: Torrentino, 1551]). If his major biographies were basically historical in format, Giovio's *Elogia* were fundamentally rhetorical; "lives written with laconic brevity," he called them.[33] They were appended to the portraits of famous individuals displayed in his museum on the shores of Lake Como. In this setting, the need to be brief but memorable forced

Giovio into overtly rhetorical techniques. His prototype was a Roman usage that was itself an example of "the rhetoric of exemplarity." *Elogia* were inscriptions on Roman funeral busts. Carried in funeral processions, they proclaimed for all to see the achievements, the *res gestae,* of the deceased. After the funeral, they were attached to the permanent bust or statue of the ancestor kept in a special room of the houses of important Roman families as a historical record and as an inducement to successive members of the family to live up to the achievements of their forebears.[34]

Unlike their prototypes, which were by nature positive, Giovio's *elogia* were rhetorical in accordance with the humanist historical conception of furnishing exempla of good and bad conduct for moral reflection. They differed from his major biographies, however, in that the criteria of selection and judgment—the hermeneutical side of the interface, one might say—now became overt. The *Elogia* of heroes included such advertisedly negative exempla as Ezzelino da Romano, "tyrant of Pavia, . . . with his fearful pallor and viper's eyes"; Cardinal Alidosi, "an example to posterity of a wicked life that should incite the clergy to lead lives of honest and upright discipline"; Cesare Borgia, "who in his bloody character and pitiless cruelty can be likened to the ancient tyrants"; and Henry VIII, who in the span of a few years turned "crueler than an enraged tiger, more rapacious than a ravaging wolf, more rabid than a mother lioness, and more poisonous than a thirsty dragon."[35] An explicitly positive exemplum was the vivid *elogium* of Antonio Grimani, a man superior to all the tricks of Fortune, who was forced to enter the state prisons in chains yet emerged to rise to the dogeship, a demonstration "that an honored name can be bruised by Fortune but never crushed."[36] Giovio's criteria for his selection and judgment in the *Elogia* would form a study in themselves, but in general they reflected the Ciceronian and Senecan moral philosophy commonplace to the humanist tradition.[37]

With the *Elogia*, Giovio's focus shifted from deeds to character. History became secondary. For the revealing of character, Giovio would frequently relate a seemingly minor incident that nonetheless revealed a major trait, proving himself in this new genre a true disciple of Plutarch, who commented in the life of Alexander, "It is not always in the most distinguished achievements that a man's virtues and vices may be best discerned; very often an action of small note, a short saying, or a jest will distinguish a person's real character more than battles in which thousands fall, or the greatest armaments or sieges of cities."[38] Giovio's

Elogia stressed vividness and memorability. The historian Ferdinand Gregorovius, in a happy metaphor, termed them "a species of historical fresco painting."[39]

Many of the striking depictions of Renaissance figures in Burckhardt's *Civilization of the Renaissance* were in fact derived from Giovio's *Elogia*, as, for example, Pomponio Leto descending the Quirinal before dawn, holding his lantern before him like another Diogenes. Giovio's portraits of captains and rulers bristled with memorable images: the impetuous Bartolomeo d'Alviano, short in stature but with piercing eyes (cf. Quintilian on Homer's portrait of Tydeus, 3.7.12); the indomitable Antonio de Leyva commanding his troops from a litter; Pompeo Colonna, with helmet in the camp and surplice at the altar; Cortez burning with desire for Mexican gold (*animo ingens cupido*). It was Giovio's efforts in the *Elogia* to be brief and memorable that, more than anything, linked them to the classical rhetorical tradition.

Not only did Giovio focus his *Elogia* on character rather than on history, he used rhetorical techniques in writing them, loosening the bond between text and life. With analysis of character supplanting the canons of history and rhetoric the conventions of historical style, the standard of absolute truth employed in historical biography yielded to the rhetorical standards of vividness and persuasiveness. The *Elogia* have been the despair of many a scholar attempting to verify otherwise unsubstantiated stories or incidents contained in them. In part because of the speed with which they were written, Giovio was not overly scrupulous about verifying gossip, particularly when it illuminated aspects of an individual's character that he wanted to dramatize, as in his otherwise unverified charge that Giles of Viterbo gave himself an ascetic pallor by eating cumin and inhaling fumes from burning damp straw. No doubt this bit of Roman curial gossip served as an illustration of the strain of hypocrisy Giovio detected in the character of that learned but pompous and not altogether consistent cleric.[40]

In a well-turned phrase, John Addington Symonds spoke of those occasions when "the legend has caught the spirit of the truth." Giovio himself cited the classical rhetorical tradition whereby the historian (and biographer) "was given a slight latitude through ancient privilege to be able to aggravate or lighten people's vices in which they sinned, and the opposite, with florid or jejune eloquence to raise or lower the virtues according to the counterbalances and their merits."[41] Thomas Babington Macaulay, a disciple of the classical tradition, gave the most eloquent apology for the technique: "The best portraits are perhaps those in which there is a slight mixture of caricature, and we are not certain that the best histories are not those in which a little of the exaggeration of fictitious narrative is judiciously employed. Something is lost in accuracy, but much is gained in effect. The fainter lines are neglected; but the great characteristic features are imprinted on the mind for ever."[42] Still, Giovio's use of material of dubious authenticity to create a "true" portrait of character produced the paradox noted by Kahn, whereby the rhetoric employed to make humanist texts persuasive might itself undermine their claims to persuasion.[43]

Giovio was well acquainted with major prototypes of classical biography, not only Plutarch and Suetonius, but also the short lives of commanders by Cornelius Nepos (whom he knew as Probus), and the biographical-doxographical compendium of Diogenes Laertius on ancient philosophers.[44] Of these, the most visibly influential on his *Elogia* was Suetonius, with his use of racy and memorable detail for delineating character. Nepos, in his largely laudatory lives, also concentrated on character over history, and Diogenes Laertius would certainly have been a good precedent for the use of anecdotal material. Presumably Giovio either knew or knew of humanist revivals of the genre of short biography, such as Petrarch's *De viris illustribus* (especially the compendium made for the Carrara family), Boccaccio's moralizing *De mulieribus claris,* or the *De viris aetate sua claris* of Enea Silvio Piccolomini.[45]

Bartolomeo Facio's *De viris illustribus,* modeled on the lives of Pius II and dedicated to their author, was to some extent a precedent for Giovio's *Elogia,* particularly as Facio included lives of artists, sculptors, and scholars who did not subsequently become important cardinals or popes.[46] A recent precedent were the short lives composed by Giovio's friend and admirer, Jacopo Sadoleto, for the *Illustrium imagines* of Andrea Fulvio (Rome: Mazzocchi, 1517), a collection of small medallion portraits printed from woodblocks.[47] Unlike Petrarch's inspiring exempla, however, or the laudatory sketches of Facio and Sadoleto, Giovio's *Elogia* abounded in biting judgments on personal, professional, and moral shortcomings. In this regard, they were far more reflective of the classical rhetorical tradition.

Giovio's *Elogia* seem to have reflected Quintilian's precepts for praise and blame (*laus* and *vituperatio*), a genre that in Rome figured as practical oratory, whereas in the Greek tradition it had been considered part of epideictic rhetoric.[48] In Quintilian's analysis of the genre, character was foremost. "Praise should be based," he said, "on an individual's physical and mental qualities in relation to external circumstances."[49] Deeds were to be praised or blamed in relation to background and ancestry, the times in which they occurred, and their legacy to the future. Thus, one individual might fall short of a distinguished background while another ennobled humble origins with illustrious deeds (3.7.10). Physical attributes were less important than the use made of them. Overcoming handicaps was cause for true praise, just as misusing gifts was cause for vituperation. Wealth, power, and influence were the surest test for good or evil character (3.7.14). (One thinks of the proverb cited by Guicciardini to conclude his *Storia d'Italia, Magistratus virum ostendit*.) Among the virtues Quintilian specifically mentioned as meriting praise were fortitude, justice, and self-control (3.7.15). Character could be analyzed, he said, either chronologically, from childhood, or analytically, discussing individual deeds in terms of specific virtues or vices.

Whether by chance or by design, in one way or another Giovio's *Elogia* exemplified virtually all of Quintilian's precepts for the rhetoric of praise and blame. His approach was analytical rather than chronological, and he constantly evaluated his subjects with respect to the past, their times, and their legacy to posterity. As Quintilian recommended, Giovio often included in the subject's background the portents that accompanied his birth or heralded his demise. Again and again, he compared a subject's life with his background. Thus, for example, Giovio marveled that a person of such noble appearance and magnanimity as Columbus could have been born in "a mean and ignoble" Ligurian town (8:369–71). In Sabellico's "iron strength of intellect" Giovio affected to see the legacy of the humanist's blacksmith father (8:77–78). To form a quick impression of his subject, Giovio invariably related features and physique to achievements. The "rather rustic" features of Pontano, for example, he contrasted with the "polish" of his literary style (8:76–77), as he contrasted Agostino Nifo's uncouth appearance with his urbane wit (8:115–16).

Originally Giovio's *Elogia* were written only of the deceased. He had postponed writing *elogia* of the living whose portraits he also possessed, his reason being that "the praises of the living ought to be weighed in the scrupulous balance of a severer criticism, for fear that my unfailing friendship with men of letters and the very sincerity of manifest goodwill in which we have always rejoiced should weaken the sinews of clear judgment and prevent frankness alike of praise or blame."[50] Giovio was not waiting, in the Greek tradition, for the whole life to reveal itself lest the end gainsay the middle and vitiate its value as an icon. He wanted the liberty of frankly depicting the combination of strengths and weaknesses that defined a particular person.[51]

In the rhetorical tradition, Giovio freely engaged in moral comment, even on personal traits. For example, he frequently reproached scholars for marring otherwise justifiable pretensions to intellectual distinction and high culture by crude manners or an unseemly life-style, as in the "plebeian and sordid manners" and "impudent gourmandise" of Pietro Alcionio (8:133).[52] He often reproached captains and rulers with lack of self-control, as in Alessandro de' Medici's immoderation—ultimately fatal—in pursuing amours (8:389–90). Moral space, as Charles Taylor has argued, was the fundamental area for the emergence of the sense of self, and the same was true for the analogous concept of character.[53] Giovio appropriated the conventional pieties regarding the worth of exempla, and to define his subjects, he engaged more frankly than most humanists in the rhetorical exercise of praise and blame, one of the chief means, since antiquity, for the individuation of character.[54]

But Giovio was just as interested, if not more so, in the configuration of individual traits. Indeed, much of the material of the *Elogia* did not lend itself so much to "Plutarchan" exercises of high moral judgment as to reflection on the quirks and foibles that characterized and defined an individual human being. With their rich admixture of moral deficiencies and personal foibles, Giovio's *Elogia* were intended as word-portraits to be appended to the portraits above them in the expectation that the ensemble of word and features would convey a complete picture of a real individual. It might even be said, using Hampton's apt phrase, that the ensemble of *elogium* and portrait was intended to serve "as the occasion for reflection on the constitution of the self," because Giovio's preoccupation with illuminating personal peculiarities as well as strengths and moral shortcomings could have had no other purpose than promoting within the reader-viewer a process of reflection on the varied components of particular personalities.[55] In the *Elogia,* in fact, Giovio was always grasping for biographical detail that rounded out an individual personality with the subject's sense of self, particularly in relation to others, as, for example, Pontano's excessively severe criticism of others but widely noted touchiness regarding himself, or the embarrassingly laudatory inscription Filippo Decio devised for his own tomb, or the grammarian Battista Pio's stubbornness in employing linguistic archaisms despite the disapproval of everyone else.[56]

In the lack of formally developed concepts of personality, Giovio was in effect providing a montage of image, traits, and actions on which the reader-viewer could exercise intuitive faculties of perception and categorization. His innovation was to bring together complementary verbal and pictorial representations to recreate not only individual character in the classical sense but also a discrete personality in the modern sense. The *elogia* were character sketches in that they placed the individual in an external moral framework, but they anticipated personality theory in that they attempted a rudimentary global perspective.[57]

Linda Klinger has shown that Giovio's museum created a framework allowing a conceptualization of "likeness," intellectually grounded and historically structured. Giovio successfully challenged poetic constructs of verisimilitude as a quality of portrayal, she argues, and forced the viewer to consider the image as an object functioning within the realm of historical truth.[58] As opposed to a "rhetoric of exemplarity," Giovio's *Elogia* might be said to have embodied a "rhetoric of individuality." In the practice of rhetoric, as Lyons points out, there is always a tension between the exemplum, grounded in historical reality, and the ideological framework that it is intended to reinforce.[59] From the rhetorical standpoint, Giovio's *elogia* burst the bounds of exemplarity to acquire independent vitality through the individuality of their subjects. One of the first to follow the methods developed by Giovio in the *Elogia* was Giorgio Vasari. Giovio's role in the genesis of the *Lives of the Artists* is well known. In the memoir of his own life and work, Vasari narrated the scene that took place about the dinner table of Cardinal Alessandro Farnese in 1546, when Giovio, who had just completed the *Elogia*, was dilating on his plan of composing the lives of celebrated artists and Vasari was urged to help him with the particulars.[60] After Giovio saw the work that Vasari already had in progress, however, he became its enthusiastic promoter, encouraging the artist to complete it and offering his services as editor, services he performed—to what extent is unknown—in the winter of 1547–48.[61] Whereas earlier art historians argued that Vasari's work was well under way by the time Giovio saw it and was therefore unlikely to have been influenced by Giovio's scheme, in point of fact, there were many echoes of Giovio's *Elogia* in the *Lives*, a circumstance scarcely surprising in view of the fact that Giovio had been one of Vasari's mentors during the whole time he had been composing his *Lives* and that Giovio himself was the author of the earliest lives of Leonardo, Raphael, and Michelangelo.

Recent scholarship has emphasized Vasari's debt to the humanist milieu into which Giovio and the courtiers of Ippolito de' Medici first introduced him in 1532.[62] It was most probably from Giovio and his humanist friends that Vasari derived the view of history expressed in the preface to the second part of the *Lives*. "When I first took to describing these lives," he told the reader, "it was not my intention to make a note of the artists and an inventory, so to speak, of their works...." Rather, he said, he had imitated the historians, "who have not been content simply to narrate events," but who "have investigated the modes, means, and ways that valiant men have used in managing affairs, and have contrived to touch on the errors as well as the fine *coups,* defenses and choices sometimes made in the government of affairs ... which is the true soul of history, and that which in truth teaches men how to live and makes them prudent...."[63] In other words, the *Lives of the Artists* were also to be "Plutarchan."

For Vasari, as for Giovio in the *Elogia,* character became the key to understanding both life and works. Thus, for example, the "cruel" personality of Andrea del Castagno explained not only his part in the assassination of Domenico Veneziano, but aspects of his style as well. Partly because it was difficult, with the lack of a developed critical vocabulary, to draw distinctions between artists on the basis of style, Vasari attempted to bring exterior events into accord with interior ones and to present a unity of personality between the artists and their work, creating plastic portraits of artistic individualities. Personality he emphasized as the most accessible principle of individuation and, as Giovio in the *Elogia,* for the delineation of personality he appropriated anecdotal materials, even ones of dubious authenticity.[64]

The prevailing medieval view that human beings acted in accordance with their social roles, their physical constitutions (humors, temperaments), or the stars was enlarged in the Renaissance by reemphasis on the classical notion of individual character. Aided by rhetorical theory and practice, the making of "Plutarchan" judgments became the principal component of the individuation of character. In his evolution from biographical historian to capsule biographer and collector of portraits, Giovio not only used "Plutarchan" judgments to impress on the consciousness of Europe the view that individual character was the well-spring of action but also offered his contemporaries new techniques for global individuations that anticipated modern concepts of personality.[65]

A final word might be added on an alternative form of life-writing popularized by Giovio, the *impresa,* or device, a lifelong interest that came to fruition in his posthumously published *Dialogo delle imprese,* which he had dedicated in 1551 to Cosimo I de' Medici.[66] Although it continues to elude efforts at uniform definition, the *impresa* was a common courtly phenomenon in the Renaissance. Basically, it consisted of an emblem and motto that required some culture to decipher and that alluded in some way to the bearer's philosophy of life. Giovio's treatise constituted the first attempt to systematize the theory and practice of making *imprese.* Rejecting the more arcane possibilities of symbolism, Giovio insisted that the *impresa* both conceal and reveal, concealing the message from the vulgar but revealing it to the educated. An ideal *impresa* consisted of a body—the emblem—and a soul—the motto. To enhance the aspect of concealment, the motto had to be in a language foreign to the bearer. Rather than a talisman of mystical, interior meaning, the *impresa* was for Giovio a form of *explicatio,* an outward revelation of inner truth. Its energy came from the Renaissance delight in conceits, in ingenuity, in the ambiguity of polyvalent allusion. A perfect example of an *impresa* was Vespasian's anchor with a dolphin and the motto, *Festina lente* [Make haste slowly].

Obviously, the *impresa* had the potential to function as an aid to memory and a symbol about which to group perceptions of an individual's life, works, and character. Like the portrait or *elogium,* the *impresa* had an explicative function. For example, the device of Leo X, a yoke with the motto *Suave*—a witty allusion to his rule of reconquered Florence—expressed the pope's personality and the spirit of his pontificate. Cosimo I's device, Capricorn—his horoscope—with the motto *Fidem fati virtute sequemur* [By virtue we keep faith with our destiny], not only revealed the duke's confidence in his destiny and statecraft, but also symbolized his foreign and domestic policy, linking him to his overlord, Charles V, who had the same horoscope, as well as to Augustus, whose victory over Anthony at Actium occurred on the same day as Cosimo's over the Florentine exiles at Montemurlo.[67] In the *Elogia,* Giovio sometimes mentioned a particularly appropriate *impresa,* as, for example, the comet adopted by Ippolito de' Medici, the effect being to intensify the verbal portrait by suggesting the subject's own sense of self.[68]

While the intentional ambiguity of many *imprese* diminished their value as biographical aids, nonetheless the *impresa* remained an intriguing component of the nascent sense of personality in the early modern era.[69] Like an *exemplum* or a name, it could serve as the fixture for a gathering of concepts or attributes, similar to the fashion in which, as Hampton points out, the fig tree, the locus of Augustine's conversion, became a synecdoche for his life.[70] Kristin Lippincott, in fact, stresses the use of *imprese* on portrait medals to give a glimpse into the subject's ambitions or essence, the obverse showing the body, the reverse the spirit.[71] Giovio's nomenclature for the emblem of an *impresa,* the corpus, also recalls Hampton's suggestion that the heroic body was a text to be read in itself.[72]

NOTES

Burckhardt quotation from *The Civilization of the Renaissance in Italy*, trans. S. G. C. Middlemore (New York: Modern Library, 1954), 179. In addition to the editors and press readers, my colleagues at Davidson, Dr. Nina E. Serebrennikov and Dr. Steven H. Lonsdale, have made helpful suggestions for this essay.

1. "Insignium aliquot procerum vitae imitatione Plutarchi summae gravitatis philosophi, a me, licentiore stilo perscriptae etc." *Pavli Iovii Novocomensis Episcopi Nvcerini Illustrium Virorum Vitae* (Florence: Torrentino, 1549), fol. a ii.

2. On biographical history, see Eric Cochrane, *Historians and Historiography in the Italian Renaissance* (Chicago: University of Chicago Press, 1981), 52–58.

3. Paolo Giovio, *Illustrium virorum vitae* (Florence: Torrentino, 1551), 157. On Campano, the essential study is Riccardo Fubini, "Umanesimo curiale del Quattrocento: Nuovi studi su Giovann'Antonio Campano," *Rivista Storica Italiana* 88 (1976): 745–55. On Platina and papal biography, see Fubini's "Papato e storiografia nel Quattrocento: Storia, biografia e propaganda in un recente studio," *Studi medievali* 18 (1977): 321–51. On Decembrio and Crivelli, see Gary Ianziti, *Humanistic Historiography under the Sforzas* (Oxford: Clarendon Press, 1988).

4. For an illuminating discussion of the problems faced by Bruni in reconstructing a historical life of Cicero from the life by Plutarch, see E. B. Fryde, "The 'New Cicero' of Leonardo Bruni," *English Historical Review* 95 (1980): 533–52.

5. Bruni made such a distinction regarding his *Laudatio Florentinae Urbis,* "aliud ist historia, aliud laudatio." Leonardo Bruni, *Epistularum libri,* ed. Lorenzo Mehus (Florence: B. Paperini, 1741), 2:112.

6. Ianziti, "The Making of the *Commentaries,*" in *Humanistic Historiography under the Sforzas,* chap. 7.

7. For an interesting analysis of Filelfo's problems in criticizing the Sforza, see Diana Robin's *Filelfo in Milan* (Princeton, NJ: Princeton University Press, 1991), esp. chap. 2.

8. A good introduction to the literature on ancient biography is Arnaldo Momigliano, *The Development of Greek Biography* (Cambridge, MA: Harvard University Press, 1971). Momigliano was still influenced, however, by the tradition of German scholarship and the somewhat forced distinction drawn by Leo between the style of Plutarch, which was viewed as historical in nature, and the style of Suetonius, which was thought to be traceable to the school of Alexandria and its biographies of artists and writers. The close links of ancient biography to history have been emphasized by Bruno Gentili and Giovanni Cerri, *Storia e biografia nel pensiero antico* (Bari: Laterza, 1983). I am obliged to Professor James Michael Weiss for reinforcing my view that the humanists were generally indifferent to such methodological divergences as may have existed in ancient biography.

9. *Leonis Decimi vita; Hadriani Sexti vita; Pompei Columnae Cardinalis vita* in *Pauli Iovii opera* (Rome: Istituto Poligrafico dello Stato, 1956–), 6, *Vitarum pars prior,* ed. Michele Cataudella. *De vita Magni Sfortiae; De vita et rebus gestis Consalvi Ferdinandi Cordubae cognomento Magni; De vita et rebus gestis Ferdinandi Davali cognomento Piscarii* in *Pauli Iovii Novocomensis Episcopi Nucerini Illustrium Virorum Vitae* (Florence: Torrentino, 1549 and 1551). *Liber de vita et rebus gestis Alfonsi Atestini* (Florence: Torrentino, 1550).

10. Lodrisio Crivelli, *De vita rebusque gestis Sfortiae bellicosissimi ducis ac initiis Francisci Sfortiae Vicecomitis eius filii Mediolanensium Ducis ilustrissimi,* in *Rerum Italicarum scriptores,* ed. L. A. Muratori (Milan: ex typographia Societatis palatinae, 1723–51), 19:628–732; Giovanni Simonetta, *De rebus gestis Francisci Sfortiae commentarii,* ed. G. Soranzo, in *Rerum Italicarum scriptores,* 2d ed., ed. G. Carducci et al. (Città di Castello and Bologna: S. Lapi, 1900–), xxi, 2; Giorgio Merula, *Antiquitates Vicecomitum,* in *Thesaurus antiquitatum et historiarum Italiae,* ed. J. G. Graevius (Leiden: P. Van der Aa, 1704–25), iii, 1. For all these, see Ianziti, *Humanistic Historiography.*

11. See T. C. P. Zimmermann, "Francesco Guicciardini and Paolo Giovio," *Annali d'Italianistica* 2 (1984): 39–42. On Platina's *Lives,* see Cochrane, *Historians and Historiography,* 54–56.

12. To Ercole II d'Este, 30 August 1549: *Iovii opera,* 2:139.

13. For an introduction to the view of history as moral philosophy, see Myron P. Gilmore, "The Renaissance Conception of the Lessons of History," in William

H. Werkmeister, ed., *Facets of the Renaissance* (Los Angeles: University of Southern California Press, 1959), 73–86. The phrase "philosophy teaching by example" derived from Dionysius of Halicarnassus (Donald R. Kelley, *Renaissance Humanism* [Boston: Twayne, 1991], 97). Two recent studies of the exemplum as rhetoric are John D. Lyons, *Exemplum: The Rhetoric of Example in Early Modern France and Italy* (Princeton, NJ: Princeton University Press, 1990) and Timothy Hampton, *Writing from History: The Rhetoric of Exemplarity in Renaissance Literature* (Ithaca, NY: Cornell University Press, 1990). Lyons stresses the tension in the rhetorical use of the exemplum between the demands of the present argument in which it is employed and fidelity to the historical context from which it is drawn. See also the article by Randolph Starn, "Reinventing Heroes in Renaissance Italy," in *Art and History*, ed. R. C. Rotberg and T. K. Rabb (Cambridge: Cambridge University Press, 1988), 67–84.

14. See Giovio's *elogium* of Vergerio in *Iovii opera*, 8:129.

15. Como, Società Storica Comense, Archivio Aliati, 28.5, 371^v–373^r.

16. Victoria Kahn, *Rhetoric, Prudence, and Skepticism in the Renaissance* (Ithaca, NY: Cornell University Press, 1985), 21.

17. Hampton, *Writing from History*, 3.

18. On acts as texts for Renaissance exemplarists, see Hampton, *Writing from History*, 10.

19. The most extensive discussion of humanist historical method occurs in Pontano's dialogue the *Actius*. See the critical edition by Carmelo Previtera, ed., in Giovanni Pontano, *I dialoghi* (Florence: Sansoni, 1943), 127–239. For Pontano's views on historical exempla, see 229. On the paradox of exemplarity and anachronism, see Hampton, *Writing from History*, esp. 16. On *res* and *verba*, see Lyons, *Exemplum*, 14, who places moral purpose in the domain of *res*, the exemplum itself, and sees the end of *verba* as making the exemplum more acceptable through the pleasure of literature; and Ernesto Grassi, *Renaissance Humanism: Studies in Philosophy and Poetics*, trans. Walter Veit (Binghampton: MRTS, 1988), chaps. 1–2 and esp. pp. 37–44.

20. For the relationship of brevity to historical truth, see the *Actius*, esp. 213ff. and 231ff. Method for Pontano consisted chiefly in means for clear and succinct presentation of significant events (*explicatio, ordo, dispositio*). The Ciceronian injunction to tell all the truth was reflected, although somewhat more weakly, in his pronouncements, "Brevitas autem erit talis, ut rerum summas paucis complectatur; diligentia tanta, ut nihil omittat quod iudicetur memoratu dignum; ... Nam praeter veritatem nihil potest esse commendabile. Quid obsecro, tam est adversum quam vanitas historiae, quae vitae magistra esse dicitur?" ibid., 231. On the importance of Cicero's canon of truth to Renaissance exemplarity, see Hampton, *Writing from History*, 6.

21. The best statement of this view is again found in Pontano's *Actius*, 229: "Ac mihi quidem res gestas memoriae qui mandant officioque funguntur

tradendi ad posteros res praeteritas non minore fortasse laude digni videantur quam qui leges tradidere vivendi. Illi enim praecepta, exempla hi nobis tradidere; quippe cum proprium eorum officium ac munus sit sustentare ingenio suo vitae nostrae imbecillitatem atque mortalitati ire obviam, ne, quantum in ipsis est, dicta factaque memoratu digna resque praeclare atque excellenter gestas tempus obscuret neve eae omnino e memoria excidant; quaeque imitatione atque congnitione digna sunt, aevo ea ne intercidant, quibus mortale genus ad virtutem excitetur et gloriam; ut qui legunt, qui de iis loquuntur intelligant omnes quo ore quoque animo laudentur honesta, vituperentur turpia et improba; etc."

22. On Facio's debate with Valla, see Linda Gardiner Janik, "Lorenzo Valla: The Primacy of Rhetoric and the De-moralization of History," *History and Theory* 12 (1973): 389–404. As Janik points out (401), there were contradictions between Valla's view that history was rhetoric and his insistence that the allegiance of the historian was not to the moral capacity of his audience but to facts. In his historicist moods, Valla felt that the historian could not preempt the judgment of the reader. See also Hampton's discussion of the "irony" of negative traits in the exemplar (Hampton, *Writing from History*, 26ff). Examples of humanist biography that omitted negative aspects of the subject were Campano's life of Braccio and Manetti's life of Nicholas V. See Cochrane, *Historians and Historiography*, 52–53.

23. *Vita Petri Gravinae a P. Iovio ad Iohannem Franciscum Campaneum* in Gravina, *Poemata,* ed. Scipione Capece (Naples: Sultzbach, 1532).

24. *Iovii opera,* 1:174. On Giovio's use of Quintilian, see ahead.

25. Examples of the former given by Giovio are the *De vita Caesarum* by Suetonius, the *Historia Augusta,* which Giovio attributed to Aelius Spartianus and Aelius Lampridius only, and the *De viris illustribus* of Cornelius Nepos, which Giovio still attributed to Probus. Examples of the latter given by Giovio are the lives of the philosophers of Diogenes Laertius, the lives of Plutarch, and "Pliny in the book of illustrious grammarians." Exactly what Giovio meant by this last is uncertain. He probably meant Suetonius's *De grammaticis et rhetoribus,* the principal surviving part of his *De viris illustribus.* Diogenes Laertius's lives had been translated into Latin in the quattrocento by Ambrogio Traversari. See Charles M. Stinger, *Humanism and the Church Fathers* (Albany: SUNY Press, 1977), 71–77.

26. In a letter to Giovio of 30 Jan. 155[1], Cosimo I de' Medici acknowledged the difference between biography and history by admonishing Giovio that "truth being the nerve of history, . . . it will be difficult to maintain credit if Your Lordship turn wholly to the *elogia* in which it is permitted in a certain manner to pass over and shade the truth." Giovio, *Lettere volgari,* ed. L. Domenichi (Venice: Sessa, 1560), fols. 71ᵛ–72ʳ.

27. *IO,* 1:178. Giovio apparently used the name "Antippo [Xanthippus?]" for Dionysius's critic, but the identification does not make sense, and he retold

the episode exactly as related by Diodorus Siculus, 15.5.6. The letter survives only in a sixteenth-century printed version.

28. On his aversion to flattery, see Giovio's remarks to Tommaso Cambi, advising against the adulation of Charles V: "et senza adulatione a Cesare, con le quale impropriamente pensando laudare, vituperano Sua M.tà et dano, che ridere a'galanthuomini,..." in "Paolo Giovio: Invenzione per la faciata della casa in Napoli di Tomaso Cambio, 1540," ed. Stefano Della Torre, *Atti del convegno Paolo Giovio, il rinascimento e la memoria* (Como: Società Storica Comense, 1985), 221–23.

29. *Iovii opera*, 1:176.

30. Ibid., 6:95.

31. The Enlightenment historian William Roscoe took vigorous exception to the passage in the life of Gonsalo in which Giovio attempted to mitigate Gonsalo's betrayal of his pledge of safe-conduct to Cesare Borgia on the grounds that he had been ordered to do so by his master, Ferdinand of Aragon. William Roscoe, *The Life and Pontificate of Leo X*, 2 vols. (London: Chatto & Windus, 1876), 1:265.

32. Preface to book 7 of the *Elogia virorum bellica virtute illustrium: Iovii opera*, 8:479.

33. "Horum enim vitas per elogia ipsis supposita tabulis, laconica brevitate conscriptas etc." *Iovii opera*, 8:235. The *Elogia* of writers were first published in 1546 (Venice: Tramezzino), those of rulers, diplomats, and generals in 1551 (Florence: Torrentino). Both series are found in volume 8 of the *Iovii opera*, edited by Renzo Meregazzi.

34. For a discussion of the precedents for Giovio's portrait collection and *elogia* see the introduction by Renzo Meregazzi to volume 8 of the *Iovii opera* and Paul Ortwin Rave, "Paolo Giovio und die Bildnisvitenbücher des Humanismus," *Jahrbuch der Berliner Museen* 1 (1959): 119–54. For a description of the busts and their role, see Polybius, 6.53.

35. *Iovii opera*, 8:262–68, 380–82, 376–78, 463–64.

36. Ibid., 8:410–12.

37. Hampton notes that the humanists talked about exemplarity in a vocabulary appropriated from Roman moral philosophy (Hampton, *Writing from History*, 6). Giovio was most deeply influenced by Cicero's *Tusculans*. See *Iovii opera*, 9:138.

38. Cited by P. G. Walsh, *Livy* (Cambridge: Cambridge University Press, 1961), 88.

39. *History of the City of Rome* (London: George Bell, 1900), bk. 14, chap. 4.

40. *Iovii opera*, 8:109–10. Although a leading proponent of ecclesiastical reform, Giles of Viterbo still possessed at his death in 1532 three episcopacies (Barbara McClung Hallman, *Italian Cardinals, Reform, and the Church as Property, 1492–1563* [Berkeley: University of California Press, 1985], 24). An ex-

ample of an otherwise unverified account is the attractive story Giovio tells in the *elogium* of Linacre of his encounter in the Vatican Library with Ermolao Barbaro. See Charles Schmitt, *The Aristotelian Tradition and Renaissance Universities* (London: Variorum, 1984), 41, n1. An example of haste in writing would be the slip whereby Giovio in the life of Filippo Decio records that he had been recruited to Pavia from Pisa, whereas he had in fact been recruited from Padua (1505). Giovio is right, though, in that he had taught at Pisa for many years before that. On haste in composition and his lack of scrupulous documentation, see Italo Gallo, "Piceni e Picentini: Paolo Giovio e la patria di Pomponio Leto," *Rassegna Storica Salernitana*, n.s. 3 (June 1986), 44. But lack of independent corroboration does not necessarily invalidate Giovio's information, since he was preserving evidence of character traits that might have been disregarded in more laudatory biography. Most often, what appears in the *Elogia* to have been gossip indicated personal shortcomings, such as crude manners, which undermined the subject's otherwise justifiable pretensions to intellectual distinction and high culture.

41. "Sapete bene che l'istoria dee esser sincera, né punto bisogna in essa scherzare se non in una certa e poca latitudine donata allo scrittore per antico privilegio di potere aggravare e alleggerire le persone de' vizii, ne' quali peccano; come per lo contrario con florida e digiuna eloquenza alzare e abbassare le virtù secondo i contrapesi e meriti loro" (*Iovii opera*, 1:177). Giovio doubtless had in mind loci such as Cicero's *Brutus*, II.42, "Tuo vero, inquit, arbitratu quoniam quidem concessum est rhetoribus ementiri in historiis, ut aliquid dicere possint argutius." On the impact of this view, see Beatrice R. Reynolds, "Shifting Currents in Historical Criticism," *Renaissance Essays*, ed. P. O. Kristeller and P. P. Wiener (New York: Harper, 1968), 118. By Hellenistic times, in fact, the border between biography and fiction had been nearly obliterated by "biographies" such as Clitarchus's life of Alexander the Great. Michael Grant, *Roman Literature* (Harmondsworth: Penguin, 1958), 114.

42. Cited by Harold Acton, *Nancy Mitford* (London: Hamish Hamilton, 1975), xvi.

43. Kahn, *Rhetoric, Prudence, and Skepticism*, 26. She also cites (p. 43) Pontano's argument in his *De sermone* that, using a pragmatic standard, doctors, rulers, and priests all tell untruths for the purpose of helping people.

44. Among ancient biographies, Giovio mentions Suetonius's *De vita Caesarum*. He does not specifically mention the obvious prototype for the *elogia* of scholars, Suetonius's *De viris illustribus*, lives of literary figures, of which the *De grammaticis et rhetoribus* survives along with a few lives of Roman writers, but he does mention lives of grammarians by Pliny, which may have been a confusion of the moment (*Iovii opera*, 1:174). Giovio knew the *De viris illustribus* of Cornelius Nepos, although they were attributed to Probus (ed. prin., Venice: N. Jenson, 1471) until proven by Parrasio to be by Nepos (J. E. Sandys, *History of*

Classical Scholarship, 3 vols. [Cambridge: Cambridge University Press, 1920], 2:486). See *Iovii opera,* loc. cit. Of the sixteen books of Nepos's parallel lives of distinguished Romans and foreigners comprising his *De viris illustribus,* only one section survives, the *Vitae excellentium imperatorum.* Giovio was also familiar with Diogenes Laertius's lives of the philosophers (loc. cit.), translated by Ambrogio Traversari by 1433 and first printed in Venice by Jensen in 1475. On Traversari's translation, see Charles Stinger, *Humanism and the Church Fathers* (Albany: SUNY Press, 1977), 71–77. Giovio did not mention, but may have known, the anonymous and very sketchy *De viris illustribus,* Roman biographies ranging from Proca to Pompey and sometimes attributed to Pliny. He mentioned several authors of the *Historia Augusta,* including Aelius Spartianus and Trebellius Pollio (Giambattista Giovio, "Elogio di Mons. Paolo Giovio," in *Elogii italiani,* ed. Andrea Rubbi [Venice: P. Marcuzzi, 1782–83], 8:74–75).

45. For a recent study of Petrarch's lives, see Benjamin G. Kohl, "Petrarch's Prefaces to *De viris illustribus,*" *History and Theory* 13 (1974): 132–44. See also Hampton, *Writing from History,* 26–27. For a recent study of Enea Silvio's, see Paolo Viti, "Osservazioni sul *De viris aetate sua claris* di Enea Silvio Piccolomini," in *Pio II e la cultura del suo tempo,* ed. Luisa Rotondi Secchi Tarugi (Milan: Guerini, 1991), 199–214. Boccaccio's *De mulieribus claris* has been translated into English by Guido A. Guarino (New Brunswick: Rutgers University Press, 1963). Giovio nowhere mentions any of these.

46. Bartolomeo Facio, *De viris illustribus liber* (Florence: J. P. Giovanelli, 1745). On Facio, a secretary of Alfonso of Naples, see P. O. Kristeller, "The Humanist Bartolomeo Facio and his Unknown Correspondence," in Charles H. Carter, ed., *From the Renaissance to the Counter-Reformation: Essays in Honor of Garrett Mattingly* (New York: Random House, 1965), 56–74. Facio's aversion to including negative traits, expressed in his polemics with Valla, made his lives more like exempla. See Linda Gardiner Janik, "Lorenzo Valla: The Primacy of Rhetoric and the De-Moralization of History," *History and Theory* 12 (1973): 389–404. There is no indication whether Giovio was conversant with vernacular biography, most notably the lives of Vespasiano da Bisticci.

47. Cecil H. Clough, "Italian Renaissance Portraiture and Printed Portrait-Books," in *The Italian Book, 1465–1800: Studies Presented to Dennis E. Rhodes,* ed. Denis V. Reidy (London: British Library, 1993), 188. The *Illustrium imagines* were edited by Theodore Besterman and reprinted by the Collegium Graphicum in 1972.

48. *Institutio Oratoria,* 3.7. For an introduction to the Renaissance revivial of the *ars laudandi et vituperandi,* see John W. O'Malley, "The New Rhetoric: Ars Laudandi et Vituperandi," in *Praise and Blame in Renaissance Rome* (Durham, NC: Duke University Press, 1979), chap. 2. Kahn points out (38) that as the political and legal dimensions of rhetoric fell away during the Renaissance, only the rhetoric of praise and blame remained. She also calls attention (39) to

Aristotle's admission that epideictic does seem to have a practical dimension in that praising is tantamount to recommending a course of action. Giovio nowhere specifically acknowledged following Quintilian, but for evident debts, see my article, "Paolo Giovio and the Evolution of Renaissance Art Criticism," in *Cultural Aspects of the Italian Renaissance,* ed. Cecil H. Clough (Manchester: Manchester University Press, 1976), 406–24. Giovio does not seem particularly indebted to the more generalized precepts for praise and blame in the pseudo-Ciceronian *Rhetorica ad Herennium.*

49. "Ipsius vero laus hominis ex animo et corpore et extra positis peti debet." 3.7.12.

50. *Iovii opera,* 8:39. Translation by Florence Alden Gragg, *An Italian Portrait Gallery* (Boston: Chapman & Grimes, 1935), 28. See also the preface to book 7 of the *Elogia* of heroes (*Iovii opera,* 8:479).

51. See Hampton, *Writing from History,* 26–27. Mayer has called attention to one short life written by Giovio that did attempt to idealize his subject, and that was the life of Cardinal Pole in the *Descriptio Britanniae,* but that, Mayer has shown, was for a special purpose (Thomas F. Mayer, "Reginald Pole in Paolo Giovio's *Descriptio:* A Strategy for Reconversion," *Sixteenth Century Journal* 16 [1985]: 431–50).

52. On Alcionio's gourmandise, see Kenneth Gouwens, "Ciceronianism and Collective Identity: Defining the Boundaries of the Roman Academy, 1525," *Journal of Medieval and Renaissance Studies* 23 (1993): 184–85.

53. Charles Taylor, "The Self in Moral Space,", in his *Sources of the Self: The Making of the Modern Identity* (Cambridge, MA: Harvard University Press, 1989), chap. 2. My article, "Confession and Autobiography in the Early Renaissance," *Renaissance Studies in Honor of Hans Baron,* ed. Anthony Molho and John A. Tedeschi (DeKalb: Northern Illinois University Press, 1971), 119–40, argues a similar point. Although the root of the English word *character* is a Greek word meaning an identifying mark or impress, English usage generally gives *character* an implicit moral component. This perpetuates the classical practice of treating individuals as moral and psychological agents and individuating them not only by their traits, beliefs, desires, self-conception, and actions, but also by outside judgments with respect to an ethical framework. While not the whole of character, Aristotle's notion of ethos was certainly its core. Personality, on the other hand, is a modern, nonjudgmental concept of the totality of the self, including that component of it developed from the ancient concept of persona (the face presented to the world), namely, the structure of outer and inner qualities actualized by social intercourse (as in, "She has a nice personality"). Lacking the nomothetic aspect of character, personality is more individualizing, concerned with identity rather than appraisal in terms of norms. The ancients certainly recognized the existence and psychology of individuality and selfhood

but did not develop a theoretical basis for them, stressing instead the validity of social norms. Ancient literature often seems more interested in types than in individuals. It is certainly ironic that something as central to humanity as character should have been so poorly conceptualized. For individual character, the Greeks used mainly the term *phusis,* the Romans the terms *natura* or *indoles.* In distinguishing the ancient approach to character, I have based myself on *Characterization and Individuality in Greek Literature,* ed. C. B. R. Pelling (Oxford: Clarendon Press, 1990), especially the editor's introduction and conclusion; Christopher Gill, "The Character-Personality Distiction," 1–31; and Stephen Halliwell, "Traditional Greek Conceptions of Character," 32–59.

54. In explaining the origin of his collection, Giovio had declared that the purpose of the "true images of illustrious men of letters" was "so that through emulation of their example good mortals might be inflamed to seek glory" (*Iovii opera,* 1:92).

55. Hampton, *Writing from History,* xi. Hampton does, in fact, mention (27 n. 45) Giovio's collection, but under a misunderstanding owing to secondhand acquaintance.

56. On Pio, see Carlo Dionisotti, "Giovan Battista Pio e Mario Equicola," in *Umanisti e il volgare fra Quattrocento e Cinquecento* (Florence: Le Monnier, 1968).

57. For the character-personality distinction, see above n. 51.

58. Linda S. Klinger, "The Portrait Collection of Paolo Giovio," Ph.D. diss., Princeton University, 1991. Although he was ultimately forced to print the *Elogia* without woodcuts, in 1544 Giovio had declared to Daniele Barbaro that doing so would be absurd, since without effigies the *Elogia* would be "mute and lifeless [*sine genio*]" (*Iovii opera,* 2:4).

59. Lyons, *Exemplum,* 14.

60. I cannot agree on the dating with Vasari's biographer, Boase, who moves the episode from the time of Vasari's collaboration with Giovio on the Sala dei Cento Giorni to 1543 (T. S. R. Boase, *Giorgio Vasari* [Princeton, NJ: Princeton University Press, 1979], 44).

61. *Iovii opera,* 2:118. Giovio suggested the title, reflecting Nepos, "Le vite de gli eccellenti artefici." See the introduction of Carlo Ragghianti to Vasari's *Vite,* 4 vols. (Milan: Rizzoli, 1949), 1:9.

62. See especially Anna Maria Brizio, "La prima e la seconda edizione delle *Vite,*" in *Studi Vasariani* (Florence, 1952), 85, and Zygmunt Waźbiński, "L'idée de l'histoire dans la première et la seconde édition des *Vies* de Vasari," in *Il Vasari storiografo e artista* (Florence: Istituto Nazionale di Studi sul Rinascimento, 1976), 6; and Julian Kliemann, "Su alcuni concetti umanistici del pensiero e del mondo figurativo vasariani," in *Giorgio Vasari tra decorazione ambientale e storiografia artistica,* ed. Gian Carlo Garfagnini (Florence: Olschki,

1985), 80–82. E. H. Gombrich has revealed Vasari's familiarity with the rhetoric of Cicero in his article "Vasari's *Lives* and Cicero's *Brutus*," *Journal of the Warburg and Courtauld Institutes* 23 (1960): 309–11.

63. Cited from the edition of Rosana Bettarini and Paola Barocchi, 8 vols. (Florence: Sansoni, 1966–69), 3:3–4.

64. For Vasari's emphasis on plasticity and for his use of anecdotal materials, see Julius Schlosser Magnino, *La letteratura artistica*, 3d ed. (Florence: Nuova Italia, 1964), 310–12. The chief means of description available to Vasari for works of art was the classical *ekphrasis*. See Svetlana Alpers, "Ekphrasis and aesthetic attitudes in Vasari's *Lives*," *Journal of the Warburg and Courtauld Institutes* 23 (1960), esp. 193.

65. Giovio's *Elogia* were immensely popular. Klinger, "The Portrait Collection of Paolo Giovio," 202, has found thirty-two editions within fifty years, including translations into French, German, and Italian. On modern concepts of personality, see note 53.

66. The *Dialogo delle imprese* was first published posthumously in 1555. It has been edited by Ernesto Travi and Mariagrazia Penco in the *Iovii opera*, 9:353–443. There are also useful notes in the edition by Maria Luisa Doglio (Rome: Bulzoni, 1978).

67. *Iovii opera*, 9:386, 389–90.

68. Ibid., 8:447.

69. Two interesting new studies of the *impresa* are Maude Bregogli-Russo, *L'impresa come ritratto del Rinascimento* (Naples: Loffredo, 1990) and Kristen Lippincott, "The Genesis and Significance of the Fifteenth-century Italian Impresa," in *Chivalry in the Renaissance*, ed. Sydney Anglo (Woodbridge, Suffolk: Boydell Press, 1990), 49–76.

70. Hampton, *Writing from History*, 28.

71. Lippincott, "Genesis and Significance of Fifteenth-century Italian Impresa," 71–72. The Kress collection of portrait medallions in the National Gallery, Washington, D.C., is particularly rich in medallions with *imprese*.

72. Hampton, *Writing from History*, 29; cf. Starn, "Reinventing Heroes."

2

Giorgio Vasari's *Vita di Michelangelo Buonarroti* and the Shade of Donatello

Barbara J. Watts

Giorgio Vasari's (1511–74) *Le vite de più excellenti pittori, scultori, et architettori,* first published in 1550, revised, enlarged, and republished in 1568, was a landmark in early modern life-writing.[1] The three-volume opus, which contained biographies of the leading Italian artists active from about 1250 through 1550, was the first biographical compilation devoted exclusively to visual artists. Previously, the genre was reserved for groups that traditionally were deemed historically significant: rulers, saints, diplomats, and, later, poets. Vasari's *Lives* thus asserted that artists' lives were comparable to those of other *uomini illustri*, and that that artistic activity was worthy of commemoration.[2] More specifically, it posited the equality of the visual and verbal arts by providing a biographical compilation of artists' lives, so too artists. In the second edition of the *Lives,* Vasari expressed this assertion pictorially as well as verbally. Prompted by Paolo Giovio's collection of portraits of *uomini illustri,* he prefaced each life with the artist's portrait, thereby placing his opus within a pictorial tradition as well as a literary one.[3] The structure of the volume further supported the importance of artistic activity. It was arranged chronologically and divided into three parts, each introduced by a preface that provides a synoptic survey of the period's artistic achievements.[4] Set into this context, the artists of Vasari's *Lives* become the dramatis personae of an established and significant historical continuum.

Classical and contemporary texts served as Vasari's chief sources in writing the *Lives.* For material on the artists themselves, he drew upon fourteenth- and fifteenth-century chronicles, *novelle,* and writings on art, among others, Lorenzo Ghiberti's *Commentaries* and Cristoforo Landino's characterization of the art of Florentine masters in the preface to the 1481 Florence *Commedia*.[5] For the larger structural and cognitive frameworks for his opus, however, he looked to other sources. Ancient writers, notably Pliny the Elder, had presented the history of art as a progression toward perfection reached in the age of Alexander.[6] Vasari's dependence on Pliny's history of art and artists in *Natural History* is most obvious. Vasari used this model for the *storia* of art in his own age, showing its rebirth as a rising continuum, each generation building upon the achievements of the former.[7] Like Leon Battista Alberti (*Della pittura* 1436), he borrowed topoi from classical histories and treatises on the arts.[8] Thus, his excursuses on education, social status, and the role of imitation, as well as his anecdotes on themes such as the aping of nature and artistic competitions, may be traced to classical sources.[9] Vasari's thinly disguised classical borrowings were doubtless intended to elicit a comparison between the artistic luminaries of the ancient world and those of his own age. Furthermore, they support the major thesis of the *Lives*'s prefaces, that Italian artists had reenacted the cycle of artistic progress that culminated in a golden age of the pictorial arts, and that sixteenth-century artists had achieved classical perfection, making them the equals of artists of the ancient world.

Although Vasari relied strongly on Pliny for matters concerning art and artists, he was also influenced by classical theories of life-writing, which he knew from humanist texts if not directly from ancient sources. Indeed, both the organization of the text and the structure of the individual *vite* suggest a careful blend of ancient and contemporary models. As T. C. Price Zimmermann has shown in the preceding chapter, Paolo Giovio's lives draw upon classical models but reflect the precise shape of no one of them. So, too, with those of Vasari. For determining the order of the lives, the *Lives of Illustrious Philosophers* by Diogenes Laertius served Vasari, as it had other Renaissance compilers of lives of a single profession.[10] Like them, he grouped masters and pupils together and ordered the artists' lives to reflect the progressive development of Italy's geographical schools. The lives themselves evoke other models. Like the Plutarchan life, a typical Vasarian *vita* first sets forth the subject's personal and artistic character, often linking it to the events of his early life. The subsequent account departs from the Plutarchan paradigm, however, for its organization and content are structured not by the artist's character, but by his professional achievements. Yet like Plutarch, and more closely at hand, Giovio, Vasari includes anecdotes that are resonant of the subject's personality and character. Usually these incidental events cast the artist in a favorable light, but not always. Vasari did not omit a subject's artistic and personal shortcomings, for, as he observed in the preface to part II of the *Lives,* the best historians "have tried to point out their [subjects'] mistakes as well as the fine strokes" (83). The lives also recall the model of Suetonius: after treating the artist's career, Vasari usually returns to the person, portraying temperament and character through a series of facts and vignettes. For Vasari, character determines artistic strengths and shortcomings. Thus, Andrea del Sarto possessed a "timidity of spirit and a yielding simple nature," defects that "deprived his work of the ornament, magnificence, and wealth of style seen in many other painters."[11] This example illustrates a biographical trope that is central to Vasari's text, one that seldom appears in earlier biographies of artists: character describes not just the artist, but also his art. Vasari's metaphoric extension is reciprocal. Thus, *terribilità* not only describes Michelangelo's art, it also denotes his character.[12] Similarly, the gentle and courteous Raphael is a "harmonizer" in both life and art. Possessing a sweet and loving disposition, he thus made paintings of "grace and sweetness." In art, Raphael harmonized diverse trends, forming from many different styles a single manner, a "smooth and graceful style" (297, 318). Correspondingly, in life, Raphael created harmony, bringing those craftsmen who worked with him to forsake querulousness for courtesy and "to live in a state of natural harmony and agreement" (322).

In writing the *Lives,* Vasari looked to medieval models as well as to those classical and contemporary. Hagiographical texts, such as Jacobus de Voragine's *Legenda Aurea,* were especially suited to Vasari's purpose of extolling artists, and he adapted formulae for the lives of saints in his accounts of their births, deaths, and obsequies.[13] The medieval model of the spiritual pilgrimage also played a significant role in the *Lives.* As Paul Barolsky has observed, Vasari's presentation of artistic progress, though it follows classical models, is indebted to Dante's *Commedia,* which records the poet's *aescesis* toward Divine Revelation.[14] Indeed, the structural and thematic parallels between the *Lives* and the *Commedia* suggest that Vasari conceived the development of Renaissance art as an aesthetic pilgrimage analogous to Dante's spiritual one. Vasari, as did Dante, divided his *storia* into three parts. For both poet and biographer, the first part is characterized by infernal darkness, and in it, the artist cum pilgrim sets out on a path toward enlightenment.[15] The second part of the *Lives,* like Dante's *Purgatorio,* details the purgation of defects and the painstaking acquisition of knowledge and virtue. Dante's *Paradiso* is devoted to those who have achieved perfection. In it, he presents the Church Triumphant in the ascending spheres of the heavens, each representing a higher degree of enlightenment. His journey culminates with the beatific vision. Following the poet's schema, Vasari, in the third part of the *Lives,* presents the artists of the High Renaissance who have achieved artistic perfection, and his opus culminates in the revelation of artistic divinity—Michelangelo Buonarroti (1475–1564), the subject of this chapter.

That Dante's *Commedia* served as a model for Vasari's *Lives* is suggestive with respect to how the text should be read. As a narrative, the *Commedia* has a diachronic structure. Dante-pilgrim moves forward in time and place, always progressing toward enlightenment. The text is also synchronic, however. As Charles S. Singleton has shown, when moving forward in Dante's text, one must also continually look back, for each passage may cast in a new light the one that preceded it.[16] Thus, as the *Inferno* colors our reading of the *Purgatorio* and *Paradiso,* so too do the *Purgatorio* and *Paradiso* alter and enlarge our understanding of the *Inferno.* This authorial directive "to look back in retrospect," as Singleton termed it, is also characteristic of Vasari's *Lives.* In a diachronic reading of the text, Vasari's life of Michelangelo represents the desired end of the artistic pilgrimage toward perfection, and its variations on themes seem to be repetitions that are endemic to biographical compilations. When the *Lives* is read synchronically, however, these variations echo one another, endowing the text with resonances that otherwise remain unheard. This subtext binds the individual biographies to one another, making the *Lives* an integrated text whose full meaning is revealed only when the work is considered as a whole. This is very much the case with Vasari's *Vita di Michelangelo Buonarroti,* which draws upon the tropes and topoi of the previous lives, and in so doing, crystallizes their synchronic *storia.*

Transcendent Tropes: Michelangelo and the Shade of Donatello

Vasari's life of Michelangelo was the last biography in the first edition of the *Lives,* intended to represent the culmination of the *storia* of artistic progress that the work records.[17] For Vasari, Michelangelo represented the summit of artistic achievement. In the preface to the third part of the *Lives,* Vasari wrote:

> But the man whose work transcends and eclipses that of every artist, living or dead, is the inspired Michelangelo Buonarroti, who is supreme not only in one but all three [arts]. He surpasses not only all those whose work can be said to be superior to nature but also the artists of the ancient world, whose superiority is beyond doubt. Michelangelo has triumphed over later artists, over artists of the ancient world, over nature itself, which has produced nothing, however significant, that his inspired genius, with its great powers of application, design, artistry, judgment, and grace, has not been able to surpass with ease (253–54).

Vasari's *Vita di Michelangelo Buonarroti* is focused toward demonstrating these assertions, and throughout it, the author harks back to the triumphal theme of the preface, describing work after work as reaching new heights of perfection. In addition, he uses virtually every topos that lends itself to glorifying Michelangelo. His birth, for example, is presented as an act of divine intervention, implicitly recalling Christ's advent (324). The events upon his death, the nocturnal transportation of his body from Rome to Florence, and the discovery, twenty-five days after Michelangelo died, that his body was yet fresh and undecayed, evoke comparison with legends of the saints (438).

Vasari's use of such hagiographical topoi to characterize Michelangelo sets the *vita* within the rhetorical realm of the panegyric or encomium, where events are embellished and advantageously displayed. With this mode of life-writing, the knowing reader assumes that the author may have omitted facts or played loose with them to present the subject as a worthy model for emulation. In so heavily relying on biographical and hagiographical topoi to portray Michelangelo as a moral, spiritual, and artistic paradigm, Vasari thus risked undermining the reader's sense of the *vita*'s historical veracity. In the revised *vita* of 1568, he eliminated this danger by carefully documenting his account, more so than in any other of the lives. In the major addition to the original text—the account of Michelangelo's activities from 1550 to 1564—Vasari emphasizes his authorial credibility, presenting the reader with proof after proof of his knowledge of the subject. He records events that he witnessed, summarizes actual conversations that he had with Michelangelo, and as if this were not enough, provides transcriptions from eleven of the "many" letters and poems that Michelangelo sent him during the periods when they were apart.[18] With repeated reminders of his long and close friendship with Michelangelo, Vasari thus creates the impression that he wrote the life largely from personal knowledge, much of which came from Michelangelo. Vasari's documentation, coupled with proof that Michelangelo provided him with information, constitutes a compelling argument for the veracity of his account. In addition, it creates an effective counterbalance to the biographical and hagiographical topoi that he uses to extol Michelangelo. Taken together, the laudatory topoi, documentation, and firsthand accounts fashion a Michelangelo who represents Vasari's moral and artistic ideal and who also evokes the actual, idiosyncratic persona of the artist himself.

Vasari and Michelangelo did not become friends until the early 1540s, which may explain why the 1568 *vita* contains so much more documentation than the 1550 *vita*. Vasari's emphatic assertions of the truth of his *vita* (328, 393) suggest a specific catalyst for his additions and revisions to the original text, however: Ascanio Condivi's *Vita di Michelagnolo Buonarroti raccolta per Ascanio Condivi da la Ripa Transone*, published in Rome in 1553.[19] In the preface to his life of Michelangelo, Condivi tells the reader that he was prompted to write it because "some, who, writing about this rare man, through not having (as I believe) frequented him as I have, on the one hand have said things about him which never were so, and on the other hand they have left out many things which are most noteworthy" (3). He claims that his life of Michelangelo, though written "with the method not of a good writer, but of a diligent and faithful collector," is honest and authoritative, composed of material that he gathered "from the living oracle," which he verified with "the evidence of trustworthy writings and men" (4). Condivi's life of Michelangelo, though beyond the scope of this study, is important for us, because it provides a control for Vasari's life, thereby offering a key to the nature of Vasari's rhetoric of life-writing. Both authors assert that their information comes directly from Michelangelo. In many instances, they make similar assessments of identical material, which suggests that both were responding to a single autobiographical voice. The similarities of the two lives, therefore, make their differences significant. In short, what sounds like the clear voice of Michelangelo in Condivi's life is, in Vasari's life, transmuted into the "objective" voice of the author, whose task is not only biography but also art history.

A point that both Condivi and Vasari make that suggests the rhetorical nature of Vasari's life is that of Michelangelo's artistic autonomy. Condivi virtually denies the influence of other artists. For example, he states that Michelangelo's first master, Domenico Ghirlandaio (1449–94), was jealous and "gave him no help whatever" (10), and he omits mention of the lesser Bertoldo di Giovanni (ca. 1420–91), Michelangelo's teacher at the Medici sculpture garden. Vasari makes this point more subtly, for his presentation of facts molds Michelangelo's life and art into an integrated *storia* that proclaims his artistic transcendence. In Vasari's hands, artistic autonomy thus becomes one aspect of the life's larger themes.

Throughout his *vita,* Vasari minimizes Michelangelo's debt to others, portraying him as ultimately beholden to no one for his achievements. Nonetheless, he continually alludes to preceding biographies in the *Lives,* thereby eliciting comparisons between Michelangelo and those who influenced him. These allusions support the triumphal theme of the literal text, for implicitly, each represents a contest in which Michelangelo emerges as the victor. At the same time, however, they set Michelangelo's achievement into an art historical context, confirming Vasari's model of an artistic continuum that progresses toward perfection. He thus presents Michelangelo as both the consequence of generations of artistic progress and as the titan whose achievements vanquished all others. Vasari's treatment of Michelangelo's artistic influences, therefore, glorifies Michelangelo, but it also serves the work's larger schema of the historical development of the arts in the Renaissance.

Just as a retrospective reading of Michelangelo's *vita* colors our understanding of it, so, too, it alters our perspective of the other lives in Vasari's opus. When read through the lens of Michelangelo's *vita,* the preceding biographies serve to set Michelangelo's *vita* into relief. In this context, the relation between Vasari's *Vita di Michelangelo* and his *Vita di Donato* (Donato di Niccolò Bardi, called Donatello, 1386–1466) is most significant. Among the fifteenth-century artists in the *Lives,* Donatello reigns supreme. For Vasari, he was the first to bring perfection to the arts, and he represented the embodiment of artistic genius and secular virtue. In the preface to the second part of the *Lives,* Vasari states that he was uncertain whether to place Donatello among the artists of the second Renaissance style, where chronologically he belonged, or to include him among those of the third period, for his figures "are worthy to rank both... with the work of the ancient world and also with that of the modern" (92). Donatello thus prefigures Michelangelo, whose achievements also transcend his time. As scholars have shown, the fifteenth-century sculptor had a profound influence on Michelangelo.[20] Yet in his life of Michelangelo, Vasari mentions Donatello only in passing and does not acknowledge Michelangelo's enormous debt to him.[21] To have done so openly would have undermined his assertion of Michelangelo's transcendence. Although "written out" of the literal text, Donatello is ever present in its subtext, however; for between the lines, Vasari continually calls for the shade of Michelangelo's artistic father. When Michelangelo's *vita* is read in the context of Donatello's *vita,* a complex dialectic between the two artists emerges that reveals Donatello to be Vasari's typological model for Michelangelo. Appropriate to the idealization of the third period of Renaissance art, Vasari perfects his model, and thus veils his prototype.[22]

Family Romance

The analogies between Vasari's lives of Michelangelo and Donatello are many. Some of these are topoi that recur throughout the *Lives.* Others reflect the artists' common identity as Florentine sculptors. Nonetheless, the parallels between Donatello's and Michelangelo's biographies are so numerous, and in some instances so striking, as to suggest that Vasari intended to elicit a *paragone* between them. Comparison reveals Donatello's role as precursor to Michelangelo and model for him. At the same time, it reinforces Vasari's assertion of Michelangelo's pre-eminence, for in each instance, he bests his artistic father. When the two lives are considered from the perspective of their similarities, the differences between them become significant. Vasari's accounts of the two artists' early years, for example, offer analogous family romances, but their differences establish Michelangelo's inborn and acquired superiority over Donatello.

Donatello's father was a wool carder, a member of the Ciompi, the lowest guild in Florentine society.[23] Vasari omits his humble origins and tells us that he was raised by Ruberto Martelli, a wealthy noble who recognized the young boy's talent (174). After Donatello's artistic greatness was manifest to all, the more exalted Cosimo de' Medici assumed the role of surrogate father and patron (180). Cosimo, the *pater patriae* of Florence, supplied Donatello with commissions and looked after him with paternal benevolence. When the sculptor was old and infirm, Vasari tells us, the patron commissioned works so that his friend would not be penniless (186). Obviously, Vasari's emphasis on Cosimo's beneficence was intended to please his own patron, Duke Cosimo de' Medici.[24] Nonetheless, in carefully documenting the close relationship between artist and patron, he asserts Donatello's importance. Cosimo's greatness reflects on him, and Donatello's status is elevated by the patrician's high regard.

Now let us turn to Michelangelo's family romance. Appropriate to the role of epic hero that he plays in Vasari's drama, Michelangelo comes not from humble stock, but from a noble family, and Vasari details his lineage.[25] The family had fallen upon hard times, however, and thus like Donatello, Michelangelo benefited greatly from the early patronage of a wealthy Florentine noble (326). Lorenzo de' Medici (*il Magnifico*), grandson of Donatello's benefactor Cosimo, astounded by the young boy's first sculpture, asked his father for him, explaining "that he wanted to keep him as one of his own sons" (331). Michelangelo's surrogate family history thus begins where Donatello's ends—with the Medici. Vasari emphasizes the youth's status as an equal in the Medici household: he was given a room of his own, and he always ate at Lorenzo's table with his natural sons, nobles, and dignitaries.[26] Michelangelo's relations with the Medici thus lacked the class distinction that characterized Donatello's relationship. After Lorenzo's death in 1492, he went on to even loftier heights, replacing his aristocratic surrogate father with an even nobler one. In 1508, he was called to Rome by Pope Julius II. Thenceforth, his chief patron would be the Holy Father the Pope, the vicar of Christ on earth.

Youth: Imitation and Emulation

The importance of artistic imitation is a recurring theme in Vasari's accounts of young artists' training. His model usually follows a formula that has a long literary tradition.[27] The essential element is the apprentice's acquisition of the skills that enable him to imitate his master's style and ultimately to make works that can pass for those of his master. The talented artist then assimilates diverse influences and creates his own style. Thus, for example, the young Raphael imitated Perugino's style so well that their paintings were indistinguishable from one another (285). When he subsequently went to Florence and saw the works of

Leonardo da Vinci and Michelangelo, he realized his deficiencies and studied their works intensely. As a result, Vasari informs us, "there followed a striking improvement in his style and skill" (290). Michelangelo also learned from studying the work of established masters. However, Vasari sets him apart from other young artists, for with Michelangelo, he departs from his model of artistic imitation. In both painting and sculpture, the youth did not imitate his masters, he surpassed them. So, too, Vasari differentiates Michelangelo from others in his treatment of the master-pupil relationship. The topos of the youth apprenticed to a master whose achievements he will surpass is not uncommon in the *Lives*. In such pairings, the master always recognizes the pupil's innate ability and, usually, he facilitates its realization—as with the great Cimabue and the greater Giotto (58), the modestly gifted Squarcione and the gifted Mantegna (241), and the talented Verrocchio and the prodigy Leonardo (256). In the case of Michelangelo, Vasari gives this topos a twist that enhances the reader's impression of him: neither Domenico Ghirlandaio, Michelangelo's first master, nor Bertoldo di Giovanni, his second, takes an active hand in training him. Rather, Michelangelo takes the initiative on his own, and, it seems, teaches himself.

According to Vasari, when he was fourteen, Michelangelo's father sent him to Ghirlandaio, then the leading painter in Florence. The author's account of Michelangelo's apprenticeship emphasizes the youth's precocious ability and self-confidence. "The way Michelangelo's talents and character developed astonished Domenico, who saw him doing things quite out of the ordinary for boys of his age and not only surpassing his many other pupils but also very often rivalling the achievements of the master himself" (328).

Vasari then relates vignettes that establish not Michelangelo's mastery of Ghirlandaio's style, but his superiority over him. One day, a student made a drawing after some draped figures by Ghirlandaio. Michelangelo took it, and, "using a thicker pen, he went over the contours of one of the figures and brought it to perfection; and it is marvelous to see the difference between the two styles and the superior skill and judgment of a young man so spirited and confident that he had the courage to correct what his teacher had done" (328). Another time, when Ghirlandaio was painting the choir frescoes in Santa Maria Novella, Michelangelo made a drawing of the site, showing his assistants at work amid the scaffolding and equipment:

When Domenico... saw what Michelangelo had done he said: "This boy knows more about it than I do." And he stood there astonished at the originality and skill in imitation that his inborn sense of judgement enabled so young an artist to display. Certainly the work showed all the qualities to be expected of an artist with years of experience. This was because the instinctive grace of Michelangelo's work was enhanced by study and practice; and every day he produced work that was still more inspired. (328-29)

Vasari's subsequent account elaborates on Michelangelo's facility for surpassing the achievements of others. For example, he improved upon Martin Schongauer's engraving of the *Temptations of St. Anthony,* adding color and using fish as models for the fantastic, scaly demons. He copied works with such "complete fidelity" that after tinging them so that they looked old, "they could not be told apart from the originals." Michelangelo then exchanged them for the originals, "which he admired for their excellence and which he tried to surpass in his own works" (329).

Vasari then turns to Michelangelo's early efforts in sculpture. Again, his *storia* is not one of imitation so much as emulation.[28] Ghirlandaio sent the youth to the *scuola* that Lorenzo de' Medici had established in his sculpture garden on the Via Larga. The school's teacher was Bertoldo di Giovanni, a former pupil of Donatello.[29] Vasari's account of Bertoldo suggests that Michelangelo learned nothing from him. He states that Bertoldo was aged and no longer sculpted and implies that he was as much a caretaker of the Medici collection of ancient sculpture as a teacher of the youths entrusted to him (330-32). As John Pope-Hennessey has shown, Bertoldo's influence on Michelangelo was substantive.[30] Vasari's failure to acknowledge this suggests a reluctance to admit the influence of a secondary artist upon the divine master and a desire to establish Michelangelo's artistic autonomy, thereby enhancing the picture of his marvelous early achievements.

Vasari describes three early sculptures by Michelangelo. Together they create a clear picture of his singular ability and ambition. The first he made shortly after arriving at the *scuola*. Upon seeing some clay figures that Bertoldo had instructed another student to model, Michelangelo made some in competition with him (330). Contrary to expectation, Vasari does not describe marvelous works in clay that Michelangelo modeled. Instead, he writes that Lorenzo de' Medici recognized the youth's "ambitious nature" and so encouraged him that within a few days he began a marble copy of the head of an antique faun. It was not an exact copy, however, for Michelangelo "followed his own fancy in hollowing out a mouth for the faun and giving it a tongue and all of its teeth." The result was a triumph: "Although this was the first time he had ever touched a chisel or worked in marble, Michelangelo succeeded in copying it so well that Lorenzo was flabbergasted" (330).[31]

Vasari's account of the marble faun is telling in several ways. From the start, Michelangelo did not follow the curriculum that Bertoldo set for the other apprentices: whereas they modeled clay, he sculpted unforgiving marble. Furthermore, Lorenzo de' Medici personally oversaw his work. For his first sculpture, he imitated not his master, Bertoldo, but rather his spiritual mistress, ancient art. Even so, by altering the original in his copy, he added invention to imitation.

The other two sculptures that Vasari mentions were not copies, but original works, done in relief.[32] In this medium, Michelangelo had a formidable predecessor to surpass—Donatello, Vasari's standard-bearer for the second period of Renaissance art. One of Donatello's major achievements was a new kind of relief carving, *rilievo schiacciato,* a flattened relief, in which the back plane appears to dissolve, giving the illusion of depth.[33] With this invention, Donatello solved the problem of creating a perspectival space in a three-dimensional medium, thereby bringing to sculpture what would become the chief feature of illusionism in fifteenth-century painting (174). At the beginning of his life of Donatello, Vasari praises his invention, and later he asserts the importance of all Donatello's relief sculpture for subsequent artists: "But indeed, it can be said that since Donatello's death anyone wanting to do good work in relief has been his pupil" (188).

The first relief that Vasari mentions depicted the "Battle of Hercules with the Centaurs," which scholars have identified with the unfinished *Battle of the Lapiths and Centaurs* (fig. 1), now in the Casa Buonarroti.[34] The subject, he tells us, was suggested by Politian, and Michelangelo made it from a block of marble that Lorenzo de' Medici gave him, thus reminding us of his association with humanist scholars and the Medici family. Art historians usually compare the *Lapiths and Centaurs* to the *Battle Scene,* formerly in the Medici Palace and now in the Museo Nazionale, Florence, by Bertoldo di Giovanni, which is based on a Roman battle relief on a sarcophagus in Pisa.[35] Like its model, Bertoldo's *Battle* is rendered in high relief. As Pope-Hennessey has shown, the composi-

Vasari's *Vita di Michelangelo Buonarroti* and the Shade of Donatello 75

Fig. 1. Michelangelo Buonarroti, *Battle of the Lapiths and Centaurs*. C. 1491–92. Marble relief. 84.5 cm × 90.5 cm. Casa Buonarroti, Florence. (Photo by author.)

tion and figural arrangement of Michelangelo's *Lapiths and Centaurs* are indebted to his teacher's *Battle Scene*.[36] Vasari, however, gives no credit to Bertoldo. He praises Michelangelo's relief, claiming it to be extraordinary for a mere youth: "This was so beautiful that today, to those who study it, it sometimes seems to be the work not of a young man but of a great master with a wealth of study and experience behind him (331)."

The second example that Vasari cites is a Madonna in bas-relief made "after the style of Donatello." That he mentions Donatello only after having lauded a copy of an ancient sculpture and a battle relief *all' antica* implies the sculptor's humble place in Michelangelo's hierarchy of artistic influences. The work to which Vasari refers is the *Madonna of the Stairs* (fig. 2), which obviously was influenced by Donatello's low relief sculptures, such as the *Madonna of the Clouds* (fig. 3).[37] Following Vasari's usual formula, one would expect him to praise Michelangelo's effort and to assert that within a short time he had so mastered *rilievo schiacciato* that his reliefs were indistinguishable from Donatello's. Instead, he writes that Michelangelo "acquitted himself so well that it [the relief] seems to be by Donatello himself, save that it possesses more grace

Fig. 2. Michelangelo Buonarroti, *Madonna of the Stairs*. C. 1489–92. Marble relief. 55.5 cm × 40 cm × 3 cm. Casa Buonarroti, Florence. (Photo by author.)

and design" (331). Whereas all others who worked in relief were pupils of Donatello, Michelangelo—as Vasari presents him—was not. With this early effort, he not only succeeded in imitating his predecessor, he surpassed him. Just as Michelangelo had corrected Ghirlandaio's rendering of draped figures, he improved upon Donatello's Madonnas, using the relief style his predecessor had invented to do so.

Vasari's glowing account of Michelangelo's youthful achievements is clearly prophetic. In this regard, he is like other artists in the *Lives*, for Vasari frequently employs the topos of marvelous youthful works that portend subsequent triumphs. However, by omitting all reference to the difficulty of imitating the work of others and by continually asserting that his copies were superior to the originals, he distinguishes Michelangelo from these others. Raphael imitated the work of Perugino, Leonardo, and Michelangelo, and subsequently achieved artistic greatness. Michelangelo had no need to follow such a pedestrian path to glory. As

Fig. 3. Donatello, *Madonna of the Clouds*. C. 1425–35. Marble relief. 33.9 cm × 32.4 cm. Museum of Fine Arts, Boston. Gift of Quincy A. Shaw through Quincy A. Shaw, Jr., and Mrs. Marian Shaw Houghton. (Photo courtesy of Museum of Fine Arts, Boston.)

Vasari presents him, he diligently studied the work of others but never submitted to the yoke of mere imitation. For the divine prodigy, imitation was always coupled with invention.[38] Thus born with artistic maturity, as if he sprang fully formed from the head of Zeus, Michelangelo also surpassed all those who had preceded him with Apollonian ease.

Vasari's narrative of Michelangelo's early years is also significant because it establishes his relationship to Donatello. In telling us that Bertoldo di Giovanni had been trained by Donatello, Vasari shifts the focus from Michelangelo's actual teacher to the sculptor who most influenced him and, in so doing, presents Michelangelo's artistic genealogy: he is a direct descendant of Donatello. His subsequent assertion that Michelangelo surpassed Donatello with his first *Madonna and Child* pairs the two as if master and more talented pupil. Coupled with the previous reference, this pairing signals their typological relationship, which is grounded in the text's Christian allegorical cognitive style. Like the Old Testament prophets who prefigured Christ, Donatello represents a prefiguration of Michelangelo. Christ came from the house of David; Michelangelo, whose advent, like Christ's, was divinely ordained, comes from the "house" of Donatello. As David is a type of Christ, so Donatello is a type of Michelangelo.

Triumphs between the Lines

As a prefiguration of Michelangelo, Donatello, through his works, character, and personality provided Vasari with the scaffolding for Michelangelo's *vita*. A sampling of the correspondences between their lives reveals his use of Donatello as a foil for Michelangelo. Each allusion that he evokes asserts Michelangelo's superiority over Donatello. At the same time, however, it also reminds the reader of Michelangelo's debt to him.

Donatello, Vasari tells us, restored the ancient gems and sculptures in the Medici collection (180). He thereby conveys the sculptor's acquaintance with art and objects of antiquity and reminds us of his association with Florence's leading family. Michelangelo, when living in the Medici household, also became familiar with these works. However, he did not restore them; like a humanist rather than an artisan, he "studied them" (332). Donatello, Vasari tells us, restored an ancient sculpture of *Marsyas* for Cosimo de' Medici (180). Michelangelo copied a marble faun for Lorenzo de' Medici, thus making his patron a "new" ancient work of art rather than restoring one (330). Later, he made a sleeping Cupid that a dealer sold as a newly unearthed classical sculpture (334). In 1547, when Paul III wanted his antiquities restored, Michelangelo did not undertake the task, but recommended Guglielmo della Porta for it (390–91).

For a convent of nuns in Padua, Donatello made a copy of an old, ugly, wooden St. Sebastian, repressing his own style because the sisters wanted a copy of the image they had so long venerated (182). He thus demonstrated artistic versatility, humility, and largesse. Michelangelo's biography contains several anecdotes on this theme. Each amplifies the virtues that Vasari attributed to Donatello. At the request of Menighelli, a "commonplace painter" from Valdarno, Michelangelo "would put other work aside to do simple things." He made a drawing of Sts. Roche and Anthony that his friend could use for paintings for the "country people." He also gave him a model of a crucifix. Menighelli made copies of it in papier mâchè and in other materials, which he sold throughout the countryside (429). Donatello, Vasari tells us, carved a wooden crucifix that Filippo Brunelleschi criticized for putting on the cross "the body of a peasant" (175).[39] Michelangelo, in contrast, modeled an "extremely beautiful" crucifix that suited the peasants' taste (429). Also for the nuns in Padua, Donatello took the end of an old block of marble that they had and carved a "very beautiful" *Madonna* from it (182). Michelangelo's achievement with old stone eclipses Donatello's. From an aging, faulty block that previous sculptors had damaged, he created the faultless *David* (337).

These parallels between the two artists' lives suggest a list of Donatello's achievements that Vasari referred to when writing Michelangelo's *vita,* ticking off each item as he showed that whatever Donatello did, Michelangelo did better. This is well illustrated in two pairs of analogous anecdotes, the first on the theme of the mercenary patron, the second on that of the unjust judge.

The Mercenary Patron

Vasari tells a story of Donatello's dealings with a tight-fisted Genoese merchant, who commissioned a life-size bronze head from the artist but who, upon receiving it, argued that Donatello's price was too high. Cosimo de' Medici was called in to arbitrate. The parties met in the upper court of the merchant's palace, and Cosimo had the bust placed between the battlements so that it could be well seen. Vasari writes:

> Then, when Cosimo tried to settle the matter, he found what the merchant was offering a long way from what Donatello was asking, and so he remarked that in his opinion the offer was too small. And at this the merchant, who thought it was too much, complained that, since he had finished the work in a month or a little over, Donatello would be making over half a florin a day. Donatello considered himself grossly insulted by this remark, turned on the merchant in a rage, and told him that he was the kind of man who could ruin the fruits of a year's toil in a split second; and with that he suddenly shoved the head down on to the street where it shattered into pieces and added

that the merchant had shown he was more used to bargaining for beans than for bronzes. The merchant at once regretted what he had done and promised to pay twice as much if Donatello would do the head again; but neither his promises, nor the entreaties of Cosimo, could persuade Donatello to do so. (180–81)

Vasari's anecdote is a pointed consciousness-raising device, aimed toward patrons. It also tells us much about Donatello. This generous soul, known to give away his works, becomes a hard-nosed Florentine when confronted by a philistine who tries to take advantage of him. Affronted and outraged, he vents his anger through words and action. He vilifies the patron's myopic view of artistic creation and makes his point by sending the statue shattering to the ground. Deprived of the bust, the merchant naturally desires it all the more. Donatello then has the satisfaction of refusing repeated entreaties to make another one, even at double the price.

In Vasari's analogous anecdote about Michelangelo, he, too, responds to the parsimonious patron with righteous indignation. Comparison of the two stories, however, suggests the superiority of the latter artist over the former. Angelo Doni, a collector and friend of the artist, commissioned a painting, so Michelangelo made him a tondo representing the Holy Family (fig. 4). "To show his superb mastery of painting," Michelangelo added variously posed nude figures in the background, and "he executed the work with such care and diligence that it is held beyond doubt as the most beautiful and perfect of the few panel pictures he painted" (340). Vasari's praise sets the stage for Angelo Doni's perfidious reception of the painting:

When it was ready he sent it under wrappings to Angelo's house with a note asking for payment of seventy ducats. Now Angelo, who was careful with his money, was disconcerted at being asked to spend so much on a picture, even though he knew that, in fact, it was worth even more. So he gave the messenger forty ducats and told him that that was enough. Whereupon Michelangelo returned the money with a message to say that Angelo should send back either a hundred ducats or the picture itself. Then Angelo, who liked the painting, said: 'Well, I'll give him seventy.' However, Michelangelo was still far from satisfied. Indeed, because of Angelo's breach of faith he demanded double what he had asked first of all, and this meant that to get the

Fig. 4. Michelangelo Buonarroti, *Doni Madonna*. C. 1503. Tempera on panel. 91 cm × 80 cm. Uffizi, Florence. (Photo by author.)

picture Angelo was having to pay a hundred and forty ducats. (340–41)

In both tales of tight-fisted patrons, the artist is righteously aggrieved and wins in the dispute. However, Donatello's and Michelangelo's responses reflect their substantive differences in temperament and class. In sparring with the Genoese merchant, Donatello is clearly the victor. By angrily throwing the bronze head over the balcony, he makes his point and thwarts the merchant's desire to possess it. However, he, too, loses the statue and thus also the money due him for making it. In stubbornly refusing to make another, he forgoes the opportunity to recoup his loss.

Michelangelo, in his contest with a mercenary collector, controls his temper. By raising his price and asking Doni to return the painting, he forces Doni to recognize the insult of his meager payment. With the acumen of a shrewd Florentine merchant, he then holds out for twice the original asking price—and gets it. Donatello satisfied his aggrieved pride by refusing to make a second bust. Michelangelo also satisfied his pride—but with a monetary reparation that took into account the nature of the insult he had suffered. Were the two stories compared, Florentines (known for their fiscal consciousness even during the Renaissance) assuredly would have granted Michelangelo the victor's laurel. Unlike Donatello, he did not allow his emotions to overtake his good sense, and thus he not only bested his patron, but also received a generous payment to sweeten the triumph.

The Incompetent Judge

For both Donatello and Michelangelo, Vasari tells a story on the theme of the incompetent judge.[40] Again, the two anecdotes are so similar that the allusion to Donatello in Michelangelo's story is pointed.

The Arte de' Linaiuoli commissioned Donatello to carve a statue of St. Mark for their niche at Orsanmichele (fig. 5).[41] In making the figure, Donatello apparently modified its proportions in accord with the viewpoint the spectator would have when the statue was set in its niche.[42] The consuls of the guild "lacked judgment of any kind," so when they saw the statue in Donatello's shop, they were dissatisfied and threatened to reject it. Donatello realized that the judges did not understand how *St. Mark*'s appearance would change when seen from the proper perspective. He therefore entreated them to let him install it at Orsanmichele and work on it there, promising that "he would show them an altogether different statue." The judges assented. "When they agreed," relates Vasari, "he merely covered it up for a fortnight and then, having done nothing to it, he uncovered it and amazed them all" (177–78).

The analogous story in Vasari's life of Michelangelo concerns his *David* (fig. 6). In 1504, it was decided that it should stand in front of the Palazzo Vecchio.[43] When the statue was being installed, Piero Soderini, *Gonfaloniere* of Florence, objected to David's nose, claiming that it was too big (*grosso*). As Donatello had before him, Michelangelo made his "corrections" in situ. Vasari relates:

> Michelangelo, noticing that the Gonfalonier was standing beneath the Giant and that from where he was he could not see the figure properly, to satisfy him climbed on the scaffolding by the shoulders,

Fig. 5. Donatello, *St. Mark*. 1411–13. Marble. 236 cm. Orsanmichele, Florence. (Photo by author.)

seized hold of a chisel in his left hand, together with some of the marble dust lying on the planks, and as he tapped lightly with the chisel let the dust fall little by little, without altering anything. Then he looked down at the Gonfalonier, who had stopped to watch, and said: "Now look at it." "Ah, that's much better," replied Soderini. "Now you've really brought it to life." And then Michelangelo climbed down, feeling sorry for those critics who talk nonsense in the hope of appearing well informed. (338–39)[44]

Vasari's stories of Donatello and Michelangelo and the incompetent judge are strikingly analogous.[45] Yet there is a key difference between them. Both Donatello and Michelangelo know that their statues are correct as they stand. Donatello swallows his pride, feigns the part of an obedient artisan and keeps his "pious fraud" to himself. Michelangelo, however, performs his ruse publicly, for all to see, and he advertises his fraud by using only his left hand when "correcting" the nose.[46]

Fig. 6. Michelangelo Buonarroti, *David*. 1501–4. 410 cm. Accademia, Florence. (Photo by Sally A. Struthers.)

Vasari's allusion to Donatello in the anecdote of *David*'s nose illustrates Michelangelo's greater audacity and more sophisticated wit in the face of an incompetent judge. It does more than this, however. By reminding the reader of the story of Donatello's *St. Mark* in relating the story of Michelangelo's *David,* Vasari evokes a comparison between the two statues, which reveals the *David* to be a descendent of the *St. Mark*.[47] His intense glare, furrowed brow, and clenched hand made their first appearance in Donatello's *St. Mark* and, subsequently, in the powerful, scowling prophet figures for the cathedral's *Campanile* (fig. 7).[48] The story of *David*'s nose demonstrates Michelangelo's superiority over Do-

Fig. 7. Donatello, *Jeremiah*. 1427–35. Marble. 191 cm. Museo dell'Opera del Duomo, Florence. (Photo by author.)

natello, and thus is consonant with Vasari's assertion that the statue "stole the cry" from every statue ever made (339).[49] However, it also mutely acknowledges Michelangelo's enormous debt to Donatello.[50] In prompting the reader to compare the *David* with the *St. Mark*, Vasari implicitly reaffirms the assertion made in his life of Donatello, that "artists should . . . trace the greatness of the art [sculpture] back to him rather than to anyone born in modern times" (189).

Disinterest in Material Gain: Michelangelo's Ultimate Gift

Despite the differences in temperament suggested by their responses to the mercenary patron and the unjust judge, Vasari characterizes Donatello and Michelangelo as similar in nature, particularly with regard to their moral and social values. Donatello, according to Vasari, was generous, gracious, courteous, and "more considerate towards his friends than towards himself" (186). One way he illustrates these qualities is by citing works that Donatello gave away, either in gratitude or simply out of the goodness of his heart. Thus, in gratitude to the Martelli family, he made a six-foot marble *David* and a marble *St. John the Baptist,* which he gave them "as tokens of his love and devotion" (181). When in Venice, he carved a *St. John the Baptist* for the Florentine colony there, "as a mark of his benevolence" (183). He willed his farm to the peasant who had long labored on it, telling his disgruntled relations that, as the peasant had toiled on it and not they, it was only fair that the farm go to him (187).

Donatello was particularly generous to his assistants. Vasari's account of his system for allocating the shop's income underscores both his unconcern with pecuniary matters and his liberality: "Nor did he ever set much store by money; what he had, he kept in a basket suspended by a cord from the ceiling, and all his workmen and friends could take what they wanted without asking" (186). When he died, Donatello left his belongings and unfinished work to his pupils (188–89).

If Donatello personifies generosity, Michelangelo represents the embodiment of *caritas*. Throughout his *vita,* Vasari illustrates Michelangelo's magnanimity toward those who were financially and artistically less fortunate than he.[51] Toward the end of it, he provides a compendium of gifts that the artist bestowed upon others. Michelangelo's gifts, in their sheer number, not to mention their munificence, far surpass those of all other artists in the *Lives*. Like Donatello, he gave his works to others in gratitude for kindnesses received. For example, for the prior of Santo Spirito, who let him dissect corpses in the convent hospital, he made a wooden crucifix (333). To Leoni of Arezzo, who cast a medal with his portrait, he presented several drawings and a wax model of Hercules and Antaeus (410). Furthermore, Michelangelo showered his many friends with drawings: he gave Bindo Altoviti a cartoon for the *Drunkenness of Noah* from the Sistine ceiling; he gave Tomasso de' Cavalieri numerous drawings, among them a *Jupiter and Ganymede,* a *Bacchanal,* and a likeness of Tomasso, the only portrait from life that he ever made (420); to Vittoria Colonna, he presented a *Pietà* and sent her his verses (422).

Not only were friends the recipients of Michelangelo's largesse, but also governments and rulers. In 1529, when his native Florence was besieged by the forces of the emperor and the pope, he lent the republic 1,000 crowns (369). Upon fleeing the city, the artist was welcomed by the Duke of Ferrara. Instead of accepting the duke's many gifts, Michelangelo offered him his services and 12,000 crowns (370).

Like Donatello's, Michelangelo's liberality extended to his employees. Whereas Donatello gave his work away upon his death, Michelangelo did so when he was still alive. To his assistant Antonio Mini, who needed dowries for his two sisters, Michelangelo gave his painting, *Leda and the Swan,* drawings he had made for it, two chests of models, a great number of cartoons, and some pictures he had painted (373).[52] To Ruberto Strozzi, he presented two "Captives," and to his servants Antonio and Francesco Bandini, the broken *Pietà* that he had planned for his tomb (424, 404–5).[53] So that Pietro Urbino, his longtime factotum, would not have to seek another master after he died, Michelangelo gave him "two thousand pounds in a lump sum, a gesture to be expected only from Caesars and Popes" (425). Unlike Donatello, Michelangelo did not keep an open basket of ducats in his shop. However, the works that he gave his assistants, "for which he could have obtained thousands of crowns" (424), provided them with saleable treasures far more precious than gold.

Finally, Vasari frames the greatest endeavor of Michelangelo's later years in the form of a gift. In 1546, Paul III, "inspired I feel sure by God" (385), entrusted Michelangelo with the design and construction of the new basilica of St. Peter's (fig. 8).[54] Michelangelo, then seventy-one, accepted the enormous charge, but refused remuneration for his work. Vasari writes, "[Michelangelo] wanted to demonstrate his own good will by having it declared in the papal decree that he was devoting his time to the fabric for the love of God and without any other reward.... And though the Pope several times sent him money by way of a salary he would never take it" (387).

Donatello, when in Rome, made a tabernacle for the Holy Sacrament in Old St. Peter's (183). His offering is subsumed by Michelangelo's, which, when completed, would house the tabernacle. The magnitude of Michelangelo's "gift," on which he tirelessly labored until his death in 1564, surpasses those of all other artists in the *Lives*. In refusing payment

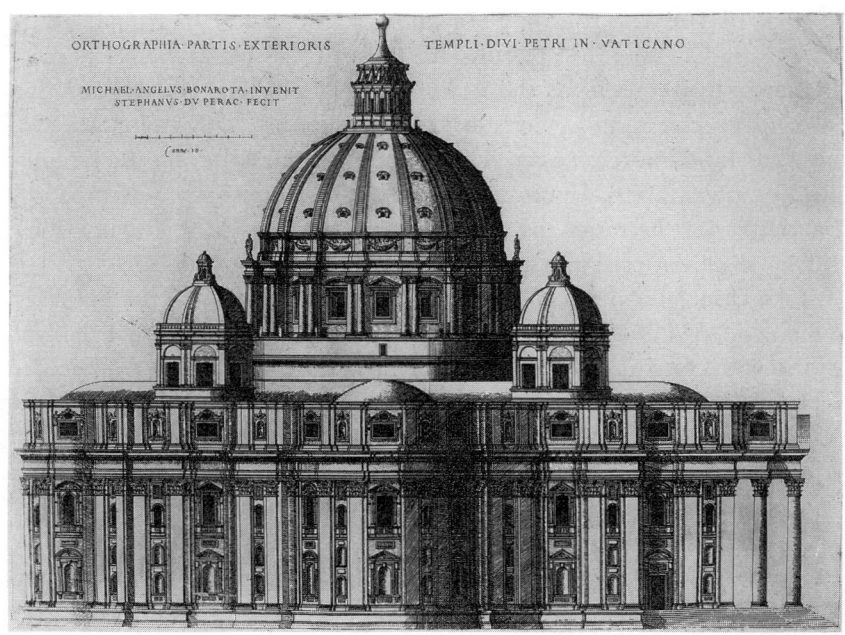

Fig. 8. Etienne Dupérac, *View of St. Peter's by Michelangelo: South Elevation of St. Peter's.* C. 1540–80. Engraving. The Metropolitan Museum of Art, New York; Harris Brisbane Dick Fund, 1941. [41.72(III,24)] (All rights reserved, The Metropolitan Museum of Art.)

for his efforts to build the new St. Peter's, working instead for "spiritual satisfaction" (397), Michelangelo placed himself under the patronage of humankind's ultimate patron, God himself. He thus recalls saints, such as Francis of Assisi, who, at God's command, rebuilt the dilapidated church of San Damiano at Assisi.[55] The implications of Michelangelo's construction of St. Peter's extends beyond hagiological allusions, however, to Christological ones. Christ, in giving the keys to Peter, told him, "Upon this rock I will build my church" (Matt. 16:18). Michelangelo's final gift makes visible and enacts Christ's metaphor: he built his church over Peter's tomb, literally upon the rock of Peter.[56]

Conclusion

The comparisons that Vasari elicits between Donatello and Michelangelo, in which the latter emerges as the victor in an unspoken competition, complements the triumphal theme that runs throughout Michelangelo's *vita*. At the same time, however, Vasari's allusions to the fifteenth-century sculptor recall Michelangelo's roots and laud Donatello by implicitly acknowledging him as having set the standard that Michelangelo had to surpass. Furthermore, when the two artists' *vite* are read together, the coincidental correspondences between their lives take on a significance that enhances both Donatello's archetypal role as precursor and Michelangelo's triumph over him. When viewed through the lens of Donatello, Michelangelo appears to relive Donatello's life and magnify his achievements.

His *David* offers the most obvious example. Early in his career, when working on the Duomo's prophet series, Donatello made a marble *David* which, in 1416, was moved from the Duomo to the Palazzo Vecchio to stand as a symbol of liberty for the beleaguered Florentine republic.[57] The young Michelangelo carved his *David* from marble that had been intended for the Duomo's prophet series. Upon completion, it too was moved to the Palazzo Vecchio, offering an updated symbol of Florentine liberty that expanded upon the classicism and intensity of Donatello's later works.[58] Similarly, for the Florence Baptistery, Donatello designed and executed the tomb of Baldassare Coscia, the deposed Pope John XXIII (176). It was a multistoried wall tomb, with allegorical figures in shell niches surmounted by a classical sarcophagus and an effigy of Coscia. For Julius II (Giuliano della Rovere), who reestablished the authority of the papacy, Michelangelo designed the largest and most elaborate papal tomb ever, intended for St. Peter's basilica. His plans for it enlarged upon Donatello's conception, incorporating its elements into a more monumental, freestanding structure (342–46).[59] Donatello made bronze and terracotta reliefs for the newly built sacristy in San Lorenzo, where his first benefactor, Cosimo de' Medici, was subsequently buried (183–84). His last works for the Medici, finished after his death, were two pulpits for the church's nave, whose reliefs treated the Passion of Christ with unprecedented intensity (330). Michelangelo, in turn, constructed the New Sacristy of San Lorenzo, which was to house the tombs of his first patron, Lorenzo *il Magnifico,* and his brother Giuliano, and as well, the artist's figured tombs for the Medici dukes, Giuliano and Lorenzo (404). Furthermore, he continued Donatello's personal exploration of Christ's Passion in his last works: a series of drawings of the Crucifixion, and two sculpted *Pietàs*, one of which he worked on until six days before he died.[60] Indeed, when one becomes aware of Donatello's presence in Michelangelo's *vita*, it seems that between the lines of Vasari's text, the spirit of Donatello watches his achievements being reinvented on a grander scale.

At the conclusion of Donatello's *vita*, Vasari records an epitaph that Vincenzo Borghini wrote in a book of drawings he had compiled. In the margins of two facing pages that contained drawings by Donatello and Michelangelo, Borghini wrote: "Either the spirit of Donatello moves Buonarroti, or that of Buonarroti first moved Donatello" (190).[61] By recording Borghini's tribute to the two artists in Donatello's *vita*, Vasari transforms it into an epitaph for Donatello, with Michelangelo serving as the matrix for judgment and praise. In thus honoring the fifteenth-century sculptor, Vasari also pays homage to the greater achievements of his successor. His use of Borghini's epitaph is prophetic of the role that Donatello plays in his *Vita di Michelangelo*. As we have seen, the subtext reveals the spirit of Donatello moving Michelangelo; but like the literal text, it also asserts Michelangelo's transcendence over Donatello. In portraying Michelangelo as superior to his prototype, Vasari completes the circle left open by Donatello's *vita*: Donatello first brought perfection to the arts, and Michelangelo perfected his perfection. Vasari thereby reveals that the two artists were moved by the same spirit—that of the "divine Michelangelo"—which, like the transcendent First Mover, first moved Donatello.

NOTES

This chapter is based on a report that I delivered in Leonard Barkan's seminar "The Theory and Practice of Artistic Relations in the Renaissance," at the University of Michigan in the summer of 1991. The seminar was sponsored by the National Endowment for the Humanities (NEH) through its Summer Seminars for College Teachers program, in conjunction with the regents of the University of Michigan. I would like to express my gratitude to NEH for making possible a summer of research and to Leonard Barkan for his insights and encouragement. Thanks are also due to the members of the seminar, particularly Anne McEntee and Julie McGee, and to Paul Barolsky, who first introduced me to Vasari.

1. George Bull, trans., *Lives of the Artists,* vol. 1, by Giorgio Vasari (London and Baltimore: Penguin Books, 1965; Harmondsworth: Penguin Books, 1987). Quotations from Vasari's *Le Vite* follow Bull's translation; page numbers are cited parenthetically in the text. The 1550 edition was titled *Le vite de più eccellenti architetti, pittori et scultori italiani, da Cimabue insino a' tempi nostri*. . . . It was printed in Florence by the ducal printer, Lorenzo Torrentino, and comprised three parts that were published in two volumes. The 1568 edition, *Le vite de' più eccelenti pittori, scultori, et architettori, scritte di nuovo ampliate da M. Giorgio Vasari pit. et archit. aretino,* was published in three volumes and printed in Florence by Jacopo Giunti. The Italian edition that I have used is *Le Vite de' Più Eccellenti Pittori Scultori e Architettori nelle redazione del 1550 e 1568,* ed. Rosanna Bettarini and Paola Barocchi, 6 vols. (Florence: Sansoni, 1966).

2. Eric Cochrane, *Historians and Historiography in the Italian Renaissance* (Chicago: University of Chicago Press, 1981), 395– 97, and 400–401.

3. William Gaunt, ed., "Description of the Works of Giorgio Vasari," in *The Lives of the Painters, Sculptors and Architects,* 4 vols., by Giorgio Vasari (London: Dent, 1963) IV:274; Susan J. Barnes, "The *Uomini Illustri,* Humanist Culture, and the Development of a Portrait Tradition in Early Seventeenth-Century Italy," in *Cultural Differentiation and Cultural Identity in the Visual Arts,* ed. Susan J. Barnes and Walter S. Melion, Studies in the History of Art 27 (Washington, DC: National Gallery of Art, 1989), 81–94.

4. Vasari arranged the lives by schools of art and according to his view of artistic progression. Generally, however, he also ordered them according to the artists' chronological sequence. See Bull, *Lives,* 47 and 84. For Vasari's chronology and his genealogy of artists, see Paul Barolsky, *Giotto's Father and the Family of Vasari's Lives* (University Park: Pennsylvania State University Press, 1992). For a general discussion of the *Lives,* see T. S. R. Boase, *Vasari: The Man and the Book* (Princeton: Princeton University Press, 1979), 43–72 and Patricia L. Rubin, *Giorgio Vasari: Art and History* (New Haven: Yale University Press, 1994).

5. Lorenzo Ghiberti, *I Commentarii,* ed. Ottavio Morisani (Naples: Ricciardi, 1947); and Dante Alighieri, *Commento de Christoforo Landino sopra la Commedia di Danthe Alighieri Poeta Fiorentino* (Florence: Nicholo di Lorenzo della Magna, 1481). For the text of Landino's discussion of artists, see Ottavio Morisani, "Art Historians and Art Critics—III: Cristoforo Landino," *Burlington Magazine* 95 (1953): 267–70.

6. Pliny the Elder, *Natural History,* books 7 and 34–37. For Vasari's sources, see Boase, *Vasari,* 51–53; and Wolfgang Kallab, *Vasaristudien* (Vienna: Grasser & Kie, 1908).

7. See the preface to part I of the *Lives* and the address to artists at the conclusion of part III. Also see E. H. Gombrich, "The Renaissance Conception

of Artistic Progress and its Consequences," in *Norm and Form: Studies in the Art of the Renaissance* (London: Phaidon, 1966), 1–10.

8. For *Della pittura,* see Leon Battista Alberti, *On Painting,* trans. John R. Spencer (New Haven, CT, and London: Yale University Press, 1966).

9. Ernst Kris and Otto Kurz, *Legend, Myth and Magic in the Image of the Artist: An Historical Experiment* (New Haven, CT: Yale University Press, 1979), 5–6.

10. See T. C. Price Zimmermann's chapter in the present volume; see also Cochrane, *Historians and Historiography,* 394 and 400–408; and Martino Capucci, "Dalla biografia alla storia: note sulla formazione della storiografia artistica nel seicento," *Studi Secenteschi,* 9 (1968): 81–125.

11. Gaunt, *The Lives of the Painters, Sculptors and Architects,* II:303.

12. For the *terribilità* of Michelangelo's character and his art in the writings of his contemporaries, see David Summers, *Michelangelo and the Language of Art* (Princeton, NJ: Princeton University Press, 1981), 234–41.

13. For the *Legenda Aurea,* see Jacobus de Voragine, *The Golden Legend: Readings on the Saints,* 2 vols., trans. William Granger Ryan (Princeton, NJ: Princeton University Press, 1992).

14. Paul Barolsky, *Michelangelo's Nose: A Myth and Its Maker* (University Park: Pennsylvania State University Press, 1990), 63–65. This chapter is deeply indebted to Barolsky's incisive examination of Vasari and the myth of Michelangelo.

15. Ibid. See the prefaces to parts II and III, Bull, *Lives,* 84–93 and 249–54.

16. Charles S. Singleton, "The Vistas in Retrospect," *Modern Language Notes,* 81 (1966): 55–80.

17. In placing Michelangelo's *vita* last, Vasari broke with chronology, for part III includes the lives of artists who were born after Michelangelo. In the 1568 edition, he added biographies of artists still living and a brief section on Flemish artists after Michelangelo's *vita,* thus altering the original structure of the *Lives.*

18. For Michelangelo's numerous letters to Vasari, see Bull, *Lives,* 328 and 408; for the assertion that much of the 1550 life came from Michelangelo's "own lips," see 393.

19. Ascanio Condivi, *The Life of Michelangelo,* trans. Alice Sedgwick Wohl, ed. Helmut Wohl (Baton Rouge: Louisiana State University Press, 1976). Subsequent quotations from Condivi are from this translation and are noted parenthetically in the text. As Wohl observes (xv), Carl Frey (ed.) in the introduction to *Le Vite di Michelangelo Buonarroti scritte da Giorgio Vasari e da Ascanio Condivi con aggiunte e note* (Berlin: W. Hertz, 1887) convincingly argued that Vasari's 1568 life of Michelangelo is deeply indebted to Condivi's life. See also Johannes Wilde, "Michelangelo, Vasari, and Condivi," in his *Michelangelo, Six Lectures,* Oxford Studies in the History of Art and Architecture (Oxford: Claren-

don Press, 1978), 1–16, and Paola Barocchi, "Michelangelo tra le due redazioni delle *Vite* vasariane (1550– 68)," in her *Studi Vasariani* (Turin: Einaudi, 1984), 36–51.

20. Charles de Tolnay, "Donatello e Michelangelo," *Donatello e il suo tempo* (Florence: Atti dell' VIII Congresso internazionale di Studi sul Rinascimento, 1968), 259–76. See also Carlo Sisi, *Michelangelo e i maestri del Quattrocento*, exhibition catalog, Florence, Casa Buonarroti, 20 June–20 November 1985 (Florence: Cantini, 1985).

21. Bull, *Lives,* 329–31 and 425–26.

22. Barolsky, *Michelangelo's Nose,* 60, has noted the typological relation between Vasari's portrayals of Donatello and Michelangelo.

23. Although Donatello's family was plebeian, it descended from a branch of the great banking family, the Bardi. For Donatello, see H. W. Janson, *The Sculpture of Donatello,* 2d ed. (Princeton, NJ: Princeton University Press, 1963; reprint, 1979); Frederick Hartt, *Donatello: Prophet of Modern Vision* (New York: Abrams, 1973); and Bonnie A. Bennett and David G. Wilkins, *Donatello* (Mt. Kisco, NY: Moyer Bell, 1984).

24. Vasari dedicated the *Lives* to Duke Cosimo de' Medici. He entered the duke's permanent service in about 1555. See Boase, *Vasari,* 53–59.

25. For Vasari's life of Michelangelo, see Paola Barocchi, *La Vita di Michelangelo nelle redazioni del 1550 e del 1568,* 5 vols. (Milan-Naples: R. Ricciardi, 1962). The standard corpus on Michelangelo is Charles de Tolnay's *The Complete Works of Michelangelo,* 2d ed., 5 vols. (Princeton, NJ: Princeton University Press, 1969). See also Howard Hibbard, *Michelangelo,* 2d ed. (New York: Harper, 1974). For bibliography, see Luitpold Dussler, *Michelangelo— Bibliographie, 1927-1970* (Wiesbaden: Harrassowitz, 1974).

26. For fact and fiction in Vasari's account of Michelangelo's early years, see William E. Wallace, "How Did Michelangelo Become a Sculptor?" in Pierre Theberge et al., *The Genius of the Sculptor in Michelangelo's Work,* exhibition catalog, Montreal, Museum of Fine Arts, 12 June–13 September, 1992 (Montreal: Montreal Museum of Fine Arts, 1992), 151–67; and Paul Barolsky and William E. Wallace, "The Myth of Michelangelo and Il Magnifico," *Source* 12 (1993): 16–21.

27. For an introduction to the literature on artistic imitation in the Renaissance, see Thomas M. Greene, *The Light in Troy: Imitation and Discovery in Renaissance Poetry* (New Haven, CT: Yale University Press, 1982), 28–53.

28. For the distinction between imitation and emulation, see G. W. Pigman III, "Versions of Imitation in the Renaissance," *Renaissance Quarterly* 33 (1980): 1–32.

29. For Bertoldo di Giovanni, see John Pope-Hennessey, *Italian Renaissance Sculpture: An Introduction to Italian Sculpture,* Part II (London: Phaidon, 1958; New York: Random House, 1985), 302–4.

30. John Pope-Hennessey, *Italian Renaissance and High Baroque Sculpture: An Introduction to Italian Sculpture,* Part III (London: Phaidon, 1958; New York: Random House, 1985), 4–5.

31. Barolsky, *Michelangelo's Nose,* 29–30, argues that the story of Michelangelo's marble faun, which first appears in the 1568 edition of the *Lives,* is a fiction created by the artist himself.

32. These two reliefs are not mentioned in the first edition of Vasari's *Lives.*

33. For *rilievo schiacciato,* see John Pope-Hennessey, *Italian Renaissance Sculpture,* 13–22; and Bennett and Wilkins, *Donatello,* 110–11.

34. De Tolnay, *Michelangelo,* vol. 1, *The Youth of Michelangelo,* 133–40.

35. Pope-Hennessey, *Italian Renaissance Sculpture,* 304, and fig. 138.

36. Pope-Hennessey, *Italian Renaissance and High Baroque Sculpture,* 4–6.

37. The provenance of the *Madonna of the Stairs* indicates it is the one to which Vasari refers. De Tolnay, *The Youth of Michelangelo,* 125 and 127–28. Donatello's *Madonna of the Clouds* may have been in the Medici Palace. See Janson, *Sculpture of Donatello,* 86–87.

38. Michelangelo's disdain for imitation is a topos that runs throughout Vasari's *vita* of the artist. See Bull, *Lives,* 397, 418, and especially 427–28.

39. This anecdote metonymically bespeaks Donatello's humble origins.

40. For the unjust judge, see Kris and Kurz, *Legend, Myth, and Magic,* 102–5.

41. Bull, *Lives,* 177. Vasari states that the Cloth Guild's commission for *St. Mark* had been given to both Filippo Brunelleschi and Donatello, but that Filippo let his friend finish it.

42. Consult Robert Munman, *Optical Corrections in the Sculpture of Donatello: Transactions of the American Philosophical Society,* vol. 75, part 2 (Philadelphia: American Philosophical Society, 1985), 15–18. For a summary of the earlier literature on Donatello's "optical corrections" with regard to Vasari's anecdote about the *St. Mark,* and a dissenting opinion, see Janson, *Sculpture of Donatello,* 20–21.

43. Michelangelo's *David* thus displaced Donatello's bronze *Judith and Holofernes,* which, since 1495, had stood in front of the Palazzo Vecchio as a symbol of liberty. See Janson, *Sculpture of Donatello,* 198–99.

44. The story of *David*'s nose does not appear in the 1550 edition of the *Lives.*

45. The similarities between these two stories were observed by Hans Kauffmann, *Donatello: eine Einführung in sein Bilden und Denken* (Berlin: G. Grotesche, 1935), 210, n. 130, and has been discussed by Janson, *Sculpture of Donatello,* 20–21.

46. A right-handed sculptor would hold the chisel in the left hand and the hammer in the right. In Vasari's account of Michelangelo "correcting" the *David*'s nose, the artist uses the chisel but not the hammer and thus uses only his

left hand. Vasari's account therefore implicitly indicates that Michelangelo performed the feigned action with his left or "sinister" hand. I am grateful to Paul Joannides for clarification on this point.

47. Vasari states that when Michelangelo used the images of others, they were so transformed that scarcely anyone could recognize the source. His allusion to *St. Mark* in the story of the *David* suggests his recognition of Michelangelo's source. Soderini's comment, "Now you've really brought it to life," may also have been intended to allude to Donatello, for in his life of the sculptor, Vasari continually emphasizes the vivacity of his figures and his ability to bring stone to life. See Bull, *Lives,* 177–79 and 425.

48. David Summers has likened the *David* to physiognomic descriptions of the courageous character, particularly his clouded brow and leonine scowl. If the facial features of the *David* recall the lion, so also do the clouded brow of *St. Mark* and the leonine scowls of Donatello's prophet figures, thereby providing a physiognomic genealogy for the *David*. As Summers observed, Michelangelo's leonine characterization of David is appropriate, for the lion is an ancient, libertarian symbol of Florence. The allusion is also especially appropriate for St. Mark the Evangelist, whose symbol is the lion. See Summers, "David's Scowl," in *Collaboration in Italian Renaissance Art,* ed. Wendy Steadman Sheard and John T. Paoletti (New Haven, CT: Yale University Press, 1978), 113–24.

49. In his list of great artists that Michelangelo surpassed with the *David,* Vasari mentions only ancient artists and thus does not mention Donatello. "*A tolto il grido*": as Barolsky, *Michelangelo's Nose,* 60, has observed, here Vasari alludes to Dante's discussion of fame in *Purgatorio* 11.95–97; Oderisi da Gubbio tells Dante that once Cimabue held the field, but now Giotto has the cry. His allusion to Giotto's triumph over Cimabue suggests Michelangelo's analogous triumph over Donatello, particularly because Cimabue and Donatello each worked in one medium, whereas Giotto and Michelangelo excelled in all three arts: painting, sculpture, and architecture. Vasari's reference also draws a comparison between Dante and Michelangelo. In this regard, see *Purgatorio* 11.98–99.

50. According to Vasari, when asked what he thought of Donatello's *St. Mark,* Michelangelo replied that St. Mark's face seemed to be that of a virtuous man, and that if the evangelist really were as Donatello had portrayed him, he would believe all that he had written (Bull, *Lives,* 425–26). This anecdote may have a bearing on the political and religious significance of Michelangelo's *David*. The Gospel of St. Mark (11:7 and 12:29 and 35) quotes Psalms 109 and 117, both of which characterize God as David's protector against the enemies who surround him.

51. Barolsky, *Michelangelo's Nose,* 60, has observed that Vasari's repeated use of the verb *donare* in telling of Michelangelo's gifts is a pun on Donatello's name, intended to recall Donatello and his generosity.

52. For the lost *Leda and the Swan,* see Hibbard, *Michelangelo,* 223–26.

53. Vasari's "two captives" refers to two of the unfinished *Slaves* that Michelangelo originally carved for the tomb of Julius II. See Hibbard, *Michelangelo,* 151–55.

54. The new St. Peter's was begun by Bramante in 1506. Michelangelo took charge of the project following the death of Antonio da Sangallo the Younger in 1546.

55. See also the story in Bonaventure's life of Innocent III's dream, in which he sees Francis supporting the falling church of St. John Lateran, in Marion A. Habic, ed., *St. Francis of Assisi, Writings and Early Biographies: English Omnibus of the Sources* (Chicago: Franciscan Herald Press, 1973), 243–44 and 640–41.

56. See Barolsky, *Michelangelo's Nose,* 85–88, regarding Michelangelo's work on St. Peter's in relation to the role of Dante's St. Peter in the *Paradiso.*

57. Sources indicate that Donatello carved a statue of David for the Duomo's prophet series, but whether this statue is to be identified with the marble *David* is a matter of debate. In 1416, when Donatello completed or reworked the statue, an inscription was added indicating David's political significance, and it was installed inside the Palazzo Vecchio. For recent discussions of the Duomo's prophet figures and Donatello's marble *David,* consult Manfred Wundrum, "Donatello und Nanni di Banco negli anni 1408–1409," in his *Donatello e il suo tempo* (Florence: *Atti dell' VIII convegno Internazionale di Stud: sul Rinascimento Firenze-Padova 1966,* 1968), 69–75; and Pope-Hennessey, *Donatello,* 42–45 and 320–23.

58. Bull, *Lives,* 338; Charles Seymour, *Michelangelo's David: A Search for Identity* (Pittsburgh: University of Pittsburgh, 1967; New York: Norton, 1974).

59. This is not to imply that the Coscia tomb was Michelangelo's chief model for the Julius tomb, which he began in 1505. Plans were altered several times, and eventually the monument became a wall tomb, installed in San Pietro in Vincoli, Rome, in 1545.

60. Hibbard, *Michelangelo,* 288.

61. This epitaph was not included in the first edition of the *Lives.* For Borghini's role in the second edition, see Boase, *Vasari,* 44–47.

3

Burying the Brethren:
Lutheran Funeral Sermons as Life-Writing

Robert Kolb

"Examples have more power than rules," observed Lorenz Mathesius as he preached over the coffin of his colleague, Johann Pfeffinger, the reformer of Leipzig and longtime pastor and professor there,[1] repeating a commonplace observation on life-writing in the theory of ancient, medieval, and Renaissance writers. Mathesius and his sixteenth-century Lutheran contemporaries simply accepted this aphorism as a truism. Examples served as important teaching devices for the cultivation of Christian values and piety for the students of Martin Luther and Philip Melanchthon. They maintained full faith in the power of God's gift of rhetoric, as Melanchthon had explained and refined it, in persuading their hearers of the truths they wished to convey, and they regarded examples as a fundamental form for communicating at least some of these truths. Nonetheless, their disciples seldom turned their pens to full-scale sketches of contemporary exemplary lives.

This fact is surprising in view of the rich historical tradition that Melanchthon fostered among his students. This tradition produced a spate of chronicles as well as the new mode of historical analysis grounded in Melanchthonian method formulated by the Magdeburg Centuriators.[2] Recording the past as a mirror of God's activity—of the conflict between good and evil, between God's truth and Satan's lies— was important for the followers of Luther and Melanchthon. It is impossible to explain fully why they neglected life-writing. Indeed, Luther's message focused on God's action and control of human history, and even God's command to love the neighbor; this focus could be highlighted through the study of the broad sweep of human events, as was done in the *Chronicle* of Melanchthon's student Johann Carion or in the history of the Christian church, the *Magdeburg Centuries* (which did include topics on individuals of significance for the church). So it is possible that they believed that biographies might more easily undermine the fundamental message of the Reformation, straying from an emphasis on God's mercy, grace, and power and might by making heroes of their subjects. The models at hand warned of such dangers: ancient exercises in life-writing praised individual accomplishment; medieval hagiography praised magical manipulation by people regarded as worthy on the basis of their own good works. Martyrology offered another possible model, but Lutherans made less of martyrology than did other Protestants and Roman Catholics of the period. In writing of martyrs, they defined the term broadly, in its root sense of "witnesses to the faith," and this enabled them to include Luther and others who had presented such a witness within the company of contemporary "martyrs." Furthermore, when they did treat the lives of those who had died for the faith, the emphasis fell more on the message delivered than on the sufferings and agonies of the martyr's final days or moments.[3] Although the Wittenbergers refined old genres of historical reporting and developed a new one in the *Magdeburg Centuries,* they avoided, for the most part, writing the lives of individuals.

It is indeed true that several of their students composed longer or shorter sketches of Luther's life, some reflecting palely certain elements of medieval hagiography, all reflecting the new humanistic rhetoric and its appreciation for the power of example and praise.[4] Joachim Camerarius produced, such a humanistic paean of Melanchthon's life, a polemic against critics within the Lutheran ranks.[5] But apart from these two heroes of the faith, German Lutherans of the Reformation period celebrated the lives of contemporaries chiefly in sermons and orations prepared for funerals. In these addresses we can observe how the Lutheran clergy utilized one important element of Melanchthon's pioneering work in rhetoric, the loci method—the assembling of examples—, to shape the public image and appreciation of their pastoral colleagues. These pastors seem blissfully unaware of tensions between reality and report in their proclamation. Reports on public lives found in funeral sermons reflect sermonic standards and forms. Although they undoubtedly tried to avoid inaccuracy in reporting reality, they were not concerned with the details of biography but, rather, with the impact of their report on the piety and perceptions of their people.

The study of "Leichenpredigten" has become a growth industry in recent historical scholarship.[6] Relatively rare in the Middle Ages, the literary phenomenon of the printed funeral address crested in the first half of the seventeenth century, but its roots can be traced back to Wittenberg in 1525, when Luther preached two sermons over the bier of Frederick the Wise and Melanchthon delivered an oration in appreciation of the prince, according to contemporary humanist style.[7] Throughout the sixteenth century, above all among German Lutherans, the genre took shape, in several forms with varying elements.[8] Luther's funeral sermons on Frederick and, seven years later, on Frederick's brother Elector John, had presented a model of sober textual exposition, with little mention of the deceased at all. Melanchthon's funeral orations opened up greater possibilities for using the person's practice of vocation and virtues to encourage pious living among those attending the funerals. Their students produced brief books which contained a variety of textual sermons, biographical sketches, a form that mixed the two in varying proportions, and Latin poetry reflecting varying degrees of literary skill.

This study focuses on the way in which Lutheran pastors apotheosized their colleagues in funeral addresses in the second half of the sixteenth century. One survey of funeral sermons found that, next to the nobility, which accounted for one fourth of the items in the sample, pastors were most frequently the subjects of such published works (16.7 percent).[9] This genre was neither hagiography nor martyrology in the medieval sense. It avoided any attribution of special merit or special powers to its subjects, and none of them had died the traditional martyr's death—even though an emphasis on their sufferings for the gospel often provides a whiff of that tradition. Instead, the genre aimed at organizing the experiences of a new Christian model of evangelical piety; its clerical selections attempted to form and inform an image of the new Evangelical estate of pastor and the tasks of that estate in the confessionalization process.

In funeral messages on pastors, the several themes common to all such sermons are found: consolation for the survivors, warnings regarding the frailty of human life and the threats of sin in an evil world, hope in the resurrection of all believers, and so on.[10] In addition, these funeral sermons set before the congregation two themes: God's providence for his servants (particularly in the midst of tribulation and persecution) and a model for the discharge of one particular calling, that of pastor.[11] The confession of the preachers' theology in these sermons focused on God's love and power at the same time it praised the practice of vocation and virtue by these pastors. These addresses defined and defended their interpretation of the Reformation message, demonstrating how the confessional polemic of the period determined much of the perception of their experiences. These sermons served as vehicles for praising the heroic defense of God's Word that the deceased had upheld within the hard-fought polemical battles of the time. The preachers thereby fielded their own contributions to the effort to fight for confessional integrity as they reinforced the departed's stand by warning the congregation against the false teaching that he had opposed. Throughout, they demonstrated that public confession of the faith, of the proper doctrine of the church, with the attendant suffering for the faith that often accompanied such confession, formed an integral and integrating part of the pastor's existence in the minds of colleagues. They believed that God had called them to secure the gift of Luther's message, and this they viewed as their central task.

Only secondarily could these funeral sermons provide models and inspiration for the lay people's practice of their piety because the sermons focused largely on clerical gifts and virtues. These preachers instead employed their funeral sermons to construct an exemplary picture of the new social stratum of Evangelical pastor and the correct practice of that office, so that the parishioners would appreciate and treasure good pastors and the message they taught and preached appropriately.

Most Lutheran pastors in sixteenth-century Germany learned to preach under the direct or indirect guidance of Philip Melanchthon. He had prepared widely used texts on rhetoric and homiletics. These had channeled the ancient rhetorical tradition into forms suitable for Lutheran preaching.[12] In Melanchthon's *Rhetoric* and *Dialectic* attention was given to the classical genus *demonstrativum*.[13] This genus had provided the standard topics or commonplaces to guide those who devised praise of human creatures: homeland, gender, birth, abilities, education, way of life, teaching or ideas, accomplishments, rewards, manner of death, and reputation after death.[14] Melanchthon's disciples altered these topics for use in their funeral addresses.

In these addresses the preachers at times engaged in basic textual exposition of a biblical text, sometimes with little reference to the deceased, sometimes with a shorter or longer overview of his life. In other instances their funeral message took topical form, either in sermons proceeding from a biblical text or in orations shaped by the humanistic rhetorical prescriptions for praising the departed. The formulation of appropriate topics for organizing and teaching pertinent material in these topics—the loci method—formed an important part of Melanchthon's development of his own rhetoric. This method was employed widely in the exemplary literature of the late sixteenth century by Lutherans.[15] In the funeral addresses, the commonplaces of ancient rhetoric for praise of individuals survived only in part. Topics of homeland and gender vanished. Circumstances of birth seldom received attention. These topics focused only on the individual and on elements irrelevant to his proclamation of God's Word. When they treated biographical detail at all, the preachers did tell the individual's own story, but other traditional topics enabled them to display God's gifts and activity in the life of the departed servant of the Word; that was their chief concern. Thus, abilities, education, moral example, doctrinal positions, accomplishments of office, and the manner of death did remain, along with other categories that offered the opportunity to praise God, as Melanchthon suggested such Christian orations of praise for human creatures should.[16] His disciples filled the categories that became commonplaces for Lutheran funeral addresses with a variety of materials that served to convey their message to hearers and readers as they set forth their image of the ideal pastor. Their focus fell more on deeds than on character, though both enabled the preachers to praise the God who governed both. The deeds and the character of their subjects gave the preachers opportunity to confess their faith in God's providence.

In this period, images of the ideal Christian life were also being developed by German Lutheran preachers in sermons on the ancient saints and martyrs of the church. Such sermons, with their dual focus on God's grace and on the human practice of virtue and vocation, offer a point of comparison for assessing how funeral addresses cultivated piety. They frequently focused on how Christians could see the goodness and providence of God in the lives of the saints.[17] Contemporary funeral sermons often echoed this topic of God's watchful care of his people. Hieronymus Mencel, for instance, reminded his hearers that "the Lord God knows how to rescue the godly from trial" (1 Pet. 2:9a), celebrating the presence and providence of God in the life of Simon Musaeus.[18] Augustin Tham made a similar observation as he began his sermon at Mencel's funeral: we learn how marvelously God rules and guides his dear Christians, not only from the Word of God and the examples of the ancient fathers and the whole church, but also from the daily experience of contemporaries.[19]

Another locus frequently struck in Lutheran preaching on the saints was seldom expressed in comment on deceased pastors: the theme of human frailty and sinfulness. Important in cultivating the Lutheran practice of repentance, the topic seems logical and appropriate for sermons aimed at fostering pious living and consoling sinful believers. Preaching on the foibles and transgressions of the ancient saints could not only call for repentance and warn of divine judgment; it could also offer much comfort to those who were struggling with their own sins.[20] Not so, apparently, with contemporary pastors. Only occasionally would one mention the deceased brother's flaws and faults, as did Lukas Osiander, and he offered an excuse for Jakob Andreae who, Osiander conceded, had repeatedly offended others as he pursued his program for resolving the strife within German Lutheranism. "Andreae wanted to offend no one.... He had his failures and weaknesses (as a human creature and not an angel), and he did not always do the right that he wanted to do but rather the wrong that he did not want to do (Rom. 7:19). Nonetheless, he did not plan to do wrong but to avoid it."[21] It was perhaps fitting that Caspar Heldelin more forthrightly acknowledged the sins of his friend, Matthias Flacius Illyricus, who had suffered much defending his radical understanding of original sin. Flacius had always battled the "old Adam" within himself. Weaknesses and frailties afflicted him, but they did not overcome him as he fought to subdue them throughout his life, Heldelin reported, reflecting Flacius's conviction regarding the perversity of sin—and undoubtedly the reality of his tempestuous life.[22] Such comments occurred exceedingly seldom as these pastors laid their colleagues to rest. What principles of pastoral care might have been used to apply comfort and provide an example for living in faith in God's forgiveness were set aside so that the proper standards for the pastoral office could be upheld.

Within the recital of the events of their colleagues' lives are found several standard loci, topics natural to the description of any career and a part of the ancient rhetorical tradition Melanchthon had helped revive.[23] Family background initiated many such recitals, though, apart from Georg Major's providing a family tree for Prince Georg of Anhalt, they did not follow ancient practice in going beyond the parental generation.[24] Schooling offered clues to the development of these reformers and was sometimes treated in detail.[25]

Funeral messages on Lutheran pastors often focused on the sufferings they had incurred battling the enemies of God's Word and the ways in which God's strength sustained them in these battles. Though not martyrology, these funeral addresses did emphasize the heroic witness of their subjects as they risked much against hostile foes in both church and state. Such discussions reveal the struggle of the confessional groups of the Reformation to define their raison d'être and their message. Flacius himself had been "hounded as Jonah was in Ninevah," persecuted not only by officials of church and state, but even by students at the University of Jena. A faculty colleague had organized their public mockery of Flacius, and the students had also stormed his home. Heldelin promised his hearers that God's wrath would be poured out upon Germany because it treated its pastors in such fashion.[26] Not just fellow Lutherans slugging it out in controversy, but especially oppression by Roman Catholics won special mention, sometimes highlighted with anecdotes, often referred to only in a general way. Mathesius could only observe, as he recounted Johann Pfeffinger's forced exile from Sonnenwald at a time when his wife was pregnant, that the church is indeed a pilgrim on earth. (His Lutheran opponents had merely slandered him.)[27] Conrad Schlüsselburg successfully wove this theme of Satanic attack through false teachers into his rather detailed sketch of the career of Johann Wigand, a pastor and professor who had battled ecclesiastical foes on many fronts.[28] Wigand had also stood up to princes and city officials. Schlüsselburg praised Wigand's forthright opposition to "Caesaropapism," "the confusion of ecclesiastical and political power, by which earthly lords, at court and in the cities, under the pretext of exercising custody of both tables [of God's law], steal for themselves the spiritual sword."[29]

Alongside this theme of suffering at the hands of ecclesiastical and political foes, the topic of the "cross of family life" received prominent, though brief, treatment in many funeral sermons. Illness was sometimes mentioned, but the central feature of the topic "Hauskreuz" was the loss of one, two, or three wives, and one or more children.[30] In each case, review of the cross of family life proved that God provides for and preserves his own.

The preachers wanted to highlight not only the faithful exercise of the calling or office of husband and father. They emphasized even more strongly the topic of the virtue of the proper exercise of the calling of pastor, of shepherd of God's flock. In summaries of what they included in the responsibilities of this office, they outlined and depicted their ideal for service in the pastoral ministry. As good students of Melanchthon, they employed this topic to build the image of the calling, role, and activities of the Lutheran clergy.

Often this depiction was exhausted with a brief summary, a series of pertinent phrases. Mencel described Heinrich Roth as a man who had come into his office through an orderly call—no fly-by-night Anabaptist type, he. With diligence, faithfulness, great effort, and toil, he had shown his love for the people of his congregation. He had taught according to the catechism, preached faithfully and well, rejected and sharply condemned sin and evil. By doing so, Mencel observed, pursuing his theme of the persecution of pastors, he had drawn the devil to his throat.[31] He visited the sick to comfort them and admonish them. He had proved himself a faithful curate of souls in hearing confession. His diligence and his Christian manner also commended his exercise of office to his people.[32]

Metaphor was often employed to reinforce such a point and to strengthen the locus. Heldelin used the image of the carriage driver who had faithfully kept the Lord's wagon and goods on the right route and assiduously guarded them during their transport in his care.[33] Josua Opitz depicted Nicholas Gallus as a reliable, industrious carpenter who with one hand built the Lord's house through salutary teaching and with the other used the sword of the Holy Spirit to tear down the devil's house. He had stood with trumpet in hand as a watchman to warn God's people of those who would lead them astray from his Word.[34]

Indeed, the chief task of the pastoral office was to preach the Word. Gallus had proclaimed the heritage that Luther had passed on to him, a criterion often used by these heirs of Wittenberg for judging their contemporaries. Gallus divided law and gospel for his people—calling for repentance through the law and giving them the comfort of God's grace and the forgiveness of sins through the gospel. Furthermore, his sermons had aided the newborn in producing good works as the fruits of their saving faith.[35] With this brief outline, Opitz laid down succinctly a perfect program for Lutheran preaching. Mencel noted that Roth had preached so well that people came to hear him from other congregations—a practice which in most cases would not have been welcomed but which seemed appropriate, after the fact, to his comrade in arms in the battles within the Mansfeld ministerium.[36]

Preaching the Word effectively arose, for the humanistically trained students of Luther and Melanchthon, from the study of the biblical text in the original languages. Georg Silberschlag, although he had not studied at Wittenberg, had appropriated the Wittenberg ideal. Andreas Poach reported that he had read the Hebrew Bible many times, and the text was as familiar to him as was the catechism's text. He had learned Chaldean (Aramaic) as well, and he compared the texts in Hebrew, Aramaic, Greek, and German as he studied them. He read also some of the prophets in Latin. Silberschlag could write in Hebrew as well as he could write in Latin. He answered correspondence from Jews in Hebrew. He also read Luther with great diligence.[37]

Preaching the Word involved cultivating Christian living as well as instruction in Christian teaching. Jakob Andreae, for instance, received praise for regularly criticizing the drunkenness, fornication, greed, pride, cursing, and every kind of presumptuous and unchristian action he had encountered among his people.[38]

In carrying out their responsibilities in the pastoral office, these leaders had needed certain gifts from God. Wigand lauded Erasmus Sarcerius's logical and methodical way of thinking, which enabled him to issue sharp judgments against "coarse heretics but also against subtle, crafty, sophistic cunning false teachers. He could separate the truth from error as one skilled at refining the lead from silver, the weeds from the wheat" (gifts vital for defending the proper confession of the faith).[39] Osiander described Andreae as one whom the Almighty had fashioned as a superb warrior and a spiritual soldier. From his youth, he had a most complete command in all subjects of study, so that he could excel over his contemporaries with ease. His natural eloquence had enabled him to preach before princes at a young age (eighteen); he had assumed a city pastorate a little later.[40] Heerbrand cited Homer's description of Nestor's mellifluous tongue in praise of Andreae's homiletic gifts.[41] Pastors also needed to be learned, and Major praised Georg of Anhalt by describing the learned conversations he had had with physicians, lawyers, and theologians, including the members of the Wittenberg faculty.[42]

Such gifts served the congregation but did not serve as a model for the lives of its members. Surprisingly, in view of their prominence in Lutheran preaching on the lives of the ancient saints, neither did the virtues of the pastor's life.[43] The funeral sermons treat the pastor's virtues so casually that it seems as though the preachers were not hoping to foster virtuous living or to motivate Christian love so much as to remind their people of what they already knew about standards for the Christian life.

The theory was in place: Georg Mylius told his hearers at the beginning of his sermon at the bier of Nikolaus Selnecker that examples sway human creatures mightily.⁴⁴ Indeed, occasionally the preachers attempted to sway the audience to reduplicate the virtues of their pastors. In spite of their sorrow, Major's audience was urged to celebrate Georg of Anhalt's going to the heavenly home and to hold onto the memory of his confession of the faith and his practice of Christian virtues by emulating him in these ways.⁴⁵ Poach labeled Silberschlag's life "a genuine sample"—in the sense of a sample of a product—of the Christian life. But his list of Silberschlag's virtues included only discipline, moderation, and honesty, by comparison a very short list.⁴⁶ The list was a favorite device for rehearsing the virtues the parishioners were to follow, hardly a persuasive rhetorical device for hearers (though perhaps a helpful catalog for readers). Opitz did no more than remind his readers that Gallus's life had presented "a pattern for good works," for he was not greedy nor proud nor haughty. He did not seek praise and honor for himself. He was humble, kind, good, his heart sincere, pious, and faithful, without hypocrisy. He had always been ready to serve everyone and exploited no one. He strove to honor God and to care for the poor, divided church in its disrepair.⁴⁷

Perhaps as something of a reverse reflection of the polemic that plagued these pastors, their colleagues were eager to praise the virtue of friendship with others, particularly with other pastors. Winsheim's praise of Melanchthon's friendship with Luther served unique purposes, reinforcing Philip's reputation as Martin's associate at a time when foes were criticizing him for betraying Luther's cause.⁴⁸ But a certain poignancy haunts Mencel's description of Conrad Porta as one "who particularly loved peace and brotherly unity. He got along well with all his colleagues, and he strove to restore peace immediately when something went amiss or there was disagreement" among the colleagues in the Mansfeld ministerium. It had not been the case, as a matter of fact, during Porta's and Mencel's troubled time in Mansfeld County that friends got along well. Old friendships had broken sharply and tragically in a dispute over Flacius's definition of original sin. This reaction to the personal side of the polemic that divided former friends reveals how distasteful such division must have been for the likes of Mencel, even if he believed firmly in its necessity.⁴⁹ Similarly, the list of friends that proved for Schlüsselburg how "sincere and constant" a friend Wigand had been reveals too much.⁵⁰ Throughout most of his life, Wigand had stood shoulder to shoulder with Tilemann Heshusius, or Hesshus. Heshusius's name does not appear on the list because the two had fallen into a violent dispute in the decade before Wigand's death. Such personal tragedies did not serve the goal of the topic of personal virtue or pastoral image, and so not even a hint of them could be heard in the funeral addresses.

Perhaps the most important single topic within the chronological tracing of the career was the topic of the pastor's blessed and peaceful death. No blessed and peaceful death, obviously no blessed and peaceful life preceding, was a medieval rule of assessment for saints and sinners alike. Johann Cochlaeus had taken special care to attribute devilish presence to the hour of Luther's death,[51] and so it is little wonder that the Lutheran preachers made special efforts to trace carefully, in finest detail in some cases, how the gospel had set at peace the mind and heart of each pastor. Confession of sins and absolution, the Lord's Supper, confession of faith and Bible reading, occasionally accompanied by hymn singing, marked the last days and last words of all these pastors.[52] Although not a cleric, the physician Matthaeus Ratzeburger had worked closely with Luther. In charting Ratzeburger's last days of devotion and prayer, over the course of four and a half months and forty-eight quarto pages, Poach presented a Lutheran "art of dying," complete with Bible readings, prayers, hymns, and hopeful reflection upon Luther's picture, hanging on the wall of Ratzeburger's bedroom, inviting the physician to join his old friend who had died thirteen years earlier.[53] The topic of the blessed death undoubtedly instructed and consoled many a reader.

Within the topics that Melanchthon's students used, several devices typical of Renaissance rhetorical usage helped convey their teaching and admonition. Simple summaries and descriptions often served to present a commonplace. Frequently, finer touches enriched these descriptions: an occasional classical citation, a well-chosen metaphor, or the anecdotal account that demonstrated a particular virtue of the deceased. Heerbrand praised Andreae's gift for public speaking not only by citing Homer, but also by reciting a story that proved his oratorical prowess. In the mid-1550s, Andreae had been passing through Weissenstein when he happened upon a Jew strung up by the feet between two dogs who were chewing on his flesh. Hearing the Jew reciting psalms, Andreae began to proclaim the gospel to him. The dogs ceased their attack and turned their rapt attention to the preacher. The Jew was converted, cut down, and baptized, having been snatched "from the jaws of the devil"—with obvious reference to canine jaws (perhaps not coincidentally, a humanistic emblem for vice) as well—by Andreae's preaching.[54]

Another favorite device these preachers employed to convey their message regarding the lives of their colleagues was what Heinrich Bornkamm has called Luther's use of biblical texts as a "mirror of life."[55] This interpretative device was neither allegorical nor typological. Instead, it used the text as a backdrop against which to highlight the gifts, virtues, or sufferings of the deceased. In this case, the biblical text combined with the preacher's goal of cultivating a proper understanding of the clerical office and Christian living to dictate the selection of the materials reported from the individual's life. For the sake of cultivating the piety and perceptions of the hearers, the preachers constructed a framework for assessing reality from the text, undoubtedly familiar to at least the better-educated people in the congregation; and they created a dialogue between this framework and the recollections of their pastor that were still alive in the minds of the parishioners—and could be imagined by readers who had not known the deceased. This often imaginative and lively combination of text and contemporary experience depicted what the congregation was supposed to remember of the life of its former pastors. Mencel had chosen the reference to Lot in 2 Peter 2:7–9 as his text for Musaeus's funeral sermon. In great detail he compared Musaeus's struggle against "Manichaean" Mansfelder (a reference to their defense of Flacius's so-called "Manichaean" doctrine of original sin) to Lot's struggle in the role into which Mencel cast him, that of the pastor whom the Holy Spirit had posted to the pulpit of Sodom.[56] Mathesius drew parallels between Aaron's death, described in his text (Num. 20:22–29), and Pfeffinger's death.[57] Primus Truber's continuing battle against papal error and oppression had made the encouragement that Paul gave Timothy for his ministry (2 Tim. 4:5–8) come alive in his own day, Andreae was convinced. Interestingly, Osiander used the same text over Andreae's bier, describing his life in parallel fashion.[58]

An interesting variation on this "mirror of life" device appears in Mencel's account of Porta's career in Eisleben. Biblical texts on which he had preached at three significant points in that career foreshadowed the events that lay before him. His first assigned text when he began preaching at the church of Saint Nikolaus had included the ancient prophet Samuel's insistence that he had neither taken anything from God's people unjustly nor injured anyone, but had only sought God's honor and their welfare (1 Sam. 12:1- 6), a passage that would typify Porta's ministry. When he was installed as pastor at Saint Peter's, the gospel lesson for the day, the eighth Sunday after Trinity (Matt. 7:15–

23), contained a warning against false prophets, such as the followers of Flacius, against whom Porta would soon have to battle. The Sunday before his death, he had preached on the gospel lesson for the twentieth Sunday after Trinity (Matt. 22:1–14), on the heavenly banquet, to which he was about to be welcomed.[59]

On their way to the heavenly banquet, he and his fellow pastors had reflected in their lives God's power and providence and the proper practice of many of the virtues and one of the vocations God had designed for human life. To make use of the examples of both God's activity and human actions that lay in the lives of their deceased colleagues, German Lutheran pastors in the late Reformation developed a catalog of commonplaces or topics—examples—that aided them in framing their rehearsal of what was useful in the lives of the departed brethren. Philip Melanchthon had shown them how to gather and frame such categories or loci. Melanchthon and Luther had begun to model how funeral addresses could be used to cultivate piety. From their suggestions, their followers employed the humanistic tools at hand in the Wittenberg legacy to proclaim God's providence and the human practice of virtue and vocation as they furthered their programs for confessional stabilization and integrity.

NOTES

1. Lorenz Mathesius, *Leichpredigt/Gehalten bey dem begrebnus des Ehrwirdigen... Herrn Johan Pfeffingers... Sampt einem einfaltigen vnd nuetzlichen Bericht/von dem leben vnd wandel/auch von der Lere/Christlicher Tugenden/vnd endtlichen Abschied desselbigen von dieser Welt...* (Leipzig: Johann Martoff, 1573), Aiij^r.

2. See Wilhelm Maurer, *Der junge Melanchthon zwischen Humanismus und Reformation, Band 1. Der Humanist* (Göttingen: Vandenhoeck & Ruprecht, 1967), 99–128; and Robert Kolb, "Philip's Foes but Followers Nonetheless: Late Humanism among the Gnesio-Lutherans?" in Manfred P. Fleischer, ed., *The Harvest of Humanism in Central Europe: Essays in Honor of Lewis W. Spitz* (Saint Louis: Concordia, 1991) 163–65, 167–72. On Luther's view and use of history, see John M. Headley, *Luther's View of Church History* (New Haven, CT: Yale University Press, 1963). Lutherans did sketch lives of some biblical and patristic saints as models of piety: see James Michael Weiss, "Luther and His Colleagues on the Lives of the Saints," *Harvard Library Bulletin* 33 (1979): 174–95; and Robert Kolb, *For All the Saints: Changing Perceptions of Martyr-*

dom and Sainthood in the Lutheran Reformation (Macon, GA: Mercer University Press, 1987), 33–102.

3. Kolb, *For All the Saints,* 77–78, 58–87, 139–158.

4. Ibid., 102–38.

5. Joachim Camerarius, *De Philippi Melanchthon ortv, totivs vitae cvrricvlo et morte... narratio...* (Leipzig: Ernst Vogelin, 1566). See the chapter by Timothy J. Wengert, "'With Friends Like This...': The Biography of Philip Melanchthon by Joachim Camerarius," in this volume.

6. See particularly, Eberhard Winckler, *Die Leichenpredigt im deutschen Luthertum bis Spener* (Munich: Kaiser, 1967), and several volumes by Rudolph Lenz, ed., *Leichenpredigten als Quelle historischer Wissenschaften,* 3 vols. (Cologne and Vienna: Böhlau, 1975; Marburg: Schwarz, 1975, 1981); idem, ed., *Studien zur deutschsprachigen Leichenpredigt der frühen Neuzeit* (Marburg: Schwarz, 1981); and *De mortuis nil nisi bene?* (Sigmaringen: Thorbecke, 1990).

7. *D. Martin Luthers Werke* (Weimar: Böhlau, 1883–), 17, 1:196–227 (Frederick) and 36:237–70 (John); *Corpus Reformatorum* XI (Halle: Schwetschke, 1843), 90–98. On Melanchthon's oration, see Eberhard Winckler, "Melanchthons lateinische Leichenrede auf Kurfürst Friedrich den Weisen," *Zeitschrift für Religions-und Geistesgeschichte* XVIII (1966): 33–42. See also, for the highly influential sermons preached at Luthers's death, Justus Jonas, Michael Coelius, and Johannes Aurifaber, *Vom Christlichen abschied aus diesem toedlichen leben des Ehrwirdigen Herrn D. Martini Lutheri/bericht...* (Magdeburg: Christian Rödinger, 1546).

8. Winckler, *Die Leichenpredigt,* 9–11, Rudolf Lenz, "Leichenpredigten: Eine bislang vernachlässigte Quellengattung, Geschichte, Forschungstand, methodologische Probleme, Bibliographie," *Archiv für Kulturgeschichte* 56 (1974): 296–312. Melanchthon's followers used and integrated the *oratio funebris,* the *oratio de vita,* and the *oratio parentalis* with biblical textual exposition.

9. Lenz, "Vorkommen, Aufkommen, und Verteilung der Leichenpredigten, Untersuchungen zu ihrer regionalen Distribution, zur zeitlichen Häufigkeit und zu Geschlecht, Stand und Beruf der Verstorbenen," *Studien,* 244.

10. Winckler, *Die Leichenpredigt,* 52–57.

11. Winfried Zeller, "Leichenpredigt und Erbauungsliteratur," in Rudolf Lenz, ed. *Leichenpredigten als,* 1:67.

12. Uwe Schnell, *Die homiletische Theorie Philipp Melanchthons* (Berlin and Hamburg: Lutherisches Verlagshaus, 1968), 17–53.

13. Although, he regarded this genus as unsuitable for preaching because the task of the preacher could not be to praise an individual. He focused on the genus didacticum in his homiletical theory and assisted his readers in using it, along with exhortation and consolation, to bring God's Word to their congregations, both through "interpretation," the exposition of the biblical text, and through

"method," the discussion of some element from the text in topical form. See Schnell, *Die homiletische Theorie Philipp Melanchthons,* 64–73, 94–109.

14. *Corpus Reformatorum* XIII (Halle: Schwetschke, 1847); *Elementa rhetorices* (Wittenberg: Georg Rhav, 1542), 448–54, on the genus *demonstrativum* and *loci communes; Erotemata Dialectices* (3d ed. of 1547, reprint Leipzig: Johannes Steinman, 1580), 659–62, on the *loci personarum.*

15. Ernst Heinrich Rehermann, "Die protestantischen Exempelsammlungen des 16. und 17. Jahrhunderts. Versuch einer Übersicht und Charakterisierung nach Aufbau und Inhalt," in *Volkserzählung und Reformation,* ed. Wolfgang Brückner (Berlin: Schmidt, 1974), 580–646; on the use of loci communes, see esp. 580–88. Cf. Heidemarie Schade, "Andreas Hondorffs Promptuarium Exemplorum," ibid., 647–703.

16. *Corpus Reformatorum* XIII: 449, 659.

17. Robert Kolb, "Festivals of the Saints in Late Reformation Lutheran Preaching," *The Historian* 52 (1990): 613–26.

18. Hieronymus Mencel, *Eine Predigt Vber den Spruch Petri. 2. Gott hat erloeset den Gerechten Loth/etc. Bey der Christlichen Begrebnis... Simonis Musaei...* (Halle: Urban Gaubisch, 1577), G2^r.

19. Augustin Tham, *Leichpredigt Bey der begrebnis des/Herrn M. Hieronymi Mencelij...* (Eisleben: Urban Gaubisch, 1590), A2^{r-v}.

20. Kolb, "Festivals," 624–25.

21. Lucas Osiander, *Ein Predig/Bey der Leych... Jacobi Andreae... Sampt einem kurtzen Summarischen Bericht/welcher gestaldt/Ehrngedachter Herr D. Jacobus Andreae seinem Abschied... Christlich vnd Selig genommen* (Tübingen: Alexander Hock, 1590), sig. D^r, cf. sig. B^v; cf. similar material in Hieronymus Mencel, *Erklerung des spruchs S. Pauli Philip l. Christus ist mein Leben/etc. Bey der Christlichen Begrebnis... M. Conradi Portae...* (Eisleben: Andreas Petri, 1586), sig. Fiij^v.

22. Caspar Heldelin, *Eine Christlich predigt vber der Leiche des... M. Matthiae Flacij Illyrici...* (n.p., 1575), sig. Piij^v.

23. Horst Schmidt-Grave, *Leichenreden und Leichenpredigten Tübinger Professoren (1550–1750), Untersuchungen zur biographischen Geschichtsschreibung in der frühen Neuzeit* (Tübingen: Mohr [Siebeck], 1984), 11–15.

24. Georg Major, *Oratio de reverendissimo... principe Georgio Principe in Anhalt...* (Wittenberg, 1554), sig. Aiiij^r-Av^v.

25. E.g., Tham, *Mencel,* Eij^r, or Jakob Heerbrand, *Oratio fvnebris, de vita, & obitu... D. Jacobi Andreae...* (Tübingen: Alexander Hock, 1590), sig. [A4]$^{r-v}$.

26. Heldelin, *Flacius,* sigs. Niij^r–Piij^v; Qij^r; on the student attacks, sigs. L^v–M^v; cf. similar material in Mencel, *Musaeus,* sigs. A3^{r-v}, C^r.

27. Matthesius, *Pfeffinger,* sigs. Ciij^r, [Diiij]$^{r-v}$.

28. Conrad Schlüsselburg, *Oratio funebris, de vita et obitv... D. Joannis*

Wigandi... (Frankfurt am Main: Johann Spies, 1591), sigs. A2^r-B^r. Wigand had written a special study of persecution, *De persecutione piorvm*... (Frankfurt am Main: Corvinus, 1580); on it see Robert Kolb, *Confessing the Faith, Reformers Define the Church* (Saint Louis: Concordia, 1991), 92–95.

29. Schlüsselburg, *Wigand*, 48.

30. E.g., Josua Opitz, *Eine Christliche Leichpredigt. Bey dem Begrebnuss des... Herrn Nicolai Galli*... (Regensburg: Hans Burger, 1570), sig. Bij^v; Tham, *Mencel*, sig. F^{r-v}; Mathesius, *Pfeffinger*, sigs. E^v, Hiij^r; Schlüsselburg, *Wigand*, 48–50; Mencel, *Porta*, sig. F^v; Heldelin, *Flacius*, sig. M^v.

31. The same point was made by Andreas Poach, *Eine Predigt aus dem Propheten Hosea/Cap: 4. Vber der Leiche M. Georgij Silberschlags*... (n.p., 1572), sig. B^v.

32. Hieronymus Mencel, *Vier Christliche Predigten... Bey den Christlichen Begrebnissen/der... Herrn M. Heinrich Rothen... M. Johan Stammen*... (Eisleben: Urban Gaubisch, 1575), sigs. H^v– H2^v.

33. Heldelin, *Flacius*, sig. A^r.

34. Opitz, *Gallus*, sig. [Aiiij]^r.

35. Ibid., sig. [Aiiij]^v.

36. Mencel, *Roth*, sig. [B4]^v.

37. Poach, *Silberschlag*, sig. E^r.

38. Osiander, *Andreae*, sig. [Ciiij]^v.

39. Johann Wigand, *Leichpredigt/Bey der Begrebnis Erasmi Sarcerii*... (Magdeburg: Kirchner, 1560), sig. Cij^r; cf. similar material in Heldelin, *Flacius*, sigs. N^r, Nij^v.

40. Osiander, *Andreae*, sigs. Aiij^v-[Ciiij]^r.

41. Heerbrand, *Andreae*, sig. D^v.

42. Major, *Anhalt*, sig. Bij^r.

43. Kolb, "Festivals," 623–24.

44. Georg Mylius, *Christliche Predigt/Bey der Leiche des... Herrn: Nicolai Selnecceri*... (Leipzig: Johann Beyer, 1592), sig. Aij^v.

45. Major, *Anhalt*, sig. [Bvij]^r.

46. Poach, *Silberschlag*, sig. E^v.

47. Opitz, *Gallus*, sig. B^v-Bij^r.

48. Veit Winsheim, *Oratio habita in fvnere reverendi et clarissimi viri Philippi Melanthonis*... (Wittenberg: Petrus Seitz, 1560).

49. Mencel, *Porta*, sig. Fiij^r.

50. Schlüsselburg, *Wigand*, 50; cf. Tham, *Mencel*, sig. F^v.

51. *Commentaria Ioannis Cochlaei, de actis et scriptis Martini Lvtheri Saxonis*... (Mainz: Franz Behem, 1549).

52. Jakob Andreae, *Christliche Leichpredig/Bey der Begraebnus des... Herrn/Primus Trubern*... (Tübingen: Georg Gruppenbach, 1586), 57; Heerbrand, *Andreae*, sigs. H^r–[H4]^r; Mathesius, *Pfeffinger*, [Hiiij]^r–[Iiiij]^r; Mencel,

Musaeus, sig. G2ʳ; Mencel, *Porta,* sigs. [Fiiij]ʳ–Gʳ; Mencel, *Roth,* sigs. H3ʳ– Kᵛ; Opitz, *Gallus,* sigs. Biijʳ–[Biiij]ʳ; Osiander, *Andreae,* sigs. Diijʳ–[Eiiij]ʳ; Poach, *Silberschlag,* sigs. E2ʳ–E3ʳ; Schlüsselburg, *Wigand,* 54–57; Tham, *Mencel,* sigs. Fijr– Fiijv; Wigand, *Sarcerius,* sigs. Diijʳ⁻ᵛ; Winsheim, *Melanchthon,* sigs. Dijʳ– [Diij]ʳ.

53. Andreas Poach, *Vom Christlichen Abschied aus diesem sterblichen Leben des lieben thewren Mannes Matthei Ratzenbergers . . .* (Jena: Thomas Rhebart, 1559), sigs. Bijʳ-Giijʳ.

54. Heerbrand, *Andreae,* sigs. B2ᵛ–B3ʳ.

55. Heinrich Bornkamm, *Luther and the Old Testament,* trans. Eric W. and Ruth C. Gritsch (Philadelphia: Fortress, 1969), 11–44.

56. Mencel, *Musaeus,* sigs. Cʳ–Gᵛ.

57. Mathesius, *Pfeffinger,* sigs. [Hiiij]ᵛ–Iijᵛ; cf. similar materials in Poach, *Silberschlag,* sig. [C4]ᵛ; and Heldelin, *Flacius,* e.g. sigs. Gʳ, [Hiiij]ʳ.

58. Andreae, *Truber,* e.g., 25, 47; Osiander, *Andreae,* sigs. A2ʳ–Dijᵛ.

59. Mencel, *Porta,* sigs. F–Fijʳ.

4

"With Friends Like This...": The Biography of Philip Melanchthon by Joachim Camerarius

Timothy J. Wengert

In 1566 Joachim Camerarius published in Leipzig a biography of Philip Melanchthon (1497–1560), evangelical reformer and teacher at the University of Wittenberg.[1] It is easily one of the most influential biographies of its time. According to the thorough bibliographic work of Wilhelm Hammer, it was reprinted twelve times: once in 1566, once in 1591, twice in 1592, three times in the seventeenth century, twice in the eighteenth, and thrice more in the nineteenth.[2] Until the flourishing of biography in the nineteenth century, this work served as the single most important source for the life of Melanchthon.[3]

This biography influenced its readers in three different ways. First, Camerarius wrote it as a piece of practice rhetoric, demonstrating how to describe the life of someone with the stature of Melanchthon. Second, this biography arose in the charged atmosphere of intra-Lutheran theological battles and fights over the role the now dead Melanchthon would play in the theology of his students. It became a piece of polemic directed especially at the detractors of Melanchthon. These two influences fit LaCapra's two poles of life-writing by combining technical rhetoric with the biographer's own ideology on the canvas of someone's life story.[4] Third, because this work was the first, and remained until the nineteenth century practically the only, important biography of Melanchthon, it has continued to exercise a tremendous influence on later depictions of his life.[5]

Biographers who have respected neither the rhetorical genre nor the polemical edge to this work have accepted uncritically Camerarius's portrayal of Melanchthon's character, despite the fact that contemporary sources contain other, quite different views of the second Reformer from Wittenberg. In so doing, they have transformed his narrative into myth. In the main, historians steer clear of such complicated transhistorical issues for good reason. The nature of history writing focuses upon the particular, and often within the plodding, scholarly genre that marks the modern genre of historical narrative lurks an uncritical acceptance of similar works from earlier times on terms foreign to the style and objective of these older writers. Thus, although the notion that sixteenth-century biography has a rhetorical edge may seem obvious, the fact remains that later historians have often ignored that very notion. Once the idea is stated, it forces reevaluation not simply of the historian's sources, but also the historian's own rhetoric and its dependence on narrative and myth.

Part of the meaning of historical texts lies in their use and misuse. One must discuss the continued life of Camerarius's narration because the response of later readers tells us something, albeit not everything, about the text itself. This is not to eliminate questions of author's intent and original meaning as some philosophers of language would do. However, one of the most fascinating parts of the historical enterprise itself is the way in which each generation appropriates the texts and their meanings.

Biography as Rhetoric

Joachim Camerarius (1500–1574) was a humanist during the flowering of languages and letters in sixteenth-century Germany. First trained under Georg Helt von Forchheim at the University of Leipzig, where he enrolled in 1512 and obtained a bachelor of arts degree in 1518 under Richard Crocus and Peter Mosellanus, Camerarius was known even at a young age for his command of the Greek language. After receiving a master of arts degree under Eoban Hessus at the University of Erfurt in 1520, Camerarius came to Wittenberg to study with the man who was to become his lifelong friend and correspondent, Philip Melanchthon. At Melanchthon's recommendation, Camerarius became teacher of Greek and of Latin histories at the newly founded Gymnasium in Nuremberg, where he stayed (somewhat unhappily) until 1535 when, again at the urging of Melanchthon, he became a professor in the arts faculty at the University of Tübingen. In 1541, Melanchthon's recommendation brought him a professorship at the University of Leipzig where, with the exception of a short period during the Smalcald War, he spent the rest of his life.

His publications include theological works, pedagogical aids, such as a book on rhetoric, and editions of and commentaries on classical works, including Cicero and Quintilian. He also wrote three *narrationes,* narrations of the lives of his contemporaries Eoban Hessus; George, prince of Anhalt; and Philip Melanchthon.[6] These works typify Renaissance lifewriting and, more specifically, imitate Philip Melanchthon's own work. Although Melanchthon wrote no full-length *narratio,* he was well known for his funeral orations. His oration delivered at the death of Luther was probably the most widely reproduced speech he gave. It makes striking use of the prose and categories of German humanism to describe the Reformer.[7]

While working on his biography of Melanchthon, Camerarius published the second edition of his book on rhetoric, *Elementa Rhetoricae.*[8] In that book he describes a *narratio* in some detail. A *narration,* using Cicero's definition, is an exposition of exploits, real or fictitious. Narrations of real events either comprise the entire work or are simply some small section of a larger work, intended in this latter case to support and confirm an orator's arguments.[9] As we shall see, the life of Melanchthon falls under the second category.

Camerarius discusses the content of narration in different categories throughout the *Elementa.* He lists the possible categories of topics, including individuals, which he subdivides into properties of natures, distinctions of conditions, age, and sex.[10] Under history, Camerarius makes a crucial distinction between annals, which use plain speech, and history, which employs an "elocutio splendida, copiosa atque ornata singularis" [a brilliant delivery, abundant and extraordinarily well-furnished]. Whatever has been put forward in the way of praise or blame in such histories, he adds, must not be overlooked.[11]

Under these self-professed guidelines, Camerarius sets out to write his biography of Melanchthon. It is without a doubt "elocutio splendida." Sentences run for miles, using the entire wealth of expression and vocabulary so loved by the Latinists of the time. For example, if Erasmus, in his Copia, could think of a hundred ways to thank someone for receiving a letter, Camerarius invented at least as many to describe the deaths of Melanchthon's friends and associates.

In fact, the very mention of someone's death calls forth at least a paragraph and sometimes an entire page or more of description of their nature, condition, and age. Since most of the deaths involve wonderful individuals, no ink is spared in singing their praises, although occasionally, as with Maurice of Saxony, whose treachery in the Smalcald War led to the defeat of his cousin, John Frederick, and who himself died in battle, some come in for criticism. In this case, Camerarius criticizes Maurice's impetuousity. As the narrative progresses and more of Melanchthon's friends and acquaintances die, the narration takes on the form of an extended eulogy. For example, in one chapter Camerarius describes the persecutions in France and the colloquies of Worms and Regensburg of 1540–41 in one page and spends three praising the lives and personalities of George Helt, his teacher, and Jerome Camermeister, his brother.[12] As is typical for these excurses, he concludes by saying, "The oration, therefore, returning to the proposition, will pursue to the end those things which remain."[13] He takes seven pages for Luther's death, describing in detail Melanchthon's relation to him.

Either before or after many of these eulogies and in connection with many of the wars, struggles, and other events in Melanchthon's life, sent by God or Fortune, Camerarius describes Melanchthon in terms of his great sorrow and perturbations of soul, which he bears with great patience and understanding.[14] Here Camerarius reveals his philosophical predilections. He was greatly influenced by the Stoics and especially their descriptions of the pathos of the soul. He uses this classical framework to describe all the narrative's characters. The result is a surprisingly static and predictable narrative in which the individuals become moral examples, as Friedrich Stähelin has pointed out in his study of all of Camerarius's attempts at biography.[15] The major ethical categories used by Camerarius are *pietas* (religion), *virtus* (morality), and *doctrina* (erudition). Stähelin also points out that the Stoics insisted on, and Camerarius accepted, the notion that friendship could occur only between good people. Thus, eulogies for those who came in contact with Melanchthon must also reflect to some degree good qualities to strengthen Melanchthon's own character.

Camerarius also investigates Melanchthon's character, under the conviction that the traits of childhood determine later behavior. Again in line with classical models, he tries to match flaws with virtues, although the virtues always seem to win. We discover a child prodigy and polymath who had mastered all the liberal arts including rhetoric, physics, and astrology, a deeply religious individual, and a Christian of impeccable virtue who, when attacked by his enemies, bore up under it all with patience and tact.¹⁶ He did have his faults, but they seem minor compared to the virtues. He had a stammer but was a wonderful rhetorician. He was overly generous. He had a hard time sleeping and was forced, against his own nature, to take wine in the evening before falling asleep. He also had a temper, which flared only for a second before he returned to his old quiet self.

We could multiply examples throughout this work. The point is, this is not narration for history's sake or for the sake of the events or people, as some of us may still practice; it is narration for the sake of rhetoric. Unlike his friend Melanchthon, who concentrated his efforts on combining rhetoric and dialectic, Camerarius defined rhetoric in terms of the late-antique tradition of the *progymnastica*.¹⁷ These were exercises that formed an important part of rhetorical training, being mentioned by Cicero and explained at length by Quintilian. But Camerarius did not simply receive suggestions from the Latin tradition; he was actively involved in reintroducing the Greek models themselves. Thus, among his writings were editions and translations of the *progymnastica* of Theon and Aphthonius. More than that, Camerarius's own book on rhetoric is styled precisely along the lines of these *progymnastica*. He uses the same technical terms for the various types of exercises and gives examples from classical literature and contemporary events. The twelve progymnastic exercises listed by Quintilian included historical narrative, encomium or denunciation of persons, comparison of persons, and chria, that is, anecdotes concerning a person. These exercises comprise Camerarius's work on Melanchthon and give it its form and purpose. We have in the life of Melanchthon narrative for narrative's sake: Camerarius applying to his friend's memory the best rhetorical skills he could offer.

Biography as Polemic

For Camerarius, Melanchthon's biography was more than rhetorical exercise; it was also polemical attack. Stähelin has pointed out several aspects of this in his analysis.¹⁸ For one thing, Camerarius mentions one of Melanchthon's living opponents, Matthias Flacius Illyricus, by name and spends three pages on his personality. In Camerarius's mind, Flacius, the gnesio-Lutheran from Croatia who trained under Melanchthon and who began his attack on Melanchthon over his stand on the so-called Leipzig Interim in 1548, serves as a counterpoint to all of Melanchthon's personal characteristics. His German was poor; he published books under strange, made-up names; despite having had good teachers, his Greek was weak and he was only a beginner in Hebrew; and he had a turbulent personality filled with ambition.[19] For another, Camerarius tries to avoid divinizing Luther, something he was sure Flacius and other gnesio-Lutherans were doing. In another work, he conveniently places Melanchthon's theology, actually the position of George Major on the question of good works, into Luther's mouth.[20]

Camerarius attacks, without naming names, Friedrich Staphylus, a former student turned Roman Catholic,[21] and Johannes Manlius, a student whose excerpts and anecdotes from Melanchthon's works and life were not greatly appreciated.[22] The identification of Manlius is somewhat clouded by the fact that other publications from this time also included excerpts of and annotations on Melanchthon's work.[23] But this does not bring us to the actual cause for Camerarius's biography. In the Prooemium addressed to the Landgrave Philip of Hesse and in a thirty-page conclusion to the book, tacked on after the description of Melanchthon's death, as well as continuously in between, Camerarius viciously attacks some people for distorting Melanchthon's writings, for besmirching his good name after his death, and for calling him a Veterator, that is, old fox.[24] Camerarius also makes clear that these offenses occurred in a controversy over the Lord's Supper. By placing this *Narratio* within the context of this dispute, an entirely different face of this writing emerges from that found in Stähelin's assessment of its rhetorical side.

In fact, one event late in Melanchthon's life brought this biography into existence. In a letter dated 1 November 1559 to Elector Frederick of the Palatinate, Melanchthon gave his response to a newly developing controversy among the clergy and professors of Heidelberg over the Lord's Supper. That letter, published in 1560 in both Latin and German, became swept up in that controversy and, even after Melanchthon's death in April 1560, was commented upon and argued over. These attacks sparked Camerarius's four-hundred-page response, defending both Melanchthon's character and theology with all the rhetorical tools at his disposal and calling for the censoring of Melanchthon's opponents.

The controversy over the meaning of the Lord's Supper arose between Tilemann Heshusius, a student of Melanchthon who had become general superintendent in Heidelberg and dean of the university's theology faculty, and Wilhelm Klebitz, a deacon and preacher in the same city.[25] Klebitz published a set of theses on the Lord's Supper for a university disputation on 4 April 1559 in which he argued that, for example, the

Words of Institution were not to be taken literally—a sure sign of a reformed position. (The theses were doubtless framed by the assistant dean, Peter Boucquin, who as rector published them in Heshusius's absence.)[26] When Heshusius returned, he declared the theses heretical and demanded from his deacon a recantation. Klebitz turned to the university for support, with the result that letters were exchanged and the opinions of outside experts solicited. One or two nasty things were said from the pulpits of Heidelberg as well. In August 1559, the newly proclaimed elector became involved and demanded an end to the dispute. By the end of the month, Heshusius had removed Klebitz from his post, and Klebitz in turn had attacked Heshusius from the pulpit. There is also the rather edifying scene in which Klebitz and another deacon fought over the chalice during a worship service, but that need not detain us here. On 1 September both men were commanded to place before the elector their personal confessions on the matter.[27] By October, Heshusius was hard at work on a much longer defense of his position.[28]

At the same time, the court turned to Philip Melanchthon for an opinion, which he gave in the form of a *Judicium,* attaching to it (or sending after it) a letter to the elector.[29] It would seem that Melanchthon had hoped to bridge the gap between the two parties by proposing the use of the biblical word *koinonia* to describe the presence of Christ in the Supper. With this word, Melanchthon wanted to avoid the transubstantiation of the papists, but also the claims of Lutheran pastors in Bremen that the bread is the substantial body of Christ, and the position of Heshusius, who had written that the bread is the true body of Christ.

This letter, rather than helping end controversies, became a cause célèbre in 1560 and beyond. Over the objections of the faculty of the University of Heidelberg it was published in 1560 in Latin and immediately translated.[30] From this translation Nicholas Gallus, an archenemy of Melanchthon, published his edition with a bitter commentary.[31] At the same time, Heshusius also published the letter with his own lengthy defense against Melanchthon's charges, in which he calls Melanchthon an old fox.[32] Joachim Mörlin, whom Melanchthon had also attacked, similarly felt called upon to write his own defense.[33] Only the dead, Erasmus Sarcerius, and, after 19 April 1560, Melanchthon himself, had nothing to say.

But Melanchthon, at least, also had his defenders. A poem published under the name of Timotheus Philophilippus, that is, "one who honors God and is a friend of Philip," appeared in 1561 and attacked Heshusius as the son of a rabbit.³⁴ Klebitz's own defense, *The Victory of Truth*, includes six pages in which fourteen of Heshusius's arguments against Melanchthon are refuted.³⁵ Paul Einhorn, who could not believe his teacher would defend a Calvinist position, published in 1563 *The Legitimate Interpretation of Philip Melanchthon's Response,* and in 1565 a *Defense, in which Philip Melanchthon's "Judgment" is more fully explained, against the Theologians who recently published some book written about the Lord's Supper.*³⁶

Joachim Mörlin's comments in a later attack in the Heidelberg controversy from 1565 epitomize the tone of this debate. He writes the following about his former teacher's claim that Luther had recanted his position on the Lord's Supper.

> I cannot let myself be persuaded by Philip, that he ever could have held such a story for true or to possess someone's report.... I write about this, as my God knows, with a heavy heart, because the fall of this man hurts me very deeply.³⁷

Precisely in this highly charged situation, Camerarius penned his biography as a massive attack against Melanchthon's opponents on this very issue. Whereas the other opponents in this dispute, with the lone exception of Timotheus Philophilippus, were throwing syllogisms across the printed page at one another, Camerarius used the best weapon at his disposal, rhetoric.³⁸

This means that Camerarius does not debate the issue, how to understand Christ's presence in the Lord's Supper, but the personalities and behavior of the chief players in the drama. Even when discussing the offensive letter, he is more concerned about its private nature, about its less-than-elegant or polished style, and about the fact that, true to his personality, Melanchthon wrote such a "private" letter to avoid the very kind of controversy that arose once it was published. Melanchthon, the prophet, had predicted in that letter the kind of dangers and divisions that the Lord's Supper debate would cause.³⁹

Camerarius's charges are as fierce as they are rhetorical. One from this number (Heshusius) provoked Melanchthon not only in life, but after his death, in order that he could show his powers of persuasion by arguing with him. Camerarius rejoins that had Melanchthon lived, he could have easily refuted him and preserved the peace and tranquillity of the republic and the pure integrity of heavenly doctrine and of the studies of the humanities at the same time. His opponents were also impudent. Another of them (Gallus) translated the dispute (in this case the offending letter with annotations) "so that little old ladies could also read and know these things."[40] Rather than answer their arguments, Camerarius ridicules them. They deal in *sophismata,* fallacious conclusions. The reason for the debate over the Lord's Supper was not piety, but "importunate vehemence and boastful confidence."[41]

The attacks are not limited to the first and last pages of the narrative but fill it at every turn. The vituperative and personal attack against Flacius, who, incidentally, had also attacked Camerarius in an earlier dispute, must also be seen in this light. Camerarius claims that Flacius was really the source of all later debates, a claim that has influenced scholarship on the sharp-tongued Croatian ever since. Contacts among the various opponents of Melanchthon abound. Thus, it is hardly accidental that the copy of Heshusius's treatise on the presence of Christ in the Supper in the Herzog August Bibliothek was a part of Flacius's private library and contains the inscription in Heshusius's hand: "To the Reverend Mr. Dr. Matthias Flacius Illyricus, from his beloved brother Tilemann Heshusius."[42] But these contacts do not mean that Flacius was a ringleader of a plot to overthrow Melanchthon.

The main point of Camerarius's *Narratio* does not become clear until near the end, when, after describing the awful behavior of Melanchthon's opponents, he appeals to the powers-that-be to take measures to suppress them. Those who have the *officium patriae,* as he calls it, should see that these people are reprimanded and restrained from these attacks.

The *Narratio* is not merely an attack on Melanchthon's enemies, it is also a defense of Melanchthon's own character. Melanchthon is not an old fox, slinking around in the bushes waiting to attack some defenseless rabbit. This countercharacter sketch takes up the bulk of the biography. Building upon an image that Melanchthon had already fashioned through his letters and public behavior during his lifetime, Camerarius portrays a Stoic hero, beset by cares, labors, sollicitudes, sorrows, and finally miseries.[43] Unlike Heshusius, he was admired by all, worked hard, did not affect titles, gently corrected those who erred, and preserved for the world illustrious and spectacular *doctrina.*[44]

Camerarius must show that the personal attacks on Melanchthon are totally unjustified. To counteract this *iudicium,* which could be used to show Melanchthon's lack of respect for a student, his underhanded ways, and his abandonment of the evangelical cause, he consistently portrays Melanchthon as peace-loving, always willing to bend over backward for someone, going to great lengths to avoid any kind of confrontation. As a student in Tübingen, he abhorred the disputations of the scholastics.[45] He studied for the sake of the truth, not for glory.[46] True, he had a temper—one way to explain his attack on poor Heshusius—but it flared up for a moment and then was gone, expelled by the force of his own [good] nature.[47] Even his love for astrology is explained as a teaching technique.[48] Camerarius even goes so far as to defend Melanchthon's slight speech impediment and the way he moved his hands and raised his eyebrows when he spoke.[49]

At the same time, Camerarius must defend Melanchthon's behavior in certain crucial situations. One case involved a dispute over the second edition of Melanchthon's theological textbook, the *Loci communes,* in 1536. After describing the vehement, immoderate, and inhuman behavior of the opponents, he describes Melanchthon with his hand steady on the tiller, fostering the study of the best arts and disciplines, handing on the simple doctrine of heavenly truth, cleansing it of all prickly disputations through pure and proper speech. He was impervious to the charges around him and did everything with moderation, so that even Luther approved.[50]

Another place Camerarius does his rhetorical best to diffuse the arguments of his enemies comes in the relation between Luther and Melanchthon. Given his limited range of possible descriptions, Camerarius has little choice but to describe Luther and Melanchthon's behavior in terms of friendship. From their first encounter in 1518, we read of Melanchthon's insight into Luther's goodness and Luther's love for Melanchthon's intelligence. Near the end of Luther's life, Camerarius describes things this way.

> But Philip Melanchthon, to his own like a quiet harbor, was so harassed by storms that he was almost overturned—either oppressed or beaten by the iniquity and hatred of some, who incited against him Martin Luther's spirit by an atrocity of accusations, of which the chief was moderation and leniency, to which it was said the adversaries [of the Evangelicals] induced him.... Then [in 1544] were renewed with not only some vehemence but plainly with savagery disputations concerning Christ's most sacred action of the mystical supper in the church, which is the communication [Melanchthon's favorite word] of the body and blood of our Lord Jesus Christ.

After describing how some tried to exaggerate Luther's teaching, he concludes, "But these things were like a little cloud that quickly at that time rained down and then that disturbance was easily calmed, both by some who restrained the blindly incited rage and by Philip Melanchthon, who constantly brought to bear his accustomed moderation and patience."[51]

Biography as Fact?

How well did Camerarius succeed? So well that later gnesio-Lutheran church historians—to say nothing of Philippists—picked up the rhetorical and polemical images of Melanchthon constructed by Camerarius and, without questioning them, used them in their own depictions of Melanchthon, thereby turning them into myths. The myths are manifold: the relation between Luther and Melanchthon transformed into a friendship; the personality of Melanchthon as being moderate and patient; Melanchthon's attempts to avoid theological conflict at all costs; his straightforward, honest, and calm manner. Even many of the crises and events that Camerarius must explain in the polemical situation of 1565 have remained the loci communes for many biographies of Melanchthon ever since.

The image that Camerarius carefully constructed for Melanchthon has remained indelibly printed in later biographies down to the present. Many scholars or Lutherans in the know, when asked to describe Melanchthon's personality, would use words like quiet, irenic, moderate, or compromising. It is no accident that one biography in English bears the subtitle "The quiet reformer," and another, "Reformer without honor."

Not only have later generations of historians believed Camerarius, they have used his psychogram of Melanchthon to conclude that the reformer was always uncertain, never capable of taking a theological position and holding it, guilty of "pussy-footing around." Thus, in the mid-nineteenth century, Karl von Helmolt could write of Melanchthon's desire to keep his *Iudicium* against Heshusius secret, that "it shows us the writer of the Augsburg Confession and its Apology, the Preceptor of Germany, in the trembling, immasculate existence with which he made an appearance all over after Luther's departure."[52]

Some have so believed Camerarius's characterization of the relation between Luther and Melanchthon as a friendship that they have constructed entire theories to explain the breaks, shifts, and tensions within that friendship.⁵³ The situation is complicated by the fact that so many of Melanchthon's letters first passed through Camerarius's hands. Thus, for example, by careful editing, Camerarius projects his own anxiety over Luther's marriage onto Melanchthon himself.

We do not have space to examine all the examples of the formulation and continuation of these myths, wrung out of Camerarius's narration. For present-day historians, however, there remain some fascinating questions. What if the gnesio-Lutherans were depicted not simply as interested in hairsplitting and exaggeration of Luther, but as representing a crucial part of the development of Lutheran self-identity in the mid-sixteenth century, whose arguments must be taken seriously on their own terms? What if Melanchthon could be portrayed as vindictive, having an uncontrollable temper and a penchant for holding a grudge? What if he could be shown as going out of his way to keep his students in their place? What if Melanchthon could be pictured as having held and maintained a consistent theological program throughout his life, and what if the historian could imagine one of the tools for maintaining his position was behind-the-scenes political maneuvering and manipulation? What if Luther and Melanchthon were painted, as Heinz Scheible has so admirably done, as colleagues, not friends?

Camerarius's biography succeeded beyond his wildest dreams. Its program has found its way into countless other biographies and textbooks on the Reformation. It also has managed quite successfully until very recently to block almost all other approaches to Melanchthon's character, behavior, and theology. Once loosed from its original moorings as a piece of rhetorical polemic, in the hands of positivist historians it furnished material to create a myth large enough to be used even by Melanchthon's opponents to their advantage, so that we now imagine the Preceptor of Germany to be more a persecuted weakling than the powerful thinker and person a historian might construe his writings and letters to reveal. It remains to be seen if a yarn spinner of our age can escape the heroic shadow that the rhetor, Camerarius, has cast into the present and can create a new narration worthy of mythologization in the present.

NOTES

1. DE ‖ PHILIPPI ‖ MELANCHTHONIS ‖ ORTV, TOTIVS VI- ‖ TAE CVRRICVLO ET ‖ MORTE, ‖ IMPLICATA RERVM MEMO- ‖ RABILIVM TEMPORIS ILLIVS HO- ‖

minumque mentione atque indicio, cum ‖ expositionis serie cohae- ‖ rentium: ‖ NARRATIO DILIGENS ‖ ET ACCVRATA ‖ Ioachimi Camerarii ‖ PABEPERG. ‖ [Woodcut] ‖ LIPSIAE ‖ CVM PRIVILEGIO. ‖ 4°. Colophon: LIPSIAE ‖ Excudebat Ernestus Voegelin ‖ Constantiensis. ‖ ANNO 1566. ‖ 423 pages + [10 at the front, 1 blank (e7) + 9 at the back] leaves. In the same year, the same printer published the book again with a slightly different type for the title page and the same number of pages, with the blank page (f8) after the nine unnumbered leaves at the end of the book. These are both described in Wilhelm Hammer, *Die Melanchthonforschung im Wandel der Jahrhunderte*, 3 vols. (Gütersloh: Gerd Mohn, 1967–81), 1, no. 365 & 366, hereafter cited as H 365 & 366.

2. H 366A, 605A, 622, 622a, 733, 837, 890, 1039, 1373, 1594, 1595, and 1761, respectively.

3. I cite throughout the edition of 1777, edited with explanatory footnotes by Theodore Strobel, the foremost Melanchthon scholar of the eighteenth century, and entitled: IOACHIMI CAMERARII ‖ DE VITA ‖ PHILIPPI ‖ MELANCHTHONIS ‖ NARRATIO. ‖ RECENSVIT, ‖ NOTAS, DOCVMENTA, BIBLIOTHECAM ‖ LIBRORVM MELANCHTHONIS ‖ ALIAQVE ‖ ADDIDIT ‖ GE. THEODOR. STROBELIVS ‖ ART. MAG. ECCLESIAEQVE WOEHRDENSIS PASTOR. ‖ PRAEFATVS EST ‖ IOANNES AVG. NOESSELT. ‖ HALAE ‖ SVMTIBVS IOANNIS IAC. GEBAVERI. ‖ MDCCLXXVII. ‖ 8°, 592 pp., hereafter cited as VM.

4. As noted in the introduction to this volume; see esp. note 18.

5. The response of readers to a text, while perhaps not a part of the meaning of the original and certainly not a part of the author's intended meaning, nevertheless is part and parcel of the text's meaning understood as *Wirkungsgeschichte*.

6. For the information in these two paragraphs, see Theodore Kolde, "Joachim Camerarius," *Realencyclopädie für protestantische Theologie und Kirche*, 24 vols. (Leipzig, 1896–1913), 3:687–89. Camerarius also contributed two other pieces to Melanchthon's biography: a poem published at the time of his death, which is also included in the *narratio,* and a highly edited edition of letters. On how to read the latter, see Judith Henderson, "On Reading the Rhetoric of the Renaissance Letter," in Heinrich Plett, ed., *Renaissance-Rhetorik* (Munich: Wilhelm Fink, 1993), 143–62.

7. See James Michael Weiss, "Erasmus at Luther's Funeral: Melanchthon's Commemorations of Luther in 1546," *Sixteenth Century Journal* 16 (1985): 91–114. Like Camerarius, Melanchthon also combined humanist rhetoric with an ideological agenda in his biographical pieces. See Heinz Scheible, "Melanchthons biographische Reden: Literarische Form und akademischer Unterricht," in Walter Berschin, ed., *Biographie zwischen Renaissance und Barock: Zwölf Studien* (Heidelberg: Mattes Verlag, 1993).

8. I have used ELEMENTA ‖ RHETORICAE, ‖ SIVE CAPITA EXER- ‖ CITATIONVM STVDII PVERILIS ‖ ET STILI, AD COMPARANDVM ‖ VTRIVSQVE LINGVAE ‖ FACVLTATEM, ‖ COLLECTA ‖ A ‖ IOACHIMO ‖ CAMERARIO, ‖ NVNCQVE DENVO CVM ‖ emendatiora,

tum locis aliquot ‖ auctiora, in lucem edita ‖ LIPSIAE ‖ IN OFFICINA ‖ VOEGELIANA ‖ cum Priuilegio Quinquenij. ‖ ANNO ‖ M.D.LXIIII. ‖ 8°, 401 numbered pages + [26 1/2 + 1 blank] l leaves. The later preface is dated 17 February 1562 and the earlier 11 June 1540.

9. Ibid., 19.

10. Ibid., 48f.

11. Ibid., 96f. "Si quid in laude, si quid in vicio positum sit, non praeteribitur."

12. The chapter divisions were added in the seventeenth century and range from two to eight pages.

13. VM 212–16, here, 216: "Rediens igitur ad propositum oratio ea, quae restant, persequatur." He has as many ways of saying this as there are deaths to report.

14. This is also true for his description of Luther's marriage. "Ex quo facto maximum dolorem cepit Philippus, non quod illud [Lutherum] damnaret, sed quod occasionem dari cerneret inimicis et malevolis." From a letter to Camerarius, dated 16 June 1525 (MBW 408; =CR 1:753–56), we discover that the scruples in this matter belonged to Camerarius, not Melanchthon. Moreover, Camerarius edited that very letter in such a way as to make it look as if Melanchthon was the one who was troubled.

15. Friedrich Stähelin, *Humanismus und Reformation im bürgerlichen Raum: Eine Untersuchung der biographischen Schriften des Joachim Camerarius* (Leipzig: M. Heinsius Nachfolger, 1936), 47, 62, 66. He also argues (46f. and 82) persuasively that Camerarius follows the models of Plutarch and that he portrays God in terms of the fates, moving the wheel of history, 88–91.

16. VM 55–88.

17. The following connections were first pointed out to me by Dr. Judith Henderson, professor of the history of rhetoric at the University of Saskatchewan. For the best description of this rhetorical tradition, see George A. Kennedy, *Greek Rhetoric under Christian Emperors* (Princeton, NJ: University Press, 1983), 52–132.

18. Stähelin, *Humanismus* and *Reformation*, 54–59, 74, 78.

19. VM 274–76. The section on Flacius continues to 285. This description follows the form of *vituperatio*, also part of the *progymnastica*.

20. See Stähelin, *Humanismus und Reformation*, 59, n. 2, in reference to *Querela Luteri*. This work was attacked by Nicholas Gallus.

21. See Paul Tschakert, "Friedrich Staphylus," *Realencyclopädie für protestantische Theologie und Kirche*, 24 vols. (Leipzig, 1896–1913), 18:771–76.

22. See H 300, where, besides Camerarius, Hammer lists the opinion of Caspar Peucer, who produced the approved edition of Melanchthon's works in the 1560s. Manlius, or Menlin from Onoltzbach, appears in the Wittenberg Matrikel under 8 January 1548. See Karl Eduard Foerstemann, *Album Acade-*

miae vitebergensis ab a. Ch. MDII usque ad a. MDCII (Leipzig: Halis, 1841), 1:237.

23. Besides what is discussed in the rest of this chapter, there is Paul Crell's "Epitome brevis et vtilis praecipuae doctrinae quae in Locis Theologicis Domini Philippi Melanthonis de singulis Articulis traditur," (H 281 and H 306); or Richard Smith's "Refutatio Locorum communiorum Phil. Melanchthonis," published in Paris in 1563 (H 334).

24. VM XIXf. and 365–96; the "old fox" on 87 and 375.

25. For all the complexities of this debate, see Peter Barton, *Um Luthers Erbe: Studien und Texte zur Spätreformation; Tilemann Heshusius (1527–59)*, (Witten: Luther-Verlag, 1972), 196–225. Barton is convinced that the controversy was orchestrated by Thomas Erastus and Peter Boucquin on the crypto-Calvinist side. Klebitz first appears in the Heidelberg *Matrikelbuch* on 6 March 1558, where it is noted that he is beginning in theology and that already on 26 January he had arrived as deacon and afternoon preacher (*pomeridianus concionator*). See Gustav Toepke, ed., *Die Matrikel der Universität Heidelberg von 1386 bis 1662*, pt. 2: *Von 1554 bis 1662* (Heidelberg: C. Winter, 1886), 2:13. On 2:14 we discover that Thomas Erastus matriculated on 3 May 1558.

26. They were answered by two pastors, Maximillian Morlin and John Stossel, in counterpropositions to have been debated on 3–4 June 1560, entitled: PROPOSITIO= ‖ NES, IN QVIBVS VERA ‖ DE COENA DOMINI SENTENTIA, ‖ iuxta confessionem Augustanam, ad= ‖ uersus quorundam Sacramentariorum ‖ certamina Heydelber= ‖ gensi, 3. & 4. Iunij, pro= ‖ positae, Anno ‖ 1560. ‖ [Leaf] ‖ ADIECTA SVNT SI- ‖ mul impia Sacramentariorum ‖ Themata, Heydelberge ‖ disputata. ‖ [Decoration] ‖ 8°. Colophon: Erphordiae Georgius Bawman excudebat ‖ [8] leaves. As is clear from the title, Klebitz's offending theses were also printed here.

27. As Barton explains (*Luther's Erbe*, 207), Heshusius's confession, "Doctoris Tilemani Heshusij Bekantniss vom Nachtmal Jesu Christi dem Churfürsten Pfaltzgrauen beym Rein vberantwortet, Anno M.D.Lix den j. septembris," was published thirteen times and became a kind of confessional document among some gnesio-Lutherans. It is reprinted by Barton at 208–14.

28. DE PRAESENTIA ‖ CORPORIS ‖ CHRISTI IN ‖ COENA DOMINI. ‖ D. TILEMANVS HESHVSIVS VVE- ‖ SALIENSIS. ‖ IHENAE ‖ ANNO M.D.LX. ‖ 8°, colophon: IENAE excudebat Donatus Ri= ‖ tzenhain, Anno M.D.LX. ‖ Mense Iulio. ‖ [149 + 3 blank] leaves. The preface is dated 20 October 1559.

29. Most recently printed in SA 6:482–86.

30. Among other editions is that from Tübingen: IVDICIVM D. ‖ PHILIPPI ME= ‖ LANTHONIS DE CONTROVER ‖ SIA COENAE DOMINI, AD ILLVSTRISSI= ‖ MVM PRINCIPEM AC DOMINVM, D. ‖ FREDERICVM COMITEM PA ‖ latinum Rheni, Sacri Romani Impe- ‖ rij Archidapiferum, Electo ‖ rem, Bauariae Du- ‖ cem. &c. ‖ Adiecta est & alia eiusdem autoris eiusdemque argu= ‖ menti Epistola. ‖ ANNO. 1560. ‖ 4° [Tübingen: Widow of Ulrich Morhart]. This printing also contains a

letter dated 21 March 1560. One translation reads: Bericht vnd Ratschlag des ‖ Herren Philippi Melanthonis / vom stritt ‖ des Hayligen Nachtmals / vnd zenckischen Kirchen= ‖ dienern / An den Durchleüchtigsten Hochgepor= ‖ nen Fursten vnd Herren / Herrn Friderichen ‖ Pfaltzgrauen / bey Rhein / des Heyligen ‖ Römischen Reichs Ertztruchseßen ‖ vnd Churfursten / Hertzogen ‖ in Bayrn / etc[etera]. ‖ [Leaf] ‖ Zü Heydelberg ‖ Anno 1560. ‖ 4° Printed most likely in Lübeck by Johann Balhorn, Sr.

31. H 233. See also H 232 and H 235. H 232 bears the date November 1560.

32. H 239: *Responsio ad Praeiudicium Philippi Melanthonis,* most likely published in Magdeburg by Wolfgang Kirchner. Heshusius also reprinted his book on the presence of the body of Christ in the Lord's Supper with an appendix of an older letter by Joachim Westphal to the pastors of Hamburg in which Westphal had extracted from older letters and opinions of Melanchthon a position supporting the real presence of Christ in the elements. This edition of Westphal is not in Hammer (cf. H 138 & 139). Its call number in the Herzog August Bibliothek is: Aa 177 (7) Alv.: DE PRAESENTIA ‖ CORPORIS ‖ CHRISTI, IN ‖ Coena Domini. ‖ D. Tilemanus Heshu- ‖ sius Vvesaliensis. ‖ Item, ‖ Clarissimi uiri D. Philippi Me= ‖ lanthonis sententia, de Coena Do= ‖ mini, ex scriptis eius collecta, a Ioa= ‖ chimo Vvestphalo, Ministro ‖ Ecclesiae Hamburgensis. ‖ MAGDEBVRGAE, ‖ ANNO ‖ 1561. ‖ 8°, 268 pages + [1] leaf.

33. See H 251. This was most likely printed in Magdeburg by Wolfgang Kirchner.

34. Also missing from Hammer. This single folio sheet begins AD TOLLMAN= ‖ NVM HESHVSIVM. ‖ It is dated 1561, call number 95.10 Quod 2º (308).

35. Also not in Hammer. VICTORIA ‖ VERITATIS, ‖ AC RVINA PA= ‖ PATVS SAXO- ‖ NICI. ‖ RESPONSIO VVIL= ‖ HELMI KLEBITII NECESSA- ‖ ria ad Argumenta Doct. Tile- ‖ manni Heshusij. ‖ PRO DEFENSIONE IVSTA ‖ I. ‖ Causae Christianae, & Verae. ‖ II. ‖ Illustrissimi Electoris Palatini. ‖ III. ‖ Philippi Melanchthonis. ‖ IIII. ‖ Senatus Ecclasiastici. [sic!] ‖ ROMAN. XII. ‖ NVLLI MALVM PRO MA- ‖ LO REDDATIS. ‖ FRIBVRGI ‖ DANIEL DELENVS ‖ Execudebat. Anno ‖ M.D.LXI. ‖ 4°. [35 + 1 blank] leaves. The preface is dated 14 May 1561. Melanchthon's letter is discussed on pages E[i] ro–[E4] vo. Nicholas Durand de Villegagnon (H 295 and H 339) also offered his view. (61.4 Theol. 4°[1] in the Herzog August Bibliothek may offer a slightly different version from those described by Hammer.) See also the response of Peter Boucquin, H 304, *Iudicii Philippi Melanchthonis de Coena Domini iusta Defensio, Aduersus iniustam vim T. Heshusij [et] N. Villagangnonis,* published in Geneva in 1562.

36. H 338 and H 360, respectively. The first is a line-by-line explanation of Melanchthon's letter and the second is a defense of the first. On 24 March 1545, a Paul Einhorn of Nortlingen was enrolled at the University of Wittenberg (Album 1:220).

37. H 357 and H 357A: *Wider die Landlügen der Heidelbergischen Theolo-*

gen (Eisleben: Andrew Petri, 1565). "Ich kan es aber auch vom Philippo mich nicht bereden lassen / das er solch gedichte jemals solt für war gehalten / oder des jemands bericht haben / Ach HERR Gott / hette er ein einiges wort dieser meinung vom Luthero gehabt / wie solte er das gehöret haben in alle Welt / sonderlich in Pfalzgrefischen Iuditio.... Ich schreibe das weis mein Gott / mit betrübtem hertzen dauon / denn des Mannes fall thut mir vber die massen wehe /...."

38. *Elementa rhetoricae*, 1. "Cum sit in ratione studiorum huius scholae [Leipzig] propositum, non modo Dialecticum disputandi exercitium, sed Rhetoricum quoque orationis Latinae, bonae... volui saepe studiosis literarum humanitatis hac de institutione exponere sententiam doctorum."

39. VM 365–68.

40. VM 370: "ut aniculae etiam legere et cognoscere possint." Camerarius also attacks Frederick Staphylus.

41. VM 376: "sed importuna vehementia et superba confidentia."

42. Call number: G 59 Helmst. 8°(3). The stamped leather cover includes the initials M F I and the date 1561.

43. VM 397.

44. VM 390.

45. VM 22.

46. VM 28.

47. VM 58–60. In the same context, Camerarius describes another of Melanchthon's vices: leaving letters lying about.

48. VM 76–82.

49. VM 69. This against Friedrich Staphylus and Erasmus Sarcerius, who used to make fun of Melanchthon by imitating his peculiarities.

50. VM 159. The number of such descriptions is countless.

51. VM 209f.

52. Karl von Helmolt, *Tilemann Heßhus, zuletzt Doctor und erster Professor der Theologie zu Helmstedt, und seine sieben Exilia* (Leipzig: Dörffling und Franke, 1859), 46.

53. See Heinz Scheible, "Luther & Melanchthon," *Lutheran Quarterly*, n.s., 3 (1990): 317–39, who unmasks this myth in the works of Lohse, Maurer, and others.

5

Manipulating Reputations: Sir Thomas More, Sir Thomas Elyot, and the Conclusion of William Roper's *Lyfe of Sir Thomas Moore, Knighte*

F. W. Conrad

The manner in which authors of early modern biographical narratives occasionally employed rhetorical invention to manipulate the reputations of their subjects promises to become, if it is not already, an important focus of scholarly attention. A common feature in recent studies of such narratives has been the demonstration of a discernable variance between the historical representations contained in a particular biographical narrative and what can be independently learned about the life portrayed. In other words, when the veracity of statements made by early modern life-writers can be checked, they are often found wanting. Two important consequences derive from this discovery. First, modern scholars no longer tend to regard the literary representations of Renaissance and Reformation figures by their near contemporaries as reliable sources and, increasingly, are challenging the conclusions of earlier scholarship more inclined to accept at face value the claims made in such texts. Secondly, early modern biographers are no longer summarily assigned the subordinate role of faithful reporter, and they are beginning to be acknowledged as self-conscious literary artists.

William Roper's celebrated *Lyfe of Sir Thomas Moore, Knighte*—composed about the year 1557 but not printed until 1626—serves as a case in point. Not without cause, Roper's biographical narrative of his famous father-in-law has traditionally been regarded as a faithful and "apparently artless" memoir.[1] Roper never sought to publish the narrative during the course of his lifetime, and he clearly states in the work's preface that the desire of friends served as his inspiration to set forth "such matters towching [More's] life as I could at this present call to remembraunce."[2] Indeed, the fact that Roper made his manuscript available as a resource to Nicholas Harpsfield, a family friend whom he had commissioned to compose a more comprehensive narrative of More's life, reinforces the image of *The Lyfe of Sir Thomas Moore, Knighte* as a chronologically ordered collection of twenty-year-old personal recollections.

More recent scholarship, however, has emphasized the selectivity of Roper's remembrances and his conscious artistry in crafting a favorable portrayal of his father-in-law. With respect to the reliability of Roper's *Lyfe* as a historical source, the researches of Sir Geoffrey Elton, John Guy, Alistair Fox, and Richard Marius have exposed dimensions of the life evidently lived by More that are not easily reconciled with the more saintly image projected by Roper.[3] With respect to Roper's careful crafting of *The Lyfe,* studies by Judith H. Anderson and Jonathan Crewe have discerned an authorial concern for arrangement, design, balance, and symmetry throughout the narrative.[4] As a result of these investigations, the artificial character of Roper's *Lyfe* is now beyond dispute. Certainly Nicholas Harpsfield's willingness to incorporate verbatim and only slightly edited passages of *The Lyfe* directly into his own biography of More suggests that Roper achieved a considerable degree of polish; and any possibility of continuing to characterize *The Lyfe* as an informal series of personal recollections is effectively precluded by John Maguire's demonstration that, just as Harpsfield would later write with Roper's manuscript in front of him, Roper composed his biographical narrative with the text of More's correspondence at his side.[5]

What has yet to be investigated is the nature and degree of the artifice Roper employed in portraying the life of his famous father-in-law. One would like to know not only the extent to which Roper consciously strayed from historical fact in *The Lyfe* when creating his literary portrait of More, but also the extent to which contemporary rhetorical standards sanctioned the incorporation of manifestly fictitious material into biographical narratives. The present chapter seeks to address both these questions. First, it establishes that, according to the canons of Renaissance rhetoric, biography, like history, was considered a type of narrative prose, and that writers of biographical narratives might legitimately and repeatedly incorporate imaginative material into their texts provided such inventions preserved historical verisimilitude. Secondly, it identifies a hitherto unrecognized historical invention that constitutes the concluding paragraph of the *The Lyfe of Sir Thomas Moore, Knighte,* analyzes its various functions in the text, and demonstrates that in this particular instance, Roper deliberately fabricated.

In order properly to appreciate the concluding paragraph of William Roper's *The Lyfe of Sir Thomas Moore, Knighte,* several modern habits of thought must first be set aside. Twentieth-century readers tend to presuppose a firm dichotomy between truth and fiction, and to define biography as a nonfictional literary form. We regularly consult biographies for accurate information about historical figures, and when confronted with manifest untruths in biographical narratives, our immediate inclination is to think poorly of the author. To us, the presence of craft and artifice in biographical writing, when not subordinated to factual accuracy, is both discomforting and unacceptable.

The presuppositions of early modern life-writers and their readers, however, differed considerably from ours. According to the classically rooted canons of rhetoric upon which they were schooled, biography, like history, was considered a type of narrative prose, and the prose narration (or *narratio*) itself was defined as "a discourse expository of things which happened *or might have happened.*"[6] Under this standard, authors of ancient biographical and historical narratives might legitimately compose speeches, invent dialogue, employ hyperbole, telescope time, and polish the language of primary-source documents being quoted wherever such devices suited their literary purposes.[7] The fact that Cicero, the anonymous author of *Rhetorica ad Herennium,* Quintilian, and Theon each recognized an imaginative component to *narratio* reveals the self-imposed rigidity of ancient historians like Polybius, who tended to eschew adventitious adornment in the interests of historical accuracy.

While considerably greater than that enjoyed by contemporary authors, the compositional freedom afforded ancient historians and biographers to incorporate imaginative material into their narratives was not absolute. With respect to the limits of historical license, we have a highly significant distinction, set down in a clear statement by the first century B.C. grammarian Asclepiades of Myrlea and related by Sextus Empiricus.[8] In it, three categories of history are discerned: *alethes historia,* or "true history," for what is literally true; *pseudes historia,* or "false history," for what is wholly imaginary; and *plasmata, hos genomena,* or "fiction as might happen," for imaginative writing. In the first two categories, no reader could be in doubt as to the quality of belief expected. Exemplars of the first category, such as historical chronicles, are to be accepted as purely factual accounts; exemplars of the second category, such as Lucian's *True History,* in which the author himself acknowledges the fictional character of his text, are to be regarded as complete fantasies. In the third category, however, the quality of truth of a given text depends upon the art and conscience of the writer, and its correct apprehension depends upon the literary experience of the reader. Authors of such compositions began with a core of factual history, which they subsequently embellished and supplemented with plausible invention in the interests of entertainment and edification. In other words, a conscious literary historian or biographer, like a Tragic Poet or the author of a historical romance, might enhance historical stories and characters by whatever means might serve a higher poetical truth.[9] Plutarch's contemporary audience would have understood that while his treatment of individual lives might occasionally include imaginative dialogue and speeches, the moral burden of *The Parallel Lives*—namely, that Greeks were much like Romans—was to be accepted seriously.

An indication of the subordinate status of literal truth in ancient historical and biographical writing is afforded by Cicero's epistolary invitation to Lucceius to memorialize his career in a *narratio.*[10] Although no such work appears ever to have been undertaken, Cicero's letter is carefully written and stands as an important document in the history of criticism. Cicero was clearly interested in having Lucceius write an authoritative account, and at the very end of the letter offers to send him notes. He also suggests that such a narrative might offer valuable political lessons to contemporaries. By far Cicero's greatest concern, however, was that Lucceius's finished *narratio* be as attractive as possible to readers. Strict factual accuracy was neither something Cicero expected nor something he desired:

> What if the record does not appear to you so eminently deserving of eulogy? ... I ask you again, not mincing my words, to write of this theme more enthusiastically than perhaps you feel. Waive the laws of history for this once. Do not scorn personal bias if it urge you strongly in my favor.... Concede to the affection between us just a little more even than the truth will license.[11]

Like his learned contemporaries, Cicero recognized the potential of narrative to supply *veritas, utilitas,* and *delectatio.* Of the three, what mattered most was the literary quality of the work itself, which alone could induce a reader to be moved and to pay attention.

What makes appreciation of the classical rhetorical standards governing the composition of biographical and historical narratives so important for the prospective student of Roper's *Lyfe of Sir Thomas Moore, Knighte* is the fact that sixteenth-century English rhetorical ideals were essentially identical. Just as various early humanist treatises on the subject of how history should be written, such as George of Trebizond's *Rhetoricorum libri quinque* (c. 1434), had recognized history as a species of prose narration comprised of both fact and plausible invention, so, too, many of the histories written by quattrocento humanists, such as Leonardo Bruni's *Historiae Florentini populi* (c. 1415–44), were clearly composed in accordance with this standard.[12] During the reigns of the first two Tudor monarchs, similar examples begin to appear in English literary history. Bernard André's Latin biography of his royal patron, for instance, *Vita Henrici Septimi* (1501–3), was carefully composed to achieve the standards of eloquence and verisimilitude appropriate to an orator's *narratio.*[13] Indeed, several years later, Leonard Coxe's *The Arte or Crafte of Rhethoryke* (1532), the first rhetorical handbook to be published in English, identified biography as a species of narrative prose characterized less by factual accuracy than by ornate language:

> The Narracion or tale wherin persones are praysed / is the declarynge of theyr lyfe and doynges after the fasshyon of an hystorye....
>
> And so to conclude, an oracion Demonstratiue wherein persones are lauded / is an historycall exposycyon of all his lyfe in order. And there is no difference beetweene this kynde and an history / saue that in histories we be more briefe and vse lesse curiositie. Here all thynges be augmented and coloured with as much ornamentes of eloquence as can be had.[14]

Like Cicero before him, and numerous Renaissance authors after him, Coxe here emphasizes the importance of a pleasant and persuasive style over determination of what actually happened, and why.[15]

As confirmed by examination of Erasmus's *De copia verborum ac rerum* (1511), a work Myron Gilmore once aptly characterized as the

Renaissance Latin equivalent of Fowler's *Modern English Usage,* Renaissance and Reformation biographers aspired not to produce an objectively truthful account, but to write with sufficient verisimilitude that readers would find their works compelling.[16] More clearly than any other Renaissance text, the *De copia* established the bounds of rhetorical propriety with respect to narrative invention. According to Erasmus, authors of biographical narratives were free to invent dialogue and compose letters and speeches wherever it suited their literary purposes:

> Particularly appropriate to character delineation is *dialogismos,* dialogue, in which we supply each person with utterances appropriate to his age, type, country, way of life, cast of mind, and character. Utterances of this kind may be introduced into historical writing, hence all the speeches in Thucydides, Sallust, and Livy. Letters and striking sayings may also be composed, and even thoughts expressed, as of a man talking to himself, though this is commoner in the poets.[17]

> The exposition of facts can be greatly enhanced by the figure which some call *sermocinatio* "dialogue" in which we assign suitable utterances to one or more persons.... In this the historical writers are particularly worthy of admiration, for everyone accepts that they are allowed to put speeches into the mouths of their characters. I refer to pagan historians. It is doubtful whether Christian ones may do the same, except that something similar seems to be done in the story of the seven Maccabees, and, apart from others who have written lives of the martyrs, St. Ambrose seems to have allowed himself to do so in his *Life of St. Agnes.*[18]

Authors desiring to include such inventions in their historical narratives need only strive to preserve verisimilitude and be respectful of the Christian religion:

> If entirely fictional narratives are introduced as if they were true because they will help us to get our point across, we must make them as much like the real thing as possible. There are well-known features, listed in the handbooks of rhetoric, which make a story credible. As an example of this type we may mention the story about Memmius in Cicero, and possibly the one about Volteius in Horace. I observe that some people have been excessively fond of this sort of thing and,

relying on the gullibility of the crowd, have imported into Christian literature the most stupid miraculous events as if they were absolutely true.[19]

Erasmus's legitimation of the use of rhetorical invention in the foregoing passages is of enormous significance. Quickly adopted as a rhetoric textbook in schools and universities throughout northern Europe, the *De copia* passed through more than 150 editions between 1512 and 1600.

A cursory examination of three sixteenth-century biographical narratives, each composed by a prominent European humanist, reveals the readiness of Renaissance authors to take advantage of the degree of compositional freedom sanctioned by Erasmus's *De copia*. In his *La Vita di Castruccio Castracani da Lucca* (1520), an idealized biography of a fourteenth-century *condottiere* who subsequently became ruler of Lucca, Niccolò Machiavelli attributed to Castruccio several *sententiae* appropriated from the pages of Diogenes Laertius's *Lives and Opinions of the Eminent Philosophers*.[20] Similarly, Antonio de Guevara's immensely popular *Libro Aureo de Marco Aurelio, Emperador y Eloquentissimo Orador* (1529), a fictional biography of the Roman emperor Marcus Aurelius written in highly mannered Spanish prose, included numerous imaginary speeches and letters.[21] In conscious imitation of De Guevara, Sir Thomas Elyot composed an idealized biography of the Roman emperor Alexander Severus, entitled *The Image of Governance* (1541), which intermixed translated portions of Alexander's *vita* in the *Scriptores Historiae Augustae* with a large number of manifestly fictitious speeches, conversations, and letters.[22] The geographical diversity of these texts, together with the range and frequency of the rhetorical inventions employed therein, is particularly instructive. As we turn to examine the concluding paragraph of William Roper's biographical narrative of his famous father-in-law, we should keep in mind the rhetorical rules under which he wrote and the considerable gulf that separates them from modern standards of biographical writing.

> So passed Sir Thomas Moore out of this world to god, vppon the very same daye in which himself had most desired.
>
> Soone after whose deathe came intelligence thereof to the Emperour Chareles. Wheruppon he sent for Sir Thomas Elliott, our english Embassadour, and said vnto him: "My Lord Embassador, we vnderstand that the Kinge, your master, hath put his faithfull seruaunt and

grave, wise Councelour, Sir Thomas Moore, to deathe." Wherunto Sir Thomas Elliott awneswered that he vnderstood nothing thereof. "Well," said the Emperour, "it is too true. And this will we say, that if we had bine maister of such a servante, of whose doings our selfe haue had these many yeares no small experience, we wold rather haue lost the best city of our dominions then haue lost such a worthy councellour." Which matter was by the same Sir Thomas Elliott to my self, to my wife [More's daughter, Margaret], to maister [John] Clement and his wife [More's foster-daughter, Margaret Gigs], to master John Haywood and his wife [More's niece, Joan Rastell], and [vnto] diuers other his Friends accordingly reported.

Such is the conclusion of William Roper's *The Lyfe of Sir Thomas Moore, Knighte,* and according to the introduction prefixed to the familiar Yale edition of the text, it is a "magnificent" conclusion.[23] Instead of engaging in an extended and passionate eulogy, or dwelling upon the details of his subject's execution in the manner of John Foxe's account of Nicholas Ridley's end in the *Acts and Monuments,*[24] Roper opts to transport his readers to the court of Charles V. There the emperor himself conveys a brief memorial tribute to the then resident English ambassador Sir Thomas Elyot: "we wold rather haue lost the best city of our dominions then haue lost such a worthy councellour." Roper's rhetorical restraint here serves to emphasize the idealized image of his father-in-law presented throughout *The Lyfe:* more than a mere series of episodes regulated by the caprice of Fortune, More's life was lived in harmony with historical patterns beyond human design. First we learn that Sir Thomas dies, in fulfillment of his hopes, on the eve of the day honoring an earlier martyred English saint named Thomas who had similarly resisted another King Henry's incursions into ecclesiastical power. Immediately thereafter, Charles V's sententious judgment echoes the prescience of More's earlier assessment of Henry VIII: "If my head [could] winne him a castle in Fraunce . . . it should not faile to goe."[25]

Judging by the frequency with which Roper's conclusion was incorporated into subsequent biographies of More, its literary virtues were recognized and admired by early modern readers as well. *The Life and Death of Sir Thomas More* composed by Nicholas Harpsfield in 1557 repeats Roper's conclusion almost verbatim, as does the 1599 biography of More credited to the otherwise unidentified "Ro: Ba:":

Who is it then but this woorthy man, for whose woorthines the late noble and newe Charles the mayne, I meane Charles the fift, gaue out such a singuler and exquisite testimonie and praise? For when intelligence came to him of Sir Thomas Mores death, he sent for Sir Thomas Eliott, our englishe Ambassadour, [and saide to him: "My lord Ambassadour], We vnderstande that the king, your master, hath put his faithfull seruaunt and graue, wise Counsailour, Sir Thomas More, to death." Whervnto Sir Thomas Eliot aunswered that he heard nothing thereof. "Well," saide the Emperour, "it is too true. And this will we say, that if we had beene master of such a seruaunt, of whose doinges our selfe haue had these manye yeres no small experience, we would rather haue lost the best Citie of our dominions then haue lost suche a worthy Counsailour." (Harpsfield)[26]

Charles the Emperour, the [fift] of that name, a most reverent and victorious Prince, gaue a singular testimonie of the praise of this man. For when intelligence came to hym of Sir Thomas More his death, he sent presentlie for Sir Thomas Eliot, our English ambassadour then with hym, to whom said the Emperour, "We vnderstand that the king your maister hath put to death his faithfull servaunt, his grave and wise Counsellour, Thomas More." Wherevnto our Ambassadour aunswered that he hard nothing thereof. "Well," quoth the Emperour, "it is too true. And this wee will say, that if we had bene maister of such a servaunt, of whose doinges our selfe haue had these manie yeares no smale experience, we should rather haue lost ye best Citie of our dominion then haue forgone so worthie a Counsailour." (Ro: Ba:)[27]

Two other early modern biographies of More—a 1588 Latin *vita* written by Thomas Stapleton and a vernacular account written about 1631 by family member Cresacre More—employ variant forms of Roper and Harpsfield's conclusion:

Finally I will cite a testimony to the same effect which I obtained through trustworthy witnesses. It is a noble tribute and deserves to be for ever remembered. The Emperor Charles V, no less penetrating in his judgments than he was brave and fortunate in war, on hearing that More and Fisher had been put to death, spoke as follows to Thomas Eliot, who at the time was Henry's ambassador at his Court.

> "If I had had in my dominions two such lights, I would rather have lost my strongest city than have allowed myself to be deprived of them, much less permitted them to be unjustly put to death." High praise from a noble prince! Indeed the thing speaks for itself. The cause of his death was most unjust, the manner infamous. More's admirable patience, his piety, his learning, and his other incomparable virtues proclaim him happy in so noble a martyrdom, and Henry infamous for so unjust a sentence. (Thomas Stapleton)[28]

> Last of all I will recounte, what the good Emperour Charles the Fift sayd vnto *Sir Thomas Eliott* than the king's Embassadour in his Court, after he had heard of Bishopp *Fisher* and SIR THOMAS MORE'S martyrdomes; on a time he spoke of it to *Sir Thomas Eliott,* who seemed to excuse the matter by making some doubt of the reporte, to whom the Emperour replyed: It is too true; but yf we had had two such lights in all our kingdomes, as these men were, we could rather have chosen to haue lost two of the best and strongest townes in all our Empire, then suffer ourselues to be depriued of them, much lesse to endure to haue them wrongfully taken from vs. (Cresacre More)[29]

Interestingly, the expansion of Charles V's eulogy by both Stapleton and Cresacre More to include Bishop John Fisher is not as original as it first appears. Writing about the year 1576, the anonymous author of the earliest biography of Fisher chose to adapt Roper's conclusion to suit his own literary purposes:

> Likewise the most noble and Christian emperor, Charles V, at such time as Sir Thomas More was beheaded and word thereof brought to him, sent speedily for Sir Thomas Elliot, the king's ambassador there resident with him, and asked him whether he heard any such news or no; who answered him that he heard no such thing. "Yes," said the Emperor, "it is true and too true that Sir Thomas More is now executed to death, as a good bishop hath lately been before." And with it (giving a sigh) said: "Alas what meant the king to kill two such men? For," said he, "the Bishop was such a one, as for all purposes, I think, the king had not the like again in all his realm, neither yet was to be matched through Christendom; so that," he said, "the king your master hath in killing that bishop killed at one blow

all the bishops in England," meaning no doubt that this bishop considering his pastoral care and constant profession of his bishoply duty in defence of the Church, in respect of the rest of his brethren did only deserve the name of a bishop." "And Sir Thomas More," said he, "was well known for a man of such profound wisdom, cunning and virtue that, if he had been towards me as he was towards the king your master, I had rather have lost the best city in all my dominion, than such a man."[30]

Clearly, more might be said about the manner in which individual authors elected to appropriate and modify prior accounts of Charles V's conversation with Thomas Elyot to suit their own literary ends. For our present purposes, however, it is sufficient merely to note that Roper's "magnificent" conclusion, both directly and indirectly, has exerted considerable influence upon subsequent perceptions of Thomas More.

For all its artful "magnificence" and historiographical influence, however, the veracity of *The Lyfe of Sir Thomas Moore*'s final paragraph is highly suspect. Despite the apparent authority conferred by both the vividness of Roper's account and its repetition in subsequent biographies of More, the conversation Roper depicts cannot possibly have taken place. At issue is not so much the emperor's high regard for More, or even the phrasing attributed to Charles,[31] but the specific occasion of the audience. Elyot's term as imperial ambassador came to a close no later than mid-April 1532, and from that date onward, he and Charles were to remain hundreds of miles apart. At the time of More's resignation of the chancellorship the following month (16 May 1532), Elyot was already in Brussels attempting to aid in the capture of William Tyndale.[32] The then resident English ambassador was Thomas Cranmer. At the time of More's death on 6 June 1535, Elyot was probably still engaged in the survey of Oxfordshire monastic properties that preceded compilation of the *Valor Ecclesiasticus*.[33] The resident English ambassador was Richard Pate.[34] Hence, if Charles V did indeed make such a comment to Elyot, the only plausible scenario would have Sir Thomas reiterating to Roper and other members of the family comments the emperor made upon receipt of 1531 diplomatic correspondence suggesting More was anxious to resign his office.[35]

Of the two possible explanations for the chronological confusion of Roper's conclusion—accidental human error or conscious authorial manipulation—the former opinion was advanced by E. V. Hitchcock in the

Early English Text Society edition of *The Lyfe,* and her judgment appears never to have been challenged.[36] Hitchcock's determination rests primarily upon Roper's portrayal of himself as a reluctant author in the work's preface. According to Roper, his biography of More was composed "at the desire of divers worshyppfull freinds" and sets forth "such matters towching his life as I could at this present call to remembraunce. Amonge which things, very many notable things (not meete to haue bine forgotten) throughe neckligens and long contynuans of tyme are slipped out of my mynde." For Hitchcock, these remarks, especially when interpreted in the light of Roper's subsequent decision to make his text available to Nicholas Harpsfield, whom he had commissioned to compose a more comprehensive biography of More, effectively eliminated the need for any scholarly investigation of Roper's methods as a biographer. Since *The Lyfe* was neither a full-scale biography nor a work designed to be published, any factual errors discovered could be summarily dismissed as "minor blemishes" attributable to "neckligens."

A careful examination of Roper's conclusion, however, raises serious doubts about the adequacy of Hitchcock's "carelessness" thesis. Certainly the phrasing of *The Lyfe of Sir Thomas Moore, Knighte*'s final paragraph gives every indication of having been carefully crafted to arouse sympathy for its subject. First, Charles V confirms to Thomas Elyot the fact of More's execution in compliance with the will of Henry VIII by means of a hyperbolic string of alliterative monosyllables: "it is too true." Next, the emperor conveys the depth of his sadness, and by inference Henry VIII's folly, by suggesting that the value of faithful servants such as More is beyond material measure: "And this will we say, that if we had bine maister of such a servante, of whose doings our selfe haue had these many yeares no small experience, we wold rather haue lost the best city of our dominions then haue lost such a worthy councellour." Finally, as a means of authenticating Charles V's superlative testimonial, Roper asserts that he learned of the emperor's opinions directly from Sir Thomas Elyot himself in the presence of a host of witnesses: "Which matter was by the same Sir Thomas Elliott to my self, to my wife, to maister Clement and his wife, to master John Haywood and his wife, and [vnto] diuers other his Friends accordingly reported." *The Lyfe of Sir Thomas Moore, Knighte*'s conclusion, therefore, in addition to complementing earlier passages in the text, leaves its readers with a vivid impression of Henry VIII as villain and Thomas More as innocent victim. Given the subtlety of Roper's dramatic construction and the prominent position of the Elyot passage, human error, whether in the form of faulty memory or mere carelessness, appears too simplistic an explanation for the chronological confusion of *The Lyfe*'s final paragraph.

We are left with the strong possibility that Roper's misdating of Elyot's embassy results from deliberate distortion. As has been previously demonstrated in this chapter, contemporary standards of biographical writing admitted the judicious mixture of creative invention with historical fact for the purposes of creating a more moving portrait. Might Roper, lacking what he deemed a suitable memorial tribute with which to conclude his narrative, simply have composed one in accordance with current rhetorical standards? Recommended by both his position of authority and his favorable disposition toward More, Charles V would surely have appeared a suitable figure to deliver More's eulogy. Moreover, the fact that Sir Thomas Elyot had once served as English ambassador to Charles V, and was no longer alive to refute any attributed statements, made him a convenient choice to receive and relay the emperor's sententious judgment. In terms of verisimilitude and decorum, such a historical fiction had much to recommend it.

Certainly by electing to conclude his account of More with a eulogy voiced by Charles V, Roper brought his text into compliance with one of the established rhetorical standards for English biographical narrative. As made clear by Leonard Coxe's *Arte or Crafte of Rhethoryke,* learned sixteenth-century Englishmen would have expected a biographical narrative on the life of Sir Thomas More to include an account of reactions to his death:

> The Narracion or tale wherin persones are praysed / is the declarynge of theyr lyfe and doynges after the fasshyon of an hystorye. The places out of the whiche it is sought are: The persones byrthe. His chyldhode. His adolescencie. His mannes state. His olde age. His dethe and what foloweth after.[37]

Dissatisfied with the brief commentary upon the treatment of death in biographical narratives he found in his principal sources—namely, the rhetorical treatises of Philip Melanchthon—Coxe recommended the account of Lorenzo de Medici's death contained in a published epistle of Angelo Poliziano (Politian) as a "very goodly ensample" for prospective authors.[38] Even more specific in identifying "Thynges that have happened aboute his death" as a fundamental component of biography was Thomas Wilson's *Arte of Rhetorique,* first published in 1553, the most comprehensive vernacular rhetorical manual available to Roper. According to Wilson, several aspects of a biographical subject's death afforded opportunities for praise:

> At the tyme of his departyng, his sufferaunce of all sicknesse, may muche commende his worthinesse. As his strong harte, and cherefull pacience even to the ende, cannot want great praise. The love of all men towardes hym, and the lamentyng generally for his lacke, helpe well moste highly to set furthe his honour.[39]

The comments of Coxe and Wilson are significant because of the fact that sixteenth-century British authors were becoming increasingly sensitive to issues of rhetorical propriety. Veré Rubel has demonstrated the great extent to which the ornament and diction of the poems in *Tottel's Miscellany* were informed by the recently rediscovered precepts of the classical rhetorics, and A. L. Bennett has shown how English Renaissance authors of memorial verses on the death of great men tended to follow the biographical arrangement of topics recommended by Coxe and Wilson.[40]

By far the weightiest evidence in support of the contention that *The Lyfe*'s conclusion constitutes a self-conscious and self-serving historical invention, however, is Roper's willingness to manipulate evidence elsewhere in his text. John Guy, for instance, has noted the partiality of Roper's image of More as lord chancellor, and of still greater significance, Judith Anderson has shown how William selectively edits the text of one of his father-in-law's letters to produce a more favorable characterization.[41] In the specific letter in question, addressed to Henry VIII and dated 5 March 1534, More recalls the comments made by the king upon his resignation of the chancellorship two years earlier:

> It pleased your Highnes ferther to say vn to me, that for the service which I byfore had done you (*which it than lyked your goodnes far aboue my deseruing to commend*) that in any suit that I should after haue vn to your Highnes, which either should concerne my honor (that word it lyked your Highnes to vse vn to me) or that should perteyne vn to my profit, I should fynd your Highnes good and graciouse lord vn to me.[42]

Roper's version of the same conversation is clearly modeled upon More's text, but it deliberately omits the preceding italicized passage:

> so pleased it his highnes [further] to say vnto him, that for the service that he before had done hym, in anye sute which he should after haue vnto him, that either should concerne his honor (for that word it liked his highnes to vse vnto him) or that should appertaine vnto his profitt, he should find his highnes good and gratious Lord vnto him.[43]

The effect achieved by this seemingly minor change is by no means insignificant. By eliminating any reference to More's dissent from his king's favorable judgment, Sir Thomas's prior service is made to appear fully deserving of Henry's gratitude.

The obvious inference to be drawn from the foregoing example is that the chronological confusion of Roper's conclusion also results from deliberate distortion. Even if we accept that interpretation, however, one question remains to be addressed—namely, why did Roper name Thomas Elyot in *The Lyfe*'s final paragraph instead of the actual English ambassador at the time of More's execution, Richard Pate? Given the subtle character of Roper's conclusion, the fact that Elyot had died in 1546 and therefore posed no threat of challenging Roper's representation appears, at best, to be an incomplete explanation. Mention of Elyot—like More, an esteemed humanist and outspoken critic of Henry VIII's divorce—must have afforded additional literary benefits sufficient to justify deviation from the factual record. Through an investigation of the historical relationship between More and Elyot, the remainder of this chapter will attempt to ascertain some of the benefits Roper may have had in mind when he penned his text's "magnificent" conclusion.

Not insignificant among Roper's motives may have been self-promotion. Elyot's reputation as a scholar and author in the 1550s was considerable. In his *Treatise of Schemes and Tropes* (1550), for instance, Richard Sherry praised Elyot's successful efforts to augment the English vernacular; not only had Sir Thomas imported sound matter through translation, but his original compositions provided English readers with models of elevated and distinguished expression worthy of emulation.[44] Although *The Boke Named the Governour* (1531) is now the most celebrated of the numerous works Elyot published during the course of his life, Roper's contemporaries would have been equally familiar with two others: Elyot's Latin-English *Dictionary,* originally completed in 1538, which was then the most comprehensive work of its kind; and his extremely popular medical regimen entitled *The Castel of Helthe*, first published in 1536.[45] Roper's text, therefore, leaves readers with an image of its author comfortable in the company of some of the most prominent English prose writers of the age—Sir Thomas More, Sir Thomas Elyot, and the dramatist John Heywood. Whatever other purposes it may serve, the conclusion of *The Lyfe of Sir Thomas Moore* suggests a claim to serious literary accomplishment.

It does not follow, however, that the grouping of the final sentence is wholly artificial. All indications are that Elyot, like Thomas Lupset and Juan Luis Vives, was an occasional member of More's household school at Bucklersbury, and it would be difficult to overestimate the formative influence that experience had upon his career.[46] At Bucklersbury, Sir Thomas witnessed firsthand the benefits of the liberal curriculum he would later advocate in his own works.[47] No doubt More's unorthodox practice of providing humanistic training for women informed Elyot's praise of the learned ancient Syrian queen Zenobia in his 1540 dialogue *The Defence of Good Women*.[48] Moreover, the pedagogical exercises of translation and retranslation commonly practiced by students at Bucklersbury promoted Elyot's competence in literary English and interest in translating Latin and Greek works.[49] It is a virtual certainty that Elyot would have met Roper, Clement, and Heywood during his visits to More's household, and one suspects that periodic contacts among members of the group continued over the course of their lives. When wishing to incorporate proper definitions of medicinal herbs into his *Dictionary*, for instance, Sir Thomas was forced to seek assistance from "men of sounder learning," and Dr. John Clement's knowledge of English flora was reputed second to none.[50]

Despite the evidence suggesting an affinity between More and Elyot, however, there is a danger of exaggerating the identity of their interests. Certainly Elyot is unmentioned in the vast bulk of More's extant writings. Moreover, Elyot took great pains to proclaim a distinction in two letters he wrote to Thomas Cromwell during the mid-1530s. Writing about the time of the Pilgrimage of Grace, he urged Cromwell to "lay a part the remembraunce of the amity betwene me and Sir Thomas More which was but *Vsque ad aras*, as is the proverb, consydering that I was never so moche addict unto hym as I was unto truthe and fidelity toward my soveraigne lorde, as Godd is my Judge."[51] In other words, Elyot claimed his private feelings for More were insufficient to prompt treason-able conduct. An earlier letter to Cromwell written just after the issuance of a December 1535 proclamation ordering the surrender of printed works by John Fisher makes clear the basis of Elyot's position.[52] In it Sir Thomas explains that his disregard for "the pompouse authoritie of the Busshop of Rome," and the English clergy's "dissolute forme of lyving" and "sondry abusions of their authorities" had been the cause of "no little contencion betwixt me and suche persones as ye have thowght that I have specially favored": "neither they mowght persuade me to approve that which both faith and my raison condemned; nor I mowght dissuade theim from the excusing of that, which all the worlde abhorred, which obstinacy of bothe partes relentid the grete affection betwene us and withdrue oure familiar repayr."[53]

Since Elyot's letters were written after More's imprisonment and execution, the possibility of special pleading cannot be dismissed. Nevertheless, his contentions appear to be borne out by a comparative analysis of *The Apology of Sir Thomas More, Knight* and Elyot's "merry treatise" *Pasquil the Playne,* works evidently composed contemporaneously in late 1532 and early 1533.[54] More's work, as is well known, sought to defend the practices of the contemporary English clergy against charges of corruption. Elyot's dialogue, on the other hand, exhibits considerable despair over the prospects of clerical reform and seems to support the argument of More's antagonist, Christopher St. German, that the authority of spiritual governors should rest in their irresistible moral characters and life-styles.[55] The same sense of disillusionment is more clearly manifested in a letter Elyot despatched to John Hackett a short time after *Pasquil*'s publication. Belief that the spiritualty had "digged the diche that thei be now fallen in," he told the English ambassador in the Low Countries, "causith many goode men the lass to pitie theim."[56] The conclusion of Roper's *Lyfe of Sir Thomas Moore,* therefore, suggests a greater sympathy for More than the historical Sir Thomas Elyot appears to have held, and in so doing, cloaks the degree of fissure in the ranks of those opposed to Henry VIII's divorce of Catherine of Aragon.

One further factor influencing the composition of Roper's conclusion remains to be discussed. As first noted forty years ago by H. W. Donner,[57] there exists an interesting parallel between the statement attributed to Charles V in the conclusion of Roper's *Lyfe* and a passage from Elyot's 1533 dialogue *Of the Knowledge Which Maketh a Wise Man*— an imaginary discussion between Plato and the Cyrenaic philosopher

Aristippus, two former members of the court of the Syracusan tyrant Dionysius. Whereas Aristippus—who pronounced the pleasure of the moment to be the supreme good—had gained the nickname "the king's dog" for his pleasing subservience there, Plato had been bound into slavery after informing Dionysius that his words were beginning to savor of tyranny.[58] Eventually Plato was released and made his way back to his native city, where, coincidentally, Aristippus had retired a short time prior to Plato's disgrace at court. The dialogue begins with a chance meeting of the two rivals about the year 386 B.C. as both are returning to Athens in the company of their servants, Plato for the first time since his encounter with Dionysius. When Aristippus asks how it is that Plato has come to exchange his former high favor for the costume of a slave, Plato relates his experience. When Aristippus condemns Plato's conduct as foolhardy, the future founder of the Academy offers a philosophical justification for his unsuccessful effort to counsel Dionysius as the two ride together into the city.

For our present purposes, the crucial moment in *Of the Knowledge Which Maketh a Wise Man* occurs near the midpoint of Elyot's dialogue when, still convinced of Plato's folly, Aristippus challenges his rival to explain the benefits of his present misfortune. Specifically, he wants to know why scorpions, poisonous herbs, and other apparent human ills should be considered providential:

> ARI: If thou canste brynge that well to passe, I wylle than saye that the fame and renome of thy wysedome / that is spronge through oute Grece, is well employed. And I wyll affirme also, that kynge Dyonise, whan he gaue the [as a slave] to Polidis was more liberall than wyse. *For he hadde bene better to haue gyuen to hym six the beste cities in Sicile, than to haue departed from suche a counsayllour.*[59]

Struck by the similarity of Elyot's phrasing here with that of Roper's conclusion, Donner proceeds to note several parallels between Elyot's depiction of Plato's career at the court of Dionysius and More's experience with Henry VIII.[60] Both counsellors, for instance, readily find favor and engage their respective monarchs in pleasant academic conversation during time free from more pressing business;[61] neither ruler can stand to be apart from his favorite for an extended length of time;[62] both counsellors fall from favor through their rigid adherence to moral standards of conduct deemed politically reckless by contemporaries.[63] On the basis of such parallels, and inspired by Professor A. W. Reed's conjecture that two Heywood plays—*The Pardoner and Frere* and *Johan Johan*—were published by William Rastell in 1533 to aid More, Donner makes the claim that Elyot's dialogue, issued sometime before Easter of that year, was also written to support More.[64]

We have already seen, however, that by the date of *Of the Knowledge Which Maketh a Wise Man*'s publication, More and Elyot had split over the strength of their commitments to the established institutional church. Prima facie, therefore, it is unlikely that Elyot had much interest in writing on behalf of his former mentor. It is also worth remembering that in early 1533 the oath of supremacy was not yet an issue, and More's chief antagonists were not Henry VIII and Cromwell but Christopher St. German and John Frith. The one work undeniably published near Easter of that year to assist Sir Thomas More was his son John More's translation of Frederick Nausea's *Sermon of the Sacrament of the Aulter*.[65] As a cursory comparison of titles suggests, the topical gulf between it and *Of the Knowledge Which Maketh a Wise Man* is considerable. Elyot's text has nothing to do with the Eucharistic controversy; Nausea's *Sermon* is not concerned with the difficulties of counseling a tyrant.[66]

Moreover, Elyot's own political fortunes in early 1533 were particularly precarious and hardly allowed time for addressing the plight of others. During the June 1532 royal audience upon return from his embassy to the court of Charles V, Sir Thomas evidently expressed considerable reservation about Henry's motives in pursuing a divorce, and from that moment onward, his loyalty and goodwill toward the king were considered suspect.[67] Indeed, Elyot's publication early the following year of a controversial dialogue entitled *Pasquil the Playne* served only to heighten such suspicions.[68] Originally issued anonymously in anticipation of the fourth session of the Reformation Parliament (during which was passed the Act in Restraint of Appeals), *Pasquil* offered pointed criticisms of rulers who had become slaves to their passions, and the self-serving flatterers who promoted or tolerated such views in their masters. Despite the "plausible deniability" defense inherent in fictional representation, someone in authority was particularly bothered by the possible application of Elyot's scenario to the English political landscape. Not only was Sir Thomas obliged to claim authorship and quickly reissue *Pasquil* in a less potentially incendiary form, but shortly thereafter, in the preface to his next work, *Of the Knowledge Which Maketh a*

Wise Man, he explicitly condemned those who would read his works as allegorical commentaries on contemporary politics.[69] Hence, through his fictional depiction of a counsellor's obligation to rebuke his erring sovereign, Sir Thomas sought to explain the principles that had governed his own previous conduct with Henry VIII, and thereby restore his estimation.

We can now better appreciate not only Cromwell's concern with Elyot's loyalty in the mid-1530s, but Roper's literary artistry in depicting his father-in-law's Christian piety and its concomitant worldly consequences.[70] His text's "magnificent" final paragraph not only echoes earlier passages in the *Lyfe,* but deceptively presents a learned critic of the royal divorce as sympathetic to More's plight. Moreover, by cleverly appropriating a sentence from Elyot's *Of the Knowledge Which Maketh a Wise Man,* Roper implicitly compares More's relationship with Henry VIII to the experience of Plato with the tyrant Dionysius in Syracuse. In other words, he suggests the exemplar of the virtuous counselor willing to suffer for his candor that Elyot had established for his own defense serves also as a model for More's conduct. Whatever Sir Thomas Elyot may have told Roper and his relatives about Charles V's respect for More, if anything, he seems to have provided him with a literary paradigm for the wise and courageous counselor-hero of his text. There is an element of truth in the statement that More's posthumous reputation was created at the expense of Elyot's historical identity.[71]

In advancing such a claim, my principal purpose is neither to challenge the saintly image of Sir Thomas More presented in Roper's text, nor to elevate the reputation of Sir Thomas Elyot among Tudor historians, but, rather, to call attention to the degree of compositional freedom afforded Renaissance and Reformation biographers by recognized contemporary rhetorical standards. As we have seen, according to those standards, writers of biographical narratives might legitimately and repeatedly incorporate imaginative material into their texts, provided such inventions preserved historical verisimilitude and conveyed edification. As we have also seen, sixteenth-century biographers were not hesitant to include historical inventions in their narratives. Machiavelli transplanted several *sententiae* from the pages of Diogenes Laertius into the mouth of Castruccio Castracani at the end of his *Vita di Castruccio;* William Roper appropriated a passage from Sir Thomas Elyot's *Of the Knowledge Which Maketh a Wise Man* when composing the conclusion of his *Lyfe of Sir Thomas Moore, Knighte;* and the anonymous author of the earliest life of Bishop John Fisher adapted the imaginative conclusion of Roper's *Lyfe* to suit his own literary purposes. When analyzing early modern biographies, it is worth remembering the critical assessment of Machiavelli's *Vita di Castruccio* made by Zanobi Buondelmonti, one of the work's dedicatees. Instead of reproving Machiavelli for importing anachronistic and historically inaccurate material into his narrative, Buondelmonti merely criticized his friend for not integrating the numerous imported sayings more skillfully.[72]

NOTES

1. Donald A. Stauffer, *English Biography Before 1700* (New York: Russell and Russell, 1930), 133.

2. William Roper, *The Lyfe of Sir Thomas Moore, Knighte*, ed. E. V. Hitchcock, Early English Text Society, original series 197 (London: Oxford University Press, 1935), 4.

3. G. R. Elton, "Sir Thomas More and the Opposition to Henry VIII," *Bulletin of the Institute for Historical Research* 41 (1968): 19–34; J. A. Guy, *The Public Career of Sir Thomas More* (New Haven, CT: Yale University Press, 1980); idem, "Thomas More and Christopher St. German: The Battle of the Books," in Alistair Fox and John Guy, *Reassessing the Henrician Age: Humanism, Politics and Reform 1500–1550* (Oxford: Basil Blackwell, 1986), 95–120; Alistair Fox, *Thomas More: History and Providence* (Oxford: Basil Blackwell, 1982); Richard Marius, *Thomas More: A Biography* (New York: Alfred A. Knopf, 1984).

4. Judith H. Anderson, *Biographical Truth: The Representation of Historical Persons in Tudor-Stuart Writing* (New Haven, CT: Yale University Press, 1984), 43–46; Jonathan Crewe, *Trials of Authorship: Anterior Forms and Poetic Reconstruction from Wyatt to Shakespeare* (Berkeley: University of California Press, 1990), 79–100.

5. John Maguire, "William Roper's *Life of More*: The Working Methods of a Tudor Biographer," *Moreana* 23 (1969): 59–65. For a similar example, see Germain Marc'hadour, "Thomas Stapleton's Use of More's *English Works* (1557) in his *Vita Thomas Mori* (1588)," in A. Dalzell, C. Fantazzi, and R. J. Schoeck, eds., *Acta Conventus Neo-Latini Torontonensis: Proceedings of the Seventh International Congress of Neo-Latin Studies*, (Binghamton, NY: Medieval and Renaissance Texts and Studies, 1991), 83–90.

6. *Ad Herennium* I, vii–ix, emphasis added; cf. Quintilian, *Institutio Oratoria* II, iv, 1 ff.; Cicero, *De Inventione* XIX–XXI.

7. The use of imaginary dialogue and speeches in ancient historiography is well known. For an example of hyperbole, see 3 Maccabees 5:2, where the

approximately seventy-five elephants Ptolemy IV had at Raphia are represented as having multiplied to five hundred in the course of a single generation. For instances of telescoping time, see *Bellum Iugurthinum,* in which Sallust variously fails to indicate a winter between the campaigns of 107 and 106 (92:5–9), characterizes an interval of fifteen years as "a few years" (9:4), and passes over a period of twelve years with the word "immediately" (9:3). For an example of the language of a primary source being polished, compare Sallust's version of a letter Lentulus addressed to Catiline in *Bellum Catilinae* (44:5) with the version of the same letter cited in Cicero's Catilinarian orations (3 *In Catilinam* 5:12).

8. Sextus Empiricus, *Adversus Grammaticos* 252.

9. It appears that the earliest romances contained a nucleus of history that was elaborated for an edifying effect. Eventually the historical element was reduced to a mere background for the love story that preempted the foreground, but the extant romances do preserve the form of history. See the introductions to *Three Greek Romances,* ed. and trans. Moses Hadas (Garden City, NJ: Doubleday, 1953); and Heliodorus, *An Ethiopian Romance,* trans. Moses Hadas (Ann Arbor: University of Michigan Press, 1957).

10. *Cicero's Letters to His Friends,* 2 vols., trans. D. R. Shackleton Bailey (New York: Penguin, 1978), 1:72–77. Cicero's actual Latin reads as follows: "Quid, si illa tibi non tanto opere videntur oranda? ... Itaque te plane etiam atque etiam rogo, ut et ornes ea vehementius etiam, quam fortasse sentis, et in eo leges historiae neglegas, gratiamque illam, ... eam, si me tibi vehementius commendabit, ne aspernere, amorique nostro plusculum etiam, quam concedat veritas, largiare" (*Epistulae ad familiares* V. xii. 2–3).

11. Ibid.

12. Robert Black, "Benedetto Accolti and the Beginnings of Humanist Historiography," *English Historical Review* 96 (1981): 51–52, 55–58.

13. C. W. T. Blackwell, "Humanism and Politics in English Royal Biography: The Use of Cicero, Plutarch and Sallust in the *Vita Henrici Quinti* (1438) by Titus Livius de Frulovisi and the *Vita Henrici Septimi* (1500–1503) by Bernard André" in I. D. McFarlane, ed., *Acta Conventus Neo-Latini Sanctandreani: Proceedings of the Fifth International Congress of Neo-Latin Studies* (Binghamton, NY: Medieval and Renaissance Texts and Studies, 1986), 437–38.

14. Leonard Coxe, *The Arte or Crafte of Rhethoryke,* ed. F. I. Carpenter (Chicago: University of Chicago Press, 1899), 55–58.

15. Peter Burke, *The Renaissance Sense of the Past* (London: Edward Arnold, 1969), 105.

16. Myron P. Gilmore, *Humanists and Jurists: Six Studies in the Renaissance* (Cambridge, MA: Harvard University Press, 1963), 94.

17. Desiderius Erasmus, *De copia verborum ac rerum,* trans. Betty I. Knott, in *Collected Works of Erasmus* 24 (Toronto: University of Toronto Press, 1978), 586. Erasmus's actual Latin reads as follows: "Ad hanc formam praecipue perti-

net schema dialogismos, id est sermocinatio, quoties vnicuique sermonem accommodamus, aetati, generi, patriae, vitae instituto, animo, moribusque congruentem. Nam huiusmodi sermones in historia licet affingere: vnde tot Thucydidis, Salustii, Liuii orationes effinguntur, et epistolae, et apophthegmata; demum et cogitationes, veluti hominis secum loquentis, quanquam hoc poetis familiarius." *Opera Omnia Desiderii Erasmi Roterodami*, I, Part 6 (Amsterdam: North-Holland, 1988), 212.

18. Erasmus, *De copia*, 649–50. Erasmus's Latin reads as follows: "Narratio vehementer locupletatur schemate quod quidam appellant sermocinationem, qua vni aut pluribus personis affingimus sermonem congruentem.... Neque quicquam est admirabilius in historiarum scriptoribus: nam historicis hoc omnium suffragiis permissum est orationem personis affingere. De ethnicis loquor. An idem liceat christianis in dubio est, nisi quod simile factum videtur in historia septem Maccabaeorum; ac, prater alios qui martyrum vitas conscripserunt, idem sibi permisisse videtur diuus Ambrosius in Vita beatae Agnetis." *Opera Omnia Desiderii Erasmi Roterodami*, I, Part 6, 272.

19. Erasmus, *De copia*, 634–35. Erasmus's Latin reads as follows: "Iam fictae narrationes rerum gestarum, si persuadendi gratia pro veris adhibeantur, quam maxime fieri potest ad verisimilitudinem componantur oportet. Sunt autem ex arte rhetorica notae partes, quibus probabilitas constat. Cuiusmodi est fabula de Memmio apud Ciceronem, et fortasse de Vulteio apud Horatium. Genus hoc video nonnullis nimium placuisse, qui vulgi credulitate freti, stultissima quaedam miraculorum ostenta pro certissimis inuexerunt christianorum literis." *Opera Omnia Desiderii Erasmi Roterodami*, I, Part 6, 256. Cf. *Collected Works of Erasmus* 26, 618; and *Opera Omnia*, I, Part 6, 242, where, according to Erasmus, "the illustrative example, properly so called" is defined as "a reference to a genuine or apparently genuine occurrence designed to induce people to accept what we are saying [exemplum (est autem rei gestae, aut perinde vt gestae, vtilis ad persuadendum commemoratio)]."

20. Giorgio Barberi Squarotti, "*La vita di Castruccio o la storia come invenzione*," *L'Approdo letterario* 59–60 (1972): 89–113.

21. De Guevara's *Libro Aureo* was published in Spanish in 1529 in Antwerp and Paris. It was quickly translated into Castilian and subsequently translated from Castilian into French by R. Berthault. Berthault's French translation first appeared in 1531 and served as the basis for Lord Berners's English translation, completed shortly before his death on 10 March 1532. Between the date of its initial publication in 1535 and 1586, Berners's *Golden Boke* went through no fewer than fifteen editions. De Guevara also issued an amplified version of *Libro Aureo* in 1529, which he titled *Libro de Emperador Marco Aurelio con Relox de Principes*. Thomas North's English translation of the *Relox*, made from an earlier French translation, was published in 1557 under the title *The Diall of Princes*.

22. A facsimile of *The Image of Governance* is included in Sir Thomas Elyot, *Four Political Treatises,* ed. Lillian Gottesman (Gainesville, FL: Scholars' Facsmiles and Reprints, 1967), 203–426.

23. Roper, *Lyfe,* 103–4; *Two Early Tudor Lives,* ed. R. S. Sylvester and D. S. Harding (New Haven, CT: Yale University Press, 1962), xx–xxi.

24. John Foxe, *Actes and Monuments of Matters most Speciall and Memorable, Happenyng in the Church,* 6th ed., 2 vols. (London: H. Lownes for Company of Stationers, 1610), 1065 col. A; reprinted in John Foxe, *The Acts and Monuments,* 4th ed., 8 vols., ed. J. Pratt (London: Religious Tract Society, 1877), 7:550–51.

25. Roper, *Lyfe,* 21; *Two Early Tudor Lives,* 208.

26. Nicholas Harpsfield, *The Life and Death of Sir Thomas Moore, knight, sometymes Lord High Chauncellor of England,* ed. E. V. Hitchcock, Early English Text Society, original series 186 (London: Oxford University Press, 1935), 103–4.

27. Ro: Ba:, *The Lyfe of Syr Thomas More Sometymes Lord Chauncellor of England,* ed. E. V. Hitchcock, Early English Text Society, original series 222 (London: Oxford University Press, 1950), 264–65.

28. Thomas Stapleton, *The Life of Sir Thomas More,* trans. P. E. Hallett (London: Fordham University Press, 1928), 226. Originally composed in Latin, Stapleton's biography of More was published in 1588 at Douai as part of a larger project which included *vitae* of Thomas the Apostle and Thomas Becket: *Tres Thomae sev De S. Thomae Apostoli rebus gestis, De S. Thomae Archiepiscopo Cantuariensi & Martyre, D. Thomae Moi Angliae quondam Cancellarij Vita.* Stapleton's Latin reads as follows: "Illud postremo loco ponam, quod a fide dignis accepi, nobilissimum in hac causa & sempiterna memoria dignum testimonium. Carolus V. Imperator, Princeps non minus judicio acer, quam bello fortis & felix, audita Roffensis & Mori nece, Thomae Elioto, tunc Henrici apud eum Legato, haec verba dixit: Ego si in meis regnis duo hujusmodi lumina haberem, quamlibet munitissimam civitatem potius periclitari sinerem, quam me illis privari, nedum injuste tolle permitterem. Haec ille. Praestantissimi principis praeclarum elogium fuit. Et vero res loquitur, causa mortis iniquissima, genus infame, Mori patientia admirabilis, pietas, eruditio, aliaeque virtutes incomparabiles loquuntur, felicem tam nobili martyrio Morum, infamem tali judicio Henricum."

29. Cresacre More, *D.O.M.S. The Life and Death of Sir Thomas Moore, Lord High Chancellour of England* (Scolar Press facsimile: Menston, 1971), sig. 3B 3[r-v].

30. *Saint John Fisher: The Earliest English Life,* ed. Philip Hughes (London: Burns, Oates and Washbourne, Ltd., 1935), 189–90. More scholarly, original spelling editions of the *Life* exist in the form of *The Life of Fisher,* ed. R. Bayne, Early English Text Society, extra series 117 (London, 1921), 128–29; and Fran-

cis Van Ortroy, "*Vie du Bienheureux Martyr Jean Fisher,*" *Annalecta Bollandiana* 12 (1893): 205–6. The latter includes transcriptions of both the English manuscript and the subsequent Latin translation commonly attributed to Richard Hall. Hall's Latin rendering of the passage cited reads as follows: "*Carolus V, catholicissimus et invictissimus imperator, postquam Thomas Morus capitis supplicio affectus fuisset, accepto eius rei nuntio, Thomam Eliottum, regis Angliae lagatum, ad se vocatum rogavit annon aliquid huiusmodi audivisset. Cui ille: nihil se prorsus accepisse. Rursum imperator:* Immo, *inquit,* est verissimum Thomam Morum capite esse truncatum, sicut et ante eum sanctissimus quidam episcopus eodem supplicii genere occubuit. *Magnoque et alto suspirio ducto:* Ah! *inquit,* quid sibi voluit rex vester, cum hos tales et tantos viros trucidavit? Nam, ut de episcopo illo loquar, non puto aut in vestro regno, aut in reliquis totius orbis christiani dicionibus, si cuncta respicias, similem inveniri posse; illoque uno e medio tollendo censetur universos regni sui episcopos iugulasse. *Hoc nimirum dicere voluit, quod si sollicitudo pastoralis officii et in fidei catholicae ac ecclesiae defensione digna episcopo constantia spectaretur, ille solus inter reliquos suos confratres nomen episcopi mereretur.* Ad Thomam autem Morum quod attinet, inquit, tantae apud omnes sapientiae et eruditionis habebatur ut, si meus civis ac subditus fuisset, maluissem amplissimam et opulentissimam totius imperii mei civitatem, quam illum unum hominem, perdidisse.*"

31. According to a widespread tradition, after hearing the news of Castiglione's death in Toledo in 1529, the emperor exclaimed: "Yo vos digo que es muerto uno de los mejores caballeros del mundo." When confronted with the Hanse pretensions to a monopoly of the trade on the Baltic, Charles is reported to have said that "he would rather miss three royal crowns than that his Burgunders should be excluded from the Sound"; cited in H. W. Donner, "The Emperor and Sir Thomas Elyot," *Review of English Studies,* n.s., 2 (1951): 55–59.

32. K. J. Wilson, "The Letters of Sir Thomas Elyot," *Studies in Philology* 73 (1976), 2; *Records of the Reformation: The Divorce 1527–1533,* ed. Nicholas Pocock, 2 vols. (Oxford: Clarendon Press, 1870), 2:249.

33. Wilson, "Letters of Sir Thomas Elyot," 24. For evidence that the letter in question should be dated late 1535 or early 1536, see David Knowles, *The Religious Orders in England, Volume III: The Tudor Age* (Cambridge: Cambridge University Press, 1959), 242–43.

34. A. F. Pollard, "Sir Thomas More and Sir Thomas Elyot," *Times Literary Supplement* (17 July 1930), 592.

35. This now standard supposition is advanced by both Hitchcock (Harpsfield, *Life,* 354) and Stanford Lehmberg, *Sir Thomas Elyot, Tudor Humanist* (Austin: University of Texas Press, 1960), 109.

36. Roper, *Lyfe,* xliv, xlvi–xlvii, 3–4.

37. Coxe, *Arte or Crafte of Rhethoryke,* 55.

38. Ibid.

39. Thomas Wilson, *The Arte of Rhetorique,* ed. T. J. Derrick (New York, 1982), 47. Rather than follow the example of Coxe in directing readers to existing texts as models, Wilson composed a sample commendation of the lives of the duke of Suffolk and his brother to illustrate the precepts articulated in the *Rhetorique.*

40. Veré Rubel, *Poetic Diction in the English Renaissance* (New York: Modern Language Association of America, 1941), 86f.; A. L. Bennett, "The Principal Rhetorical Conventions in the Renaissance Personal Elegy," *Studies in Philology* 51 (1954): 107–26.

41. Guy, *Public Career,* 80–93; Anderson, *Biographical Truth,* 42.

42. *The Correspondence of Thomas More,* ed. E. F. Rogers (Princeton, NJ: Princeton University Press, 1947), 489.

43. Roper, *Lyfe,* 52.

44. Richard Sherry, *A Treatise of Schemes & Tropes* (London: John Day, 1550), sig. A ii^{r-v}.

45. DeWitt T. Starnes, *Renaissance Dictionaries: English-Latin and Latin-English* (Austin: University of Texas Press, 1954), 45–84; Paul Slack, "Mirrors of Health and Treasures of Poor Men: The Uses of the Vernacular Medical Literature of Tudor England," in Charles Webster, ed., *Health, Medicine and Mortality in the Sixteenth Century* (Cambridge: Cambridge University Press, 1979), 247–50.

46. Lehmberg, *Sir Thomas Elyot,* 18–19. A good summary of the school's personnel and practices is contained in E. E. Reynolds, *Margaret Roper, Eldest Daughter of Sir Thomas More* (New York: P. J. Kenedy and Sons, 1960), 12–29.

47. For example, Elyot's translation of Plutarch's essay, *The Education or Bringing up of Children* (London: Thomas Berthelet, c. 1529); and Book One of *The Boke Named the Governour* (London: Thomas Berthelet, 1531).

48. Elyot's wife, Margaret, was also a student in More's school.

49. J. A. Gee, "Margaret Roper's English Version of Erasmus' *Precatio Dominica* and the Apprenticeship behind Early Tudor Translation," *Review of English Studies* 13 (1937): 265–71.

50. Charles E. Raven, *English Naturalists from Neckam to Ray: A Study of the Making of the Modern World* (Cambridge: Cambridge University Press, 1947), 68–69. Elyot's comments on the difficulties of botanical identification can be found in the first paragraph of the Latin epistle to the readers prefixed to his 1538 *Dictionary.*

51. Wilson, "Letters of Sir Thomas Elyot," 31. The proverb in question concerns the competing claims of law, religion, and friendship in the context of swearing an oath—specifically, the refusal of Pericles to perjure himself for the sake of a friend (Aulus Gellius, *Noctes Atticae* I, 3, 20). In the enlarged 1542 and 1545 editions of Elyot's dictionary, retitled *Bibliotheca Eliotae, vsque ad aras*

esse amicum is glossed as "to do all the pleasure that a man can for his frend, sauing his conscience." K. J. Wilson's short note, "*Vsque ad aras:* Thomas Elyot's Friendship with Thomas More," in McFarland, *Acta Conventus Neo-Latini Sanctandreani: Proceedings of the Fifth International Congress of Neo-Latin Studies,* 531–35 also deserves mention in this context.

52. *Tudor Royal Proclamations, Volume I: The Early Tudors,* ed. P. L. Hughes and J. F. Larkin (New Haven, CT: Yale University Press, 1964), no. 161. The correct date of this proclamation is established by R. W. Heinze, *The Proclamations of the Tudor Kings* (Cambridge: Cambridge University Press, 1976), 22–23.

53. Wilson, "Letters of Sir Thomas Elyot," 26–27. Here again Wilson's provisional dating of the letter in question is misleading.

54. Judging by More's comments in *The Debellation of Salem and Bizance,* his *Apology* was published near Easter, which in 1533 fell on April 13. The slightly earlier publication date of *Pasquil the Playne* is established by a letter from Elyot to Cromwell accompanying copies of his dialogue *Of the Knowledge Which Maketh a Wise Man* which alludes to the reception of *Pasquil* in its proem. Since Elyot's extant letters appear always to observe his correspondents' latest eminence, and Cromwell is addressed as Treasurer of the King's Jewels, it follows that Sir Thomas's letter was dispatched prior to his friend's appointment as chancellor of the exchequer on 12 April 1533.

55. Elyot, *Four Political Treatises,* 56–58, 68; Marius, *Thomas More,* 434–38.

56. Wilson, "Letters of Sir Thomas Elyot," 17.

57. Donner, "The Emperor and Sir Thomas Elyot," 56.

58. Diogenes Laertius, "Aristippus," *Lives of the Eminent Philosophers,* 2. 66. Although many features of the dialogue are his own interpolations, Elyot's principal source for Plato's experience at the court of Dionysius was Diogenes Laertius ("Plato," *Lives of the Eminent Philosophers,* 3:18–21). For Sir Thomas's own testimony that Diogenes's text served as an inspiration for his dialogue, see Sir Thomas Elyot, *Of the Knowledge Which Maketh a Wise Man,* ed. E. J. Howard (Oxford: Anchor Press, 1946), 11–12.

59. Howard, *Of the Knowledge,* 143, emphasis added.

60. Donner, "The Emperor and Sir Thomas Elyot," 56–57. I have modified and expanded Donner's list of parallels.

61. Roper, *Lyfe,* 11; *Two Tudor Lives,* 201–2; Howard, *Of the Knowledge,* 204–5.

62. Roper, *Lyfe,* 11–12; *Two Tudor Lives,* 202; Howard, *Of the Knowledge,* 18–19.

63. Roper, *Lyfe,* 51, 71–72; *Two Tudor Lives,* 225, 236–37; Howard, *Of the Knowledge,* 22–23, 192–232; Crewe, *Trials of Authorship,* 87–90.

64. Donner, "The Emperor and Sir Thomas Elyot," 57. For the dating of *Of the Knowledge,* see note 23.

65. Elizabeth Brooke Blackburn, "John More's 'A Sermon of the... Aulter,' " *Moreana* 2 (1964): 5–36.

66. In this context, it is worth remembering that Sir Thomas More wrote four separate works on the subject of the Eucharist: the *Letter to Frith; An Answer to a Poisoned Book; A Treatise upon the Passion;* and *A Treatise to Receive the Blessed Body of Our Lord.*

67. Chapuys to Charles V, 5 June 1532: *Letters and Papers, Foreign and Domestic of the Reign of Henry VIII,* 21 vols., ed. J. S. Brewer, J. Gairdner, and R. H. Brodie (London: Longman, 1862–1910), 5:1,077; Wilson, "Letters of Sir Thomas Elyot," 9.

68. For a discussion of the content and publishing history of *Pasquil the Playne,* see F. W. Conrad, "The Problem of Counsel Reconsidered: The Case of Sir Thomas Elyot," in Paul A. Fideler and T. F. Mayer, eds., *Political Thought and the Tudor Commonwealth: Deep Structure, Discourse and Disguise* (London: Routledge, 1992), 75–107.

69. Howard, *Of the Knowledge,* 4.

70. Crewe, *Trials of Authorship,* 84, plausibly suggests that Roper's celebration of More's "suicidal" yet "saving" folly was informed by his appreciation of Erasmus's *Encomium moriae.*

71. The influence of Roper's *Lyfe* on subsequent perceptions of More is well established. The effect of its image of Elyot can be seen in the following fanciful portion of Sidney Lee's 1889 entry on Sir Thomas, which remains uncorrected in the *Dictionary of National Biography:* "in 1535 [Elyot] again became ambassador to Charles V. In all probability he left England in May, and joined the emperor at Barcelona, whence he proceeded with him on the expedition to Tunis. He seems to have been in the emperor's suite at Naples at the end of the year, and there learned from the emperor himself the news of the execution of his friend Sir Thomas More, which took place on 6 July 1535 (William Roper, *Life of Sir T. More*)." Despite his exclusive mention of Roper, Lee also relies upon the introduction to Sir H. H. S. Croft's critical edition of *The Boke Named the Governour,* 2 vols. (London: C. Kegan Paul and Co., 1880), where Elyot's hypothetical travels with Charles V through Spain and Italy in 1535 are described in detail (1:cxvii–cxiv).

72. The pertinent portion of Buondelmonti's letter to Machiavelli, dated 6 September 1520, reads as follows: "Notossi bene certi luoghi i quali, se bene stanno, bene si potrebbono non di meno migliorare; come è quella parte ultima dei ditterii et de' tratti ingegnosi et acuti detti del detto Castrucci, la quale non tornerebbe se non meglio piú breve, perché, oltre all'essere troppi quegli suoi detti o sali, ve no è una parte che furono ad altri et antichi et moderni savi attribuiti; un'altra non ha quella vivacità né quella grandeza che si richiederebbe

a un tanto huomo. Ma ve ne restano tanti buoni che si possono di lui adurre, che la sua vita ne resta richa assai. l'altre annotationi sono piú tosto circha alle parole che circha alle altre parte: delle quali tutte cose ci reserbereno a parlare a bocha con piú piacere assai."

6
Characterizations of the "Obscure Men" of Cologne: A Study in Pre-Reformation Collective Authorship

James V. Mehl

In the spring of 1518, Erasmus wrote to his humanist friend in Cologne, Johannes Caesarius: "The man who invented the title *Obscurorum virorum* did civilization a bad turn: if the title had not given away the joke, those letters would still be read everywhere to this day as though they were written in support of the Dominicans." Erasmus had even heard about a "noble doctor of divinity" in Louvain who had purchased twenty copies of the book to give as presents, shortly before a papal bull had been issued condemning the scandalous text.[1] But in an earlier letter to Caesarius (16 August 1517), Erasmus had expressed strong disapproval of the *Epistolae obscurorum virorum* [the *Letters of Obscure Men*] (fig. 1), adding that "the wit might have proved entertaining if it had not set such an offensive precedent."[2] Erasmus was especially disturbed by the lewd language and personal attacks in the letters, including the mention of his own name. He expressed similar concerns to another friend and leader of the humanists in the "home town" of the obscure men, Count Hermann von Neuenahr, who had been won over to the cause of Reuchlin.[3] James Overfield has recently argued that Erasmus's evaluation of the *Letters* was typical of the humanists' response to the satire during the Reuchlin affair in early sixteenth-century Germany.[4] Thus, the interpretations of those later historians who used the excessive characterizations in the letters to generalize about the opposition of humanism and scholasticism, according to Overfield, need to be revised; the comedy of demented, sex-crazed obscurantist scholastics flailing aimlessly against the supporters of Reuchlin should not be singled out as evidence for the existence of hostile "camps" of humanists and scholastics.[5]

Such appraisals of the *Letters of Obscure Men* by Overfield and Erasmus raise new and perhaps even more difficult questions about the role, significance, and later fame of the satirical letters. If the letters did not generate broad appeal during the Reuchlin controversy, even among the humanists, then how can their later popularity and fame be explained? Barbara Könneker has recently pointed out the significant and unique contributions of the *Epistolae* in the development of modern satire.[6] Pierre Mesnard has claimed that the particularly brutal nature of its satire marked the end of the tradition of humanist correspondence and of humanism itself.[7] Why did its authors select the letter or letter collection as the genre for their publication? What kinds of literary techniques and methods of rhetorical persuasion were employed by its authors to insure its reputation as the most famous satire in pre-Reformation Germany? How did its multiple authors, working in different places and in different times, produce a literary masterpiece? These are the questions related to the subject of the rhetorics of life-writing in early modern Europe that I will address in this chapter.

The statements by Erasmus reveal some important clues in pursuing these literary-historical issues. Erasmus denounced the letters in 1517 because their literary tone and purpose had changed. He sensed, correctly, that their satirical intention had shifted. In place of the playful mimic satire of mainly fictional obscurantists devised by Crotus Rubeanus for the first edition of the letters in 1515, the more militant Ulrich von Hutten had directed the satire in the expanded second and third editions against actual opponents in the Reuchlin case.[8] He had also interjected sweeping attacks against abuses and authorities in the Roman Church as well as specific mention of humanists such as Erasmus, Caesarius, and Hermann von Neuenahr. The broader thrust and more polemical intention of Hutten and other authors of these later editions disturbed Erasmus; they contributed to intellectual divisiveness and controversy that detracted from his own moderate reform program of Christian humanism. Despite his later denunciations and denials, Erasmus likely had specific knowledge and involvement in the literary project in its earliest stages. On his trip from England to Basel in August 1514, he had met with Reuchlin, Hutten, and Hermann von dem Busche in Mainz. During a second meeting with Hutten and Busche in Frankfurt am Main in April 1515, Erasmus may have been given a manuscript copy of some of the first letters.[9] The first edition of the *Epistolae* was printed anonymously by Heinrich Gran, in the autumn of that same year, in Hagenau.

Fig. 1. Title page from *Epistolae obscurorum virorum (Letters of Obscure Men)*, 1st ed., pt. 2. From Eduardus Böcking, ed., *Ulrichi Hutteni equitis Operum supplementum: Epistolae obscurorum vivorum cum inlustrantibus adversariisque scriptis*, 2 vols. (Leipzig, 1864–70)

It was an assistant at that press, Wolfgang Angst, who evidently sent a copy of the first edition of the satirical letters to Erasmus shortly after publication.[10] Erasmus may truly have been entertained by the humor of these early letters, as he later intimated, just as Thomas More revealed amusement and general satisfaction with the satire in correspondence a year later.[11] But the quickening tempo and shifting focus of the controversy was soon reflected in the personal denigration and sharper barbs of wit in the next editions of the letters, as well as in the more open disapproval of the literary enterprise by Erasmus, Beatus Rhenanus, and other humanists.[12] This shift in rhetorical purpose and reception of the *Epistolae* thereby illustrates the more general reorientation of humanist-scholastic debates in Germany during the early sixteenth century, as argued recently by Erika Rummel.[13] What had once been a kind of "insiders' joke" for its humanist authors and their associates had been turned into an instrument of mass media propaganda for new cultural, religious, and political causes in early Reformation Germany.[14]

The idea of circulating a collection of satirical letters came in the wake of several events showing favor to Reuchlin's cause. In March 1514, the bishop of Speyer, who had been commissioned by the Roman curia to adjudicate the case, came out strongly in Reuchlin's favor. About the same time, Reuchlin himself had collected a number of letters by prominent humanists sympathetic to his position and published them as the *Epistolae clarorum virorum* [the *Letters of Famous Men*].[15] What better way to lend additional support to the Reuchlinist side than to circulate yet another collection of letters? But this time the collection would be a mimic satire of Reuchlin's opponents recast as the "obscure men" of Cologne. The publication of both these letter collections in the early sixteenth century, as Cecil Clough has pointed out, was an important step in the development of the epistolary form as a literary genre.[16]

While Hutten and the other authors of the spurious *Epistolae obscurorum virorum* took their cue from the appearance of the more serious *Epistolae clarorum virorum*, they were also drawing on a long tradition of letter writing and of letter collections as models for life-writing during the Renaissance. Beginning with Petrarch, a number of humanists wrote neo-Latin letters and often edited them into collections as a means of literary self-expression and a way of insuring fame.[17] As with Petrarch, many of the humanists were inspired by the discovery of ancient letter collections. Thus, the classical texts of Cicero (especially his *Epistolae ad Atticum* found by Petrarch in 1345 and his *Epistolae ad familiares* discovered later), Seneca, and Pliny the Younger, among others, not only served as important models in the adoption of new rhetorical approaches in letter writing, but also encouraged a custom of letter collection among the Renaissance humanists themselves.[18] Among the most famous and widely circulated of the early manuscript letter collections were those of Coluccio Salutati, Leonardo Bruni, and Poggio Bracciolini, all of whom were accomplished letter writers and served as chancellors of the republic of Florence. However, as Clough has argued, these early manuscript letter collections were probably less influential than might be thought.[19] Their use as anthologies for instruction in humanist epistolary styles also explains the appearance of several collections of fictional letters in Italy during the early fifteenth century.[20]

The greatest interest in neo-Latin letter collections can be traced from the last three decades of the fifteenth century, an interest that continued well into the first half of the next century. The popularity and greater use of letter collections, especially among the humanists, was made possible by the invention of the printing press. Beginning in 1472, there were numerous printed editions of letter collections by leading authors of the time: Leonardo Bruni, Enea Silvio Piccolomini (both his *Epistolae in Pontificatu editae* and his *Epistolae in Cardinalatu editae*), Giovanni Antonio Campano, Giovanni Maria Filelfo, Marsilio Ficino, Giovanni Pico della Mirandola, Angelo Poliziano, and Robert Gaguin. Although all these early printed letter collections were by Italians, save for the Frenchman Gaguin, the editions were either printed or reprinted, more often than not, in the north.[21] The collections of Enea Silvio Piccolomini, a well-known humanist author and later pope, treated important events and personalities of the period and were very popular both in Italy and in the north. Certainly the most famous author of the neo-Latin letter in the north was Erasmus, whose letter collection remains an object of intense interest into our own time.[22] To promote the reform of letter writing, Conrad Celtis, Erasmus, Lorenzo Valla, and other humanists contributed manuals on that subject.[23] Some of the manuals included collections of letters to be used as examples of good style. One of the most widely used formularies in the north during the fifteenth century was the *Epistolares formulae* by the Louvain arts professor, Carolus Virulus (Menniken). Virulus's text, which was reprinted at least twenty-seven times by 1500 and was possibly used by Erasmus during his student years, consisted of 337 fictional letters.[24] Like the earlier collections of fictitious letters by Gasperino Barzizza, they could be exploited as model letters for any occasion. Thus, the humanist authors and readers of the satirical *Epistolae* would have been familiar with a long humanistic tradition of treating letter collections as literary texts and would have likely been aware of a wide variety of such letter collections from the period, primarily through the availability of printed editions during the early sixteenth century. Indeed, the appearance of the *Letters of Obscure Men* coincided with the rising tide of publication and widespread use of letter collections during the late Renaissance.

The fictional orientation of the *Epistolae* as a literary text was also in line with the rhetorical approaches of the humanist letter writers and editors of letter collections during the Renaissance. Questions regarding authorship, authenticity, and the purpose of humanistic letter writing have been raised by several recent scholars. The difficulties of assessing authorship and authenticity can be demonstrated by the ways in which the humanists put together their letter collections. In some cases, the humanist letter writers, such as Petrarch, edited their own collections, while in other instances, the collections were assembled by colleagues or other editors, often after the death of the original authors. In this guise, the letter collection took on an autobiographical character. The editor was interested primarily in the rhetorical effect of the total literary collection. The reader of the collection was no longer the original addressee of the letters but, rather, a third party in the public domain, thereby the audience—and hence the rhetorical purpose—of the letters had shifted. Such collections could be used to demonstrate (and authenticate) the learning, wisdom, and broad range of acquintances of the humanist. The surfaces, that is, the self-images, projected by the letters became the primary concern of the editors of the letter collections. To achieve the desired rhetorical effect, the author or editors would change the text of an original letter, arrange the letters in a certain complementary order, and even add fake correspondence to round out the collection.[25] Whatever authenticity the original letter collection might have contained would be further eroded by the circulation of later revised and/or abridged editions, and later editors would select individual letters or groups of letters for inclusion (and rearrangement) in entirely new letter collections, which were typically used as anthologies for instruction in epistolary style. In the latter case, an "original" letter by a "real" author was often followed by a fictitous letter in the formulary, thus making it difficult for the reader to discern actual authorship. As letters would be assembled and reassembled in a succession of new letter collections, there was an increasing degree of collective authorship and of fictionality.

The difficulties of ascertaining originality and authenticity were compounded by the publication and reprinting of numerous texts of letter collections during the later fifteenth and sixteenth centuries, thereby increasing the potential for greater fictionality and collective authorships. The evolution of this tendency by the humanists to treat letter writing and letter collections as literary enterprises, a tendency that continued through the later sixteenth century when the vernacular letter became the dominant form, has led Claudio Guillén to emphasize the fictional character of the Renaissance letter.[26] With the printing of letter collections during the later Renaissance, there was a new emphasis on focusing the rhetorical appeal to the third-party witness, that is, to the reader of the letter collection now treated as a public document. As Guillén puts it:

> The equivocal triangle, the latent voyeurism that I allude to here—the only innocent participant being the original addressee of the letter—exists or increases in the exact degree in which the moral or newsworthy epistle becomes so familiar and private as to be lacking apparently in general interest and only be of concern to immediate friends and near relatives. What was intended to be read, in principle, is actually reread; and, most important, reread by others.[27]

Just as the epistle replaced the oration as the preferred means of communication by the end of the fifteenth century, so, too, the autobiographical qualities of the Renaissance letter, according to Guillén, became the forerunners of the modern essay and novel.[28] The increasing use of vernacular languages in letter writing and letter collections during the sixteenth century was conducive to a greater sense of playfulness and reliance on humor in these texts.[29] The pervasive autobiographical orientation of these letter collections of the late Renaissance lent itself to ludic and satirical elements which characterized much of the humanist literature of the period, as may be seen in Erasmus's *Moriae encomium* and *Colloquia*. Familiarity with these more general rhetorical patterns, as expressed by the humanists in their letter writing and letter collections, should contribute not only to a clearer understanding of the place of the *Epistolae obscurorum virorum* in this Renaissance literary tradition, but also to a more accurate appraisal of the unique literary elements and historical circumstances of this particular satire.

Most scholars credit Crotus Rubeanus, a Thuringian peasant's son, with the conception of the satire, as well as the authorship of most of the forty-one letters in the first part of the *Epistolae*.[30] Crotus's experiences as a student and teacher provided him with much of the raw material for the characterizations in the letters.[31] He had traditional training in scholastic subjects at the University of Erfurt between 1498 and 1507. An outbreak of plague in 1505 had sent him briefly to Fulda, where he met Hutten as a student at the monastic school in that town. Another threat of plague had forced both Hutten and Crotus to travel to Cologne, where they matriculated at its famous university during the winter of 1505.[32] There they not only experienced firsthand the traditional academic fare as students, but may have also become acquainted with another arts student, Ortwin Gratius, and the important theologians Arnold von Tongern and Jacob Hochstraten—all of whom were singled out for special ridicule in the satirical letters. Crotus soon returned to Erfurt in order to complete his M.A. degree. He became a priest and served as headmaster at the monastic school in Fulda between 1510 and 1515. During a visit to Cologne in 1512, he had by chance met Johannes Pfefferkorn, the converted Jew who had initiated the Reuchlin case in 1507 with his publications calling for the suppression of Hebrew books. In addition to his duties as a headmaster and teacher at the monastic school, Crotus had become closely associated with the Erfurt circle of humanists led by Conrad Mutianus Rufus, whose home in nearby Gotha served as "a kind of literary censorial office" for the younger humanists around him.[33] Crotus redirected his interests to the new humanist cause and was admired by Busche, Hutten, and other members of the circle for his wit and literary abilities. Crotus was no doubt aware of his mentor's distaste for scholasticism and his criticisms of academic and religious abuses. While Mutianus was actually a rather timid intellectual canon who tried to avoid controversy, his wise and fatherly advice was both sought and shared through personal meetings and extensive correspondence. Crotus's close ties with Mutianus and his humanist associates, along with his own earlier experiences as a student of scholastic programs at Erfurt and Cologne, provided useful models for developing the characterizations of the *poetae* and *magistri* in the *Letters of Obscure Men*.[34] Crotus would invert the humanistic preoccupations of Mutianus's circle to create a new "circle" of obscurantist correspondents seeking the foolish advice of their "leader" in Cologne, Ortwin Gratius.[35]

While Crotus's efforts to undermine the traditionalist opposition were significant, there were other important contributors to the literary conspiracy. Hutten had written the first letter for the initial installment of forty-one letters, as well as seven additional letters appended to them in the second edition of 1516 (known as part I of the *EOV*). In 1517, another collection of sixty-two letters by the *viri obscuri* was published as a sequel to the first volume (known as part II of the *EOV*). Hutten had written the majority of the letters for the second part, although some of them have also been attributed to Busche and several other authors.[36]

Busche played a greater role in the literary project than has generally been recognized.[37] Returning to Cologne as an arts professor for a second time in 1508, he taught poetry and other humanistic subjects in the *bursa Laurentiana,* one of the two largest and most humanistically inclined colleges at the university. This was a more settled period in his personal life, although he was never far from controversies. Even before his arrival in the city, he had joined Gratius and other defenders of the Italian jurist, Peter of Ravenna, in a dispute with the faculty of theology.[38] But the friendship with Gratius soon turned sour. Early in 1509, under increasing pressure from university authorities, Gratius changed sides in the conflict with Peter of Ravenna. It was also at that point that Gratius supervised the publication of his Latin translations of several anti-Jewish pamphlets by Pfefferkorn and Victor von Karben at the Quentell press, where he was employed as a part-time editor. Later that year, Busche and Gratius engaged in a brief, but bitter, disagreement over the introduction of Donatus into the arts curriculum. Gratius used his position as an editor to respond in kind, in a printed prefatory letter, to the personal attacks that had been made against his good name and character by Busche.[39] Their personal enmity spilled over into the Reuchlin affair. After initially siding with Pfefferkorn and the conservative theologians, Busche was persuaded to join Reuchlin's cause by 1514. In that year, he probably wrote the first draft of the *Triumphus Capnionis,* in which Reuchlin stands in triumph over Gratius, Tongern, Hochstraten, and other defeated opponents.[40] As a further act of personal revenge, Busche probably recommended Gratius as the addressee of the satirical letters at that time. Busche's own contributions to the letters include personal information about Gratius and the situation in Cologne, an "insider's" knowledge made possible by his continuous residence in the city until 1516. Busche may have even arranged for the publication of two early editions of the *Epistolae* in Cologne.[41]

In any case, Crotus and the other authors would have been receptive to the suggestion of Gratius's name as a focal point for the satire. He was, from their perspective, a logical and deserving choice for the parody. In his *Defensio* of 1513, as well as in earlier writings, Reuchlin himself had responded to Gratius's heightened involvement in the controversy by calling him "an ass, a half-Gentile, a barbarian, an illiterate, a mercenary corrector of books, a most worthless and degenerate good-for-nothing, a sophistical and laughable human being, a silly poet, an awkward metrist, and the scum of every wickedness and treachery." To ridicule his position at the university, Reuchlin had dubbed him a "perversor bonarum artium," rather than a professor of liberal arts, and revealed him as an "agent of the theological faculty."[42] Furthermore, Gratius was considered a "turncoat" humanist. Besides teaching humanistic subjects in the *bursa Cucana,* one of the smaller colleges at the university, he had led the annual quodlibetical disputations with Peter of Ravenna in 1507. Gratius's arguments favoring the *humaniora* were published a year later as the *Orationes quodlibeticae.*[43] His humanism, however, was of a more moderate kind, seeking coexistence, rather than conflict, within the dominant scholastic culture of the late medieval university. At the Quentell press, he edited and supervised the printing of a number of texts recommended by the humanists. He wrote a number of poems and letters, in the humanist manner, to serve as introductions for these books. But his humanist critics considered his poetry uncreative and hackneyed.[44] Gratius's sudden change of sides in the Peter of Ravenna case, his dispute with Busche, his aggressive collaboration with Pfefforkorn and the theologians, and his attacks against Reuchlin made him a renegade to the humanist cause and marked him as the central figure for satirical mockery in the *Letters of Obscure Men.* Gratius's reputation as a humanist was permanently damaged, and his name was employed as a satirical caricature in a number of controversies thereafter.

Several recent studies have contributed to our understanding of how Crotus and the other authors achieved their literary success. Reinhard Becker has pointed out their reliance on a long tradition of medieval anticlerical satire. Gratius and his obscurantist correspondents have all succumbed to the Seven Deadly Sins, especially those of fleshly pleasure, *luxuria* and *gula.*[45] In letter after letter Gratius's advice is sought for success in amorous affairs, because he had quite a reputation as a lover—his liaisons with Pfefferkorn's wife, the maiden at Quentell, and other unattractive women were among the popular topics of gossip for the depraved clerics.[46] His former students and friends prided themselves in their knowledge of the local brands of beer and wine—beverages consumed in great quantities during academic banquets and other informal occasions. The crudeness and lewdness of such details in the letters were inspired by the humanist *facetiae* literature as well as the vernacular traditions of the *Fastnachsspiel*.[47] Overindulgence in food and drink exacerbated their already demented mental state. Becker argues that the authors were most original in the depiction of the *viri obscuri* as scholars and poets.[48] Just as Gratius's shifting preoccupations in real life had made him vulnerable to charges of hypocrisy, mediocrity, and stupidity, these same qualities were exaggerated in the satire. His students and pretentious "scholarly" friends were but carbon copies of their mentor.[49] In the first letter of the *Epistolae*, Hutten describes an academic "Feast of Aristotle" in which a mock disputation is held to determine whether the title "magister nostrandus" or "noster magistrandus" is more fitting for candidates taking the degree of Doctor of Divinity. Other equally ridiculous disputations, debates, and inquiries follow to illustrate the intellectual shallowness of the traditional scholastic subjects and methodologies as well as the affectations of the stuffy professors.[50] They lived in a world of fools.[51] Such examples were part of a longer tradition of university satire; parodies of scholasticism were typically given at the conclusion of quodlibetical disputations in the German universities.[52] Ortwin's shortcomings as a poet were highlighted when a number of the correspondents sought his advice in composing poems and his criticism of their labored meters. Crotus was especially effective in his mimic satire of these would-be village "poets," who constructed verses as though they were hammering together a shoe or building a chair.[53] The crudeness of their poetry was matched only by the lasciviousness of their sexual exploits.

There were other abuses of language to prove the incompetence of the "obscure men." Misuse of the epistolary form that, as discussed previously, was the preferred genre of communication for the humanists by the early sixteenth century, revealed the illiteracy and false pretensions of the obscurantists. Becker has shown how Crotus and the other authors exaggerated and distorted the first and last parts of the letters, the *salutatio* and *conclusio,* to achieve their satirical purpose.[54] In the first letter of part I, for example, Hutten begins with the salutation, "Thomas Langschneiderius, duly qualified, albeit unworthy, Bachelor in Theology, sendeth greeting to the supereminent and high-scientifical Herr Ortwin Gratius of Deventer, Poet, Orator, and Philosopher—Theologian too, and whatsoever else he listeth." And the letter concludes: "Farewell—and take it not amiss that I write to you thus familiarly, for you told me once on a time that you loved me as a brother, and desired to advance me to all things, even if it should cost you a pretty penny."[55] That the correspondents are really a motley crew of country bumpkins is proven by their names in the salutations: Plumilegus (Featherplucker), Scherscleifferius (Knifegrinder), Mistladerius (Manureloader), Mammotrectus Buntemantellus (Breastfondler Brightcoat), to mention but a few.[56] Perhaps Crotus, as a kind of self-irony, had in mind his own peasant origins in concocting these names, but Reinhard Hahn has recently demonstrated that Langschneiderius (Tall Tailor), the sender of the first letter, as well as a number of the characters in part II (Wüstenfeld, Ochsenfart, Warmsemmel, and Kachelofen), were names of actual persons known to Hutten in Leipzig.[57] The addition of the Latin nominative singular (us) to the names betrayed their presumptions to be humanists, just as Gratius was still posing as a humanist. When the Latinate ending was on a German name, it created a macaronic Latin, a satirical usage with a long literary tradition in Germany and other parts of Europe. Besides the sprinkling of macaronic terms and phrases, *Küchenlatein,* or *kitchen Latin,* was the predominant language used in the mimic correspondence.[58] This was a distinctive German evolution of Latin in the late medieval universities, whereby the classical Latin styles had degenerated in the common conversation of students and academics who spoke in a doggerel Latin using the word order of German. Such ludic mixing of Latin and German—known as *Barbarolexis*—reached a high point in the disputation exercises of the German universities around 1500, thus contributing to the parody of the quodlibetical questions in the *Epistolae.*[59] Winfried Frey has translated a passage from the letters into so-called Lübke-English, which will give us an example of the linguistic confusion—as well as the lack of any meaningful communication—in the letters: "I believe that the devil is in these poets. They destroy all universities. And I have heard from an old Master of Arts of Leipzig, that when he young was, then this university were orderly, because in 20 miles around not one poet were."[60] This specific passage is also significant because the first sentence, "I believe that the devil is in these poets," is a quotation from St. Jerome that had been used by reactionary preachers in Germany to condemn the humanists and their learning.[61]

Finally, Crotus, Hutten, and the other authors included conceptual labels and metaphors which made clear their superior learning and their awareness of living in new times. Karl-Heinz Gerschmann has pointed out their playful interjection of the terms *antiqui, novi,* and *moderni* to refer, on the one hand, to the "wegestreit" between the "antiqui" and "moderni" (that is, the conflict between the two dominant philosophical traditions, the realists and the nominalists) in the late medieval German universities.[62] At the University of Cologne, the actual philosophical split was between the Albertists and the Thomists, a competition that is mentioned in several of the letters.[63] In the second part (letters II.43 and II.50), Hutten introduced the possibility of a new, third way, "the way of Christ." In this context the "moderns" were those humanist-theologians, such as Reuchlin and Erasmus, who approached the study of theology and the scriptures armed with a knowledge of ancient Hebrew, Greek, and Latin. Hutten was reorienting the purpose of the satirical letters to promote the religious, social, and political renewal of Germany.[64] But in other letters, the terms *moderni, novi,* and *antiqui* imply that the humanists are the moderns and the classical authors are the ancients. This reflects the new Renaissance understanding of history and the role of the humanists in the cultural revival, first in Italy and then in the north. The terms *obscurus* and *clarus* were used by Reuchlin and his supporters to draw attention to their own intellectual superiority and fame, in contrast to the stupidity and mental darkness of their scholastic opponents.[65] But *obscurus* and *clarus* were also related to the important Renaissance metaphor of light and dark. Petrarch had been the first humanist to reverse the historical meaning of that metaphor to visualize his hopes for a cultural rebirth in fourteenth-century Italy.[66] In their own way, Crotus, Hutten, and the other authors promoted this new "modern" sense of history through their characterizations of the *viri obscuri* as outmoded medieval scholastics who should be replaced by the humanists as the best hope for cultural renewal.

Perhaps my remarks will contribute to a clearer understanding of how the authors of the *Letters of Obscure Men* were ultimately successful in their literary satire, in spite of the mixed reviews of their efforts by Erasmus and other humanists of that time. This example of early modern life-writing is complicated by its multiple authorship and by its sequential publication over several years. The *Epistolae* were conceived, written, and circulated by several humanists associated with the Erfurt circle as a strategy to undermine the opponents of Reuchlin. In addition to Crotus Rubeanus and Ulrich von Hutten, the primary authors of the letters, Hermann von dem Busche played an important role in the project, especially through his advancement of Gratius's name as the "leader" of the "obscure men" of Cologne. The authors relied on a variety of literary techniques in their mimic satire of the "obscure men," adapting the traditions of anticlerical satire, university satire, and fool literature for their own purposes. Manipulation of language and of the epistolary form was crucial in achieving the desired literary and rhetorical effect. Crotus created characters and situations that exploited and exaggerated the shortcomings and pretensions of Reuchlin's opponents, while Hutten was more direct in his satire and introduced issues and ideas that would be taken up shortly during the Reformation. Literary consistency and persuasion were enhanced by the mixing of fictional characters with real-life personalities, such as Gratius, and by having them all miscommunicate in a dog-eared Latin. After the first and second parts of the letters were published as a single volume in 1556, readers could better appreciate the *Epistolae* as a masterpiece of literature.

The satirical characterizations and burlesque humor of the letters appealed to a wide variety of authors and readers during the sixteenth and later centuries. The *viri obscuri* served as a model for satirical attacks in the pamphlet literature of the early Reformation, as can be seen in the *Eccius dedolatus*.[67] Rabelais included a number of book titles by "obscure men" in the Library of St. Victor, a literary convention which influenced, in turn, the German vernacular tradition through the writings of Johann Fischart.[68] The *Epistolae* have continued to serve as an important literary source and model for satirical writings in a number of political disputes and other controversies down to our own time.[69] Indeed, such polemical usages contributed to the historical conception and modern, secular (and negative) definition of the term *Dunkelmänner* (obscure men, obscurantists) by the nineteenth century.[70]

The literary success of the *Epistolae obscurorum virorum* was due, in large part, to the unique mixture of rhetorical-stylistic elements its humanist authors had employed to achieve their specific satirical and polemical purposes in the context of the Reuchlin controversy. But they also selected one of the most popular literary forms during the early sixteenth century—the printed letter collection—as the vehicle to circulate their satire. Not only had the letter and the letter collection evolved as one of the most important genres of Renaissance literature, but the autobiographical tendencies in the collections contributed to their increasingly fictional character. The literary potential for ludic and satirical qualities was thereby enhanced in such collections. The immediate inspiration and model for Hutten and the other authors was the letter collection that Reuchlin had published in his own defense, the *Epistolae clarorum virorum*. Their sequel, the *Letters of Obscure Men*, which was a consciously ironical inversion of that more serious collection, also incorporated characteristics of autobiography, fictionality, and collective authorship that could be found in a long tradition of Renaissance letter collections. The *Epistolae obscurorum virorum*, as a result, is a particularly good example of the development of life-writing through letter collections during and after the late Renaissance. The success of the *Epistolae* can further be measured by the durability of its contribution—the characterization of the *viri obscuri* (the "obscure men")—as a literary type into our own time.

NOTES

1. Erasmus to Caesarius, Louvain, 5 April 1518, in *Collected Works of Erasmus*, ed. Peter G. Bietenholz et al. [cited hereafter as *CWE*] (Toronto: University of Toronto Press, 1974–), 5:359; *Opus epistolarum Des. Erasmi Roterodami*, 12 vols., ed. P. S. Allen [cited hereafter as *Opus epist.*], (Oxford: Clarendon, 1906–58), 3:262–63 (Ep. 808).

2. *CWE*, 5:66; *Opus epist.*, 3:44–46 (Ep. 622).

3. Erasmus to Hermann von Neuenahr, Louvain, 25 August 1517, *CWE*, 5:83–85; *Opus epist.*, 3:58–59 (Ep. 636). On Neuenahr, see Charles G. Nauert, Jr., "Graf Hermann von Neuenahr and the Limits of Humanism in Cologne," *Historical Reflections/Réflexions Historiques* 15 (1988): 65–79. For more general discussions of humanist activity in Cologne at the time of the *Epistolae*, see Erich Meuthen, *Kölner Universitätsgeschichte, I: Die alte Universität* (Cologne and Vienna: Böhlau, 1988), 203–62; and James V. Mehl, "Humanism in the Home Town of the 'Obscure Men,'" in idem, ed., *Humanismus in Köln/Humanism in Cologne*, (Cologne/Weimar/Vienna: Böhlau, 1991), 1–38.

4. James H. Overfield, *Humanism and Scholasticism in Late Medieval Germany* (Princeton, NJ: Princeton University Press, 1984), 284–97. For other accounts of the Reuchlin controversy, see Hajo Holborn's "Introduction" to the *Letters of Obscure Men*, trans. Francis Stokes (London: Chatto and Windus, 1909; Philadelphia: University of Pennsylvania Press, 1964); Max Brod, *Johannes Reuchlin und sein Kampf* (Stuttgart: Kohlhammer, 1965); and Winfried Frey, "Multum teneo de tali libro: Die Epistolae Obscurorum Virorum," in Peter Laub, ed., *Ulrich von Hutten: Ritter, Humanist, Publizist, 1488–1523: Katalog*

zur Ausstellung des Landes Hessen anläßlich des 500. Geburtstages (Kassel: Hessischer Museumsband, 1988), 197–209, at 199–202.

5. See also the recent study by Erich Meuthen, "Die 'Epistolae obscurorum virorum,'" in Walter Brandmüller, Herbert Immenkötter, and Erwin Iserloh, eds., *Ecclesia Militans: Studien zur Konzilien- und Reformationsgeschichte,* 2 vols. (Paderborn: Ferdinand Schöningh, 1988), 2:53–80, who stresses that the *Epistolae* should not be interpreted simply as a conflict between humanists and the Cologne scholastics, because there were already tensions and disputes among humanists and scholastics in the city itself when the satire was published.

6. Barbara Könneker, *Satire im 16. Jahrhundert: Epoche-Werke-Wirkung* (Munich: C. H. Beck, 1991), states their importance in three areas: (1) "Als erste neuzeitliche Satire, die ihre Entstehung einem aktuellen Anlaß, dem Reuchlinstreit und der aus ihm sich ergebenden Spaltung der zeitgenössischen Gelehrtenwelt verdankte, konzentrierte sich ihr satirischer Angriff erstmals auf eine ganz bestimmte Personengruppe, die sich durch ihre Parteinahme gegen Reuchlin und seine Anhänger gewissermaßen selbst definierte" (104); (2) "Die Sonderstellung der *Epistolae* gegenuber der satirischen Literatur der Vergangenheit beruht daher u.a. auch darauf, dass sie früheste Beispiel einer persönlichen Satire sind, in der bekannte und z.T. hochangesehene zeitgenössische Persönlichkeiten nicht nur beiläufig erwähnt oder in ihrer öffentlichen Funktion kritisiert, sondern speziell auch in ihrer Intimsphäre zur Zielscheibe des Spotts und der Verunglimpfung gemacht werden" (107); and (3) "Originell waren sie hier nicht in der Erfindung des Einzelmotivs, sondern in der Art, in der sie es verstanden, aus zahlreichen überlieferten solcher Motive einen neuartigen satirischen Typus, den 'vir obscurus,' zu formen" (110).

7. Pierre Mesnard, "Le commerce épistolaire, comme expression sociale de l'individualisme humaniste," in *Individu et société a la Renaissance,* Université Libre de Bruxelles, Travaux de l'Institut pour l'Étude de la Renaissance et de l'Humanisme, 3 (Brussels: Presses Universitaires de Bruxelles; Paris: Presses Universitaires de France, 1967), 15–31, at 22–23.

8. Critical editions of the *Epistolae* include *Epistolae obscurorum virorum,* ed. Aloys Bömer, 2 vols. (Heidelberg: Weissbach, 1924; Aalen: Scientia Verlag, 1978); and *Ulrichi Hutteni, equitis Germani, opera quae reperiri potuerunt omnia,* ed. Eduard Böcking [cited hereafter as *UH*], 5 vols., suppl. 2 vols. (Leipzig: Teubner, 1859–70; Aalen: O. Zeller, 1963), suppl. 1:1–80, 181–300. For the relationship of the *Epistolae* to other genres of neo-Latin satire, see Jozef IJsewijn, "Neo-Latin Satire: *sermo* and *satyra menippea,*" in R. R. Bolgar, ed., *Classical Influences on European Culture, A.D. 1500–1700* (Cambridge: Cambridge University Press, 1976), 41–55, at 41 n. 2.

9. Reinhard Hahn, "Huttens Anteil an den *Epistolae obscurorum virorum,*" *Pirckheimer Jahrbuch,* 4 (1988): 79–111, at 87–88; Barbara Könneker, "Ulrich von Hutten," in Peter G. Bietenholz and Thomas B. Deutscher, eds., *Contempo-*

raries of Erasmus [cited hereafter as *CE*], 3 vols. (Toronto: University of Toronto Press, 1985–87), 2:217–20, at 217; *CE*, 1:233. On Hutten, see also Lewis W. Spitz, *The Religious Renaissance of the German Humanists* (Cambridge, MA: Harvard University Press, 1963), 110–29; Hajo Holborn, *Ulrich von Hutten and the German Reformation*, trans. Roland H. Bainton (New Haven, CT: Yale University Press, 1937); Eckhard Bernstein, *Ulrich von Hutten* (Reinbek bei Hamburg: Rowohlt, 1988). See also Bernstein's "Creating Humanist Myths: Two Poems by Ulrich von Hutten," in Alexander Dalzell, Charles Fantazzi, and Richard J. Schoeck, eds., *Acta Conventus Neo-Latini Torontonensis* (Binghamton, NY: Medieval and Renaissance Texts and Studies, 1991), 249–60, where the "Carmen rithmicale" in II.9 is treated.

10. Wolfgang Angst was a humanist, a supporter of Reuchlin, and a close friend of Hutten who likely collaborated with the authors in arranging for the printing of the first edition in Hagenau; *CE*, 1:58. See also Angst's letter to Erasmus, Hagenau, 19 October [1515], which accompanied the gift of this copy, in *CWE*, 3:184–85; in *Opus epist.* , 2:152–53 (Ep. 363).

11. More to Erasmus, London, 31 October [1516], in *CWE*, 4:116; in *Opus epist.*, 2:372 (Ep. 481).

12. Overfield, *Humanism and Scholasticism*, 296.

13. Erika Rummel, "*Et cum theologo bella poeta gerit:* The Conflict between Humanists and Scholastics Revisited," *Sixteenth Century Journal* 23 (1992): 713–26.

14. Winfried Frey was the first to describe the Latin wordplay and the satire of late scholasticism in the letters as "ein Insider- Spaß," in "Die 'Epistolae obscurorum virorum'—ein antijudisches Pamphlet?" in Norbert Altenhofer and Renate Heuer, eds., *Archiv Bibliographia Judaica, Jahrbuch 1* (Bad Soden: A. and V. Woywod, 1985), 147–72, at 152. See also Könneker, *Satire*, 104.

15. Reuchlin issued a similar volume of collected letters toward the end of the controversy, the *Illustrium virorum epistolae* (1519). See Mesnard, "Le commerce épistolaire," 21–23, who also discusses the widespread use of the letter among German humanists during the later fifteenth and early sixteenth centuries.

16. Cecil H. Clough, "The Cult of Antiquity: Letters and Letter Collections," in idem, ed., *Cultural Aspects of the Italian Renaissance: Essays in Honour of Paul Oskar Kristeller* (Manchester: Manchester University Press, 1976), 33–67, at 33. See also Claudio Guillén, "Notes toward the Study of the Renaissance Letter," in Barbara Kiefer Lewalski, ed., *Renaissance Genres: Essays on Theory, History, and Interpretation* (Cambridge, MA: Harvard University Press, 1986), 70–101, at 71; Judith Rice Henderson, "Defining the Genre of the Letter: Juan Luis Vives' *De Conscribendis Epistolis*," *Renaissance and Reformation/Renaissance et Réforme*, n.s., 7 (1983): 89–105, at 89; as well as the collected essays in Franz Josef Worstbrock, ed., *Der Brief im Zeitalter der Renaissance*, Mitteilung der Kommission für Humanismusforschung, 9 (Weinheim: Verlag

Chemie, 1983). On the development of the humanist epistolary style, especially during the sixteenth century, see Marc Fumaroli, "Genèse de l'épistolographie classique: rhétorique humaniste de la lettre, de Pétrarque a Juste Lipse," *Revue d'histoire littéraire de la France* 78 (1978): 886–905.

17. Clough, "The Cult of Antiquity," 34–35; Mesnard, "Le commerce épistolaire," 17, 24–26.

18. Clough, "The Cult of Antiquity," 43, states that there were at least fifty-two editions of Cicero's *Epistolae ad familiares* by 1501, and he estimates that some five thousand printed copies of the text were made available every year.

19. Ibid., 38, although Clough mentions (40) that "Bruni's collection was the most sought after and one suspects that it was his that considerably moulded taste for such collections." Clough also cites (37) a miscellany of manuscripts transcribed by Agostino Santucci during his student days at the University of Padua in the 1420s, which includes letters and orations by Pier Paolo Vergerio, Gasperino Barzizza, Guarino Guarini, Poggio, and other distinguished humanists, as evidence that such collections were often used for instructional purposes.

20. Clough, "The Cult of Antiquity," 40, maintains, for example, that the fictional letter collection of Barzizza, dating from about 1420, was essentially a formulary to teach style.

21. Ibid., 41ff. For specific listings and information regarding these early editions of letter collections and related materials, see Clough's appendixes, 49–61.

22. Guillén, "Renaissance Letter," 91.

23. These late Renaissance manuals on letter writing are treated in a number of studies. On Celtis's *Tractatus de condendis epistolis* (1492), see Lewis W. Spitz, *Conrad Celtis: The German Arch-Humanist* (Cambridge, MA: Harvard University Press, 1957), 24. On Erasmus's *Opus de conscribendis epistolis* (1522), see the introduction by Jean-Claude Margolin to the critical edition of that text in *Opera omnia Desiderii Erasmi* [cited hereafter as ASD] (Amsterdam: North-Holland Publishing Company, 1971), I-2:157–203; Aloïs Gerlo, "The *Opus de Conscribendis Epistolis* of Erasmus and the Tradition of the *Ars Epistolica*," in R. R. Bolgar, ed., *Classical Influences on European Culture A.D. 500–1500* (Cambridge: Cambridge University Press, 1971), 103–14; as well as several articles by Judith Rice Henderson: "Erasmus on the Art of Letter-Writing," in James J. Murphy, ed., *Renaissance Eloquence* (Berkeley and Los Angeles: University of California Press, 1983), 331–55; "Despauterius' *Syntaxis* (1509): The Earliest Publication of Erasmus' *De conscribendis epistolis*," *Humanistica Lovaniensia*, 37 (1988): 175–210; "The Enigma of Erasmus' *Conficiendarum epistolarum formula*," *Renaissance and Reformation/Renaissance et Réforme* 25 (1989): 313–30; and "The Composition of Erasmus' *Opus*

de conscribendis epistolis: Evidence for the Growth of a Mind," in Alexander Dalzell, Charles Fantazzi, and Richard J. Schoeck, eds., *Acta Conventus Neo-Latini Torontonensis* (Binghamton, NY: Medieval and Renaissance Texts and Studies, 1991), 147–54. On Vives' *De conscribendis Epistolis* (1536), see Henderson, "Defining the Genre of the Letter: Juan Luis Vives' *De Conscribendis Epistolis,*" cited in n. 16.

24. Clough, "The Cult of Antiquity," 47–48, 59–60. On Virul, see Jozefus IJsewijn, "The Coming of Humanism to the Low Countries," in Heiko A. Oberman and Thomas A. Brady, Jr., eds., *Itinerarium Italicum: The Profile of the Italian Renaissance in the Mirror of its European Transformations* (Leiden: Brill, 1975), 193–301, at 219–20, 243–44, 300.

25. See Clough, "The Cult of Antiquity," 35, for examples of such editing by Petrarch and Pietro Bembo.

26. Guillén, "Renaissance Letter," 85: "The letter as literacy, as writing committed in fact, if not always in theory, to its own potentialities and peculiarities as writing, had tended, since at least classical times in Greece, toward fictionality. This is the essential legacy that will evolve and fructify during the Renaissance."

27. Ibid., 100.

28. Ibid., 98–99; see also Fumaroli, "Genèse," 888. For a related study pointing out the difficulties of interpreting collaborative authorships in modern autobiography, see Philippe Lejeune's "The Autobiography of Those Who Do Not Write," in his *On Autobiography,* ed. Paul John Eakin and trans. Katherine Leary (Minneapolis: University of Minnesota Press, 1989), 185–215. On the decline of the oration, see Clough, "The Cult of Antiquity," 44.

29. Guillén, "Renaissance Letter," 92–100, discusses especially the vernacular letter collections of Pietro Aretino and Fray Antonio de Guevara. See also Fumaroli, "Genèse," 894–96.

30. In a seminal study based on linguistic analysis of the letters, Walter Brecht, *Die Verfasser der Epistolae obscurorum virorum* (Strasbourg: Trübner, 1904), argued that Crotus was the author of part I and Hutten the author of part II. But later scholars attributed some of the letters to other authors; see note 36 for further discussion of the authorship problem.

31. On Crotus, see Reinhard Paul Becker, *A War of Fools: The Letters of Obscure Men; A Study of the Satire and the Satirized* (Bern/Frankfurt am Main/Las Vegas: Peter Lang, 1981), 58–60; *CE,* 1:362–63.

32. Meuthen, "Die 'Epistolae obscurorum virorum,'" 61.

33. Spitz, *The Religious Renaissance,* 130.

34. Becker, *War of Fools,* 64–66.

35. Crotus and the other authors may have also intended here an inversion, for satirical purposes, of the themes of friendship and advice that could be found in the "moral epistle," as explained by Guillén, "Renaissance Letter," 78–79: "During the Renaissance the 'moral epistle' in verse is really a footnote to the

achievement of Horace. The framework of the epistle in Horace is the friendly advice given by an older man to a younger man who is not as advanced as he is in the long road to experience and wisdom. The enveloping feeling and practice of friendship make possible the epistolary persona—the formulation of counsel without didactic pride—and, above all, the attachment of existential and concrete features to what otherwise might be abstract moral philosophy. In this tradition the relationship is normally masculine."

36. Thomas W. Best, *The Humanist Ulrich von Hutten: A Reappraisal of his Humor* (Chapel Hill: University of North Carolina Press, 1969), 6–12, maintains that clear evidence exists for Hutten's authorship of only I.1 and II.55 but agrees with Brecht and Bömer that most of the letters in part I's appendix and in part II were written by Hutten. Bömer, "Hermann von dem Busches Anteil an den *Epistolae obscurorum virorum*," in *Aus Vergangenheit und Gegenwart: Festgabe Friedrich Philippi* (Münster: Regensbergschen Buchhandlung und Buchdruckerei, 1923), 86–99, argues for Busche's authorship of I.19, I.36, and perhaps I.12 and I.39, as well as II.61 and II.62, while Hutten's friends in Bologna, such as Jakob Fuchs, probably had a hand in the writing of II.13, II.17, II.29, and II.42, which clearly were not in Hutten's style; see also Bömer, *Epistolae,* 1:101–2. Furthermore, in his "Verfasser und Drucker der *Epistolae obscurorum virorum:* Kritik einer neuen Hypothese," *Zentralblatt für Bibliothekswesen* 4 (1924): 1–12, Bömer did not completely refute Paul Merker's thesis that the Strasbourg humanist, Nicolaus Gerbelius, wrote the entire appendix to part I and fifteen letters in part II; see Merker's *Der Verfasser des Eccius Dedolatus und anderer Reformationsdialoge: mit einem Beitrag zur Verfasserfrage der Epistolae obscurorum virorum* (Halle: M. Niemeyer, 1923), 289–314. Best, *Ulrich von Hutten,* 21, concluded skeptically that "we cannot know with absolute certainty just who the authors of this satirical classic were and just which letters each wrote."

37. On Busche, see Mehl, "Hermann von dem Busche's *Vallum humanitatis* (1518): A German Defense of the Renaissance *Studia Humanitatis*," *Renaissance Quarterly,* 42 (1989): 480–506, at 482–87.

38. Nauert, "Peter of Ravenna and the 'Obscure Men' of Cologne: A Case of Pre-Reformation Controversy," in Anthony Molho and John A. Tedeschi, eds., *Renaissance Studies in Honor of Hans Baron* (DeKalb, IL: Northern Illinois University Press, 1971), 609–40, at 614.

39. Mehl, "The 1509 Dispute over Donatus: Humanist Editor as Controversialist," *Publishing History* 16 (1984): 7–19. Clough, "The Cult of Antiquity," 46, discusses the use of the printed letter, which developed into the tract and short treatise, in several scholarly controversies in Italy during the late fifteenth and early sixteenth centuries.

40. The text of the *Triumphus Capnionis* is in *UH,* 3:413–47. Best, *Ulrich*

von Hutten, 48–50, argues for Busche's authorship of the earliest manuscript version, revised slightly perhaps by Nicolaus Gerbelius, then put into final form for publication by Hutten in 1517.

41. However, Bömer's contention, in his "Verfasser und Drucker der *Epistolae obscurorum virorum,*" that the Cologne printer Heinrich von Neuss published editions of the letters in 1516 and 1517 (*UH* nos. 3 and 4), has been called into question by Jozef Benzing, "Wer ist der Drucker der 'Epistolae obscurorum virorum' (Bömer 3 und 5)?" *Das Antiquariat* 11 (1955): 57–59.

42. As cited in *UH,* suppl. 2:572 n. 34: "asinus . . . semipagani, hominis barbari, analphabeti, mercenarii correctoris impressorum, nequissimi et perditissimi nebulonis, cavillatoris et ridicularii hominis, amusi versificis, metrificis, faecis omnis sceleris et perfidiae, bonarum artium perversoris, mandatarii theologisticae facultatis."

43. Mehl, "Ortwin Gratius' *Orationes Quodlibeticae:* Humanist Apology in Scholastic Form," *Journal of Medieval and Renaissance Studies* 11 (1981): 57–69.

44. Becker, *War of Fools,* 54. See also the more recent sharp attacks against Gratius's credentials as a humanist and a poet made by Jacques Chomarat, "Les Hommes obscurs et la poésie," in Joël Lefebvre, ed., *L'Humanisme Allemand (1480–1540)* (Munich: Fink; Paris: Vrin, 1979), 261–83.

45. Becker, *War of Fools,* 85–106, 175–76.

46. Winfried Frey has recently cited the adulterous affair with Pfefferkorn's sex-starved, libertine wife as but one of a number of anti-Jewish and anti-Semitic depictions in the letters, thus rendering the *Epistolae* "an anti-Jewish pamphlet": "Die 'Epistolae obscurorum virorum'—ein antijudisches Pamphlet?" (cited in note 14). While these depictions would likely strike a late twentieth-century reader as distasteful and truly anti-Semitic, it should be kept in mind that such characterizations of the Jews probably contributed to the appeal and persuasion of the satire during its own time and in later centuries. Heiko A. Oberman, *The Roots of Anti-Semitism,* trans. James I. Porter (Philadelphia: Fortress Press, 1984), and other scholars have discussed the pervasiveness of anti-Jewish bias during the sixteenth century, including leading figures such as Erasmus and Luther.

47. Könneker, *Satire,* 110. Gossip and rumor, according to Guillén, "Renaissance Letter," 100, were also common themes in the vernacular letter collections of the sixteenth century.

48. Becker, *War of Fools,* 107–67, 177–81.

49. See note 35.

50. See, for example, the parodies in I.13, I.28, I.36, I.37, I.42, II.1, II.10, II.23, II.26, II.28, II.47, II.50, and II.61. See also Günther Mensching, "Die Kölner Spätscholastik in der Satire der *Epistolae obscurorum virorum,*" in A.

Zimmermann, ed., *Die Kölner Universität im Mittelalter: geistige Wurzeln und soziale Wirklichkeit,* Miscellania Mediaevalia, 20 (Berlin: Walter de Gruyter, 1989), 508–23.

51. Specific references are made in the letters to Erasmus's *Moriae encomium* (II.49) and Sebastian Brant's *Narrenschiff* (II.9, II.68), which served as literary models for the authors of the *Epistolae.* For example, in II.52 Hutten based a portrayal of Gratius, who sits listlessly in his library with wisk in hand to dust the unused books, on Brant's "Von unnutzen buchern" in the *Narrenschiff;* see Hahn, "Huttens Anteil," 107–8. See also Joël Lefebvre, *Les Fols et La Folie: Etude sur les genres du comique et la création littéraire en Allemagne pendant la Renaissance* (Paris: C. Klincksieck, 1968), 262–64, on Erasmus, the *Moria,* and the *Epistolae.*

52. Becker, *War of Fools,* 22–28, 131–33; Hahn, "Huttens Anteil," 91–96.

53. See also Becker, *War of Fools,* 162, who relates this characterization to the German "Meistersinger" tradition.

54. Ibid., 69–84, 169–74. See also Henderson, "Defining the Genre of the Letter," 95, on the exaggeration of the salutation.

55. *Letters of Obscure Men* (Stokes translation, 1964), 5–8. See also the salutation in II.16 for an especially exaggerated example.

56. This theme is explored further in my "Language, Class, and Mimic Satire in the Characterization of Correspondents in the *Epistolae obscurorum virorum,*" *Sixteenth Century Journal* 25 (1994): 289–305. See also Becker, *War of Fools,* 81; Meuthen, "Die 'Epistolae obscurorum virorum,'" 54; Frey, "Multum teneo," 202–3.

57. Hahn, "Huttens Anteil," 90–91.

58. Becker, *War of Fools,* 131–33; Hahn, "Huttens Anteil," 108 n. 91; Mensching, "Die Kölner Spätscholastik," 513. On the historical development of "Küchenlatein," see Paul Lehmann, *Erforschung des Mittelalters: Ausgewählte Abhandlungen und Aufsätze* (Leipzig: Karl W. Hiersemann, 1941), 46–62, as well as the related collection of essays in Peter Burke, *Küchenlatein: Sprache und Umgangssprache in der frühen Neuzeit,* trans. Robin Cackett (Berlin: Wagenbach, 1989). For a technical discussion of how the authors manipulated the orthography and syntax of the language for satirical effect, see Bengt Löfstedt, "Zur Sprache der 'Epistolae obscurorum virorum,'" *Mittellateinisches Jahrbuch* 18 (1983): 271–89.

59. Günter Hess, *Deutsche-Lateinische Narrenzunft: Studien zum Verhältnis von Volkssprache und Latinität in der satirischen Literatur des 16. Jahrhunderts* (Munich: C. H. Beck, 1971), 175–221.

60. Frey, "Multum teneo," 204.

61. See Mehl, "Hermann von dem Busche's *Vallum humanitatis,*" 498. The satire of reactionary preachers here and elsewhere in the letters was directed primarily against Hochstraten, Conrad Köllin, and other members of the Order

of Preachers (Dominicans) in Cologne who had strenuously opposed Reuchlin. See also Becker, *War of Fools,* 121–24.

62. Karl-Heinz Gerschmann, "'Antiqui—Novi—Moderni' in den 'Epistolae obscurorum virorum,'" *Archiv für Begriffsgeschichte* 11 (1967): 23–36.

63. See II.45. Meuthen, "Die 'Epistolae obcsurorum virorum,'" 66–69, explains the references to the Cologne "Copulata" in I.11, I.19, and II.9.

64. This interpretation is also pressed by Hahn, "Huttens Anteil," 98–104.

65. See also Erasmus's discussion of "perspicuitas," or "claritas," and "obscuritas" as stylistic characteristics to be pursued in humanistic letter writing, in ASD I–2:217–22. On the importance of clarity as a stylistic element in Renaissance rhetoric, see Richard A. Lanham, *The Motives of Eloquence: Literary Rhetoric in the Renaissance* (New Haven, CT, and London: Yale University Press, 1976), 20–25.

66. Theodor E. Mommsen, "Petrarch's Conception of the 'Dark Ages,'" *Speculum* 17 (1942): 226–42. See also Robert E. Proctor, *Education's Great Amnesia: Reconsidering the Humanities from Petrarch to Freud* (Bloomington and Indianapolis: Indiana University Press, 1988), for a more recent discussion of Petrarch's contribution to the new sense of historical self-awareness.

67. Könneker, *Satire,* 155–68; idem, *Die deutsche Literatur der Reformationszeit: Kommentar zu einer Epoche* (Munich: Winkler, 1975), 17–20, 84–90. See also Meuthen, "Die 'Epistolae obscurorum virorum,'" 78–79, for other examples.

68. For Rabelais, see Barbara C. Bowen, "Rabelais and the Library of Saint-Victor," in Barbara C. Bowen and Jerry C. Nash, eds., *Lapidary Inscriptions: Renaissance Essays for Donald A. Stone, Jr.* (Nicholasville, KY: French Forum, 1991), 159–70, at 164–66; Lefebvre, *Les Fols et Folie,* 164. For Fischart, see Hess, *Deutsche-Lateinische Narrenzunft,* 221–34.

69. Helmut Rogge, *Fingierte Briefe als Mittel politischer Satire* (Munich: Beck, 1966). Also related is Wilhelm Kreutz, *Die Deutschen und Ulrich von Hutten: Rezeption von Autor und Werk seit dem 16. Jahrhundert* (Munich: W. Fink, 1984).

70. Meuthen, "Die 'Epistolae obscurorum virorum,'" 76.

7
Cassandra Fedele's *Epistolae* (1488–1521): Biography as Ef-facement
Diana Robin

A Disclaimer

First of all, I want to make clear that there is some distance between my own thinking about life-writing and that of the editors of this volume, whose introduction assumes a dichotomy between life and text—as though there were some ur-reality out there that we could get our hands on, if only we were scrupulous enough or objective enough. I am in no sense worried about distinguishing between "real life" and "life-writing," nor about the danger of "threatening the life in the name of the text," nor again about "rhetoric getting in the the way of the real story." Nor am I worried about the boundaries of the genre or about what counts or does not count as autobiography. My assumptions here are—with the new theorists of autobiography, Shari Benstock, Paul John Eakin, Laurie A. Finke, Felicity Nussbaum, Caren Kaplan, James Olney, and Sidonie Smith—first, that all writing is in some sense autobiographical and, second, that the constitution of self/gender is not physiological but takes place in signification and in metaphor.[1] One further assumption: biography, as Paul de Man has argued, is not only constitutive of face, and hence of self: *prosopopeia,* maskmaking, as the ancient Greeks called biography. It is clearly privative and disfiguring as well.[2]

The "Facts" of Fedele's Life

The archival documentation for Cassandra Fedele's life is sparse. There are some parish records of where she lived; there is a copy, probably in her own hand, of her last will and testament and a contemporary's account of her funeral, but no birth or marriage records.[3] On the literary side, we have numerous fifteenth- and sixteenth-century catalogs of the lives of famous men and women and encyclopedia entries that attest to Fedele's renown as a writer, but no manuscripts of her writings other than a few individual letters of hers.[4] Her book of collected letters survives in one posthumously printed edition of her work compiled by Jacopo Filippo Tomasini, the biographer of a number of women, a client of Queen Anne of Navarre, and the Bishop of Istria. In the introduction to his edition of her letters and orations, Tomasini reports that he obtained her correspondence from three different sources. He received bundles of her letters in loose leaves from Evangelista Zagalia of Padua and Battista Fichetti of Venice; and from Alessandro d'Este, he received a bound codex of her letters.[5] During her lifetime, one pencil-slim book containing four of her letters and one oration was printed;[6] all these letters and the oration are included in Tomasini's edition of her work. We might have more reason to question the authorship of the volume if we did not have another of Tomasini's edited works to compare it with—his edition of the collected letters of Fedele's contemporary and compatriot, Laura Cereta.[7] His edition of Cereta's correspondence is an impeccable work of scholarship, faithfully compiled from two complete manuscripts of her letters.[8] While we should keep in mind that Fedele's collected letters are an editor's compilation, this should not be a deterrent to our consideration of the *Epistolae* as a woman's work any more than it is in the case of the autobiography of the fifteenth-century mystic Margery Kempe.

Other than the year of her death, 1558, there is almost no fact about Fedele's life that is not disputed. She is supposed to have been born in 1465 in Venice, but some sources record her birth date as 1456.[9] Respectful of the dictates of her contemporary Baldesar Castiglione, Fedele took care to represent her family as coming from a courtly milieu but who the Fedeles really were remains a mystery. They were not members of the Venetian patriciate, though according to Cassandra, the Fedeles were courtiers of the Visconti lords in Milan before emigrating to Venice. Other than the statement by the seventeenth-century Venetian historian Sansovino that Fedele's father, Angelo Fedele, was "respected by the members of the Venetian patriciate"—indicating that Angelo may at one time or another have been a client of some members of the nobility, we have no information about the family's economic status.[10] In her twenties, Fedele represented herself in her letters as the object of the zealous attentions of the nobility and even of royalty. She received invitations to lecture from the Venetian Doge Marco Barbarigo and from Queen Isabella and King Ferdinand of Spain, who sought permission from the Venetian republic to bring her to their court in Castile. We do not know the year in which she married, though it is believed that she was already thirty-three or thirty-four, late in life for a fifteenth-century Italian woman. We do know that her physician husband, Gian-Maria Mapelli, died about twenty-two years after they married, in 1520 or 1521. After his death, Fedele appears to have moved in with her sister's family, unable to find work and dependent on her younger siblings and nephews for the most minimal kind of support. Through the intervention of Pope Paul III, Fedele was appointed prioress of the orphanage San Domenico di Castello in Venice at the age of eighty-two, where she lived until her death.[11]

Letters and the Courtly Milieu

By the last quarter of the fifteenth century in Italy, a few women had joined the almost solely male ranks of humanist patrons, scholars, and writers. Almost all the women who became active as humanists were members of four princely families whose courts in the Renaissance were centers of literary and artistic activity: the Gonzaga of Mantua, the Este of Ferrara, the Sforza of Milan, and the Aragonese rulers of Naples. Only two women outside this group, Laura Cereta (born 1469 in Brescia) and Cassandra Fedele, whose families belonged to the urban professional class, managed to achieve any real eminence as humanist writers in the later fifteenth century.[12]

Cereta and Fedele both left sizable letterbooks, the bound collections of personal letters and epistolary treatises, in Latin, that were the stock in trade of the humanists. No two letter collections could differ much more from one another than do the Cereta and Fedele epistolaries. Cereta's *Epistolae* do not fall into the genre of courtly patronage letters as do most fifteenth-century humanist letterbooks. Her seventy-two published letters address not patrons, but family members and friends: her husband, sister, mother, father, brothers, and other friends. Her book is a local affair; its subject matter is not for the most part taken up with scholarship and learned topics, but with everyday life—with so-called women's stories: descriptions of her childhood nurse, a walk on the family estate with her mother, the duties of a wife and daughter, the sufferings of her husband during his last illness, and the like.[13] Fedele's letters, on the other hand, are those of the typical male client, entreating or expressing gratitude to his patrons. In Fedele's subject matter and her choice of correspondents, there is little that distinguishes her book as the work of a woman. The book contains 123 letters, many addressed to her by well-known scholars and members of the nobility; also included in her *epistolario* are a number of poems of praise written by admiring friends about her.[14] Her letterbook forms a kind of artist's portfolio, a testimonial of her educational experience and connections, filled with samples of her work and flattering letters about her writings by prominent scholars and royalty.

Fedele's published correspondence resembles the typical humanist "collected letters," *epistolario,* or *epistolae familiares* of the sort that Leonardo Bruni, Poggio Bracciolini, Marcantonio Sabellico, Enea Silvio Piccolomini (Pope Pius II), Pier Candido Decembrio, Francesco Filelfo, and Angelo Poliziano first circulated and eventually published. Such letter collections were the most popular form of autobiography in the Renaissance.[15] These courtly letterbooks, Fedele's included, appealed to the same audience as did the courtesy books of the period, the quintessential example of which is Baldesar Castiglione's *The Book of the Courtier*. Both sorts of books were, at least in part, books of courtly etiquette that told their readers how to speak and write in different circumstances and how to behave. Filelfo, whose collected letters outsold any other work of its kind to be printed before 1520, had corresponded with the dukes of Milan, Ferrara, and Urbino, and the kings of Naples and France.[16] The royalty Fedele wrote to included every Italian queen, duchess, and marquise listed in Castiglione's register of model ladies in the *Courtier*. Fedele wrote to Queen Isabella of Spain (whom Castiglione served as papal nuncio in 1524), the queen of Hungary and the queen's sister Eleanora, and the duchess of Ferrara, whose eminent daughters were Isabella and Beatrice d'Este, marquise of Mantua and duchess of Milan, respectively. In Florence, Fedele was associated with the patronage circle of Lorenzo de' Medici, Poliziano, and Ficino. Unlike Cereta, Fedele included no family members (except one learned brother) among her correspondents, nor are her letters about domestic matters.[17]

What is very different from male humanist letterbooks about Fedele's *Epistolae* is her idiosyncratic Latin style and the construction, both in her letters and those of her admirers, of a self that is neither fully female nor male in any conventional sense; yet the self that Fedele offers her readers is, as I will demonstrate, saturated with sexuality and preconceptions about gender.[18]

Because of the number of different authors, voices, and subjectivities represented in Fedele's letter collection, the image of self that emerges here is a composite of sorts—a mosaic assembled from disparate pieces. In both Fedele's letters to her friends and those of her friends written to her, three major groups of themes that define and delimit her sexuality and persona emerge: (1) those privileging chastity, the purity of body, and the absence of sexual knowledge over learning and wisdom; (2) themes of lack, privation, deficiency, and diminution; and (3) the theme of transsexuality or hermaphroditism: Fedele's tendency, that is, to assume attributes the culture generally ascribed to males, such as *virtus* (manhood) and *gravitas* (authority), while not for a moment letting go of her female side, her *virginitas*.

Writing, Femininity, and Chastity

The attribute of chastity was usually coupled with eloquence as a precautionary measure in humanists' praises of female writers and scholars.[19] How else could women writers be flatteringly represented in a courtly milieu where the categories "woman" and "writer" were supposed to be mutually exclusive? Women who wrote and read Latin were thought deviant and were seen as a threat to society, whether in the private or public domain. In Verona, anonymous pamphleteers accused the unmarried Isotta Nogarola, the prolific writer of a generation earlier than Fedele, of criminal sexual acts.[20] In Florence, the otherwise reasonable chancellor of the republic, Leonardo Bruni, warned that "rhetoric in all its forms [was and should remain] absolutely outside the province of woman."[21] The prominent humanist and Venetian statesman Francesco Barbaro published the pronouncement that "not only the [bare] arms but indeed also the speech of a woman should never be made public."[22] A century after Bruni and Barbaro, the Mantuan-born Miss Manners of the Italian courts, Baldesar Castiglione, hardly ever allowed the ladies in his *Courtier* to open their mouths except to yawn.

But the connection between writing and sex was an old trope whose usage went all the way back to antiquity. In Latin poetry, from the first century B.C. to the Renaissance—from Catullus to Panormita—writing and reading had always been metaphors for sexual knowledge and erotic stimulation.[23] The Latin words for writing tools, book, and scroll—

stilus, calumus, volumen, libellus—were in Roman elegy and later Latin verse conventional images for representing both male and female genitalia. Accordingly, any mention of Fedele's writing, her pen, or her literary achievements in her book of letters is invariably accompanied—in an almost ticlike fashion—by praise for her virginity.

The elaborate letter praising Fedele that Poliziano sent her after their first meeting in Venice in 1491 honors Fedele's erudition and mastery of philosophy, but at the same time returns repeatedly to the theme of her virginity and her adolescence.[24] A letter in Fedele's letterbook from a woman whom Castiglione cites in the *Courtier* as his courtly ideal, the duchess of Ferrara, Eleanora of Aragon, projects a similar image of Fedele's eloquence, her intellectual brilliance, and, at the same time, her extreme youth and sexual innocence. Using various forms of the Latin *virgo,* a word that connotes youth, innocence, and chastity in a woman, Eleanora repeatedly lauds her young client. She is adorned, writes Eleanora, by the "shining purity of her illustrious maidenhood." What is more, she is both a "pure virgin" and a girl deserving of praise for her "virginal demeanor" and the "honorable nature of her life." Fedele is also a marvel for her "tender age" and an "ornament to our sex," Eleanora comments.[25] In eloquence, Eleanora compares her to Plato rather than the famous ancient women poets—Corinna, Sulpicia, Sappho—as does Poliziano in his letter to Fedele. Eleanora also compares Fedele to a garden, a common metaphor for the properly domesticated and controlled female body in antiquity and the Renaissance. Like a well-ordered arrangement in a garden of flowers and fruit trees, Eleanora writes, Cassandra represents the best mixture of nature at its freshest and most luxuriant with careful training and cultivation:

> We have read your sweet letter, which evinces the learning and eloquence not of a young girl, but rather an elderly man and a seasoned orator as well. For the letter is graced not only with elegant phrases but also with serious observations, which are all the more striking coupled with the sincerity of your maidenly youth. Just as we generally praise those gardens where lilies, violets, roses, and various kinds of apples all have their own proper places and delight us with the variety of their beauty, fragrance, and taste, so we admire and esteem you, who are an innocent maiden, yet distinguished and adorned with a noble character and extraordinary eloquence, and we think you worthy of every honor. Blessed and fortunate are you who

are so endowed with heavenly gifts and divine grace that you, at so tender an age, do such honor to our sex. From those who gave suck to you, you partook of sweet milk and that marvelous honey which they say the bees dripped, drop by drop, onto Plato's lips while he slept.[26]

The Shrinkage of the Female Self

The ideal courtly lady in Castiglione's *Courtier* is described, in sharp contrast to the ideal male courtier, by what she is not. Negatives and privatives dominate Castiglione's discourse on the female courtier and his prescriptions for her. She should not be arrogant, coy, vain, contentious, licentious, prolix, bawdy of speech, overly familiar, gossipy, insolent, scurrilous. She should not move too much when she dances, or sing and play too loudly when she makes music.[27]

Likewise, to the end that her power—verbal, intellectual, and dialectical—should not appear menacing or lacking in decorum, Fedele uses the privative force of diminutives to represent her own lack, her own insufficiency—of talent, mind, learning, and work. She is merely an *audacula*, "a pushy little woman," she constantly reassures her readers. Diminutives—the use of the suffixes *-olus, -ulus,* or *-culus* to connote the minuscule—are unusual in both classical and Renaissance Latin, and they suggest in Fedele's letters, where they typify her style, a comic tone or certainly a degree of irony. Her letters, she confesses, are only "little notes" (*literulae*), her words are "little words" (*voculis*), and her talent is a small one (*ingeniolum*). She herself is only a little manlet in a woman's skin (*homuncula*), a "little client" (*servula* [in the language of patronage]), a "small maiden" (*virguncula*), and a "very small female" (*femella* [a word attested only in Catullus]).[28] Such diminutives not only diminish and circumscribe her attributes and abilities, they lay further emphasis on her youth and thus her sexual inexperience. Even the frequent compliment paid her—that she is a jewel or ornament to her city, her country, and her sex (*decus, ornamentum*)—is diminishing of her significance and substance, reducing her to that which is superfluous, otiose, trivial, and decorative.[29]

The opening letter in Cassandra's *Epistolae* to Eleanora of Aragon's son-in-law, Gianfrancesco Gonzaga, the lord of Mantua, is thematic for the whole letterbook in the sense that it articulates her rationale for deciding to become a writer and introduces her readers to the persona she assumes throughout her book. This undated letter appears to have been written in or soon after 1489, when Gianfrancesco was appointed commander in chief of the Venetian army, because the letter praises his military prowess at length. Though Gianfrancesco would then have been only twenty-three and Cassandra twenty-four, she addresses him with exaggerated deference, as though he were much older. Her Castiglionian lack, emptiness, and nullity are repeatedly contrasted to his sufficiency of body and mind. The contrast is especially stark in Latin because of the greater flexibility of word order permitted in that language. The word that Fedele uses to downgrade herself—*virguncula* (little maiden)—directly follows her aggrandizing of Gianfrancesco as *tantum principem* (such a great prince). While she is moved by the fullness of Gianfrancesco's "clemency and goodness towards everyone," she is also embarrassed by the sheer deficiency of her own nature. And while her "little letters" are of "little or no importance," she is conscious that they will be delivered to a man of great magnitude and excellence:

> It should by no means seem strange, invincible prince, if I should take so great and difficult a burden on my shoulders, to the end that I have not hesitated in the least to write my little letters [*literulas*] to you, although at first being very much afraid, I—a very young girl [*virguncula*], writing to so great a prince—shied away from this task of writing. But then I was moved by your mercy and goodness toward everyone, which persuaded me, despite the meagerness of my talent, to write. Then also from the beginning of my labors, when I relinquished womanly tasks [*cultu foemineo relictu*], since I attended to those things which pertain not only to honor in this briefest of lives, but also to my enjoyment of the majesty of God, I considered that immortal praise would follow with me among men. Therefore I have striven because of my manly [*virili*], burning and incredible (though I hope not improper) desire for the study of the liberal arts, so that my name may be celebrated in the talk of the most excellent men. Therefore I had proposed that Platonic saying: that is, either to live beautifully or to die beautifully. This I shall believe I have done when my little letters, even if they are of little importance and learning, are delivered to the excellence and greatness of so great a man. For as it is agreed by all good men, this greatness of fortune and mind is so endowed with those things which I have called the good, that they affirm unanimously that no one is more kind, more just, or more

distinguished than you. Not even in inflicting injury. For there is such great admiration for your genius in every area—in your military prudence, in the administration of your power, and in your justice, that everyone follows and embraces you, not only with love but with a kind of veneration. What more should I wish to say about your physical strength? That you exceed Achilles in dexterity, Paris in handsomeness? Should I omit your most noble lineage, your most famous deeds, since they demand another speaker and another occasion, since my ability scarcely is up to such a task, needless to say? It is the very breadth of your gifts that makes the orator's task so very difficult and serious. Therefore I entrust and commend myself, O most illustrious prince, and all my efforts to your magnanimity.[30]

Fedele's letters to the sister of Eleanora of Aragon, Queen Beatrice of Hungary, it should be noted, express her lack and diminution vis-à-vis the queen in much the same way she had in her letters to Gianfrancesco. Here, too, Fedele apologizes for her "little letters," her "little voice," and her "small talent" (*literulis, voculis, ingenioli*):

Even if it has been my aim to suit something of my previous days' letters to your generous spirit, since it's not possible for me to make known to you, in my small voice [*voculis meis*], my obedient heart, face to face in your presence, still I have not ceased to show you in these little letters my singular loyalty and homage to you; and even if it might seem that I would be frightened away from writing you more because of the meagerness of my small talent, the dissonant sound of my words, and the inappropriateness of my thoughts than from the fear that I might hurt your erudite ears with my inelegant words or offend the magnitude of your mind so tried and tested in prudence, wisdom and in conduct of affairs, still the loftiness of your spirit has such an effect that I don't shy away from scribbling these things to you....[31]

In a pair of letters Fedele writes to Eleanora's son-in-law and other daughter, the duke and duchess of Milan, Lodovico (Il Moro) Sforza and Beatrice d'Este, congratulating each of them on the birth of their first son, we find the same diminution of self, the same rhetoric of shrinkage, the same erasure of whole parts of the self:

[Cassandra to Ludovico] By no part of your bounty to me, invincible Prince, have I been induced to be capable of responding to your magnanimity, because of the enormity of which my meager talent would even seem to be shy about giving thanks, now that the very distinguished Senate has thought it right to commend me so kindly (and much more richly than my small virtue deserves), and by Hercules, now that your commendation has given me the greatest honor. For it must be thought the greatest tribute that a little maiden such as myself should praised by such a great prince . . . [32]

[Cassandra to Beatrice d'Este] I hope you will not judge that I am an overly bold little girl for not hesitating to write to you, who are endowed with justice, fortitude, beauty, and innumerable other heroic qualities.[33]

The Female Body as "Corpus Debile"

Another trope regarding woman found in Renaissance writers from Boccaccio to Castiglione is the general physical insufficiency and feebleness of the female body (*corpus debile*). Sickness, ill health, and lack of male strength and robustness further define the female voice, further diminish the female sex as one marked by deficiency, as castrated. Fedele's feeble and ailing constitution is the subject of her letter to the queen of Hungary (Eleanora's sister Beatrice) of 12 October 1497. Fedele here explains that she is severely hampered in her ability to write a proper letter by "her infirm mind, her frail body, and trembling hand." She promises the queen that if she ever does recover, she will make up for her lack of length in the future:

> Although I have wanted to write to your highness for a long time now, most holy Queen, the ill health that has afflicted me has deterred me from the duty of writing; nor am I in fact so strong in body and mind at this time that I should be writing to you, who are endowed with such graces—were I not afraid that otherwise I should seem either neglectful or forgetful. For when Sigismondo, a man of the highest integrity, summoned me, he so inflamed me with love for you that—though I was still feeling somewhat sluggish from this chronic illness—I had to write, as much as my limited physical strength would allow, so that if I had already lost my grace in writing and had none, still I would leave a testimony of my thoughts and devotion towards

you.... But now with a weak mind, a frail body, and a trembling right hand, I am not strong enough to write any more. When I am well, if I ever am, I shall repair this brevity with many long letters. You in the meantime, most happy Queen, may you be well and blessed, and may you know that I, your little servant, have been dedicated and devoted to you for a long time now.[34]

Hermaphroditic Themes

The third major theme that emerges in Fedele's letters concerns the ambiguity surrounding her sexuality and confusion about her gender. As we suggested above, writing and femininity were not considered compatible in the early Renaissance (Boccaccio, Bruni, Barbaro, Castiglione). Is Fedele a man or a woman, then? In a letter to the duke of Milan, Fedele herself suggests that certain Venetians envy her because she is a "new man," the Roman term for men prominent in the state who were not of patrician rank: "nonnullos mortales invidere novitati meae," she writes.[35]

The layout of the opening two pages of her letterbook, facing one another in the printed edition, foregrounds the problem of Fedele's sexuality. Julius Caesar Scaliger's epigram dedicated to Fedele that faces the first page of Tomasini's edition of the *Epistolae* epitomizes the problem of her sexual identity for her contemporaries:

> If woman can neither explore the truth that lies hidden in the bosom and mind of God nor bring forth from the lofty heavens the divine spirit in nature, then you never were a woman; but you were a man.[36]

Adjacent to the page that contains the Scaliger epigram is a letter from Fedele stating that she has given up women's work (*cultu foemineo relicto*) to devote herself to the male pursuits of philosophy and the study of literature. Remarking on Fedele's abandonment of "womanly" knitting needles to take up the "manly" pen, Poliziano makes the same point in a letter addressed to her after their first meeting in 1491. In this letter, Poliziano hails Fedele suggestively with the same gender-confounding epithets that Virgil applies to his cross-dressing heroine Camilla. In Poliziano's text, the virgin Cassandra/Camilla becomes something of more value than a mere woman. She becomes an abstraction; she is the "glory" and "honor" of Italy (*decus Italiae virgo*).[37]

The Latin word *virtus* (*vir-tus:* literally, *man-hood*), moreover, a word evocative of the masculine attributes of courage, fortitude, and so on—traits necessary both in warfare and sexual pursuits in Latin literature—is provocatively applied to Fedele in a letter addressed to her by Lodovico Sforza. The duke's note to Fedele, dated 12 April 1493, is suitably avuncular and patronal in tone. By his patronage of her, he makes clear that he means to advertise both his virtue and hers, which (he tells her) is the most precious possession that she as a member of the "female sex" can have. And *virtus* (a word he repeats five times in this note) is the one subject the duke can't seem to get off his mind in this conversation with Fedele. What is striking about this letter is the duke's praise of Fedele—who, according to other friends, was all intellect, eloquence, and learning—not for her erudition or her writings, but for her moral virtue (*morali disciplina*). And Lodovico makes clear that he does not mean just womanish *virginitas* when he uses the word *virtus;* he means, he tells her, that habit (read: male habit) of character that enables us to love even our enemies. This dictum, found in both the Greeks and the gospels, he reminds Fedele, is the "true meaning of virtue."[38]

Ef-facement

If we can generalize, then, from the representation of Cassandra Fedele's persona in her *Epistolae,* a woman humanist's autobiography could be privative. It could be, according to the prescription of Castiglione and the description of de Man, an ef-facement, a denial of face rather than a "face-making" (*prosopopeia*). It might be privative, that is, in a way that was not the case in male patronage letterbooks, such as those of, say, Poggio, Filelfo, Decembrio, Bruni, or Poliziano, where the relational self that emerges is based on an enhanced sense of worth. Unlike the stock feminine traits Laura Cereta assumes in her letterbook, in Fedele's letters we have seen a constant erasure of what the culture valued as feminine, sexual, and Other. This kind of erasure of Self is not found in the autobiographical letterbooks of any of her male contemporaries that I know of. I have argued in this chapter that the composite image of Fedele we get in the *Epistolae* is marked throughout by the language of lack, deficiency, privation, and diminution. Fedele, by virtue of her own language about herself, either lacks or represents to a lesser degree the qualities of her male correspondents. Her personal characteristics have been reduced to the standard specifications of the woman scholar-writer:

she has become not a woman but a simulacrum of virginity and eloquence, and of youth and transsexual virtue. Though she became one of the most celebrated women of her time, Fedele has situated herself, in her book of letters, outside the culture and cult of individuality still thought to be the hallmark of her age.

NOTES

An earlier version of this paper was presented at the Sixteenth Century Studies Conference in St. Louis, Missouri, on 19 October 1990. I would like to thank the editors of the volume, Tom Mayer and Daniel Woolf, and the anonymous readers of the University of Michigan Press for their helpful comments and suggestions.

1. Shari Benstock, ed., *The Private Self: The Theory and Practice of Women's Autobiographical Writings* (Chapel Hill: University of North Carolina Press, 1988); Paul John Eakin, *Fictions in Autobiography: Studies in the Art of Self-Invention* (Princeton, NJ: Princeton University Press, 1985); Laurie A. Finke, *Feminist Theory, Women's Writing* (Ithaca, NY: Cornell University Press, 1992); Felicity Nussbaum, "Eighteenth-Century Women's Autobiographical Commonplaces," in Benstock, *The Private Self*, 147–76; James Olney, *Metaphors of Self: The Meaning of Autobiography* (Princeton, NJ: Princeton University Press, 1972); Sidonie Smith, *A Poetics of Women's Autobiography: Marginality and the Fictions of Self-Representation* (Bloomington: Indiana University Press, 1987); Sidonie Smith and Julia Watson, *De/Colonizing the Subject: The Politics of Gender in Women's Autobiography* (Minneapolis: University of Minnesota Press, 1992).

2. Paul de Man, "Autobiography as De-facement," *Modern Language Notes* 94 (1979): 919–30.

3. The only full-length study of Fedele that deals with archival sources is Cesira Cavazzana, "Cassandra Fedele erudita Veneziana del rinascimento," *Ateneo Veneto* 29 (1906), 2:73–91, 249–75, 361–97; see also (the very rare) Maria Petrettini, *Vita di Cassandra Fedele* (Venice: Giuseppe Grimaldo, 1852). On Fedele manuscripts, see also Adriano Capelli, "Cassandra Fedele in relazione con Lodovico Il Moro," *Archivio Storico Lombardo* 3.4 (1895): 387–91; Henry Simonsfeld, "Zur Geschichte der Cassandra Fedele," in *Studien zur Literaturgeschichte, Michael Bernays Gewidmet* (Hamburg: Leopold Voss, 1893). See also Giovanni Pesenti, "Lettere inedite del Poliziano," *Athenaeum* 3 (1915): 284–304; and idem, "Alessandra Scala, una figurina della Rinacenza fiorentina," *Giornale Storico della Letteratura Italiana* 85 (1925): 241–267.

4. *Vitae* of Cassandra Fedele were published in the following early printed

biographical dictionaries: Giacomo Alberici, *Catalogo breve degli illustri et famosi scrittori venetiani* (Bologna: G. Rossi, 1605); Jacopo Filippo Bergamo (alias J. F. Foresti), *Liber de claris scelestisque mulieribus* (Ferrara: n.p., 1497); Giuseppe Betussi, *Libro di M. Gio. Boccaccio delle Donne Illustri Tradotto per Messer Giuseppe Betussi* (Venice: n.p., 1545); Ioannis Baptista Egnatius, *De Exemplis Illustrium Virorum Venetae Civitatis atque aliarum gentium* (Venice: Aldine Press, 1554); Battista Fregosa (alias Campofregosa, alias Baptista Fulgosius), *Factorum Dictorumque Memorabilium Libri IX.* (Venice, 1483; reprint, with a supplement by Justo Gaillardo Campo, Paris: P. Cavellat, 1578); Jean Tixier de Ravisius, *De memorabilibus et claris mulieribus aliquot diversorum scriptorum opera* (Paris: S. Colin, 1521); Iacopo Filippo Tomasini, *Elogia Literis et Sapientia Illustrium ad vivum expressis imaginibus exornata* (Padua: S. Sardi, 1644).

    5. *Epistolae et orationes,* ed. Jacopo Filippo Tomasini (Padua: Franciscus Bolzetta, 1636), 44–46.

    6. Cassandra Fedele, *Oratio pro Bertuccio Lamberto* (Nuremberg: Peter Wagner, 1489).

    7. *Laurae Ceretae Epistolae,* ed. Jacopo Filippo Tomasini (Padua: Sebastiano Sardi, 1640). On Laura Cereta, the essential work is Albert Rabil, Jr., *Laura Cereta: Quattrocento Humanist* (Binghamton, NY: Medieval and Renaissance Texts and Studies, 1981); see also Ottavio Rossi, *Elogi historici di bresciani illustri* (Brescia: Bartolomeo Fontana, 1620), 196–200, 226–28; Girolamo Tiraboschi, *Storia della letteratura italiana* (Milan, 1833), 3.169; M. Palma, "Laura Cereta" in *Dizionario biografico degli italiani* (Rome, 1960–), 729–30; and E. Caccia, *Storia di Brescia, 2: La Dominazione Veneta (1426–1575),* promessa e diretta da Giovanni Treccani degli Alfieri (Brescia: Morcelliana, 1963), 486, 494–96.

    8. Vatican City, Cod. Vat. lat. 3176; and Venice, Cod. Ven. Marc. 4186.

    9. Cavazzana, "Cassandra Fedele," 80.

    10. Ibid.

    11. Ibid.

    12. On women humanists in Italy, see Margaret L. King, "Thwarted Ambitions: Six Learned Women of the Italian Renaissance," *Soundings: An Interdisciplinary Journal* 59.3 (1976): 280–305; Patricia H. Labalme, ed., *Beyond Their Sex: Learned Women of the European Past* (New York: New York University Press, 1980); Margaret L. King, "Book-Lined Cells: Women and Humanism in the Early Italian Renaissance," in Patricia H. Labalme, ed., *Beyond Their Sex: Learned Women of the European Past* (New York: New York University Press, 1980), 66–90; Margaret L. King and A. Rabil, eds., *Her Immaculate Hand: Selected Works By and About the Women Humanists of Quattrocento Italy* (Binghamton, NY: Medieval and Renaissance Texts and Studies, 1983); Margaret L. King, *Women of the Renaissance* (Chicago: University of Chicago Press,

1991). See also Anthony Grafton and Lisa Jardine, "Women Humanists: Education for What?" in their *From Humanism to the Humanities: Education and the Liberal Arts in Fifteenth- and Sixteenth Century Europe* (London: Duckworth, 1986), 29–57.

13. See above, note 7. My own translation of Cereta's *Epistolae* is forthcoming in 1995.

14. See above, notes 3 and 5. My translation of Fedele's *Complete Letters and Orations (Epistolae et Orationes)* is forthcoming.

15. On humanist letters as autobiography, see Diana Robin, *Filelfo in Milan: Writings, 1451–1477* (Princeton, NJ: Princeton University Press, 1991). On early modern female autobiography, see Mary Beth Rose, "Gender, Genre, and History: Seventeenth-Century English Women and the Art of Autobiography," in Mary Beth Rose, ed., *Women in the Middle Ages and the Renaissance: Literary and Historical Perspectives* (Syracuse, NY: Syracuse University Press, 1986), 245–78; Estelle Jelinek, *The Tradition of Women's Autobiography: From Antiquity to the Present* (Boston: Twayne, 1986); and Domna C. Stanton, *The Female Autograph* (New York: New York Literary Forum, 1984); see also note 1.

16. See Robin, *Filelfo in Milan*.

17. See above, notes 3 and 5.

18. Cf. King, "Book-lined Cells," 79.

19. Ibid., 77–79.

20. Ibid., 76.

21. Ibid., 77.

22. Ann Rosalind Jones, "City Women and Their Audiences," in M. W. Ferguson, M. Quilligan, and N. Vickers, eds., *Rewriting the Renaissance: The Discourses of Sexual Difference in Early Modern Europe* (Chicago: University of Chicago Press, 1986), 300; King and Rabil, *Her Immaculate Hand*, 13.

23. R. A. B. Mynors, ed., *C. Valerii Catulli Carmina* (Oxford: Clarendon Press, 1958); see, for example, Cat. 16.5–9: "nam castum esse decet pium poetam / ipsum, versiculos nihil necesse est; / qui tum denique habent salem ac leporem, / si sunt molliculi ac parum pudiculi / et quod pruriat incitare possunt..." [A good poet should be pure and upright himself, but his little poems don't have to be that way at all. If his verses are erotic and not exactly clean, and if they have the power to arouse prurient desires, then they do at long last possess wit and charm...] (my translation). See also the prologue to Antonio Beccadelli, *L'Ermafrodito,* ed. and trans. Jole Tognelli (Rome: Avanzini e Torraca, 1968).

24. Fedele, *Epistolae,* letter 101, pp. 155–58.

25. Fedele, *Epistolae,* letter 105, p. 162.

26. Fedele, *Epistolae,* letter 105, pp. 161–62: "Legimus tuas literas, Cassandra, suavissimas, quae profecto non adolescentis feminae sed veri senis eiusdemque gravissimi oratoris doctrinam eloquentiamque redolent. Sunt enim refertae cum verborum elegantia, tum gravitate sententiarum. Sunt etiam tuae

candore Virginitatis illustratae; nos ut laudare solemus hortos eos, in quibus lilia, violae, rosae, variaque pomorum genera suis sunt locis collocata. Quae pulchritudinis, odoris, saporis etiam varietate delectant, sic te Virginem castam ingenuis moribus singulari eloquentia egregiis virtutibus praeditam decoratamque et admiramur et diligimus et omni dignam laude censemus. Beata faelixque es quae caelesti ac divino munere usque adeo repleris et gratia ut tam tenera aetate sexui nostro sis decori. Ex iis, quae te lactaverunt uberibus, dulce suxisti lac, et illud praeclarum mel quod ferunt Apes Platonis labellis, dum in somnis esset, sensim instillasse . . ."

27. Baldesar Castiglione, *The Book of the Courtier,* trans. Charles S. Singleton (Garden City, NY: Anchor Books/Doubleday, 1959), 205–11.

28. Catullus, 55.7.

29. See, for example, Angelo Poliziano's letter eulogizing Fedele: Latin text in Fedele, *Epistolae,* 205–11; English translation in King and Rabil, *Her Immaculate Hand,* 126–27.

30. Fedele, *Epistolae,* letter 1, pp. 1–3: "Minime cuiquam, invicte Princeps, mirum videri debet, si tam magnum ac perdifficile humeris meis onus sumpserim, ut meas ad te exarare literulas haud dubitarim. Cum hoc scribendi officium ad tantum Principem ego Virguncula primo extimescens perhorruerim. Deinde tua in omnes clementia bonitate[que] mota sum, quae mei ingenii exilitatem ad scribendum suadet; tum etiam cum ab initio meorum laborum, cultu foemineo relicto, ad ea, quae non tantum ad huius brevissimae vitae honorem pertinent, sed Divinae Maiestatis praesentia fruendam me ipsam contuli, immortalem laudem consecuturam inter homines mecum reputavi. Haec igitur liberalibus studiis pro virili mea consequenda enitar, ardeoque cupiditate incredibili (neque ut arbitror improbanda) ut nostrum nomen per praestantissimorum ora celebretur. Itaque illud Platonicum exequi proposueram, quod est, 'Aut pulchre vivere, aut pulchre mori.' Hoc ipsum me nactam censebo cum meae quidem literulae, etsi parvi sint momenti ac doctrinae, ad tanti viri magnitudinem atque excellentiam reddantur. Ipsa enim, ut omnibus constat et animi bonis et fortunae referta ac praedita adeo est, ut his quae dixi bona, liberatiorem, probiorem, atque praeclariorem te neminem omnes uno ore affirment. Nec inuria quidem. Nam tui ingenii tanta omni in re est admiratio, in re militari prudentia, in administratione imperii Iustitia, ut omnes te non modo amore prosequamur atque amplectantur, sed quadam veneratione existimant. Quid si de tui corporis viribus plura in medium afferre vellem? Nonne dexteritate Achillem, robore Herculem, formositate Paridem antecellis? Omittam quoque tui nobilissimum genus eorumque praeclarissima facinora, cum alium laudatorem et locum postulent. Cui mei ingenii vires vix satis sint perlibare, nedum recensere. Est enim eorum tam latus campus ut cuilibet oratori cel maximo perdifficile ac gravissimum sit. Me igitur illustrissime Princeps, meosque omnes tuae animi magnitudini commendo atque trado."

31. Fedele, *Epistolae,* letter 21, pp. 33–35: "Etsi superioribus ante diebus mearum aliquid literarum ad tuam animi amplitudinem destinavi, tamen cum postquam tua coram praesentia meum in te obsequentissimum animum voculis meis declarare non datur, meam in te singularem observantiam fidem[que] significandam literulis his non destiti; tametsi ex ingenioli mei parvitate, ac incongrua meorum verborum oratione, atque sententiarum improprietate a scribendi officio potius deterreri viderer, qua tuam animi magnitudinem prudentia, sapientia, et multorum usu rerum expertam et eruditissimas aures tuas inornatis verbis laederem atque obtunderem: tua tamen animi celsitudo effecit, ut haec ad te exaranda non exhorruerim."

32. Fedele, *Epistolae,* letter 55, pp. 81–83: "Nulla ex parte tuorum in me meritorum, Invictissime Princeps, tuae Amplitudini respondere me posse maceror, quorum magnitudine mea quidem ingenii exilitas gratias agere diffidere videatur. Cum tam perhumane, atque multo uberius quam virtus exigua mea exigat huic, praeclarissimus Senatus me commendare non est dedignatus, tuaque aedepol commendatio plurimum meo conduxit honori. Nam me Virgunculam a tanto Principe laudari plurimi faciundum est..."

33. Fedele, *Epistolae,* letter 57, pp. 84–85: "Non ergo audaculam me iudices homunculam ad te Principem iustitia, fortitudine, venustate, heroicisque innumeris dotibus ornatam scribere haud dubitasse."

34. Fedele, *Epistolae,* letter 71, pp. 91–101: "Cupientem me ad amplitudinem tuam iam diu scribere, sacratissima Regina, valetudo gravis qua tandiu laboravi a scribendi officio deterruit, nec nunc quidem ita corpore ac animo firma sum, ut ad te tantis ornamentis praeditam scribere debeam, nisi verear, ne vel mei immemor, aut negligens videar. Nam cum ad me Sigismundus vir integerrimus accesserit, ita me amore tui quidem prius, sed tamen morbo ipso diuturno nescio quo modo ad omnia torpentem inflammavit, ut statuerim, quantum per tenues corporis vires liceret aliquo modo esse scribendum, ut si scribendo gratiam tam diu perdidi, nullamque haberem, testatum tamen apud te relinquerem animum devotionemque in te meam... Sed iam haec imbecillo animo, infirmo corpore ac trementi dextra plusquam satis plura scribere non valeo. Cum convaluero, si hoc unquam erit, brevitatem hanc et crebris et prolixis literis resarciam. Tu interea foelicissima Regina feliciter valeas, me ut servulam tibi deditissimam, ac tibi iam diu dicatam commendatam habeas..."

35. Fedele, *Epistolae,* letter 55, pp. 81–83.

36. Fedele, *Epistolae,* p. i:
Indagere valet nullum si foemina verum,
Quod lateat gremio, consilioque Dei,
Nec Genium celso naturae educere caeli:
Nunquam tu fueris foemina, sed vir eras.

37. *Aeneid,* 11.508–9; Fedele, *Epistolae,* letter 101, p. 155.

38. Fedele, *Epistolae,* letter 56, pp. 83–84.

8

A Sticking-Plaster Saint?
Autobiography and Hagiography in the Making of Reginald Pole

Thomas F. Mayer

"An image... adorned with all the virtues and excellencies which today might come together in a Christian gentleman."[1] Such was the portrait Ludovico Beccadelli, Reginald Pole's first biographer, promised his readers, and such became the dominant image of Pole.[2] If it will ever prove possible to get behind that portrait, attention must be directed not only to the dissemination of what Paolo Simoncelli calls Pole's "myth of sanctity," but also to the means Pole employed to launch his own hagiography.[3] This article studies the creation and diffusion of one particular episode in Pole's own presentation, his refusal in late 1530 to take Henry VIII's offer of the archbishopric of York in exchange for support of the king's divorce from Catherine of Aragon. Instead, as Pole came to claim, he had prophesied against the king, acting under divine inspiration. In creating his persona of prophet (together with its mirror image of martyr), Pole slid from humanist into Counter-Reformation historiography. Although in the process he played with language in the way his humanist education had taught him to do, Pole's serious approach and that of his successors led them to negate the playful intentions in much humanist historiography.[4] Thus, an originally heavily rhetorical story became a transparent account of what had happened, and the realist axiom that the saintly Pole always told the truth (or at least serious stories) came to dominate historiography.[5]

Pole first unveiled his prophetic persona in 1536 in *De unitate*, his savage attack on Henry, and only gradually worked it into the story of his climactic interview with the king.[6] How this retroactive control developed emerges from an analysis of the intricate relationship between

Pole's own writings and those of his biographers. The accounts Beccadelli, Andras Dudic, and Nicholas Harpsfield gave depended directly on the point Pole had reached in his reconstruction when they knew him. Pole first adverted to the event in the immediate aftermath of *De unitate*, in the form of Latin and English renderings of a reply to the king's council. Two years later, in 1539, when he and Beccadelli spent six months together in Spain, Pole still told much the same story, which Beccadelli faithfully reproduced as "what Sig. Reginaldo told me," the only one of these authors to make that claim. (Beccadelli had also been at Padua in 1533–36 at the tail end of Pole's extended stay and then became secretary to Pole's close ally Gasparo Contarini, who loaned him to Pole in 1539.)[7] A decade further on, Pole returned to the episode in a 1549 draft letter to Protector Somerset, before producing his final reckoning in two prefaces to *De unitate*, both addressed to Edward VI and written between mid-1553 and mid-1555 (despite the king's death two years earlier); Angelo Maria Querini printed one of these in the eighteenth century, but the other has not been previously noticed.[8] Within the next few years, Pole probably gave copies of this preface to Dudic, whom he met about 1550, and to Harpsfield, archdeacon of Canterbury during Pole's tenure as archbishop.[9] Alexius Horányi claimed that Dudic met Pole at Maguzzano in 1550, and Dudic may have been Pole's secretary after Pole's return to England in the 1550s; he certainly was profoundly impressed by Pole.[10] Judging from the number of preferments Harpsfield received from Pole, they, too, must have been close.[11]

In the Latin of the letter to the council, Pole rhetorically asked the Duke of Norfolk, "If I had wished to assent to the king's opinion, would anyone have been preferred to me in the archbishopric"?[12] Although Pole made a great deal of his opposition, he admitted that he would have liked the benefice. Seeing that the sole road to advancement ran through support for the divorce, Pole gave in to various blandishments "and directly I decided to satisfy the king." Once Henry was notified of Pole's resolve, "he met me in the door of a secret ambulatory in the house of York at Westminster (I can never forget that place).... When I saw him ... I could no longer say what I had previously thought out," despite the "human chain" between them, reflected in the king's face, "which I loved above the rest."[13] It is perhaps significant that this is the only version of the interview that reached the eyes of anyone who could pass on its relation to what had passed between the two royal cousins.[14]

This simple story of a change of mind became much more complicated by the mid-1550s; fortunately, although the second version of the preface to Edward is longer than the first, they do not vary significantly in content (I quote the more readily available printed version). When telling Henry's son about his original resolution to cooperate with his father, Pole added the editorial comment "and so I really judged, blinded in my effort following men more than obeying God." Once the interview began, strange things happened. Pole saw himself singled out by divine favor in such a way that

> when . . . I tried to enter the case, here I do not say I hesitated to have explained insufficiently what I wanted to say, but, oh divine goodness! so my tongue was plainly hampered, and my mouth obstructed, that I could not utter a word about what I had considered. When I yet began to speak, I said everything which attacked his opinion, as whose defender I had been expected to come.

Pole explained that his love for God and king—no longer king alone— was responsible for his change of heart.[15] Much the same account appears in the letter to Somerset. In addition to confirming that Pole's new story of his prophetic inspiration had supplanted the straightforward report of 1537, this second account offers a large clue about how Pole used autobiography to suit his rhetorical purposes. In the letter to Somerset, the story functioned as an exemplum designed to shame the protector by illustrating how Henry, "having an opportunity of knowing my sincerity in a matter very contrary to his feelings, would not, however, be angry with me nor ridicule me as you do."[16]

Harpsfield, Beccadelli, and Dudic, in that order, produced their renditions of the tale between about 1557 and 1562, almost reversing the sequence in which they came into contact with Pole.[17] The last two texts have frequently been taken as mirror images, a perception the two authors encouraged.[18] In fact, their accounts here differ most. Harpsfield veered between them. While all began by having Pole resort to prayer, Beccadelli kept it simple ("but in this deliberation, [Pole] turn[ed] to prayer, as he was wont to do"), Dudic dramatized ("while Pole was engaged in this so difficult and so dangerous deliberation, he eagerly fled to God, and prayed that in such a time he might not fail"), and Harpsfield went Dudic one better and spelled out for what exactly Pole prayed, making him ask "God to direct and govern his doings in this matter, that they might be conformable to truth, right and justice, and to His blessed will and pleasure." Despite the general similarity of Dudic's text to Harpsfield's, this could be one of several spots at which Dudic carefully criticized Pole, having him pray for inerrancy and then immediately waver. Pole himself said nothing about any kind of prayer in his letter to Edward.[19]

After this request for divine advice, Beccadelli adhered closely to Pole's original story in the letter to the council, while the other two reproduced Pole's later versions. According to Beccadelli, Pole discovered that

> he could never enter ... into the spirit to conform himself to the king's will ..., but he resolved to speak freely as he thought, and not as a flatterer, but truly as a relative and servant, since, the truth known, one must abstain from offending against it. The which he did with much eloquence and modesty, nor did he wish that anyone aside from the king should know his opinion.[20]

Pole's becoming modesty and faith in the power of the "truth" to convert Henry disappeared in the other two accounts. Instead of a direct refusal to support the king, Harpsfield and Dudic had Pole painfully work out a compromise, which God then prevented him from offering the king. Once their Pole recovered from the dumb fit featured in Pole's later reworkings, these two portrayed Pole telling Henry the opposite of what he had intended to say.

Strong verbal resemblances clinch the case for Harpsfield's and Dudic's dependence on Pole's finished versions. For example, where Pole wrote to Edward that "ne verbum quidem effari potuerim," Dudic merely cast that into the third person as "nullum verbum effari posset," and Harpsfield, departing from his usual practice, embroidered that into "he could not, if his life had stood on it, a great while utter one word." Pole continued "cum autem loqui tandem coepissem, omnia dixerim" [When, however, I began to talk, I said everything] against Henry, and Dudic once more followed with "[t]andem vero cum loqui coepisset, ejusmodi fuit ejus oratio, ut alia omnia diceret" [Yet truly, when he began to speak, this was his speech, that he said all the other things (against the king)], while Harpsfield wrote more expansively "[a]fterward, when he came to himself and recovered his speech, he spake quite contrary to that thing which he was determined to have spoken, and showed the king very plainly and openly that he wonderfully disliked the divorce."[21]

All these texts were plainly intended as hagiography. Dudic made his aim as explicit as Beccadelli's opening sentence: he had set out not only to translate Beccadelli's original, but also to modify it in order to demonstrate that Pole was on a par for sanctity with the martyred Thomas More and John Fisher. Dudic also adopted Beccadelli's conclusion that Pole belonged in the company of martyrs.[22] Pole looks a little out of place in Harpsfield's legal treatise on the validity of Henry's marriage to Catherine, but his figure was intended to function in much the same way as it had for Dudic, as an example of "the most notable captains" who fought against the divorce, again along with More and Fisher. By promoting Pole to equality with them, Dudic and Harpsfield completed the absorption of Pole's persona of martyr, which Pole had fashioned in *De unitate* by implicitly comparing himself to Fisher and More.[23]

The motives behind these authors' reactions to Pole's self-presentation need more work.[24] The problem is especially acute in the case of Dudic's adaptation. On the one hand, Dudic had a collaborator, Giovanni Battista Binardi, about whom little is known. Thus far we have scarcely more than Dudic's own account of his relations with Binardi, who had been one of Pole's secretaries, and to whom Dudic apparently deferred. He had asked Binardi for help because of his own artistic failings, and he went on to emphasize how much substance Binardi had contributed, in addition to having "polished ... this whole image of Pole" [totam hanc Poli effigiem].[25]

Ludovico Castelvetro's polemical attack on Binardi offers the only biography I have unearthed.[26] According to Castelvetro, Binardi came from very humble origins (one of the points Castelvetro considered most damaging) and had worked his way up as a tutor until he had gained an assignment as secretary to Cardinal Bernardino Maffei. On Maffei's death in 1553, Binardi had immediately passed to Pole's service. Perhaps the most scandalous suggestion Castelvetro made—one that students of Pole have ignored—is that Binardi, hoping for preferment, hired his pen to Pole, writing many works in Italian—especially letters and a treatise on the sacraments—which were then translated into Latin and published as Pole's own.[27] Or perhaps Castelvetro's assertion is a garbled version of Beccadelli's claim—which might be more reliable—that Binardi had served as Pole's *Latin* translator.[28] If both these stories are true, the corpus of "Pole's" work will need serious reduction! According to the spy Francisco Delgado, Binardi had custody of Pole's manuscripts when they were in England.[29] On Pole's death, Binardi accompanied his lifelong companion Alvise Priuli to Paris and then set off for Italy alone.[30] Shortly thereafter, he played a major role in the planned edition of Pole's works.[31] Binardi eventually entered the service of Cardinal Bernardo Navagero, by whom Castelvetro supposed he was richly rewarded.

Castelvetro offered the summary judgment (although it may apply only to Binardi's tenure as visitor of Roman prisons) that "he was in all his actions vain and simple [*semplice*], if not a persecutor." This last suggests that the root of Castelvetro's animus to Binardi was religious. If so, it may have sprouted from Castelvetro's difficulties in Modena in the early 1540s when he had been a member of a "heretical" conventicle whose beliefs Pole and his allies had been called upon to investigate and correct.[32] The notoriously irascible Castelvetro's account of Binardi and his involvement in Pole's works may have been meant to repay Pole. One of Castelvetro's accusers was another ally of Pole, Pietro Bertano.[33] Then again, Castelvetro had earlier been friendly with Binardi, and Binardi (and Gianfrancesco Stella) had a very high opinion of Castelvetro's literary theories as late as 1559; this put them in a distinct minority in a major literary dispute.[34] Thus, Binardi would appear to have had the perfect qualifications of a "ghost writer," if Castelvetro can be trusted. To this moment, alas, no manuscript of Dudic's work has surfaced.[35]

On the other hand, Dudic's own later conversion to Calvinism has cast a shadow over his work. G. B. Morandi argued that Dudic was actually attacking Pole from a crypto-Protestant position.[36] Domenico Caccamo, Gigliola Fragnito, and Lech Szczucki all reject Morandi's thesis.[37] Nevertheless, one of the coauthors of Dudic's life may have meant to make a number of subtle criticisms of Pole. In addition to the possibly negative comparison to other heroes who had died for the faith, for example, it was similarly noted that two of the four men created cardinal with Pole had gone on to become pope. "Dudic" noted this again when discussing the same two serving together with Pole as legates to the first session of Trent.[38] But in 1556, Dudic had extravagantly praised Pole, together with their mutual friend Paolo Manuzio, for their "true religion of Christ, by whom I was confirmed in the faith and by whose examples I was invited to spend life piously and holily."[39] Near the end of his life, Dudic expressed a similar opinion in offering his study of Pole as a model for a series of biographies of men "whom our age raises to the level of the fathers [of the church]."⁴⁰ Thus the theory of Dudic the crypto-critic may not work, but if these apparently negative comments actually were Binardi's, the situation becomes even more complicated. Likewise, the meaning of Beccadelli's ties to Pole's allies the *spirituali*, in whose defense Beccadelli is generally agreed to have written, requires further attention.⁴¹ Furthermore, Harpsfield's legendary zeal for the Counter-Reformation may not explain his handling of the image of Pole as well as further attention to his numerous historical works.⁴²

The accident of print denied much immediate impact to Beccadelli's and Harpsfield's intentions and motives, for Dudic alone achieved the honor of type in the sixteenth century. This may be explained by the fact that Dudic had a compelling motive to seek patronage from Emperor Ferdinand, to whom he dedicated the *Vita*. Beccadelli, by contrast, had lost hope of further preferment after the death of his patron Marcello Cervini (the short-lived pope Marcellus II), even if he had not yet broken irrevocably with Cardinal Morone when he wrote his "Vita."⁴³ Or perhaps Beccadelli really was sufficiently pleased with Dudic's text to abandon his own original.

The mere availability of Dudic's text no doubt accounts in part for the appearance of his dramatic adaptation of Pole's own reworked image in the second edition of Nicholas Sander's *De origine ac progressu schismatis anglicani*. Given the wide circulation of this work, it is worth trying to determine who modified Sander's account of Henry's first divorce in order to emphasize Pole's role. Sander himself could not have selected this particular "remarkably truthful" vignette, to adapt T. G. Law's characterization of the whole work.⁴⁴ The first edition of 1585 (Cologne, but actually Rheims) contains only a compressed reference to Pole's contretemps with Henry. As Sander put it, since "nothing" in England could compare to Pole, "therefore first the king offered him an archiepiscopal prerogative, if yet he should first promise, by eloquent words, that he would support the king's divorce by all effort. When Pole heard such a foul added condition, he rightly refused to sit in the chair of pestilence."⁴⁵ Before a new edition of *De origine* appeared in Rome the following year, Dudic's version of the interview had replaced this passage. While the second edition usually follows Dudic almost literally, it also contains details from Pole's own late versions that do not appear in Dudic, for example, the fact that Henry met Pole in a small, internal chamber. These could have come from Pole's own letters, provided once again by Hosius, but it is curious that Sander, who had been Hosius's theologian at Trent and then followed him to Poland, did not include them.[46] Alternatively, whoever prepared the second edition might somehow have had access to a copy of Beccadelli's text, which also contains these details.

In any case, how these changes were made between editions is still uncertain. Until twenty years ago, it was accepted that Sander's fellow Jesuit Robert Persons bore responsibility both for the original edition and for its Roman successor. Much of the former case is conjectural and rests in the main on Joseph Gillow's etymological identification of Persons with the "Iodocus Skarnhert" who had persuaded Rishton to publish Sander's work. Despite his skepticism about "Skarnhert's" identity, J. H. Pollen did think that Persons was responsible for the second edition, arguing that because his annotations stopped early in Sander's manuscript, he must have made the rest of his additions on a copy of the 1585 edition. Eusebio Rey put forward an especially freewheeling and almost entirely unsupported argument for Persons's primacy.[47]

As flimsy as the case for Persons's original involvement was, that for his role in the second Roman edition has even weaker support and has been largely destroyed by Joseph Simons. On the basis of a comparison of the first two editions with Persons's annotations on Sander's manuscript, Simons argued that the recusant leader William Allen already had a hand in the first edition, and definitely prepared the second, into which he incorporated Persons's notes.[48] This could well be true; Persons's marginalia on Sander's manuscript did not incorporate Dudic's story.

Whoever intruded the tale, the complete supplantation of the first edition of *De origine* by the second guaranteed the survival of Pole's self-creation.[49] This critical phase began quickly. In 1587, the Rome edition was reprinted in Ingolstadt (and twice more the following year) as well as translated into French; in 1589, it was adapted into Spanish by another Jesuit, Pedro de Ribadeneira, and both it and Sander's original were recast into Italian by the Dominican Girolamo Pollini in 1594. Ribadeneira adopted the main outline of Dudic's story, but toned down the climax a little, writing merely that when Pole tried to tell Henry the compromise formula he had worked out, "se turbó, (cosa maravillosa) y de repente se cortó de tal manera, que por un buen trato no pudo hablar palabra. Despues volviendo en sí comenzó á hablar y á decir todo lo contrario de lo que habia pensado" [he became disturbed (a marvelous thing) and suddenly turned in such a manner that for a good space of time he could not speak. Afterward coming to himself, he began to speak and to say all the contrary to what he had thought out]. Pollini dedicated *L'Historia ecclesiastica della Rivoluzion d'Inghilterra* (Rome: Guglielmo Facciotti, 1594) to Allen, and it bore a privilege of Clement VIII, together with a *nihil obstat* from the famous Spanish Jesuit and moral theologian, Juan Azor. Although the first edition was apparently suppressed, Pollini brought out another three years later.[50] If Sander's history and Pole's story appeared to be standard Counter-Reformation fare at that point, in the seventeenth century they became usual features of other sorts of historiography. The catalog of the British Library lists fifteen editions of *De origine* before 1700, and that is certainly not the total. Law's judgment (in his *DNB* article on Sander) that Sander's work "formed the basis of every Roman Catholic history of the English Reformation" is no exaggeration. In one instance, the Florentine patrician Bernardo Davanzati compressed and rearranged Dudic's treatment of Pole's interview in his *Lo schisma d'Inghilterra,* except that he did not attribute Pole's dumbness to divine intervention.[51] Although Davanzati frequently followed Johannes Sleidan's *De statu religionis et reipublicae Carolo V Caesare commentarii,* he could not have in this case; Sleidan did not mention Pole before his legation of 1537.[52] Davanzati's sympathetic attitude to Pole could well have arisen from his experience in the as yet little-explored circles around Cosimo I, which had earlier displayed a good deal of interest in defending Contarini's reputation and contained a number of figures of more-or-less heterodox religion.[53] One of Cosimo's partisans, Benedetto Varchi, had a very high opinion of Pole and some of his friends.[54] The Accademia fiorentina also included Dominicans, one of whom was interested in revising heretical literature, which may suggest a tie between Pollini and Davanzati.[55] Or, the link between Davanzati and Pole could be as direct as Beccadelli, who entered the service of the Medici in 1563 at the conclusion of Trent.

Undoubtedly the most important of the later adaptations and translations of *De origine* was that of François Maucroix (1676, with at least three more editions by 1715, including one of The Hague). From it descends modern historiography of the English Reformation. Maucroix's work served as "the proximate cause" (Law) of Gilbert Burnet's *History of the Reformation,* the first volume of which, published in 1679, in turn led to Joachim Le Grand's reply in his *Histoire du divorce de Henri VIII* (Paris, 1688) and thence directly to the great burst of interest in church history in the first half of the eighteenth century.[56] Even though Maucroix had apologized for Sander's partisanship in his preface, when he chose to translate the equally partisan Dudic in 1677 as a sequel, he manifested intentions as blatantly hagiographical as most of his predecessors.[57] Maucroix gave few clues about his motives. He wrote only in his brief preface that everything Dudic had written was "la verité" [the truth] and that although he did not wish to give a eulogy of Pole, "je diray seulement, qu'il seroit difficile de trouver dans un même homme, tant de Noblesse, de Pieté & de Doctrine, que dans le celebre Cardinal POLUS" [I would only say, that it would be difficult to find in a single man so much nobility, piety, and learning as in the famous Cardinal Pole].[58] Why either work should have interested a protector of the Jansenists and a "convinced Gallican" is puzzling.[59] Perhaps this is evidence both of the reception of Pole's tolerant attitude to Protestantism and also that he was read as much less of a staunch papalist than he has been made out to be in later scholarship. Such an interpretation would fit the views expressed in *De unitate*.[60]

By the mid-eighteenth century, the time of Thomas Phillips, another sometime Jesuit and author of the first modern biography of Pole, the corner had been turned and Pole's tale come to be read fully seriously.[61] Both Phillips and his critics so took it, as the replacement of salvation history by scientific history merely substituted one objectivist epistemology for another. Gloucester Ridley, for example, insisted that he would "never rely on Pole's testimony when not supported by others," but he yet blithely assessed the York interview as an instance of "the common weakness of irresolute men, [who] fluctuating between the choice of a present and future advantage, and, loath to quit either, lose both."[62] Benjamin Pye offers an even more egregious instance. The translator and annotator of Beccadelli argued at length in his preface that "a biographer seems to be by profession a writer of panegyric" who therefore "often makes a sacrifice of truth without scruple," before concluding that "it would be absurd... to make such effusion of the fancy... the basis and ground-work of real history." Despite a few doubts about the documentary record, Pye nevertheless accorded Beccadelli's story enough credence to judge that it showed Pole in a very bad light: "he prevaricated with his prince; he deceived his friends; he acted disingenuously with himself."[63]

This outcome is the more surprising in that it ignored the conclusion reached by the dean of Anglican historians of the Reformation and the man probably most responsible for renewed interest in Pole, Bishop Burnet. But Burnet, Ridley, and Pye all held Pole to the same serious standard. Burnet flatly rejected Pole's tale as a fabrication only because, as he thought, it had no external support.[64] A key episode, invented by Pole as part of his prophetic persona, could not be expunged from historiography, even by hostile critics like Pye who displayed sensitivity to the rhetorical demands of biography. Pole's well-fashioned autobiography proved too seductive.

NOTES

A preliminary version of this article was read at the meeting of the Renaissance Society of America at Harvard in 1989. My thanks to the Gladys Krieble Delmas Foundation, Villa I Tatti: The Harvard University Center for Italian Renaissance Studies, and the National Endowment for the Humanities for their support of further work.

1. Ludovico Beccadelli, "Vita del cardinale Reginaldo Polo," in G. B. Morandi, ed., *Monumenti di varia letteratura* (Bologna: Istituto per le scienze, 1797–1804), 1:2, 277 reads *ponno*, as do most of the manuscripts; *possino* supplied from Newberry Library Case MS fE5.P7536, fol. 1r. I am at work on a critical edition and translation of Beccadelli's and Andras Dudic's lives of Pole.

2. Paolo Simoncelli, *Il caso Reginald Pole: eresia e santità nelle polemiche religiose del Cinquecento* (Rome: Edizioni di storia e letteratura, 1977), 17 and 241; and Gigliola Fragnito, "Aspetti della censura ecclesiastica nell'Europa della controriforma: l'edizione parigina delle opere di Gasparo Contarini," *Rivista di storia e letteratura religiosa,* 21 (1985): 3–48, 24. For Pole's place in English recusant historiograpy and subsequent Catholic writing, see B. H. G. Wormald, "The Historiography of the English Reformation," in T. Desmond Williams, ed., *Historical Studies,* 2 (1958): 50–58, esp. 58.

3. Simoncelli, *Caso Pole,* 17.

4. Sergio Bertelli, *Ribelli, libertini e ortodossi nella storiografia barocca* (Florence: La nuova Italia, 1973), esp. chap. 1. Richard A. Lanham, *The Motives of Eloquence: Literary Rhetoric in the Renaissance* (New Haven, CT: Yale University Press, 1976), esp. chap. 1, develops the fundamental humanist dialectic between serious and playful behavior.

5. Athanasius Zimmermann, *Kardinal Pole, sein Leben und seine Schriften. Ein Beitrag zur Kirchengeschichte des 16. Jahrhunderts* (Regensburg: F. Pustet, 1893), 36. Cf. Martin Haile [pseud. of Marie Hallé], *Life of Reginald Pole* (London: Isaac Pitman and Sons, 1911), 72.

6. Peter S. Donaldson discovered Pole's prophetic persona in *De unitate,* Pole's savage attack on Henry, but did not bring out the dialectic between it and Pole's martyr-self: "Machiavelli, Antichrist, and the Reformation: Prophetic Typology in Reginald Pole's *De unitate* and Apologia ad Carolum quintum," in

Richard L. DeMolen, ed., *Leaders of the Reformation* (Selinsgrove: Susquehanna University Press, 1984), 211–46.

7. Beccadelli, "Vita," 287. For Beccadelli's stint with Pole, see Antonio Giganti da Fossombrone, "Vita di Monsignor Lodovico Beccadelli," in G. B. Morandi, ed., *Monumenti di varia letteratura* (Bologna: Istituto per le scienze, 1797–1804), 1:1, 17. Cf. also Gigliola Fragnito, "Beccadelli, Ludovico," *Dizionario biografico degli Italiani* (Rome: Istituto della Enciclopedia italiana, 1960–).

8. The letter to Somerset bears various dates in the manuscripts, but the best is probably 12 October 1549 from Biblioteca Apostolica Vaticana [hereafter BAV] Vat. lat. 5968, fols. 258^r– 74^v. Querini's text of the preface to Edward is in *Epistolarum Reginaldi Poli* (Brescia: Rizzardi, 1744–57) [hereafter *ERP*], 4, 306–53; his dating by implication is on XXII–XXVII (endorsed indirectly by Thomas F. Dunn, "Cardinal Reginald Pole and Codex Vaticanus Latinus 5970," *Manuscripta*, 21 [1978]: 75–82, at 81). This text came from Johann Georg Schellhorn, *Amoenitates historiae ecclesiasticae et litterariae* (Frankfurt and Leipzig: Daniel Bartholomäus, 1737), 192–276; Querini later acquired the manuscript from Schellhorn. It is now part of Brescia, Biblioteca Civica Queriniana [hereafter BCQ] MS F III 7, m. 1. The presence in the Queriniana of two other pieces of the codex as it existed before Schellhorn sold it to Querini clinches its provenance. This manuscript came from Pole's friend Stanislaus Hosius via Charles XIII of Sweden, who stole it from Hosius's bishopric. From him it passed to various German bibliophiles before its sale to Querini. It might be in Seth Holland's hand. The other manuscript of the preface is Bergamo, Biblioteca Civica "Angelo Mai" [hereafter BCM], Archivio Stella, 40/76, a version in the hand of Pole's secretary, Marcantonio Faita, which must have passed into the possession of Pole's longtime business agent, Gianfrancesco Stella. (The archivist who cataloged the Archivio Stella, probably Giuseppe Bonelli himself, guessed it was dated 1548. See Giuseppe Bonelli, "Un archivio privato del Cinquecento: le Carte Stella," *Archivio storico lombardo*, 24 [1907]: 332–86, no. 93.) The presence of a marginal note in the same unknown but contemporary hand on each manuscript proves their close relationship in time. The initial impulse to the preface to Edward probably came from Gianpietro Caraffa's suggestion that Pole republish *De unitate,* as mentioned in Pole's letter to Girolamo Muzzarelli of 9 August 1553 (misdated 6 August in *ERP,* 4, no. 37, 92; original in BAV Vat. lat. 5967, fols. 358^r–65^v, with wrapper and seal; as Heinrich Lutz argues, this probably means the letter was never sent: *Nuntiaturberichte aus Deutschland,* Erste Abteilung, vol. 15, *Friedenslegation des Reginald Pole zu Kaiser Karl V. und König Heinrich II. (1553–1556)* [Tübingen, 1981], XIXn). Caraffa could have hatched his scheme, possibly intended to incriminate Pole further, at any time after their famous "reconciliation" in April 1553 (reported by Filippo Gherio to Beccadelli on 29 April in Morandi, ed., *Monumenti di varia letteratura,* 1:2, 347–53). Muzzarelli endorsed Caraffa's proposal both then and again

on 1 September (*ERP*, 5, no. 64, esp. 124; no original of his letter has been found, but there is a contemporary copy in Naples, Biblioteca Nazionale "Vittorio Emanuele III," IX. A. 14, fols. 45^r–47^v, and the copy in BCQ, MS F III 7, m. 2, fols. 7–8, may be not much later). Cf. the discussion of these two important letters in Massimo Firpo, *Inquisizione romana e Controriforma: Studi sul Cardinal Giovanni Morone e il suo processo d'eresia* (Bologna: Il Mulino, 1992), 238–50. Caraffa's urgings and the news of Edward VI's death (which reached Rome about 6 August and Maguzzano, Pole's residence, about a week later; cf. *Friedenslegation des Reginald Pole*, nos. 2 and 4) came very close together, which suggests that despite his protests to the contrary, Pole went to work immediately on the preface. The appearance of Pier Paolo Vergerio's edition of *De unitate* in Strasbourg in 1555 provides a *terminus ad quem* for the first of these prefaces, and *a quo* for the second. In the first, Pole wrote as if the anonymous edition that had spurred him to write had not yet appeared, and in the second as if it had. The balance point between these two *termini* can be dated from Pole's letter to Otto Truchsess of 19 June 1554 (*ERP*, 4, no. 53, to be used cautiously in light of its variations from the minute in BAV Vat. lat. 5967, fols. 367^r–71^v) in which Pole asked Truchsess's help in learning whether Vergerio's edition had yet appeared. Cf. Simoncelli, *Caso Pole*, 120–31, which, however, offers no further help in dating this key episode. That Edward was dead by that time poses no difficulty in dating—Pole was, after all, proposing to reprint *De unitate*, a work that addressed Henry VIII in the first person throughout. There are yet two more autograph but fragmentary versions of the preface in BAV Vat. lat. 5971, fols. 1^r–57^v and 117^r–149^v, neither covering this episode.

9. Dudic could also have gotten his copy after Pole's death from Cardinal Hosius, who encouraged Dudic to translate Beccadelli, and who was well known for his aid to English Catholic exiles, among them Nicholas Sander. A. Horányi, *Memoria Hungarorum et provincialium scriptis editis notorum*, 1 (Vienna: Anton Loew, 1775), 550, apparently building on the contemporary life of Dudic by Quirinus Reuter; Pierre Costil, *André Dudith, humaniste hongrois 1533–1589: Sa vie, son ouevre et ses manuscrits grecs* (Paris: "Les Belles Lettres," 1935), 61–73, and Domenico Caccamo, *Eretici italiani in Moravia, Polonia e Transilvania (1558–1611). Studi e documenti* (Florence: Sansoni; Chicago: The Newberry Library, 1970), 110, for Dudic's high opinion of Pole.

10. See *ERP*, 1, 257 for the MS, and H. D. Wojtyska, *Cardinal Hosius, Legate to the Council of Trent* (Rome: Gregorian University Press, 1967), 211–16 for his relations with English Catholics. See Costil, *Dudith*, 104, for Hosius's encouragement.

11. Nicholas Harpsfield, *The Life and Death of Sir Thomas Moore*, ed. E. V. Hitchcock, intro. and notes by R. W. Chambers (London, Early English Text Society, o.s., no. 186 [1932]), xxi.

12. Public Record Office, London, SP 1/116, fol. 65^r and *ERP*, 1, 182. The

English version, which was probably Pole's original (it is autographed and signed), is phrased considerably differently and much less rhetorically. The purpose of the Latin rendering, its connection to the copy in the BAV printed by Querini, and the precise relation between all three letters remains to be worked out.

13. Ibid., fol. 66^{r-v}.

14. Wilhelm Schenk argued to the contrary in *Reginald Pole, Cardinal of England* (London: Longmans, 1950), 31n, but see T. F. Mayer, "A Mission Worse than Death: Reginald Pole and the Parisian Theologians," *English Historical Review*, 103 (1988): 870–91, esp. 876–77.

15. *ERP*, 4, 330–31; BCQ, MS F III 7, m. 1, fols. 107^v–108^r; BCM, Archivio Stella, 40/76, fols. 14^v–15^r, which has the following text: "Itaque plane cupiditate hominis plusquam Dei obtemperandi obcaecatus iudicabam.... ingressum in causam quaererem si hic non dicam me in ipsa principia haesitasse me non satis expressisse quod dicere volui. Sed o bonitatem divinam ita mihi et lingua plane impedita est, et os obstructum ac ne verbum quidem ullum effari potuerim de iis quae mecum meditatus fueram, cum autem loqui inciperem, omnia dixerim quae cum sententiam oppugnarent, cuius defensor optatus veneram."

16. BAV Vat. lat. 6754, fols. 3^r–27^v; fol. 5^r has the most legible extant text. That in Vat. lat. 5968, fols. 258^r–74^v, stems more directly from Pole, but nearly all of this version can no longer be read. There are other copies in BL Add. MS 41577, fols. 3^r–27^v, dated in a different hand 8 April 1548; BL Add. MS 25425, 3–27; and Venice, Biblioteca Marciana, MSS italiani X. 24 (6527), fols. 6^r–22^v, summarized in *Calendar of State Papers and Manuscripts, Relating to English Affairs in the Archives and Collections of Venice*, ed. Rawdon Brown, 5 (London, 1873), no. 575, p. 242, where it is dated 7 September.

17. For the dates of composition, see Nicholas Harpsfield, *A Treatise on the Pretended Divorce between Henry VIII and Catharine of Aragon*, ed. Nicholas Pocock (London, Camden Series, n.s. 21 [1878]), 13–14); Morandi, *Monumenti di varia letteratura*, 1:2, 272; and Gigliola Fragnito, "Gli 'spirituali' e la fuga di Bernardino Ochino," *Rivista storica italiana*, 84 (1972): 777–811, 803n. For Dudic at Trent, see most recently Lech Szczucki, "Miedzy ortodoksja a nikodemizmem (Andrzej Dudycz na soborze trydenckim)," *Odrodzenie i Reformacja w Polsce*, 29 (1984): 49–90. I have been unable to read this article, but I am grateful to Dr. Szczucki for sending me a copy.

18. Gigliola Fragnito, *Memoria individuale e costruzione biografica* (Pubblicazioni dell'università di Urbino, serie di lettere e filosofia, Urbino, 1978), 64n, 161.

19. *ERP*, 4, 330; BCQ, F III 7, m. 1, fol. 107^v; BCM, Archivio Stella, 40/76, fol. 14^v.

20. Beccadelli, "Vita," 286–87.

21. *ERP*, 4, 330 (BCQ, F III 7, m. 1, fol. 107ᵛ–108ʳ); BCM, Archivio Stella 40/76, fol. 14ᵛ, adds a few words; Dudic, *Vita Reginaldi Poli*, in *ERP*, 1, 9; Harpsfield, *Divorce*, 206. Harpsfield's somewhat stultifying, if fully rhetorical, treatment of Pole resembles the way he rewrote William Roper's life of Thomas More. See Judith H. Anderson, *Biographical Truth: The Representation of Historical Persons in Tudor-Stuart Writing* (New Haven, CT: Yale University Press, 1984), 15, 49–51.

22. Andras Dudic, *Vita Reginaldi Poli* (Venice: Domenico and Giovanni Battista Guerrei, 1563), sig. 3ᵛ; *Vita*, in *ERP*, 1, 65, repeating Beccadelli, "Vita," 333. Querini did not reprint Dudic's preface in *ERP*, but his text is otherwise almost identical to the Venetian edition.

23. *Reginaldi Poli ad Henricum octavum Britanniae regem, pro ecclesiasticae unitatis defensione* (Rome: Antonio Blado, 1539), esp. fols. LXXXIII–XCV.

24. Quentin Skinner sketches the useful distinction between motives and intentions in "'Social Meaning' and the Explanation of Social Action," in P. Laslett, W. G. Runciman, and Q. Skinner, eds., *Philosophy, Politics and Society*, series 4 (Oxford: Blackwell, 1972): 136–57, esp. 144–47. I differ from him in suggesting that both should be taken into account, with intentions and their textual warrant controlling motives that must be established by inference from texts. This method thus comes fairly close to that espoused by Eric Cochrane in *Historians and Historiography in the Italian Renaissance* (Chicago: University of Chicago Press, 1981), xvii.

25. Dudic, *Vita*, sig. 4ʳ.

26. Castelvetro's broadside was printed in part by Girolamo Tiraboschi in *Biblioteca modenese*, 1 (Modena: Società tipografica, 1781), 274–76. The original is in the Biblioteca Estense, Modena, Alpha H 1, 11. The short biographical notice of Binardi in *Nuovi documenti su Vittoria Colonna e Reginald Pole*, ed. Sergio Pagano and Concetta Ranieri (Città del Vaticano: Archivio segreto vaticano, 1989), 47n, must be used with caution. Most previous notices have no value.

27. Given the evidence of multiple pens in all of Pole's works written during Binardi's service, there is probably more than a grain of truth in this allegation. Cf. especially the numerous versions of Pole's "De Reformatione Ecclesiae" in BAV Vat. lat. 5964. The partial manuscript in the British Library of Pole's "De sacramento," which Castelvetro singled out as Binardi's work, is in Faita's hand, and the copy in the Marciana is later, possibly made from the printed edition.

28. Fragnito, "Censura ecclesiastica," 23n.

29. J. I. Tellechea Idigoras, "Pole, Carranza y Fresneda: cara y cruz de una amistad y de una enemistad," in *Fray Bartolomé Carranza y el cardenal Pole: Un navarro en la restauracion católica de Inglaterra (1554–1558)* (Pamplona: C. S. I. C., 1977), 137 and 139 (noting his intimate involvement in the discussion of Bartolomé Carranza's *Catechismo*, later judged heretical).

30. See the letters between Binardi and Priuli in BCM, Archivio Stella, 40/160–61.

31. Fragnito, "Censura ecclesiastica," 24 and 35, together with Binardi's important letter to Giovanni Morone in BAV Vat. lat. 6414, fols. 191^r–2^v.

32. Massimo Firpo, "Gli 'spirituali,' l'Accademia di Modena e il formulario di fede del 1542: controllo del dissenso religioso e nicodemismo," *Rivista di storia e letteratura religiosa*, 20 (1984): 40–111, now in *Inquisizione romana*, 29–118.

33. T. Sandonnini, *Ludovico Castelvetro e la sua famiglia* (Bologna: Nicola Zanichelli, 1882), 42–43, 81.

34. See Binardi's letter to Stella, BCM, Archivio Stella, 40/155.

35. The manuscript in the Queriniana, MS G. V. 1, is a copy of the text printed in Venice, written by Querini's sometime amanuensis, Abbot Schannat.

36. G. B. Morandi, ed., *Monumenti di varia letteratura* (Bologna: Istituto per le scienze, 1797–1804), 1:2, 274 and his notes.

37. Caccamo, *Eretici italiani*, 112–13, argues that although Dudic's true beliefs were much more radical, he had not openly broken with the Catholic church before the end of Trent; Fragnito, "Censura ecclesiastica," 39; and Szczucki, "Andrzej Dudycz," according to the English summary.

38. *Vita*, in *ERP*, 1, 14, and 19.

39. Caccamo, *Eretici italiani*, 112–13. For Manuzio's religion, see Fragnito, "Censura ecclesiastica," 26–28, Simoncelli, *Caso Pole*, 40–42, and A. J. Schutte, "The *Lettere Volgari* and the Crisis of Evangelism in Italy," *Renaissance Quarterly*, 28 (1975): 639–88.

40. Costil, *Dudith*, 448.

41. Hubert Jedin, *Il tipo ideale del vescovo secondo la riforma cattolica* (Brescia: Morcelliana, 1950), 49, 54–55; Simoncelli, *Caso Pole*, 191–92, argues for this thesis most strenuously; but see Fragnito, *Memoria*, 157–59; and idem, "Per lo studio dell'epistographia volgare del Cinquecento: le lettere di Ludovico Beccadelli," *Bibliothèque d'humanisme et renaissance*, 43 (1981): 61–87, 64, and 87, in which she disputes current views of Beccadelli's religion. Fragnito considers Beccadelli a lifelong adherent of Contarini, but not a *spirituale* (a term she would now restrict to Pole's immediate circle). See Fragnito, "Censura ecclesiastica," esp. 36 where Beccadelli not only becomes a key instrument in the campaign to rehabilitate Pole, but also a promoter of the "banca di vescovi Contarini."

42. See his entry in Sidney Lee and Leslie Stephen, eds., *The Dictionary of National Biography* [hereafter *DNB*] (Oxford: Oxford University Press, 1917).

43. Fragnito, *Memoria individuale*, 145–55; and "Censura ecclesiastica," 32–41. Fragnito obliquely makes "Dudic's" text part of the campaign engineered by Morone, even though she theorizes that the cardinal would not have approved its anti-Carafa polemic ("Censura ecclesiastica," 39–40). The latter, like Mo-

rone's putative, but undocumented, attitude, is difficult to detect; in all the cases where Carafa is mentioned by name, "Dudic" referred to him more respectfully (and at greater length) than Beccadelli. "Dudic" also seemed much more concerned with the prerogatives of the *Sancta romana ecclesia* than Beccadelli, which also reverses Fragnito's analysis.

44. T. G. Law, "Nicholas Sanders," in *DNB*.

45. Nicholas Sander, *De origine ac progressu schismatis anglicani*, ed. Edward Rishton (Cologne [Rheims], 1585), 57. The manuscript of Sander's work confirms that these are his words and not Rishton's: English College, Rome, Liber 1388, fol. 43^r. I am greatly indebted to the Rector of the English College and to T. M. McCoog, S. J., for procuring me a photocopy of this section of Sander's MS.

46. Wojtyska, *Cardinal Hosius*, 211–12 and 216.

47. J. Gillow, *A Literary and Biographical History or Biographical Dictionary of the English Catholics*, 12 vols. (London: Burns and Oates, 1885–1905), 5:279; J. H. Pollen, "Dr. Nicholas Sanders," *English Historical Review*, 6 (1891): 18–35, esp. 24 (cf. Thomas McNevin Veech, *Dr. Nicholas Sanders and the English Reformation* [Louvain: Bibliothèque de l'Université, 1935], 234); Pedro de Ribadeneira, *Historias de la contrareforma*, ed. Eusebio Rey (Madrid: Editorial Católica, 1945), 856–60; and T. H. Clancy, *Papist Pamphleteers. The Allen-Persons Party and the Political Thought of the Counter-reformation in England, 1572–1615* (Chicago: Loyola University Press, 1964), 16.

48. Robert Persons, *Certamen ecclesiae anglicanae*, ed. Joseph S. F. Simons (Assen: Van Gorcum, 1965), 301–4.

49. Something similar happened to the tales Sander told about Sir Thomas More. See Beatrice Corrigan, "Sir Thomas More: Personage and Symbol on the Italian Stage," in D. B. J. Randall and G. W. Williams, eds., *Studies in the Continental Background of Renaissance English Literature: Essays Presented to John L. Lievsay* (Durham, N. C.: Duke University Press, 1977), 91–108.

50. For the first German editions, see *The National Union Catalogue: Pre-1956 Imprints* (London: Mansell, 1968–81); Pedro de Ribadeneira, *Historia del cisma de Inglaterra* (Cadiz: Revista Medica, 1863), chap. 16, 86. For Pollini, Piero Rebora, "Una controversia anglo-toscano nel secolo decimosesto," in *Civiltà italiana e civiltà inglese: studi e ricerche* (Florence: Le Monnier, 1936), 101–5. Cf. also Giulio Negri, S. J., *Istoria degli scrittori fiorentini* (Ferrara: Bernadino Pomatelli, 1722), 304, and for Pollini's treatment of More, Piero Rebora, "San Tommaso Moro e l'Italia," in *Civiltà italiana*, 75–79.

51. *Lo schisma d'Inghilterra e le altre operette di Bernardo Davanzati Bostichi* (Siena: F. Pigafetta, 1828), 29–30. The work first appeared posthumously in 1638. For Davanzati's wholehearted endorsement of Counter-Reformation ideals, see Leandro Perini, "Un patrizio fiorentino e il suo mondo: Bernardo Davanzati," *Studi storici*, 17 (1976): 161–70.

52. Cochrane *(Historians and Historiography,* 361) emphasizes Davanzati's dependence on Sleidan, but his further judgment that Davanzati had nothing new to add because he knew no English is neither fair nor accurate. Davanzati adduced a good deal of evidence from continental writers that Sleidan had not. Johannes Sleidan, *De statu religionis et reipublicae Carolo V Caesare commentarii* (n.p.: Eustace Vignon, 1573), treated Pole at sigs. 137^{r-v} and 169^{r-v}. Sleidan had read Pole's *De unitate* and criticized him as a controversialist whose writings did not serve to advance historical understanding (sig. Oiiii^r).

53. Fragnito, "Censura ecclesiastica," 10–11.

54. B. Varchi, *Opere,* 2 vols. (Triest: Lloyd Austriaco, 1859), 2:347. For him, see Ugo Pirotti, *Benedetto Varchi e la cultura del suo tempo* (Florence: Olschki, 1971); and Leatrice Mendelsohn, *Paragoni: Benedetto Varchi's Due Lezzioni and Cinquecento Art Theory* (Ann Arbor, MI: UMI Research Press, 1982).

55. Perini, "Davanzati," 163.

56. For some of this development, see the recent sketchy treatments in Rosemary O'Day, *The Debate on the English Reformation* (London: Methuen, 1986), 38–55; and A. G. Dickens, J. M. Tonkin, and Kenneth Powell, *The Reformation in Historical Thought* (Cambridge, MA: Harvard University Press, 1985), 105ff.

57. *Histoire du schisme d'Angleterre des Sanderus,* 1 (Lyon: Guillimin, 1685), sig. aiiii^v.

58. F. Maucroix, *Suite du schisme d'Angleterre, ou les vies des cardinaux Polus et Campege* (Lyon: Guillimin, 1685; added to vol. 2 of his translation of Sander), sig. Aii^{r-v}.

59. Renée Kohn sketched Maucroix's career in *Lettres de Maucroix* (Paris: Presses Universitaires de France, 1962), 17–35 (assessment at 27).

60. For a reading of *De unitate* as no more enamored of papal absolutism than of Henry VIII's, see T. F. Mayer, "Nursery of Resistance: Reginald Pole and his Friends," in P. A. Fideler and T. F. Mayer, eds., *Political Thought and the Tudor Commonwealth: Deep Structure, Discourse, and Disguise* (London: Routledge, 1992), 50–74.

61. Thomas Phillips, *The History of the Life of Reginald Pole* (Oxford: William Jackson, 1764), 66 followed Dudic very closely.

62. Gloucester Ridley, *A Review of Mr. Phillips's History of the Life of Reginald Pole* (London: J. Whiston, et al., 1766), 24 and 20.

63. *The Life of Cardinal Reginald Pole, Written originally in Italian by Lodovico Beccatelli,* translated by Benjamin Pye (London: Bathurst, 1766), ix, 27–28. Pye claimed in the preface (iv–v) that he had chosen to translate Beccadelli in order to correct Phillips's inaccuracies, but why Pye worked from Beccadelli's Italian instead of Dudic's Latin—as Phillips had—is unclear.

64. Gilbert Burnet, *The History of the Reformation of the Church of England,* ed. Nicholas Pocock, 6 vols. (Oxford: Clarendon Press, 1865), 4, 557–58. Burnet (545) cited the 1628 edition of Sander.

9
A Protestant Poetics of Process: Reformation Rhetorics of the Self in Sponde, de Bèze, and d'Aubigné

Catharine Randall

In *Les tragiques,* the great Calvinist epic polemic, and specifically in the books "Feux" and "Fers," the sections devoted to recounting Protestant martyrdoms, the Huguenot poet and prosateur Théodore Agrippa d'Aubigné reconstructs a series of martyrological discourses. In his recuperation of tortured confessional bodies, no one fragment can stand alone; all must interrelate to form textual coherence. D'Aubigné interweaves these portions of narrative to create a full and personalized narrative, a form of autobiography. The roll call of martyrdoms eventually extends to include d'Aubigné's own name as he inscribes himself within their salvation scenario. Theology and its constituents thus compose a morphology that comprises and inflects autobiography and its shadow forms.

Life-writing in *Les tragiques* constitutes a complex intertextuality that occurs within a dialectic of life and death. Death to this life, and life in the next, is assured to the martyrs, as well as for and by d'Aubigné himself in the space of his text through his dialogue with, and response to, the martyrs he includes. D'Aubigné's Calvinist belief in election, or predestination, informs this dialectic; as elect, d'Aubigné prophesies in his text, speaking of that which cannot be known until *after* death, as being *fore*known, and in this way creates a subgenre, what he terms the *apophétie,* in which he claims prescience regarding an event; this comes about because of a narrative subterfuge: writing after the fact, he pretends to have had foreknowledge. This propensity for playing fast and loose with facts, plastically manipulating them to privilege himself, is a clue that the martyrs as d'Aubigné records them in *Les tragiques* are actually tools he uses in a creative, self-enhancing process. The text in this way acts as the privileged medium for d'Aubigné's self-bestowed imprimatur of martyrdom, and, especially, for the exaltation of selfhood. The martyrs who inform the text work in the economy of "Feux" and "Fers" as pretexts for and intertexts of an autobiographical narrative of salvation.[1] This composite, inexplicit sort of authorial self-exaltation through the problematizing of erstwhile exemplarity forms, I suggest, a major distinction between Reformation and Renaissance life-writing, the primary literary reperiodization for which I wish to argue here.[2] These autobiographical narratives may be clandestine because of contextual constraints experienced by confessional Calvinists who wrote during periods of intense religious hostility and persecution. The surreptitious insertion of the Self into these texts, performed in and through conventional or recognizable (Calvinist martyrs were recognizable, if not conventional) *figura,* ultimately reconfiguring these *figura,* is also attributable to the nature of Calvinism itself: its near doctrinal interdiction of focus on the Self as blasphemous and counterproductive in the salvific process. If Renaissance authors have to shape themselves as authorities within a zone of influence crammed with already established *auctores,* Reformation writers contend with authority with a capital *A:* metaphysics spurs the need for metatext, a text capable of subsuming its base and moving beyond it—precisely what d'Aubigné does when he speaks of martyrs yet uses them as ciphers or springboards for his own self-expression. His gloss on his text is no true textual commentary, no four-tiered patristic exegesis, but rather an exposition, the relation of event to personal circumstance which, paradoxically, John Calvin—whom Richard Stauffer has shown to have used the first-person singular pronoun only exceedingly rarely in his sermons[3]—practiced in his biblical commentary. In a book exalting a collection of illustrious martyrs, there should be no space in which appropriately to speak about the Self. And yet d'Aubigné shows that everyone, while not themselves martyrs in the sense that saintliness could be enrobed or emulated, could speak a form of personal scripture, a self-writing, a confessional narrative which rehabilitates their humanity by resituating them in alignment with the divine.

In Reformation life-writing, the author situates his own body *in relation to* those of the martyrs; he writes himself and his reader into a textual space of election. This is a form of network, what contemporary theorists would term intertextuality: a dialogue of call and response (that recalls Calvin's structure for Genevan catechetical manuals); the emphasis is always on word and oral or textual reaction to it.⁴ Writing, by incorporating the body, becomes the zone in which reassemblage and resurrection occur. Through the collection and rearrangement of the severed and fragmented body parts of various martyrs, the Reformation life-writer becomes himself the agent who revivifies. He does not hesitate to prefigure the application of this strategy, for the future, to himself. We see this technique in Reformation figures throughout the Continent; John Donne, for example, in *Holy Sonnet* 165, by the dynamism of his words sets in motion the Second Coming:

> At the round earth's imagin'd corners, blow
> Your trumpets, Angells, and arise, arise
> From death, you numberless infinities
> Of soules, and to your scattred bodies goe.⁵

In positing d'Aubigné as a case study exemplifying features of Reformation life-writing, we shall examine micronarratives that I would classify as "martyrological," although they have not formerly been so categorized. Charles Taylor has commented on the militant organizational program of the Calvinists, the desire to work with "ordinary life" by restructuring it in a more theologically conforming way.⁶ D'Aubigné demonstrates a concern for organization so that he may find a space in which to sanction speech about the Self. In the Renaissance, humanist authors created works deemed of their own authorship through the borrowing, restating, and revising of classical topoi. Not so d'Aubigné: he borrows from no source other than Scripture, and he does not revise Scripture—that would have been deemed a blasphemous act by Calvinists. What he does is lift events out of daily experience, here, from the horrors of religious persecution, and describe them in such a way that he restructures their effect. His rhetoric aims not at *movere*, not even at *utilitas*, but at a suggestion of metaphysics contained in germ within the situation and "fleshed out" by the narrative of the martyr. His is a rhetoric of direction that both englobes and surpasses intention.

As d'Aubigné develops it, a "martyrological narrative" contains a cluster of descriptions of martyrdoms, spotlighting the words uttered by the martyr and surpassing the image his body generates, arranged strategically so as to facilitate the insertion of the author's personal perspective, and theological self-realization, into the repetition of the soteric event. D'Aubigné authors a textual composite by blending the diverse martyrs' testimonies and bodies (always particularized and individualized, never generalized as in the format for saints' bodies) together in a pattern instructive of how personal salvation transpires.⁷ In an expansive reworking of the resurrection theme, two types of bodies stand at the origin of this text: that of the confessors and that of the writer. Assimilating his body to theirs, forming it upon their model but, more important, taking up fragments of their confessional statements and reiterating them in his own sense, d'Aubigné claims that the resurrection the martyrs experience will also happen to him. This will be a *textual* resurrection: the recuperation and persistence of words. The text both embodies that pledge and figures forth the new, changed, resurrected body of d'Aubigné. Here, the flesh becomes both Word and word: while the martyrs' lives point beyond their existence to the Divine, they also serve to validate the text that grants eternity to them. D'Aubigné's human text acts like, and may even dare to claim to be, Scripture or, at least, that divine register of which Huguenot writers speak, the roll call of the elect:

I shall not forget you...
I will pull your name from the shadowy night
Your secret martyrdom, your hidden example
By my writing shall be pulled out of the shadows.⁸

In some measure, d'Aubigné's text itself is a metaphysical structure: it is both the theater for the reassemblage of testimony pointing beyond itself to God and that metatextual system of confirmation and validation which bestows value upon and recognizes the merit of the materials (martyrs, *matière*) with which it works. A sophisticated literary *dédoublement* thus characterizes Reformation rhetoric—and this is certainly borne out in other of d'Aubigné's works. His autobiography, *Sa vie à ses enfants*, shows him situating himself within his own texts, brooding on their, and his, significance, or dialoguing with himself in dreams saturated with stylistic considerations. Jean-Raymond Fanlo notes that "acting in order to die, is to place oneself within the doubled perspective of both the cadaver dying on the table at Talcy, and of the seer who loses himself in God."⁹ Once (self-) designated as saved, d'Aubigné is freed to speak about himself not merely as a component in and of a larger theological system, but also about himself as (secular) Self. D'Aubigné thus participates along with other Protestant martyrologists in creating a new genre through the interpenetration of theology, history, and literature. He develops his own rhetoric through which to textualize lives.

While I focus primarily on martyrological narratives in this chapter as those texts which furnish the occasion for the development of a Reformed rhetoric that functions as a scripture of the Self, it should be noted that other Reformed types of writing conform to this paradigm. For instance, Calvinist meditational literature is, at least at times, an autobiographical genre. Motivating the Protestant meditational project is the sin committed by the sinner and, thereby, the notion of autobiography. A "scripture of the Self" interposes itself between biblical word and recipients of both biblical and meditational texts. Only a sin-and-salvation dialectic can resolve this tension. Writing focuses on the fallen Self, to confess that unregenerate state. Yet through a confession of sin, writing—and redemption—may occur. The Calvinist meditational tracts of Jean de Sponde, d'Aubigné, and Théodore de Bèze serve to demonstrate how such writers labored under the Calvinist proscription against discussion of the Self.[10] These men wrote camouflaged works which, while apparently scripturally faithful, actually contain instances of autobiographical infiltrations or even eruptions. Meditational writing yields to life-writing, as the Self, rather than the scriptural model, predominates in the text.

Jean de Sponde in his *Méditations* appears to adhere to Calvinist injunctions instructing him to "rid [him] self... of these old rags of vices,"[11] and enjoins "all the same, nothing of yourself; it is the heavens [rather] which produce these effects."[12] He is to practice self-emptying, not self-expression: "Void yourself of your sins and fill yourself with the good things that come from God."[13] He emphasizes his inadequacy, the feebleness of his voice: "my insufficiency"; "my poor mouth";[14] he will silence himself and substitute the Word of Scripture. Sponde portrays the Calvinist Self as a microcosm of the fallen, corrupt and condemned world:

This World which squats thus within itself
Never swerves from loving that which it loves
And can love nothing other than its own misshapenness.[15]

This imploded vision of the world demonstrates the dangers of turning in on the Self, of proffering a personal perspective. Yet, by turning in and knowing one's sin, one can develop the Self beyond the confines of sin's clutches. Sponde ultimately shifts the emphasis from exterior Other (God) to interior Self, viewing selfhood as a vehicle for his own salvation: he moves away from meditation on Scripture to a scriptural meditation on himself. Within the Self he paradoxically finds sin a prerequisite to salvation:

> Enter into yourself, enter into your conscience
> You will see your salvation if you will see your sin.[16]

The Self is then enabled to write its own story, in a dialogic engagement with God: "I have allowed myself to take pen in hand, to discuss these matters freely with our God."[17] Sponde uses his own body, by means of his text, as the site of God's legitimation; in a daring move, God's reality is confirmed in and through the Self:

> I believe in this sole Word of God, in this voice
> alone which has resounded in my ears but which I
> have often pondered upon within myself and in which
> I have struggled mightily, to well confirm it, that
>   I can no longer doubt it in any way.[18]

This maneuver is similar to the doubled, textual but also metatextual, nature of d'Aubigné's *Les tragiques* on which I have already commented. God's Word is that cornucopia which has created Sponde's physical being and which unleashes and enfleshes the textual entity. The text becomes the theater for the situation of man's sinful state, yet enacts the legitimation of the writing self who records it: "God is hungry for our inner man; he watches out for our souls, not for our hands."[19] These hands which God disregards are therefore freed to write, and to write of the Self.

Both d'Aubigné's *Méditations sur les pseaumes* and de Bèze's *Chrestiennes méditations* are arguably literary documents, since the cultic purposes of the meditational genre are clearly altered and surpassed. Each demonstrates autobiographical rhetoric: the ends to which Scripture is employed are intensely personal. D'Aubigné reassigns the purpose of devotional manuals; for him, they are part of a literarily determined textual universe. He intends to use the *Méditations* stylistically to counteract the claim that biblical style is too plain or simple. He crafts the

Méditations to his own purpose, enrolling them in the lists of a battle for which they are generically unsuited. Similarly, the unusual format of the work shows d'Aubigné not as an exegete or commentator, but rather as an author capable of crafting and manipulating a text. His meditations are tripartite; they include a transcription of the Psalm from which they ostensibly devolve, an "occasion," and an "argument." Citing the Psalm in its entirety invites the reader to compare it to d'Aubigné's meditation. The differences are glaring. D'Aubigné's meditation is tailored to his own concerns. The "occasion" and "argument" heighten this situation of difference: the "occasion" is a historical contextualization of d'Aubigné's literary inspiration. Thus, through the pattern of his text, his historical Self is always interposed between biblical Word and his subsequent development. D'Aubigné takes hold of biblical material and sculpts it in his own sense. In the "occasion" for Psalm 51, he states that this meditation was written "on the subject of an act of repentance that the King, while still King of Navarre, made at La Rochelle. The author gave this meditation to the King, and it was very well received."[20] The "argument" displays originality and deviance, rather than conformity to the scriptural model. In this space between pattern and supposed reproduction, Calvinist autobiographical writing can be discerned.

Both d'Aubigné and de Bèze include Psalm 51 in their meditations. This is a particularly effective example of how the author's Self inscribes itself in the meditations, since in it David the psalmist figures himself. De Bèze and d'Aubigné adopt the David persona, rework it, and personalize it. The David persona, himself a writer of songs and verses, is a potentially liberating construct for literary production.[21] D'Aubigné and de Bèze use David as a cipher for their own expression, blurring the difference between "I" David and "I" de Bèze or d'Aubigné. D'Aubigné focuses on the body, as though to fit himself into David's lineaments. A physical relationship exists between d'Aubigné-David and God; God is his "lawyer who takes us by the hand like the children of his house."[22] Neither of these developments is contained in the original. D'Aubigné thus alters Scripture into allegory. He further adds the motif of pictorial representation, which becomes the means for his self-representation. He creates a portrait within a portrait: his own face, yet disguised, looks back at him from the mirror into which David gazes in d'Aubigné's text. Thus a self-portrait embedded in his text confronts d'Aubigné:

staring back at me . . . a horrifying portrait, a
hideous goat . . . a terrifying crocodile . . . a wolf
. . . and then without a portrait it displays as in a
mirror the same things as it mirrors my face.[23]

The emphasis is on process, not portrait. The image becomes event, which can be narrated progressively (". . . and then without a portrait . . ."); the Self is changeable and cannot be fully known; its metamorphoses can only be captured in the dynamic text, not the static image. D'Aubigné illicitly focuses on the Self, finding a multiplicity of selves inscribed *en abyme,* of which David, and by extension the Psalm, becomes only one among many figurations. The goat, the crocodile, and the wolf in the mirror do not facilitate religious expression, nor do they translate David's self-perception. Rather, they propose a personalized psychology of how d'Aubigné views himself as a sinner. D'Aubigné steps out of the David persona as though redeemed from sin through the operation of his text, mandating the resurrection of his body. "Grant me the good news of my deliverance . . . in order that these bones and marrow, melted before the fire of your anger, may be restituted in the restoration of the moribund and the reestablishment of the lost soul."[24] D'Aubigné abandons the format and content of the Psalm, substituting an autobiographical statement explicitly equated with authorship: "the author, stricken by an overwhelming sorrow upon the death of Suzanne de Lézai his wife, took Psalm 88 and made from it Sapphic verses."[25] He converts biblical material to personal, lyrical expression, appropriating Scripture as the vehicle of his own assertion.

De Bèze's meditation on the same Psalm is stamped with self-awareness. He, too, adopts the David persona and fabricates a myriad of detail that does not exist in the biblical text. De Bèze does not cite the Psalm on which he purportedly models his work, possibly to avoid the kind of tension that d'Aubigné generates through juxtaposition, or perhaps to exalt his own work as normative and independent. Instead, he uses directive paraphrase to recast Scripture in his own sense. Much of de Bèze's meditation seems to be spoken in his own voice. At times, however, David speaks of himself and to himself in a doubling process that recalls the mirror effect in d'Aubigné's meditation and the doubled quality of *Les tragiques.* De Bèze sees himself, sees himself in David, who sees himself and renders judgment on himself. "I see David . . . but in order to make myself take both sides, and in order to judge against myself."[26] De Bèze does not explicitly inscribe his own body in the text. Rather, he anatomizes a generic sinful body modeled on that of David: "treacherous tongue...bold hands stained with countless murders... this audacious tongue...this guilty heart."[27] De Bèze does, however, effect an autobiographical aperture in his text by discussing the phenomenon of authorship: David is the author of a crime, de Bèze the author of a text. The sinful persona of David is spotted with *pollutions a / encrees* [sins anchored within myself / sins inked into me] in a wordplay that locates sin in the interior person (*ancrer:* to anchor) and simultaneously implicates writing as sinful (*encrer:* to pen). David's adultery is described in terms of writing. The letter ordering Uriah's death stains writing with sin and equates individual creation—the composition of a letter deviant from God's will—with damnation. The bed on which the adulterous act occurs is "blotted" with the signs of sin as though splotches of ink marred a blank page, and the black-and-white color motif of this meditation suggests writing or printing.

I have already noted that autobiographical segments, and particularly references to the Self as author, are embedded in d'Aubigné's writing. In his autobiography, d'Aubigné discusses how he authorizes his word. Suffering, an awareness of sinful status, and literary creation link together:

> I began this work, during the wars of '77...
> where the author...thinking he was going to die
> as the result of wounds received in a great battle,
> drew up this text as a testament.... Await my death
> which cannot be far off, and then examine the fruit
> of my labor...on the lists of the martyrs I will
> say that which the angel of God has dictated that I write.[28]

D'Aubigné depicts himself as a mutilated potential martyr, to position himself among the martyrs of whom he speaks. D'Aubigné's historical treatment of his own suffering is considerably more developed as a narrative than are those he provides of the martyrs, about whom similar facts were known and available (and cited copiously by Crespin and Foxe). He thereby creates a self-representation substantial enough to stand up with the heroic martyrological figures. Structuring his (fictive and unactualized) personal martyrdom scenario as a homologue of the martyrological anecdote, d'Aubigné uses his body, pretext for the "testament" he writes, as a text upon which he comments (he gives similar treatment to the martyr Anne du Bourg, who structures his body as an annotated text at his funeral pyre: "I am only the index to a larger text."[29] Simultaneously, d'Aubigné joins his body/text to the divine Word. Creating text from body, d'Aubigné embodies his text and empowers it to act as his advocate, to produce legitimized speech about the Self. The rhetoric of death, of wrenching apart, requires text to recuperate that which has been sundered, and such a text is now authorized: the torments of the body ensure the validity of speech.

Unlike the instances he narrates of martyrdoms, d'Aubigné does not cite his own words here but, rather, relies exclusively on text as the vehicle for his personal expression and the medium of his confirmation in the martyrological persona. Lest the combined force of text and image be inadequate, he threatens his impending death assuring that it, like that of the martyrs, will bestow the stamp of his spirit-filled speech upon his writing. His authorship coextensive with his physical agony, d'Aubigné licenses himself to "say in this place that which the name of God dictates onto my paper."[30] The citation demonstrates that *Les tragiques* is the divine register ("in this place"). Indeed, while d'Aubigné in many places paraphrases scriptural verses, he also offers fragments from other of his own works, thus writing himself into his text as an authority coequal with God and perpetuating a coherent *literary* persona for himself. Rather than his text merely guaranteeing him, d'Aubigné's identity is used to validate the text. As the culmination of the central mininarrative in which he rehearses his own martyrdom, d'Aubigné records his own resurrection. He is assumed into the heavens, where he reads portions of his own text that portray martyrological tableaux; he then revives and his "esprit" rejoins his "corps." Body and text again join forces in the economy of d'Aubigné's writing.

> I, who call together ... their fears and their pains
> And then their freedom, I will be silent about my own.
> During these evil times my spirit, having left
> To murderers my body pierced in various places, ...
>   though impure, was taken up ...
> there ... I saw the beautiful secrets and
>   paintings of which I write ...
> Then, my forehead turned toward the blazing South
> There appeared ... Spectacles of past events which

> wheeled to the right
> ... There shone yet another hundred portraits in
> the distance ... [31]

D'Aubigné's resurrected posture is adamantly embodied; he reads the images, his forehead aligned with them, bodily stance thus mimicking the literary creation. This resurrection—d'Aubigné's own—is the only one visually depicted in *Les tragiques;* elsewhere, the martyrs are shown up in the heavens, but no resurrection is enacted. D'Aubigné clearly sees his text as the medium for, locus of, and proxy for, his body in the drama of election. Speech about himself is thus permitted as a tool in the salvific process.

A similar phenomenon obtains in an emblem book devoted to the Christian martyrs, in which de Bèze portrays himself in the process of textual composition. As with d'Aubigné, pain and resulting self-awareness motivate writing. As the author of *Icones,* de Bèze recalls, "in my afflictions diverse fantasies came into my mind. I had recourse to the Word of God ... thus reading sacred stories with a remarkable pleasure and profit, I was seized with the desire to strive to write in verse form such arguments."[32] For both authors, the stricken and helpless Self is involved in the act of creation. One must be martyred to be memorialized, dead in the body to live through the word.

The dominant trait of d'Aubigné's *Les tragiques* is its compendium of bodies and body parts. Yet, unlike the bodies contained in Catholic hagiographies, these bodies do not possess, nor do they eventually develop, a significance of their own. They do not function as semantic units. D'Aubigné does not lament the dissolution of the body, but rather revels in it, recording the occasions of its torture. It is in the torture scene that the body, scarred and vilified, is prepared for spiritual elevation. For d'Aubigné, the body was expressly fashioned to be tortured, so that the Word might be spoken through it. D'Aubigné's text, itself a corpus, also suffers wounding, imitating the martyrdoms it reproduces; the paper of *Les tragiques* is broken, torn away ("I hid away the crumpled and torn papers from which I had grabbed that which you see here").[33] *Tirer* ("to pull away, to yank back") is a key word in the text. In d'Aubigné's organizational and inaugural rhetoric of reformation, election and textual creation occur (as in Genesis) through separation. This wound in the body is the occasion for the word. One martyrological anecdote recounts the fate of a young girl:

> I want to separate and emphasize faithful Mary,
> Who, seeing with disdain the tomb of her life
> And the earth and the coffin and the iron bars
> Where she was to be stifled in body though not in soul
> 'It is,' so she said, 'thus that the beautiful seed of the elect
> Is both buried and sown so as to be resurrected.'³⁴

This reenactment of her death makes d'Aubigné's text both her tomb (through the image of the *tombeau*) and the site of her election ("pull aside") through his word. The body for d'Aubigné becomes an arena of testing preliminary to assimilation with the Word. This is not a model in the sense of a hagiographic exemplum: it is not meant to be copied through the visual representation of its configuration or circumstances. Instead of acting like an exemplum, the body of the martyr institutes a modeling *process* for those who read of it. This process necessitates the conjunction of word and image to compose a dynamic, textual emblem. The body itself does not have significance; God's reception, and d'Aubigné's recuperation, of the confessional word uttered bestows sense upon it. Thus, unlike the portrait characteristic of hagiographies, a process—that of reading—typifies martyrologies. Such reading replicates the oral scene in which confessional words were first enunciated and reestablishes a situation of reception and response that leads to a rhetoric of the Self (we might call this "Reformation 'reader-response'"). The suffering body surpasses itself in and through speech, and it appeals to its audience and readers to search out their own reactions to its words. For example, the caged, tormented body of an illiterate prisoner transforms into the persona of a preacher:

> Witness that for two years and six months in a high 'cathedral chair,'
> The preacher frightened his judges with his sentence.
>   In incessant verses he praised God,
>   His strong voice preached...
>   Pure truth issued forth from that cage.³⁵

The power of the word, related to the wind of the spirit, the Paraclete ("for the Spirit which expresses itself in tongues of fire.../ Words of fire came out of their mouths"³⁶), shows that language is the essential tie between God and the martyr. It is for this reason, for instance, that Protestant martyrologies such as Jean Crespin's *Histoire des martyrs* do not depict martyrs accompanied by characteristic iconography as is the case with hagiographies (St. Catherine and her wheel, for example). This would be static portraiture, encapsulating meaning in image or typical trait, and would short-circuit the movement, questioning, and direction beyond that necessitated by the Protestant processual rhetoric of self-construction.

This emphasis on verb (and *Verbum*) recurs in *Les tragiques;* rather than recreate an image, d'Aubigné rehearses events and actions. For example, the motif of the sowing of the seed likens the martyr's broken bodies to seeds that must be scattered in an earthen grave in order to germinate for the harvest. This motif replicates d'Aubigné's strategy in "Feux": he strews the text with fragmentary references ("You, O Gastine and Croquet, come out of those graves / Here will I plant your heads"[37]) which the reader must then collate to create the textual harvest of Protestant redemption. The reader is absolutely essential to the signifying process, thereby spotlighting the construction of selfhood. The body of the martyr acts as the hull of the seed: it is the container of the word which is released and activated by the destruction of the body. The martyr's exemplary role in the text thus functions as a form of fecundation. Others imitate their example because they have "mis leur semence sur" them. A similar sort of procreative reverbing, a seminary or school for selfhood, requires the reader to complete the movement of the text rather than emulate it (as would be the case with hagiographies). For this reason, d'Aubigné scatters images of himself throughout his text, in close proximity to, or interwoven with, those of the martyrs, so that his speech receives the imprimatur of the election to which their martyrdom, and his text, testifies. Imbricated in this company is a third body, that of the reader.

D'Aubigné is obsessed with *making sense* of the devastated Protestant body. Unlike martyrologists such as Crespin or Foxe, he does not aim at inclusivity; rather than compose an exhaustive compendium of martyrs, he gleans out those materials best suited to his aims. The martyrs d'Aubigné selects are not only *tesmoins* to the truth through the torture they experience, they are also representatives, for those who read the text, of the fulfillment of the requirements for salvation. This selectivity stylistically mimes d'Aubigné's concern with the doctrines of election and of prevenient grace. For this reason, his text is more literary in tenor and, especially, personalized. In the preface, d'Aubigné tellingly describes the position of his body in relation to Catholic oppressors: he uses a slingshot, like David against Goliath, to throw *cailloux blancs* at the heads of his persecutors. The white pebble, employed in the book of Revelation as a symbol of election, is also a by-product of cremation; charred pebbles (and not poeticized "ashes") are the actual remains of martyrs' bones. Joining life and death in one symbol and thereby concentrating therein the dialectic that drives his text, d'Aubigné simultaneously opens out the body—as he had refused closure to the martyrs' bodies—into a concatenation of exemplary references set to an autobiographical purpose: David and Goliath, Revelation, and the martyrs' words uttered prior to incineration weave a web of intertexts within which d'Aubigné textually situates himself and his reader. (He also likens his book to the *caillou* David throws, thereby intimately linking the stance of his body and the work he composes.) For instance, d'Aubigné relates the death of a young girl who, splotching the air with her blood, thereby writes a testimony of her ordeal, as well as that truth to which she attests: "her left hand made a sign / Completely bathed in her innocent blood. / In the air she raised this bloody hand."[38] The wordplay between *sang* (blood) and *seing* (personal seal), attests to the intimate relationship between the body and writing.

Reformation life-writing as exemplified in *Les tragiques* describes the interpenetration of theological and personal expression. Martyrs act as models for the faithful which must be actualized, extended: in short, *received* by a responsive readerly Self who is himself or herself, in this phenomenon of reception, authenticated. Martyrs thus constitute the flexible framework for the process of d'Aubigné's own self-shaping. Through narrative, d'Aubigné writes both a sacred and a secular story, licensing his own speech about the Self by embedding it in a larger, metaphysical narrative. Reformation life-writing as displayed by d'Aubigné is therefore always proximate and relational, but never precisely imitative. It is constructed through a network of personae and anecdotes accepted for their theological value, yet reinterpreted for personal aims. Embodiment, or reembodiment, is a necessary component (if ultimately surpassed) in enabling the speech of the Self. D'Aubigné's version of Reformation life-writing functions parasitically, ingesting bodily parts and snippets of the martyrs' speeches to render more substantial the construction of the Self. Such citations are not imitative, but revisionary: fragments of phrases call out for situation in sentences; the denial of the totality of the original statement necessitates a new coherent formulation, to be supplied by the inquisitive Self reading the text, desiring closure and sense. The extreme self-consciousness subtending d'Aubigné's oeuvre derives from the climate of religious persecution in which he was first impelled to display his authorial persona. Reformation life-writing does not work with the notion of *auctoritas* in the same way as does Renaissance life-writing; it opposes rather than accepts, fractures rather than unifies, restates anew rather than quotes. Above all, it ultimately situates itself in relation to Self rather than to an authority. Citations from the work of others to bolster what the Reformation writer has to say about himself or herself are conspicuously absent (as we have seen in d'Aubigné's tendency to paraphrase even the martyrs' speeches). Even in strictly theological writing, rather than theological paraliterature such as d'Aubigné's work, commentary moves from medieval exegesis, seamed with the annotations of many other previous interpreters, to exposition, in which the commentator extrapolates from (personal) life experience the applicability of the passage at hand. The narratives of the lives of others are invoked only inasmuch as they articulate the personal expression of the author. Formed in adversity, characterized by singularity, the Reformation writer acknowledges no predecessor—other than God. William Paden has observed that for Puritans, latter-day Calvinists, "the significant antithesis was not between God...and world, but between God and self."[39] D'Aubigné resolves this tension textually, using the figures of martyrs as a middle ground to highlight language, rhetoric, and text as the critical devices mediating between event and our reception of it. Reformation martyrology, and other paratheological forms of Reformation writing constitute an entirely new genre in which the focus is on at least two selves: that of the author and that of the reader.

Calvinist life-writing occurs through an accretion of images not found in the parent text, through a modification of personae with particularized representatives of the Self, and through the discussion of how writing may be redeemed from its association with sin. Individuals shape the standards of their salvation for themselves by writing. The focus on the self is necessary in order to inscribe it into a salvific text. Despite Calvinist interdictions on self-expression, Sponde, d'Aubigné, de Bèze and others write meditations that legitimize speech of and about the Self. The reader is invited to emulate their program by writing further autobiographies. The figures of selves author a new, self-expressive genre created, paradoxically, within a system established, at least in part, to inhibit the Self.

NOTES

1. For a ground-breaking recent study that discusses varieties of intertextual investigations along with its contribution to elaborations of self-constructs, consult Richard Goodkin, ed., *Autour de Racine: Studies in Intertextuality,* special issue of *Yale French Studies* 76 (1989).

2. Similar scenarios of textual engineering resulting in guarantees of salvation for the author can be found in Jean Crespin and in John Foxe. Théodore de Bèze, d'Aubigné's mentor, displays scenes of self-inscription on the divine roll. These are stunningly similar to those found in *Les tragiques:* see Catharine Randall Coats, *(Em)bodying the Word: Textual Resurrections in the Martyrological Narratives of Foxe, Crespin, de Bèze, and d'Aubigné* (New York: Peter Lang, 1992).

3. Richard Stauffer, *Dieu, la création et la providence dans la prédication de Calvin* (Berne: Peter Lang, 1978).

4. This dialogue embodies intertextuality and occurs, in the Protestant, internally through a process of *dédoublement,* which I discuss later in this chapter. William E. Paden, writing about Puritans, says that "The Protestant self must... become both accused and accuser.... the external, two-part [Catholic] dialectic of confessing and examining becomes an entirely internalized dialogue" ("Theaters of Humility and Suspicion," in Luther H. Martin et al., eds., *Technologies of the Self: A Seminar with Michel Foucault* [Amherst: University of Massachusetts Press, 1988], 75).

5. John Donne, "Holy Sonnet 24," *The Complete Works of John Donne,* ed. John T. Shawcross (New York: Anchor Books, 1967).

6. Charles Taylor, *Sources of the Self* (Cambridge, MA: Harvard University Press, 1989), 227.

7. On this, see Jacobus de Voragine's hagiographic compilation, *The Golden Legend: Readings on the Saints,* 2 vols., trans. William Granger Ryan (Princeton, NJ: Princeton University Press, 1992).

8. "Je ne t'oublieray pas... / Je tireray ton nom de la nuict tenebreuse / Ton martyr secret, ton exemple caché / Sera par mes escrits des ombres arraché," verses 993–96. All citations from d'Aubigné are from *Oeuvres complètes,* ed. Henri Weber (Paris: Pléiade, NRF, 1969). All translations are my own.

9. "Agir pour mourir, c'est se placer dans la double perspective et du cadavre qui agonise sur une table à Talcy, et du voyant qui 'se pasme' en Dieu." Jean-Luc Fanlo, *Tracés, ruptures: La composition instable des Tragiques* (Paris: Champion, 1990), 365.

10. Cf. Catharine Randall Coats, *Subverting the System: d'Aubigné and Calvinism* (Kirksville, MO: Sixteenth-Century Essays and Studies, 1990), chaps. 1 and 2.

11. "Se despouiller... de ces vieux haillons de vices." Jean de Sponde, *Médi-*

tations, eds. Alan Boase and Françoise Ruchon (Geneva: Caillier, 1969), 236. All other references in the text to Sponde are to this edition. All translations are my own.

12. "Toutesfois rien de toy, c'est les Cieux qui produisent...ces effaicts." Sponde, *Méditations*, 236.

13. "Vuyde-toy de tes maux et t'emply de[s] biens [de Dieu]." Sponde, *Méditations*, 237.

14. "Mon insuffisance"; "ma pauvre bouche." Sponde, *Méditations*, 246.

15. "Ce Monde qui croupist ainsi dedans soy-mesme / N'esloigne point jamais son coeur de ce qu'il aime / Et ne peut rien aymer que sa deformité." Sponde, *Méditations*, 248.

16. "Entrer dedans toy-mesme, entre en ta conscience / Tu verras ton salut si tu vois ton péché." Sponde, *Méditations*, 237.

17. "Je me suis dispensé de mettre la main à la plume, pour en discourir librement avec nostre Dieu." Sponde, *Méditations*, 95.

18. "Je crois à cette seule parole de Dieu, à ceste voix unique qui m'a frappé les oreilles, mais que j'ay souvent médité en moy-mesme, et en laquelle je me suis si bien exercé, si bien confirmé, que je n'en doute plus." Sponde, *Méditations*, 233.

19. "Dieu est affamé de nostre intérieur; il prend garde à nos esprits et non pas à nos mains." Sponde, *Méditations*, 184.

20. "Sur une repentance que fit le Roi, estant Roy de Navarre, à la Rochelle, l'autheur luy fit present de cette méditation laquelle fust lors très bien receue." D'Aubigné, *Méditations sur les pseaumes*, in *Oeuvres*, 536.

21. On self-portraiture through *figura*, consult Michel Beaujour, *Miroirs d'encre* (Paris: Seuil, 1980).

22. "Advocat qui nous prens par la main comme enfans de la maison." D'Aubigné, *Méditations*, in *Oeuvres*, 538.

23. "M'affronte...un portrait effroyable, un vilain bouc...un espouvantable crocodile...un loup...et puis sans portrait me fait voir dans son miroir les mesmes choses en m'y voyant." D'Aubigné, *Méditations*, in *Oeuvres*, 538.

24. "Fay-moy la nouvelle de ma délivrance par le tesmoignage intérieur de ton Esprit, qui me prononce ma grace...afin que ces os et moelles fondues devant le feu de ton courroux soyent restituees en la restauration du mourant et retablissment du perdu." D'Aubigné, *Méditations*, in *Oeuvres*, 540.

25. "L'auteur accablé d'un deuil démesuré pour la mort de Suzanne de Lézai sa femme prit le Pseaume 88 pour en tirer des vers sapphiques." D'Aubigné, *Méditations*, in *Oeuvres*, 547.

26. "Je voy David...mais pour me faire partie et juge contre moymesme...mon meschanceté sans cesse se manifeste devant mon propre esprit." Théodore de Bèze, *Chrestiennes méditations*, ed. Mario Richter (Geneva: Droz,

1965), 72. All references in the text to de Bèze are to this edition. All translations are mine.

27. "Langue traiteresse... mains audacieuses de tant de meurtres... ceste audacieuse langue... coeur coupable." De Bèze, *Chrestiennes méditations,* 71.

28. "Il ya trente-six ans et plus que cette oeuvre est fait [*sic*], assavoir aux guerres du septante et sept... où l'autheur... se tenant pour mort pour les playes receues en un grand combat, il traça comme pour testament cet ouvrage.... Attendez ma mort qui ne peut etre loin, et puis examinez mes labeurs... au roolle des martyrs je diray en ce lieu ce que sur mon papier dicte l'Esprit de Dieu." D'Aubigné, *Sa vie à ses enfants,* in *Oeuvres,* 178–79.

29. "Je ne fay qu'un indice à un plus gros ouvrage." D'Aubigné, *Les tragiques,* verse 609 in *Oeuvres,* 131.

30. "Di[re] en ce lieu, ce que sur mon papier dicte le nom de Dieu." D'Aubigné, *Les tragiques,* verse 611, in *Oeuvres,* 131.

31. "Moy, qui rallie ainsi... leurs frayeurs et leurs peines / Et puis leurs libertés, me tairay-je des miennes. / Parmi ces aspres temps l'esprit, ayant laissé /Aux assassins mon corps en divers lieux percé... / Bien qu'impur, fut mené... Pour voir les beaux secrets et tableaux que j'escris... / Doncques, mon front tourné vers le Midi ardent, / Paroissoyent... Les spectacles passez qui tournoyent sur la droicte... / Là esclatent encor cent portraits eslongnés." D'Aubigné, *Les tragiques,* verses 1191–211, in *Oeuvres,* 178–79.

32. "Il y a environ deux ans, que Dieu m'a faict la grace d'habandonner le pais auquel il est persécuté, pour le servir selon sa saincte volonté; durant lequel temps pource qu'en mes afflictions diverses fantaisies se sont présentées à mon esprit; j'ay eu mon recours à la parolle du Seigneur... la parolle duquel est toujours accompagnée de l'effect... Lisans donc les histoires sainctes avec un merveilleux plaisir et singulier prouffict, il m'est pris un désir de m'exercer à escrire envers tels arguments." De Bèze, *Icones, les vrais pourtraicts des hommes illustres,* ed. Alain DuFour (Geneva: Droz, 1972), 48–49.

33. "Je desrobay les paperasses enrottees et deschirees desquelles j'ay arraché ce que vous voyez." D'Aubigné, *Les tragiques,* in *Oeuvres,* 7.

34. "Je veux tirer à part la constante Marie, / Qui, voyant en mespris le tombeau de sa vie / Et la terre et le coffre et les barres de fer / Où elle alloit le corps et non l'âme estoffer: / 'C'est,' ce dit-elle, ainsi que le beau grain d'eslite /Et s'enterre et se seme afin qu'il ressuscite.'" D'Aubigné, *Les tragiques,* verses 529–34, in *Oeuvres,* 129.

35. "Tesmoin deux ans six mois qu'en chaire si hautaine, / Le prescheur effraya ses juges de sa peine. / De vers continuels, il louoit Dieu, / Sa voix forte preschoit... / Des pures veritez sortoient de cette cage." D'Aubigné, *Les tragiques,* verses 405–10, in *Oeuvres,* 126.

36. "Pour l'esprit qui s'explique en des langues de feu... / Les paroles de feu

sortirent de leur bouche." D'Aubigné, *Les tragiques,* verses 508–10, in *Oeuvres,* 129.

37. "Vous, Gastine et Croquet, sortez de ces tombeaux / Icy je planteray vos chefs." D'Aubigné, *Les tragiques,* verses 719–20, in *Oeuvres,* 134.

38. "Sa main gaucha seigna / Entiere dans son sang innocent se baigna. / En l'air elle hausse cette main degouttante." D'Aubigné, *Les tragiques,* verses 1067–69, in *Oeuvres,* 142.

39. Paden, "Theaters of Humility and Suspicion," 68.

10

The Rhetoric of Martyrdom: Generic Contradiction and Narrative Strategy in John Foxe's *Acts and Monuments*

D. R. Woolf

> For oftentimes the will and pleasure of God is to beautifie and adorn his kingdom with the weake and simple instruments of this world: such as in the olde Testament Amos was, who with many other of obscure and unknowne names, were called from the heards and foldes to the honour of the prophets: as likewise we read of the Apostles that were called from Fishermens craft, and put into Churches.[1]

Flowing over some two thousand folio pages and several hundred thousand words in the fourth edition of 1583, John Foxe's *Acts and Monuments of these Latter and Perillous Dayes, Touching Matters of the Church* (the title of the first edition of 1563), better known as the "Book of Martyrs," chronicles the agonies of the true Church of Christ from apostolic times, through a series of persecutions by Roman emperors, medieval popes, and English monarchs, climaxing in the most notorious of all English persecutions, that of Bloody Mary between 1553 and 1558. A great deal has been written about Foxe, his religious views, his historical methods, and his attitude to the past.[2] Many critics, beginning in Foxe's own time, have noted the ambiguities and confusions in his book; one recent author finds in the work a "critical malaise" symptomatic of a "general disorder."[3] The purposes of this chapter are to explore the problems of structure and order in Foxe's history by examining some previously overlooked aspects of his narrative strategy, including his use of medieval and Renaissance historical and literary models, and to address the rhetorical tensions that the Book of Martyrs reveals. In reading Foxe I am beginning with the following assumptions that I would hope do not require defense here: first, that any writer may borrow a variety of literary elements from the cultural conventions shared by himself and his readers;[4] second, that to draw on the conventions or the contents of a particular genre in no way obliges one to obey the rules of that genre, much less simply to create another example of it; and third, that early modern audiences, for all their sensitivity to matters of rhetoric and poetics, and perhaps because of it, were entirely capable of reading and responding to a complex narrative that mixes story forms and that freely uses or discards narrative conventions. Having stated these as starting points, I shall argue that any attempt to analyze Foxe's book according to a single inherited formal genre, or even a set of genres, oversimplifies the work, and that instead of *imitating* genres, Foxe's narrative strategy depends rather on *following* them, appropriating from them elements of plot, trope, and character that would resonate with his readership.[5] By analyzing the book in this way—by complicating our reading of the *Acts and Monuments*—we may end up closer to a sense of the ways in which Foxe would have been understood by his own socially heterogeneous audience.[6]

History, Hagiography, and the Limits of Genre

Among the medieval works on which Foxe could draw, the most obvious candidates were the various ecclesiastical historians from whom he drew the bulk of his early material, from Eusebius through Bede and Otto of Freising to the Protestant chroniclers Johann Carion and Johann Sleidan and, for the early and high medieval periods, the important *Magdeburg Centuries* initiated by Matthias Flacius Illyricus and written by a group of his associates. At one level, the *Acts and Monuments,* is simply a Protestant ecclesiastical history, differing from most medieval and sixteenth-century chronicles principally in the greater degree to which it subordinates secular events to a redemptive time scheme running inexorably toward the reformation on earth that must precede the arrival of the New Jerusalem. Foxe assuredly set out, as suggested by the title of the earliest, Latin edition of his work, *Commentarii Rerum in ecclesia gestarum,* to be the Eusebius of his own time, and there can be little doubt that among early Christian historians, the bishop of Caesarea exercised on his sixteenth-century successor a very strong influence, in particular as a guide to the proper selection and sorting of materials. Yet merely to assent to the obvious, that the *Acts and Monuments* is indeed an ecclesiastical history of Eusebian ambition and scope, will not get us terribly far. For one thing, such a flat assertion of genre provides little aid in understanding some of the problems that Foxe faced in writing the lives and deaths of several hundred men and women, ancient and modern, linked solely by their willingness to suffer for their faith (problems with which Eusebius, writing about a much shorter period and without the burden of twelve hundred years of medieval literature, had not to deal). For another, Foxe's very relationship to Eusebius, his earliest and greatest historiographic exemplar, is itself much more ambiguous than has been acknowledged, as indicated in subtle changes to the contents and the physical arrangement of successive editions of the *Acts and Monuments*. Although through virtually all the editions Foxe maintained his claim to be a historian and his work to be a universal history, he does not press this point throughout the work, nor as strongly in later editions. In 1570, for instance, he added a Eusebian-style preface "To the true Christian reader, what utilitie is to be taken by readyng of these Historyes," justifying his avoidance of the high politics and war that traditionally occupied the humanist historian. The "history" of this preface has become, in the 1576 edition, merely an address "To the Christian reader," and by 1583, the last edition Foxe had a hand in, the title to his preface no longer commends history at all but the broader and potentially more fictive category of a mere "story."[7] The 1570 edition is also, perhaps significantly, the last edition to be billed explicitly as an "ecclesiastical history." As the book grew larger and larger, and included more and more detailed accounts of the martyrs of his own time, the Eusebian paradigm became increasingly difficult to sustain. So, too, did Foxe's sense that he was telling a single-threaded story, imitating Eusebius's claim, with regard to his own predecessors, that he was endeavoring to "give them unity by historical treatment."[8]

The changes to the running headers of successive editions underline the fragmentation of the work as it expanded. The first edition bears a common running header, giving the title of the work, throughout. In the 1570 edition, arguably the closest to a Eusebian model, the "unity" of the story is forced by a split header on facing pages saying "Actes and Monuments / of the Church," a general title sandwiched in the center between marginal titles specific to the episode being recounted, for instance the martyrdom of Polycarp or the antipapalism of the emperor Henry IV. This printer's device provides a sharp reminder on every page of that edition of the providential historical connection that roots each story into a nominally unified history. The device disappears halfway through the 1570 edition (and does not return in subsequent printings), at precisely the point at which Foxe's account is ceasing to become the tale of the church through its elite and their enemies and is instead growing populated by the common folk whose presence on the stage threatens to stretch the boundaries of the historical. From the margins, the individual story now moves into the center of the page, and the providential-historical connection is from this point on a subdued presence rather than a driving narrative engine.[9]

If Eusebius, and church history in general, proved to be useful but problematic paradigms, we are left with the difficulty of explaining how, despite his progressive expansion of the text, Foxe nonetheless managed to achieve a coherent historical vision and to synthesize his mass of details into an account that made sense as a whole. To what possible genres can he have turned, other than history? An obvious candidate, if only as a foil, is hagiography, and it is undeniable that there is much about the book that makes us think of medieval saints, not least of all because Foxe's own profound faith in his ability to serve as a witness to the lives of his martyrs mirrors the narrative attitude taken by most medieval hagiographers.[10] Yet Foxe signals both his debt to and independence from the Catholic tradition of lives of saints in a dramatic way, in the "Kalender" of martyrs with which his book begins, a device that subverts as well as reinforces a hagiographic division of the year, imposing on it Protestant martyrs, listed month by month throughout the year in a way that profoundly irritated Catholic readers.[11] He also specifically attacks, in his Latin preface, such hagiographic texts as the *Golden Legend* for being utterly invented and unhistorical; and at various points in his account he denies the miracles attributed to popish saints reported by more reputable historians, such as Ranulf Higden, Bede, and Eadmer. At the same time, however, Foxe mimics this tradition by including his own answer to the miraculous: Protestant providences that, unlike the tales of hagiography, can be safely reported on the basis of credible testimony. On the death of Zwingli, for instance, he writes that "The report goeth, that after his body was cut first in foure peeces, and then consumed with fire, three daies after his death his friends came to see whether any part of him was remaining, where they found his heart in the ashes, whole and unburned: in much like manner as was also the heart of Cranmer archbishop of Canterbury, which in the ashes also was found and taken up unconsumed, as by credible information is testified" (791.A.91–B.7).

If Foxe's heroes are indeed reformed countersaints, purified of false, romish miracles, they are also more than a mirror image. Although he idealizes character and dwells on the virtues of piety, Foxe was not content simply to imitate hagiographic models. The flesh-and-blood victims of his tales do not live the lives of holy hermits. Moreover, they also inhabit a historical space, a temporal process that ranges back and forth beyond their own lives but that mirrors the transcendant eschatological scheme implicit in all medieval church history and most hagiography. The importance of history and hagiography as formative genres behind Foxe's own project is thus indisputable, though the precise relationship between those genres and the book remains troubling. But there are strong signs in the structure and contents, and especially in the rhetorical disposition of the Book of Martyrs, that Foxe, a well-educated rhetorician and the author of plays, was influenced by other, less "serious" genres, even if he did not seek to imitate them. One of these, again a medieval genre, is romance, which itself has some features in common, and shares a parentage, with the saint's life; the second, which intrudes even more strongly in the latter half of the book, is comedy.[12]

On the face of it, romance should have been even less suitable to Foxe's purposes than was hagiography, which at least pertained to the sacred. It is quite likely that Foxe, in common with many Protestant writers of his age, distrusted romance as a genre, thinking it, as we know he thought Old Comedy, frivolous, even bawdy.[13] He did, however, write two works for entertainment. The Oxford closet drama, *Titus et Gesippus*, which he penned in 1544–45, has unmistakable romance elements that can be traced to Foxe's sources, and in particular to Boccaccio; it is accurately described by its modern editor as a "romantic comedy."[14] A later play, *Christus triumphans*, composed in 1556 during Foxe's exile, allegorizes the Marian persecution and owes much less to romance; but it was termed by Foxe himself a *comoedia apocalyptica*, and both plays anticipate the comic themes that, I shall argue, would eventually intrude into the later books of the *Acts and Monuments*.[15]

Leaving aside his dramatic works, specific Renaissance exemplars of romance appear to have affected him little, and although the millennial subtext encourages a reading of the work as, instead, a kind of Christian epic, Foxe was certainly no Protestant Tasso or Ariosto. Yet even if Foxe has not imitated any specific formal genre, romance included, there are indisputably romance story elements in the design and structure of the *Acts and Monuments,* as there were in *Titus et Gesippus.* There is no central character, except the Church as a whole; nor is there an unilinear plot, beyond the providential supertext being written not by Foxe but by God. Instead, we find an interwoven narrative, consisting of a series of episodic accounts, spanning a millennium and a half, of the quest of true Christians for the One Church promised by God.[16] Though often speaking of the historian's duty to maintain the order of time and place (a point to which we will return), Foxe repeatedly exercised a narrative freedom of movement that has more in common with romance than with classical historical models: shifting time and location, his story bounces from one part of Christendom to another. The multistoried architecture of the *Acts and Monuments* has something of the structure of a good soap opera, especially in its early sections, where Foxe toggles back and forth between English and European events, relying on connecting themes and tropes rather than a single unified plot to maintain a sense of order.

> For in these diversities and alterations of times, I suppose the whole course of the church may well be comprised. The which church, because it is universall, and sparsedlie through all countries dilated, therefore in this historie standing upon such a generall argument, I shall not be bound to anie one certaine nation, more than another. (1)

In a medieval romance, the telos generally involves the hero in some sort of divinely aided transcendence of the obstacles placed in his path by a hostile and often marvelous environment, his triumph over material temptation, and the success of his "quest." Furthermore, romances at all times have nearly always focused not on the developing character of a single flawed protagonist, but on the static attributes of a variety of individuals in conflict. These are generally defined in stark terms that we would regard as naively black and white. The heroes of medieval and Renaissance romance alike are either perfect, like Galahad or Percival, or at the very least represent stable embodiments of virtues appropriate to their station: chastity, courtesy, nobility, generosity, and so on. Its villains, witches, giants, and monsters are unrepentantly and—unlike tragic dramatic villains such as Shakespeare's Richard III—unreflectively evil. The outward behavior of romance villains, indistinguishable from their inner qualities, is a function of the storyteller's need for a human agent to provide both a narrative obstacle for the heroes and a mirror for their pure acts. Romance writers such as Chrétien and the author of the Arthur cycle follow the adventures not of one character, even a superhumanly perfect being like Galahad, but of a variety of protagonists who, as Foxe said of his own martyrs, are "sparsedlie through all countries dilated." Romance cuts back and forth between story lines, and from one character to another, though generally these are set against a common foe who takes many shapes and appears in several places; sometimes romance heroes may even find themselves fighting each other. As Sir Richard Southern noted in connection with Chrétien, "the enemy is dispersed; he is everywhere and may be found everywhere"; this almost exactly describes, as we will see, Foxe's sense of the struggle between individual Christian martyrs and the forces of Satan afoot in the world, a struggle that also, not infrequently, entails struggles within the ranks of the godly; this sort of struggle, and the allegorical mode of thought that constructs it, can be found in aspects of medieval historical writing but is much more obvious in a genre closer at hand, the Tudor interlude, for instance in *King Johan,* written by Foxe's friend and mentor John Bale.[17]

It would be foolish simply to replace the assertion that Foxe was a Protestant hagiographer with some other oversimplification, such as that he was a Protestant author of romance, or even that his principal model lay in romance rather than history: this would be to fall into the same formalist trap that, I am suggesting, we need to escape. What he did was much more complicated, bringing the narrative looseness of the romance story form to bear on what was a tremendous organizational challenge, without tying himself to the limitations or the subject matter of the romance genre. The story line of the *Acts and Monuments* is a romantic one, defined less by what happens than by where events lead, to the immediate reestablishment of Protestantism in Foxe's time and, beyond that, to an implied, but as yet unrealized, final triumph of the true Church at some undefined future time known only to the Almighty. The actual finale as much as the future telos are points to which the storyteller proceeds only slowly and indirectly, as a series of tales-within-the-tale are paratactically grafted onto each other. Unlike most figures of hagiography, Foxe's subjects live in the world and play by its rules. Although some priests and bishops figure prominently in the Book of Martyrs, and though its author was himself an ordained minister with a high regard for the role of a godly clergy, Foxe was writing for a predominantly lay audience. Consequently, the vast majority of Foxe's hundreds of characters are not clerics at all, but members of the laity, whether rulers such as the emperor Henry IV, godly Lollard knights such as Sir John Oldcastle, or, in the last and most famous third of the book, the pious artisans and illiterate laborers put to death by the Marian regime.

That Foxe should choose to borrow some of the conventions of romance in casting his vision of the past should not be surprising. To find a model for such an emplotment of Christian history, he needed to look not to Chrétien or even Malory, but no further than the genre, ecclesiastical history, that provided the bulk of his material on the late Roman and medieval church. The gap between romance and historiography has itself been overstated; as several medievalists have noted, medieval chronicles, both Latin and vernacular, ecclesiastical and aristocratic, have a great deal in common with the structure of romances, often amounting to *romans à tiroir*.[18] Moreover, Walter Ong has argued forcefully that romance is the story form most highly suited to hierarchical societies in which literacy is confined to a small elite. Its episodic tales were highly suited to serial, interrupted oral performance, and the sharply polarized entities that inhabit most romances could most effectively strike the listener's senses and be retained in his or her memory. England in the later sixteenth century remained a hierarchical and marginally literate culture, albeit poised between an age of predominantly oral-scribal communication and the era of print, which was bringing with it an increase in popular literacy.[19] The *Acts and Monuments* signifies its own place in this liminal social moment by beginning and ending with the importance of reading:

> And while thou hast space, so employ thy selfe to reade, that by reading, thou maiest learne daily to know that may profit thy soule, may teach thee experience, may arme thee with patience, and instruct thee in all spirituall knowledge more and more, to thy perpetuall comfort and salvation in Christ Jesu our Lord.... (1949)

Print was the "science" given to man by God to stir up the reformation (768.A.36–49). Foxe knew as well as any that the overwhelming majority of the English population could not read, and print could help close the gap between the rude multitudes and the scripture by presenting

God's Word in alternative ways. His book provided the channel between the oral tales of martyrdoms, which required recording and replication, at the same time digesting the enormous weight of church history into a popular form that could be read by the literate but also comprehended by the vulgar. It is a work thoroughly attuned to the requirements of those on the margins of literacy, both the text itself and its accompanying illustrations relying to a great degree, as does romance, on frequent repetition with variation.[20] The text and the various charts and tables were designed for those who have the skills to consult the printed word. The woodcuts translated and simplified this information into graphic images capable of perception by the ordinary parishioner, icons that in turn would reinforce the effect of hearing the tales read aloud from time to time; frequently these illustrations were even detached from the book, colored, and stuck on walls to provide godly decoration.[21] This accounts, no doubt, for the number of copies of the 1583 edition that no longer have the pullout *A table of the X. first persecutions of the primitive church* printed by John Day in that year (and reprinted by Humfrey Lownes for the 1610 edition, from which it is often similarly missing), a chart that cross-references its images of martyrdom to the appropriate places in the text.[22]

So far I have found in Foxe hints of both the hagiographer and the romancer, and have argued that the romance story form is the more useful in explaining how the *Acts and Monuments* ends up as more than a mere series of discontinuous lives laid end to end, how it tells a story the *object* of which is the eventual triumph of the saints. This picture is still only two-dimensional. It does not explain how Foxe dealt with the obverse of the problem of continuity: namely, how to invest his martyrs, his *subjects,* with a limited individuality without making them appear essentially different. To do so, he superimposed on his romance skeleton some comic flesh and blood, putting to good effect his own experience in writing his earlier Latin *comediae.*[23] He thereby made his martyrs and Reformers seem more human, less extraordinary, and more immediate to the reader; in short, he gave a work of epic proportions and high sacred purpose a rhetoric that is distinctly "low-mimetic," grounding his own version of eschatological history in the dirt, flesh, and cloth of the experiential world.

Comparatively late in the narrative, when Foxe reached the age of the Lollards and the Tudor Reformers, he ran into a further complication: the backbone of the Reformed Church was neither the godly prince nor the reforming bishop, but the commoner. This would pose problems for any writer standing, however tentatively, on a scaffolding of romance, but to a devout Reformer and preacher who also laid claim to the title of historian, it created profound generic contradictions. The heroes of *res gestae,* like their fictitious romance counterparts, are by definition not ordinary but extraordinary. Romances, as Auerbach has taught us, are among the least "mimetic" of prose genres, partly because they are not populated by the fishermen, carpenters, bricklayers, and cooks we meet in every day life. Yet historical reality was such that these were indeed the types of individual whose lives and deaths Foxe had set himself to depict. In short, Foxe faced the problem of writing a Christian history with material of wide social heterogeneity: the very subjects he wished to memorialize fit ill with any of the traditional "high" genres.

This tension becomes apparent as the narrative approaches Foxe's own times, and it is nowhere clearer than in his treatment of the hundreds of victims of popish persecution in England from Wycliffe to the Marian regime. There are certainly a number of august figures of high seriousness and inherited social rank: Cranmer, he tells us, came from a long line of English gentry. But the purpose of the book and its several reeditions was never to extol the high and mighty; and despite its enormous influence, in this respect the *Acts and Monuments* lies at the margins rather than at the center of Tudor historiography, its concerns quite remote from those of most secular historical writing and biography as these genres were to develop under Elizabeth and the early Stuarts.[24] Instead, Foxe's book sought to demonstrate, life by life, the courage, faith, and steadfastness of the ordinary English man and woman, down to the lowest of the low, so as to encourage those more fortunate ones who lived on into Elizabeth's time to imitate their godliness. The *Acts and Monuments* is not simply a recital of the great deeds of the past; it is an injunction to vigilance and godliness for the future, directed at the broadest possible spectrum of English churchgoers. This is precisely why the government insisted on its wide availability, chaining copies of the 1570 edition in cathedral churches by order of convocation, and why it enjoyed relatively steady and continuing sales at a time when most books of similar size and expense did not.

Foxe repeatedly emphasizes the humility and baseness of his martyrs; among other things, this allows him to contrast the earthly wealth and pomp of the Catholic Church with the apostolic simplicity of the saints. Furthermore, he tends to downplay the importance of the more famous martyrdoms: the deaths of Cranmer, Ridley, Latimer, and Hooper receive more coverage than most—in part because the documentation surviving from their cases was naturally more plentiful—but they are by no means pivotal figures in the narrative, and their executions, for all the attention they have since received, do not mark any sort of climax to the work as a whole (though, as we will see further on, Cranmer is assigned a special status within the briefer range of the Marian substory). Even major continental Reformers such as Luther and Calvin do not merit exceptional treatment. Those of high station often come from humble origins. Foxe's account of the life and death of Thomas Cromwell—who figures only as one among many martyrs, rather than as a main actor in the drama of Henry VIII's Reformation—stresses the fact that Cromwell was a blacksmith's son, whose great successes derived principally from the divine education of his mind (1074). As might any biographer, Foxe stresses the small acts of hospitality and charity toward the godly that this Protestant saint performed throughout his life: for instance, Cromwell's provision of meat to a poor pregnant woman during Lent, or his kindnesses to Cranmer's godly secretary, Ralph Morice, who survived the persecutions to provide Foxe with the details of Cromwell's life (1080.B.40–1081.B40).[25] Like Cromwell, the zealous Reformer Hugh Latimer is no aristocrat but the son of a Leicestershire husbandman, and a devout papist till he was "pretily caught in the blessed net of Gods word"—a peculiar mixture of georgic and piscatorial-apostolic metaphors (1570.B.80). This praise of the low-born does not extend to all, and certainly not to the conservatives in the church. Wolsey, notorious even then as the son of an Ipswich butcher, becomes Foxe's perfect example of wealth and corruption. Foxe interjects a "brief discourse" on the cardinal "by way of digression," in the midst of his account of early Henrician martyrs. Although, as Foxe admits, "it be not greatly pertinent unto this our history," it proves an effective narrative tactic; coming as it does immediately after a lengthy series of poor martyrs, it underlines the disparity in earthly wealth and status between the saints and the leaders of the unreformed church (899ff.).[26]

The most common sort of martyr is an ordinary person in town or country who shows little outward resistance to civil authority but is prepared to perish for the faith that God has graciously granted him or her. A typical group of saints, those martyred at Colchester in April 1556, includes two weavers, a tanner, a husbandman, a sawyer, and an apothecary. In most instances, execution is semivoluntary; it follows

Fig. 1. The execution of Archbishop Cranmer. Foxe, *Acts and Monuments* (London: John Day, 1583), II, 1888. (Photo by Findlay Muir. Courtesy of the Library: University of King's College, Halifax.)

repeated attempts by the forces of popery to tempt the victim out of his beliefs and back into the safety of the Romish Church, like Satan's temptation of Christ in the wilderness. The London martyr Thomas Whittle merits more space than do the six others with whom he burns because of his initial recantation (1673ff.). His story serves as a preparative to the reader, a type foreshadowing the more famous tale of Cranmer's recantation, and of his ritualistic burning of the hand that signed it (fig. 1), an episode that brings the Marian section to its horrific climax, since Cranmer is the last of the learned martyrs, "and almost the verie middle man of all the martyrs which were burned in all her raigne besides." Though far from representing everyman, Cranmer is at least a "middle" term amid one distinctive section in the longer historical process, a median rather than an average.²⁷ In cases such as his, the accused may obtain release, or be given some hope of the remission of punishment, before the pull of faith proves too great, forcing his relapse and rearrest. Being human, the condemned martyr may even experience a brief last-minute weakness, a personal Gethsemane, before Providence steps in and strengthens his resolve, allowing him to proceed not simply courageously, but happily, and sometimes even *merrily,* into the flames. This resolve is demonstrated over and over, perhaps nowhere more strikingly than in the case of the thirteen martyrs of Stratford-le-Bow, eleven men and two women, who go "joyfully" to the stake, kissing and embracing it (fig. 2). While the men are bound, the two women are "loose in the midst without any stake"; all are "burnt in one fire, with such love to each other, and constancy in our saviour Christ, that it made all the lookers-on to marvel" (1738).²⁸

As this last passage suggests, the comic side of the Book of Martyrs emerges both from Foxe's use of such stock narrative conventions as popular celebration and from his foregrounding of common folk.²⁹ The text is also genuinely entertaining, playful, and even funny, in many places. Foxe had a sense of humor, and he leavens his standard polemical tone with a dry wit. He even employs the occasional pun—his transition into a discussion of Edward Hall's *Chronicle,* one of his most important sources for Henry VIII's reign, is spoken of as a physical moving "out of the kitchen unto the *hall,*" for instance (532.A.41, emphasis added). Digression, too, is a rhetorical tactic that can use a humorous anecdote to make a point and at the same time lighten the reader's mood. An excellent example of this comes in Foxe's account of the panic over a nonexistent fire at Oxford in 1541 during the period of Henrician reaction following the enforcement of the antiheretical Six Articles.³⁰ On the face of it an unlikely candidate for humorous treatment, the grim business of the Henrician persecutions is rendered into entertainment, and humanized, through Foxe's skillful deployment of a "merrie and pleasant narration, touching a false fearfull imagination of fire, raised among the Doctors and Maisters of Oxford in S. Maries church at the recantation of M. Malary, M. of Art of Cambridge" (1102.A.8–1103.B.60). This tale is termed by Foxe himself "a tragicall storie of a terrible fire which did no hurt" (1103.B.49–50), yet which caused the deaths of several present, who were crushed to death in the panic. "Thus it pleased almighty God to delude these deluders, that is, that these great doctors and wise men of the schooles, which thinke themselves so wise in Gods

Fig. 2. The Stratford-le-Bow martyrs. Foxe, *Acts and Monuments* (London: John Day, 1583), II, 1915. (Photo by Findlay Muir. Courtesy of the Library: University of King's College, Halifax.)

matters as though they could not erre, should see by their owne senses and judgements, how blinde and infatuated they were in these so small matters and sensible trifles" (1102.A.80–86). There is a serious point, and the story is by no means irrelevant, but it performs the same sort of dramatic function as a barroom brawl or melée might in a modern war film, lightening the somber tone of the book. Foxe, who refers to this turmoil festively as a "pageant" (1102.B.92),[31] is able to see some humor in the episode, suggesting (as so often with reference to his favored language of ruptured bodies) that had the ancient philosopher Democritus heard such a tale, he would have "laughed his heart out of his bellie" (1102.B.46).

A further comic touch comes in the occasional intrusion of the ironic, "providential joke," whereby God avenges the deaths of his saints by inflicting on sinners and persecutors ends that mirror their own deeds.

Thus Stephen Gardiner, the time-serving bishop of Winchester, is struck down after hearing of the burning of his fellow prelates Ridley and Latimer. Gardiner lies ill for fifteen days before dying,

> his bodie being miserably inflamed within (who had inflamed so manie good martyrs before).... And thereof no doubt, as most like it is, came the thrusting out of his tongue from his mouth so swoln and black, with the inflammation of his body. A spectacle worthy to be noted and beholden of all such bloudy burning persecutors. (1622.B.80–87)[32]

The knight marshall of Calais, who refused to permit a martyr to bear witness to his faith before being hanged and quartered, meets a violent death in a skirmish with the French at Boulogne (1104.A.12). Others are eaten by lice, are struck down as they walk, or commit suicide. Their grim destinies (and the unspoken torments that lie beyond death) provide a grotesque countertext to the glorious ends of the godly. And a great deal of humor comes directly from the martyrs themselves, in their ability to jest with and often intellectually humiliate their persecutors, and in the manner of their deaths. The martyrs endure pain with a stoicism that goes beyond courage and dignity. In most cases they seem positively to enjoy the torment of the flesh and the spectacle of humiliation. We are told that Bishop Hooper, upon "having his neather parts burned, and his bowels fallen out," died like a child in his bed (1373.A.64–65). The detachment of body parts and the mutilation of organs maintains its grisly appeal in entertainment media even today; in Foxe's time, it appears to have had an even more powerful allure for readers.

Metaphor, Unity, and Historical Time

Having now identified what may be seen as elements of romance and comedy in the *Acts and Monuments,* the first in its overall conception, shape, and story line, the second in its rhetorical treatment of place and character, it remains to ask what Foxe does with these mythoi; more specifically, how he handles certain narrative problems, foremost among which was to maintain the integrity and distinctness of individual martyrological identity, the existence of discrete subjects rather than hagiographic types, without subverting a central theme of the book as a whole: the essential unity and wholeness of the Church, and the spiritual sameness of its adherents through time and space. Unity, enforced by ecclesiastical discipline, was an important theme of Foxe's many theological writings. He was the earliest Reformed Englishman to author a tract on discipline, and he remained committed to the notion of a single national church, though he adapted his views in the 1560s to reflect the ecclesiology of the Elizabethan regime, and also to allow for his own greater sympathy for Anabaptists and other sectaries condemned as heretics by their fellow Protestants.[33]

If there is a Burkean "master-trope" underpinning the *Acts and Monuments,* it is certainly metaphor, the figure of sameness. What strikes the reader most about the many successive accounts of persecutions, trials, and martyrdoms is how little they differ from one another: it is almost literally true that if you have read one martyr's death, you've read them all. Like most Reformers, Foxe subscribed to a cosmology that was Augustinian in its outlines, and the church father to whom his more learned martyrs appeal most frequently is none other than Saint Augustine himself. In this universe, there is only one undifferentiated essence, namely Go(o)d, against which is measured its own antithesis, (D)evil, which is simply a lack of good. "Good" is embodied on earth in Christ and his Church Triumphant, which is sometimes, though not always, coterminous with the Visible Church. The Church is no human institution, confined by the human dimensions of time and space; rather, it is a spiritual body (the oxymoron is intentional) which seeks, and finds, a multitude of physical manifestations that at bottom are essentially alike. As the martyr John Bradford explains, the true Church has existed "sithens the creation of men, and shall be for ever," while the institutions that surround it provide mere outer clothing (1465).

The Church knows no natural boundaries. While much of his narrative concentrates on England, Foxe in no sense suggested that the English were an especially privileged "elect nation," as William Haller once thought.[34] God respects neither time nor place: the first directive to the apostles is to go forth and spread the faith to the far corners of the world, but the popes and some misguided secular rulers of the eleventh century and after made a mockery of this by investing a specific place, Rome, with both sacred significance and preeminent authority. Even a series of well-intentioned acts such as the Crusades against Islam were foolish because they mistook a particular location, Jerusalem, for the real, spiritual Church, "as [if] it had been for the chiefe and onely force and strength of our faith" (391.A.76ff.) The Reformation was not, in Foxe's eyes, about the separation of a group of godly people from the corruption of humankind; it was rather a concerted effort to bring the unreformed segments of the Christian body back into conformity with Scripture. For all his loathing of Rome, Foxe never sought the outright destruction of Roman Catholicism; rather, he hoped for the sort of eirenic reform that might one day reduce all Christendom to the same godly obedience: the body of Christ's bride made whole, anew.[35]

The real rebels in Foxe's stories are not the martyrs who guard the gospel, but the ecclesiastical and civil forces that over the course of centuries have divided Christendom, just as more recently they have severed, through mutilation, the physical bodies of the saints. If unity is the watchword of the Reformed, division is that of Rome. The apparent unity of the Catholics, like their argument that they can boast a continued descent from Christ, is specious. "Antichrist also hath his unitie, which is not to be kept," Foxe asserts. "There is no unitie but where Christ knitteth the knot among such as be his" (1292.A.26, gloss–A.38). Discord is the devil's tool; his sowing of division among the godly during Edward VI's reign weakens the Reformation and allows the Catholic clergy to recover their strength. "Experience may teach us what discord worketh on publike weales; and contrary, what a necessarie thing concorde is to the advancement especially of Gods matters appertaining to his Church" (1292.A.51–54). Fearing that without their pastor they are likely to be divided, Rowland Taylor's flock at "Burntwood" bewail his execution with the cry, "What shall we poore *scattered* lambes doe?" (1387.A.6, emphasis added).

Even the central theological issue of the Eucharist is expressed as one of division versus unity. The differences between Catholics and Protestants on this issue are made clear in the confession of one martyr, John Denley (1529.A.1–15), while Foxe has Thomas Cranmer denounce the doctrine of transubstantiation on the grounds that it confuses the metaphorical relationship of blood and wine, body and bread with a literal one (1308–9). The preacher John Bland (under examination by Foxe's future critic Nicholas Harpsfield), pushes this point further, asserting that the popish Eucharist, in positing a false literal relationship in place of a true metaphorical one, actually "divides" the body from the flesh, "the one alive by the Godhead, the other livelie by Gods spirit, and both one sacrament" (1518.A.32–5). Similarly, when he is pressed to interpret Christ's "This is my body" remark, John Newman of Maidstone, a pewterer by occupation, replies that this is "a figurative speech, one thing spoken, & another meant, as Christ saith: I am a vine, I am a doore, I am a stone &c. Is he therefore a materiall stone, a vine or a doore?" (1770.A.10).

Foxe sustains this theme of unity through an extended play with a series of metaphors in which time, place, and circumstance are reduced to epiphenomena, accidents that matter little in the unfolding of history. The sole distinction that counts for anything is that between the binary opposites, good and evil, martyr and persecutor (fig. 3). Other distinctions of character, comportment, calling, and even social degree are all dissolved in the Church Triumphant, whither all true Christians seek to return.[36]

One of the great errors of the degenerate Church of Rome, in Foxe's view, is that it was "so addict to outward shewes," so fixated on the external details of religion, that it neglected the essence of the gospel. Ceremonies and laws count for little in Foxe's cosmos, where Christians are connected by common participation in blood: the spiritual blood of Christ shed for humanity, the symbolic blood drunk by the contrite sinner in communion, and the literal blood that the true believer sheds through his own immolation. The importance of blood as a unifying motif comes across early in the *Acts and Monuments,* where Foxe echoes Tertullian's statement that "the blood of Christians is seed," which, spilled upon the ground, spreads and issues in the growth of the Church. "Such is the wisedome and providence of God," writes Foxe, "that the blood of his deare saints (like good seed) never falleth in vaine to the ground, but it bringeth some encrease" (50.A.89). Throughout the text blood is the solvent that eradicates accidental differences and unites the holy, to one another and to Christ. The widow Margery Polley declares to the crowd assembled to witness her burning, "I am come to seale with my bloud Christs gospel, for because I know that it is true" (1527.A.75); William Tyms of Essex writes his final letter to his sister in his own blood (1723.A.25). On the other side, a thirst to shed blood is the mark of the persecutor. As Foxe comments in a gloss on the examination of John

Fig. 3. Model of Foxe's theme of unity and division

Bland, the reader must "Note how these Papists seeke for matter, to sucke the bloud of poore men" (1514.A.35, gloss). In perhaps the most grisly, and notorious, death of all, Foxe relates the burning of a Guernsey woman and her two daughters, one of whom, Perotine, is pregnant.[37] The accompanying woodcut (fig. 4) shows three naked women at the stake, one of whom has a newborn infant bursting out through her womb. According to Foxe, the child was removed from the flames and then cast back in. "And so the infant baptised in his owne bloud, to fill up the number of Gods innocent saints, was both born and died a martyr, leaving behind it the world, which it never sawe, a spectacle wherein the whole world may see the Herodian crueltie of this graceless generation of catholike tormentors" (1765.A24–29).[38] In this passage, first added in the 1570 edition (2129), Foxe goes beyond the flatter account of the affair published in 1563 (1544), playing upon the traditional link of blood with guilt, pronouncing the persecutors "bloudie guiltie homicides" whose crimes cannot be washed away. "Bloud, especiallie of Christs servants, is a perilous matter," Foxe declares further on, a matter which "will not be stilled with the lawes of men" (1915.B.61–64). No human law, from whatever authority it issues, can justify such bloodletting or deny God his vengeance on the tormentor.

Just as "blood" is necessary to wash the Church clean and unite its members, so is "fire," its elementary counterpart, the truest measure of spiritual strength.[39] Again, the fire is both literal and metaphorical: the Lollard William Sawtrey (d. 1401), a clerk degraded into a layman, is "inflamed with zeale of true religion" long before he is literally burned (474.A.56–476.B.70), as is the Henrician Thomas Bilney (910). In one synthesis of the fire image with the comic theme of martyrdom as marriage, Foxe describes how the Lollard John Badby, one of the first artificers executed under Henry IV, "*consummate[d] his testimony and martyrdome in fire*" (481.A.59–60; emphasis added); in another, the Petrine figure of the fisherman Rawlins White is burned at Cardiff in his wedding garment (1415.B.37); white in name, he is also clad in white (fig. 5). Fire not only purges but also provides illumination: the body of an Ipswich preacher, Robert Samuel, becomes a torch illuminating the gospel. "The report goeth among some that were there present, and saw him burne, that his body in burning did shine as bright and white as new tried silver in the eies of them that stoode by: as I am informed by some which were there, and did behold the sight" (1547.B51–55).

As with any narrative held together by metaphor, much is made of

Fig. 4. The burning of three women at Guernsey. Foxe, *Acts and Monuments* (London: John Day, 1583), II, 1944. (Photo by Findlay Muir. Courtesy of the Library: University of King's College,

related stylistic devices such as analogy and allegory, itself the dominant trope of romance.[40] As Bishop Latimer observes in a sermon quoted extensively in the *Acts and Monuments,* all human discourse relies on such resemblances, and "everie speech... hath his metaphors and the like figurative significations, so common and vulgar to all men, that the very painters doe painte them on walles and on houses" (1574.B.36–39). Foxe felt perfectly free to make comparisons, suggest resemblances and highlight similarities, and figure type and antitype, often across vast expanses of time. The vocabularies of good and evil change remarkably little in the course of the work, and they frequently challenge the reader or hearer to become involved in the game of finding similitudes. As I have contended in this chapter, Foxe's stories were so powerful, and so influential, because his choice of language appealed to the thought processes of his Elizabethan audience, processes that revolved around net-

Fig. 5. The martyrdom of Rawlins White. Foxe, *Acts and Monuments* (London: John Day, 1583), II, 1559. (Photo by Findlay Muir. Courtesy of the Library: University of King's College, Halifax.)

works of correspondence, resemblance, and likeness. A common phrase for persecutors such as "devouring and ravening wolves" (140.A.16) can be understood on two levels, as depicting the literal wolves, which the Anglo-Saxon King Edgar is supposed to have expelled from England, and also the bloodthirsty wolves of Rome; to an even more sophisticated reader, the wolf has an emblematic significance, as an icon of gluttony, the quintessential monkish vice. Sometimes, readers are left to draw these analogies for themselves; at others, the martyrologist provides a helping hand. In one such case, Foxe likens the "curse" of a medieval pope to the "thunder" of an earlier persecutor, the emperor Domitian. "The pope's curse may well bee assimilated to Domitians thunder: if a man give eare to the noise and cracke, it seemeth a terrible thing; but if you consider the causes thereof, it is a most vaine ridicule" (152.A.88–B.1). Individual martyrs and martyrdoms mirror each other, while each in turn is an image of Christ and his Crucifixion. When the Henrician martyr Thomas Man is burned, after twice recanting and relapsing, he is delivered by the chancellor of the diocese of London to the sheriff because the Church "had no power to put him to death" (742), precisely the same reason the Pharisees used in turning Christ over to Pilate.[41] Regimes that harry the godly "stumble at the same stone as did the Jewes in persecuting Christ" (1902.B.28).

It might be argued that a historian preoccupied with sameness and resemblance has an easy task, since any event or character can be seen as the type or antitype of any other. But such sameness is a matter of inner character, not of external characteristics, and in order to demonstrate it, Foxe was paradoxically obliged to pay close attention to the small differences, to the details, if only to show how little they mattered. Thus we have not one archetypical burning, nor even a few, but dozens upon dozens, each one described in intimate detail which often includes pictorial descriptions of the room in which an examination took place or the clothing worn by the martyr, right down to Bishop Latimer's "old felt" hat (1603.A.40): we are back, again, to Foxe's low-mimetic scenography. For modern readers, the effect is to make this collection of lives more biographically convincing, but Foxe appears to have had rather the opposite purpose in mind. By localizing his characters in time and space, and by bringing out their differences in circumstance, education, social degree, and occupation, Foxe was able to demonstrate to the reader that these were mere accidents, external features that conceal inner similarities. In the case of Latimer, his outward poverty and frailty can be contrasted with his fellow sufferer Ridley, in a sort of Plutarchan parallel description that converges at the stake:

> Master Ridley had a faire blacke gowne furred, and faced with foines, such as he was wont to weare beeing bishop, and a tippet of velvet furred likewise about his neck, a velvet night cap upon his head, and a corner cap upon the same, going in a paire of slippers to the stake, and going between the Maior and an Alderman, &c.
>
> After him came Master Latimer in a poor Bristow freeze frock all worne, with his buttoned cap, and a kerchiefe on his head, all readie to the fire, a newe long shrowde hanging over his hose downe to the feet: which at the first sight, stirred mens hearts to rue upon them, beholding on the one side, the honour they sometime had, on the other, the calamitie whereunto they were fallen. (1065.A.25–28)

The suppression of difference applies to more than physically and temporally linked pairs like these two bishops. It also cuts across the ages. No matter how much each individual martyr may have lived a life of his or her own, all these differences are resolved in the process of persecution, which structurally varies little from Christ to Cranmer—*plus ça change, plus c'est la même chose*. The persecution for treason of the Lollard leader Sir John Oldcastle can thus be made to stand for all persecutions everywhere and at all times:

> He that is or shall bee acquainted with old histories and with the usuall practises of Satan the old enemie of Christ, from the first beginning of the primitive Church unto this present time, shall see this to bee no newes, but a common and (as ye would say) a quotidian fever among Christs children.... (525.B.83–88)

Foxe includes the text of the condemnation of John Rogers, the first Marian victim and, despite his clerical status, in several ways a prototype, because this document could "serve for all other sentences condemnating through the whole story to be referred to" (1352). Almost every episode is driven by the simple triadic relation of Persecutor–Martyr–Cause, whereby an initial deed (the "cause") on the part of the martyr-to-be, often some sign of Reformed religiosity such as reading from the Bible, serves as a spur to the persecutor in bringing an action. Foxe highlights this relationship, the motive machinery of his stories, in a number of places, for instance in the caption accompanying the representation of a martyr's beheading (fig. 6).

The celebrated woodcuts further support Foxe's simplification of narrative action and his suppression of historical difference. There is no evidence that Foxe himself directed the cutting of these illustrations, but both the textual cross-references and the banderoles, presenting words that Foxe attributes to particular martyrs, suggest his close collaboration with the publisher, John Day, in their design. A number of these woodcuts were made, as John N. King points out, specifically for Foxe's book by illustrators in Day's employ, and several are known to represent realistic likenesses of their subjects—Bishop Bonner is supposed to have complained that his was too accurate. On the other hand, a great many of the woodcuts, particularly where the humbler martyrs are concerned, are stereotypes rather than likenesses, and in several cases the same woodcut was used (a common Renaissance cost-saving measure not confined to Day) to depict different people or scenes: Robert Samuel of Suffolk is one of a number of martyrs so represented (fig. 7).[42] A strik-

Fig. 6. The triad of Persecutors, Martyrs, and Causes, illustrated in a beheading. Foxe, *Acts and Monuments* (London: John Day, 1583), I, 887. (Photo by Findlay Muir. Courtesy of the Library: University of King's College, Halifax.)

ingly inapposite illustration adjoins Foxe's account of the burning of Julius Palmer, a youthful fellow of Magdalen College, Oxford. The text tells us that he suffered together with *two* other men at Newberry; the uncaptioned woodcut (fig. 8) shows only Palmer and one other being burned, and both of these figures appear considerably older than the description of Palmer suggests (1761.A).[43] Other discrepancies between text and image are commonplace, and not all are accidental. Foxe's account (940) of Robert Debnam, Robert King, and Nicholas Marshe,

The Rhetoric of Martyrdom 267

The cruel burning of Robert Samuel, Martyr.

Fig. 7. A woodcut stereotype (the burning of Robert Samuel of Suffolk). Foxe, *Acts and Monuments* (London: John Day, 1583), II, 1704. (Photo by Findlay Muir. Courtesy of the Library: University of King's College, Halifax.)

the three iconoclasts hanged in 1532 for destroying the Rood of Dovercourt, states the historical, documented fact that they were executed in three different places; yet the accompanying woodcut (fig. 9) shows all three hanging together off adjoining gallows, before a crowd of gloating churchmen and onlooking soldiers. The Christian connection to be drawn from this analogy is hammered home with the image of the rood itself, surrounded by flames, superimposed at the bottom left corner: crime and punishment are compressed into a single, powerful image.[44]

Frances A. Yates has suggested that Foxe envisaged the Marian burnings as modern reenactments of the primitive persecutions and that he represented the Tudor royal reformers Henry VIII, Edward VI, and Elizabeth I as sixteenth-century Constantines, realigning the church with godly secular power.[45] It is analogy of this kind, and the metaphoric world view that underlies it, that allows Foxe to maintain but de-center time and place, the twin axes of history, by asserting the essential sameness of all martyrs and, by extension, of all times. He sets out this device early on, in the preface *Ad Doctum Lectorem* (significantly, the only

struglyng, holdyng vp their handes, and knockyng their hartes, and calling vpon Jesu vntill they had ended their mortall lyues.

Fig. 8. The burning of Julius Palmer. Foxe, *Acts and Monuments* (London: John Day, 1583), II, 1940. (Photo by Findlay Muir. Courtesy of the Library: University of King's College, Halifax.)

section of the book to be written in socially exclusive Latin), explicitly pairing new martyrs with old saints, Thomas Cranmer with Thomas Becket, Nicholas Ridley with St. Nicholas. This sort of free comparison continues throughout his account as the most humble are tied to the mighty, and figures of recent times to those of more remote. The "good" duke of Somerset similarly becomes an image of the "good" duke Humfrey of Gloucester a century earlier (1248). William Tyndale, "the apostle of England," is depicted in a woodcut (fig. 10) going to his death clad only in a loincloth, a graphic as well as a textual *imitatio Christi* (981, 985). Bishop Hooper is compared to Polycarp "as they both were joined together in one spirit" (1373), while Laurence Saunders or Sanders is likened to St. Laurence:

> And thus have yee the full historie of Laurence Sanders, whom I may well compare to S. Laurence, *or any other of the olde martyrs of Christs Church:* both for the fervent zeale of the trueth and gospell of Christ, and the most constant patience in his suffering: as also for the cruell torments that hee in his patient body did susteine in the flame of fire (1362.A.16–21, emphasis added).[46]

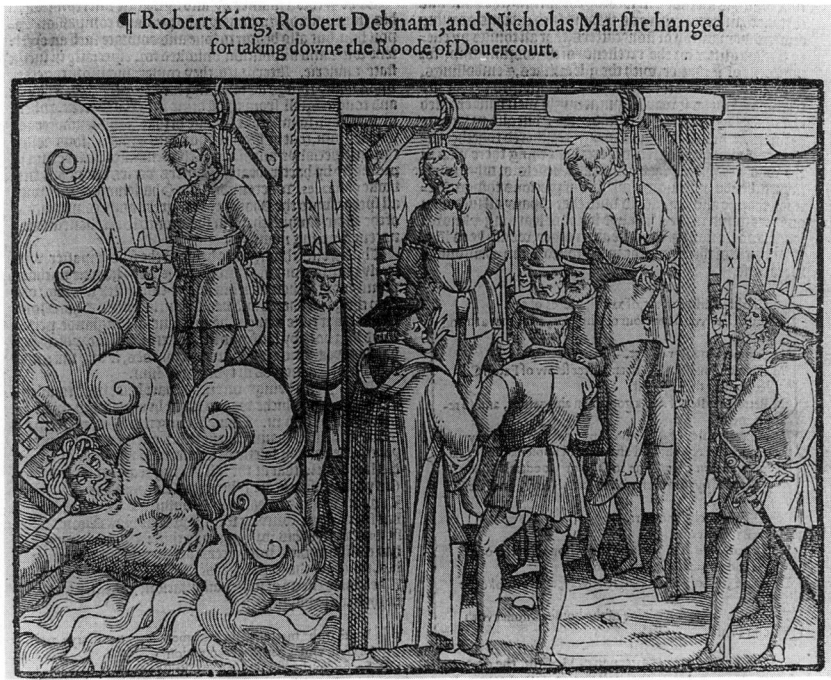

Fig. 9. The Dovercourt iconoclasts. Foxe, *Acts and Monuments* (London: John Day, 1583), I, 1031. (Photo by Findlay Muir. Courtesy of the Library: University of King's College, Halifax.)

Virtually any comparison became valid in Foxe's eyes because the martyrs were all essentially the same. The false accusation of heresy against an early sixteenth-century bricklayer is freely compared with various other examples of wrongful persecution, including those of Socrates, Aristides the Just, St. Paul, and a number of church fathers (1146.A.80–86). Underlying all these explicit analogies is a single implicit archetype, the accusation and trial of Christ himself.

Foxe's commitment to a representation of the church as an undifferentiated whole created problems of chronology. Though it follows the story of the church in order, from earliest to most recent times, the *Acts and Monuments* frequently digresses and meanders from time to time and place to place. Like any other Renaissance historian, Foxe recognized that his story was at best a rhetorical representation of past reality, not that reality itself; and he acknowledged that things took place in the

270   *The Rhetorics of Life-Writing in Early Modern Europe*

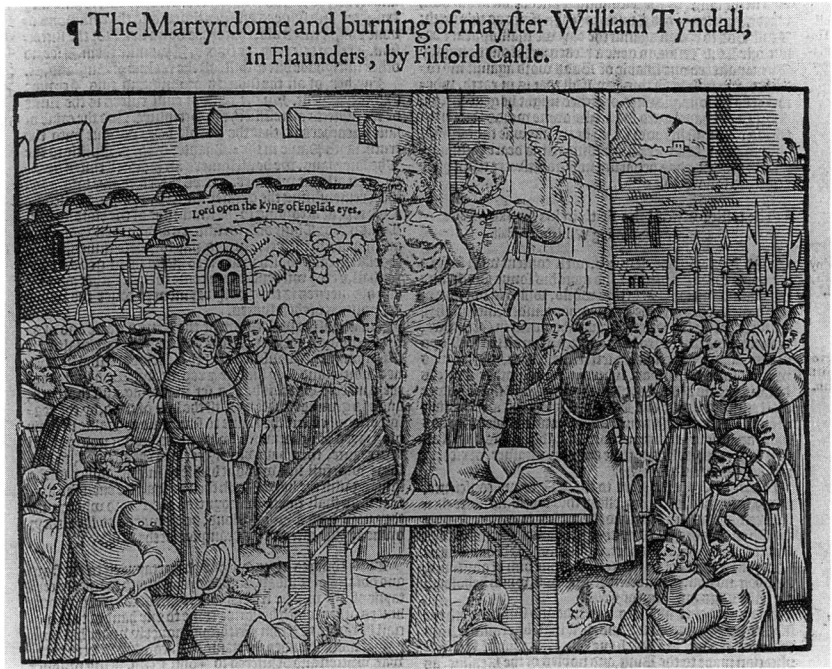

Fig. 10. The martyrdom of William Tyndale. Foxe, *Acts and Monuments* (London: John Day, 1583), I, 1079. (Photo by Findlay Muir. Courtesy of the Library: University of King's College, Halifax.)

order in which they did because it was God's will that they do so. But though the historian should emulate temporal reality as closely as possible, it was also his duty to make higher connections for the reader—if necessary, through ungainly digression. Conscious that some—especially the Catholic critics of early editions of the book—had found fault with this, Foxe defended himself by asking, "why should I be restrained from the free walke of a story writer, more then other that have gone before me?" (645.B.4–5).

This was not an avowal of narrative anarchism, nor a proto-Derridean elevation of the process of writing over its end product, the text; rather, it was a recognition that all authors, up to and including himself (and since), find that their pens often take them in unforeseen directions, across subjects unanticipated in all their preliminary planning and outlining. Foxe promised at the outset of his book to "proceed in the course of our storie, as the spirit of God shall vouchsafe to direct us," in the manner of a gospeler recording external events under divine inspiration. He was well aware of the rhetorical demands that a biographer, as much as a historian, relate events in the order that they occurred. In concluding an account of the life of Origen, which Foxe had in fact taken almost verbatim from the *Magdeburg Centuries,* he declares that "the congrue order of historie requireth next to speake of Heraclas his usher"; he thereupon relates a story that is closely connected to Origen's by proximity both in time and place. But keeping faith with the chronological outlines of history (something he needed to do in an effort to fend off Catholic critics who challenged his veracity) often conflicted with Foxe's conviction that he had to be as comprehensive as possible, and he persistently violated the order of story both to make his free comparisons of characters and to ensure that high or low, modern or ancient, almost no one was left out. He saw himself as the personal guarantor of everlasting earthly fame to those who had given over their lives to the faith, and the strict principles of life-writing could be bent or broken accordingly. An account of Persian martyrs—not among the best known of ancient Christians—is sufficiently necessary that Foxe feels compelled to "stray somewhat out of the order and course of time and place" (89–90). On some occasions, information came to hand after the relevant section of the *Acts and Monuments* had been composed. He inserts a speech of King Edgar between his accounts of Harold II's and William the Conqueror's reigns "although out of order" because "better I judge it out of order, then out of the booke" (153.A.5). Much further on, he appends an account of several previously overlooked Henrician martyrs, well out of their proper place: "Yet rather then they should utterly be omitted, I thoght here to give them a place, though somewhat out of time ... being no lesse worthy to be registred and preserved from oblivion, then other of their fellowes before them" (1162.A 69ff.). Having recounted the burning of Robert Glover, Foxe briefly mentions the excommunication of his two brothers, John and William, who survived unscathed. "I thought them not unworthie therfore in the storie to be joyned together, which in one cause and the same profession were not sundred one from the other" (1556.B.11–14); the storyteller can use his discretion to reunite in narrative those who were together in life.[47]

Foxe's devotion to the reputation of the single martyr meant that even the nameless and illiterate counted. The first piece of oral evidence to be used in the volume concerns the burning of "a certaine godly woman" under Henry VII; this was a martyrdom concerning which virtually no written information survived, but it had been witnessed by one Rowland Webbe, whose son Richard had in turn informed Foxe (708.A.58–711.B.71). Anonymous martyrs such as this deserved as much attention as their more famous brethren; if anything, they merited special praise from Foxe, both because they had been denied earthly fame by the very obliteration of their names and because they provided specimens representative of the whole army of saints. These were the "unknown soldiers" of Foxe's world war against antichrist. The poor and illiterate similarly cried out for their place on the printed page. When the Reformer John Bradford, after refusing several opportunities to recant, is finally consigned to the flames, he meets death in the company of a young chandler's apprentice named John Leafe who apparently cannot read for himself: even his own confession has to be read aloud to him in prison. A Wiltshire farmer, John Maundrell, is described as illiterate, "but when he came into any companie that could read, his booke was alwaies readie, having a very good memory," and he could recite most places in the New Testament (1719.A.35–40).

Conclusion

While at a superficial level the *Acts and Monuments* can be viewed merely as Protestant hagiography, and as a Reformed version of Foxe's main sources for the early church, Eusebius and Bede, it should be evident, I hope, that the work is much more complex in both narrative structure and rhetorical form than it has previously been deemed. Without denying the book's obvious resemblance to the various medieval Christian genres on which it draws—romance, ecclesiastical history, and hagiography—I have suggested that these collectively represent only one side of its genealogy and that it is in many ways a hybrid that cannot be well understood within the terms of formal genre criticism. If the content of the work is inspired by religious narratives of the past, then the manner in which that content is presented owes much to the tensions between these genres, tensions only partly resolved in the rhetoric of Foxe's lives. The narrative strategies that he employed spring in part from the conflict between his various duties as martyrologist, historian, and biographer, in part from his sensitivity to the reading practices and intellectual assumptions of his audience.

The *Acts and Monuments* was perhaps the most widely read book in

Reformation England, apart from the Bible, to which it was often seen as a supplement, an uncanonical "Book of Martyrs" to follow the books of prophets and chronicles in the Old Testament and the apocryphal Book of Maccabees. It is correctly regarded as being one of a kind, at least within England. But having now traced some of the many streams that flow into it, is it now possible to explore the ways in which those streams proceed out again, into other genres of Elizabethan and seventeenth-century prose and even poetry? It has long been acknowledged that such Elizabethan masterworks as the *Faerie Queene* that, more obviously than Foxe, have the generic structure of romance, also have strong religious and even apocalyptic themes.[48] It is not stretching the connection to see the *Acts and Monuments* as a missing link connecting a discredited genre like romance with the purified Protestant poetics of Spenser, and beyond him of Milton and Bunyan. Rather than limit ourselves to a study of either Elizabethan "fiction" or "fact," history or poetry, we should explore the rhetorical homologies between works such as Foxe's and Spenser's. Similarly, it might be worth considering the possibility that the later literature of roguery and crime, which features a gallows humor not unlike that shown by many of Foxe's martyrs—and which in turn ultimately found its place in the early novel—owes its parentage at least in part to the Book of Martyrs: a work with a serious message, but one its author well knew had to entertain its readers as it instructed them.

NOTES

An early version of this chapter was read at the Renaissance Society of America national meeting at Harvard University in 1989. It has been much revised since, and I have been able to expand the scope of the enquiry and conduct much additional research, thanks to generous grants from the Social Sciences and Humanities Research Council of Canada and the Faculty of Graduate Studies Research Development Fund at Dalhousie University. A short-term fellowship at the Folger Shakespeare Library permitted me to recheck my material and examine several editions of Foxe simultaneously. In addition to my coeditor and other contributors to the present volume, I am grateful to Devorah Greenberg, Arthur J. Slavin, Peter Herman, Martha Yeide, Thomas S. Freeman, and Paul Christianson for their critical comments on the chapter in its various versions. I am also indebted, for further valuable insights on Foxe, to Annabel Patterson and Patrick Collinson. None of the aforementioned bears any responsibility for the opinions expressed, nor for any errors committed.

1. John Foxe, *Acts and Monuments* (London: H. Lownes for Company of Stationers, 1610), 1872. For bibliographical details, reference may be made to the entries on Foxe in the second, revised edition of A. W. Pollard and G. R. Redgrave, *A Short-Title Catalogue of Books Printed in England, Scotland, & Ireland and of English Books Printed Abroad*, 3 vols., ed. W. A. Jackson, F. S. Ferguson, and K. F. Pantzer (London: The Bibliographical Society, 1976–92), hereafter referred to as *STC*. Foxe's book appeared in several editions, and it will be necessary to refer to several of these. As my base edition I have taken the sixth (London: H. Lownes for Company of Stationers, 1610, *STC* 11227), which appeared in two volumes under the title *Actes and Monuments of Matters most Speciall and Memorable, Happenyng in the Church, with an Universall History of the Same;* the second volume of this is entitled *The Second Volume of the Ecclesiasticall Historie,* a distinction I shall discuss below. Most references in this chapter will be to that edition and will be given in the text, generally with page number, column letter (a or b for left and right) and, where relevant, line numbers. For illustrative woodcuts, however, I have for convenience used the two-volume edition published by John Day in 1583 (*STC* 11225, the last edition published in Foxe's lifetime), which appeared under the same title, a copy of which is in the library of the University of King's College, Halifax, to whom I am grateful for permission to reproduce material; page references to the woodcuts will therefore be to the 1583 edition. There will be occasion to refer to the earlier editions, which appeared under the following titles: *Actes and Monuments of these Latter and Perillous Dayes, Touching Matters of the Church* (London: J. Day, 1563, *STC* 11222); *The First Volume of the Ecclesiasticall History contayning the Actes and Monumentes of Thynges Passed in Every Kynges Tyme in this Realme* (London: J. Day[e], 1570, *STC* 11223) [the second volume is similarly titled, but in this edition the two volumes are, for the first and only time, separately paginated]; *Actes and Monuments of these Latter and Perillous Dayes, Touching Matters of the Church* (London: J. Day[e], 1576, *STC* 11224); *Actes and Monuments of Matters most Speciall and Memorable, Happening in the Church, with an Universall history of the Same* (London: P. Short, 1596, *STC* 11226). The frequent changes in title are an obvious, and hitherto neglected, sign of an instability of genre and of an ambivalence in the mind of author and, no doubt, publisher, as to how exactly to present such a complex and unusual book.

2. The authoritative biography of Foxe, now in need of revision but mainly reliable, remains J. F. Mozley, *John Foxe and his Book* (London: SPCK, 1940); see pp. 234ff. for a list of editions of Foxe's works. More recently, see the short but useful biographical-textual study, W. W. Wooden, *John Foxe* (Boston: Twayne, 1983). For an account of Foxe firmly within the context of the hagiographic tradition and its Protestant debunking (a contextualization I am disputing here), see Helen C. White, *Tudor Books of Saints and Martyrs* (Madison:

University of Wisconsin Press, 1963), 132–95. White recognizes (169) that Foxe did not intend to write a Protestant sequel to the *Golden Legend,* but she nevertheless stresses the hagiographic aspects of his character delineation. Like Wooden and White, Catharine Randall challenges the continuity between the genres of medieval hagiography and Protestant martyrology while maintaining a view of Foxe as standing "at the intermediate position between the two poles of hagiography and martyrology": see her (Catharine Randall Coats), *(Em)bodying the Word: Textual Resurrections in the Martyrological Narratives of Foxe, Crespin, de Bèze and d'Aubigné* (New York: Peter Lang, 1992), 38; see also her chapter in the present volume. My own essay owes a considerable debt to Timothy Hampton's book, *Writing from History: the Rhetoric of Exemplarity in Renaissance Literature* (Ithaca, NY: Cornell University Press, 1990); see especially pp. 122–33 for an illuminating study of the "poetics of martyrdom." I have also profited from Michael McKeon's illuminating explorations of the growth of a sense of emplotment, together with historical consciousness, from the Middle Ages to the eighteenth century, in *The Origins of the English Novel, 1600–1740* (Baltimore: Johns Hopkins University Press, 1987), though its main concern is the seventeenth century. Finally, John R. Knott's *Discourses of Martyrdom in English Literature, 1563–1694* (Cambridge: Cambridge University Press, 1993), is the first serious attempt to study Foxe as part of a continuing tradition of persecution literature up to the later seventeenth century.

3. Stefan J. Smart, "John Foxe and 'The Story of Richard Hunne, Martyr,'" *Journal of Ecclesiastical History* 37 (1986): 1–14, at p. 14.

4. John G. Rechtien, "John Foxe's Comprehensive Collection of Commonplaces: A Renaissance Memory System for Students and Theologians," *Sixteenth Century Journal* 9 (1978): 83–89, for Foxe's rhetorical training.

5. I am here "imitating," in what he would no doubt regard as a transformative way, the taxonomy of imitation worked out by G. W. Pigman III in his incisive essay, "Versions of Imitation in the Renaissance," *Renaissance Quarterly* 33 (1980): 1–32; Pigman's comments refer principally to versions of imitation involving the transportation of phrases, sentences, or passages from one work into another, rather than the wholesale mixing of genres that I shall here be arguing occurs in Foxe; or perhaps Foxe's application of techniques worked out in romance, comedy, hagiography, and chronicle to the history of the church deserves the term *emulation,* the hallmark of which, for Pigman, is "an awareness of the historical distance between present and past," a feature that I do not believe, for reasons that will become clear further on, distinguishes Foxe's sense of the unfolding of history.

6. A number of Tudor historical texts, such as the *Acts and Monuments,* seem ripe for a reappraisal in the wake of recent literary theory. In her essay, "Rethinking Tudor Historiography," *South Atlantic Quarterly* 92 (1993), 185–208, Annabel Patterson has made such a plea on behalf of a book that has until

now been taken even less seriously in literary and historiographical terms, Holinshed's *Chronicles,* published in 1577 and revised and enlarged by several contributors in 1587; her book *Reading Holinshed's Chronicles* (Chicago: University of Chicago Press, 1994) should redirect historiographical attention from the much-studied humanist historians toward the generally maligned sixteenth-century chroniclers who, unlike Foxe, have until now had few champions.

7. The original 1563 preface is billed as "A declaration concerning the utilitie and profite of thys history." This point should not be overstated, because the terms *story* and *history* were nearly interchangeable in the sixteenth century, but the shifts in usage suggest, once again, some uncertainty about exactly how to bill the work.

8. Eusebius, *The Ecclesiastical History,* 2 vols., trans. Kirsopp Lake (London and Cambridge, MA: Loeb, 1949), I.1.2–5.

9. The last occurrence of the split header is at vol. I, p. 647 of the 1570 edition; it is not employed in volume II.

10. As D. Karl Uitti points out in his study of French romance, "participation in the telling of a saint's life was itself an act of faith, an act of witness": *Story, Myth, and Celebration in Old French Narrative Poetry, 1050–1200* (Princeton, NJ: Princeton University Press, 1973), 26.

11. The Kalender appears in the 1563 edition, complete with an almanac for the seasons, but was removed in the 1570 edition, that which cathedral churches were required to possess. Absent again in 1576, it returned in the 1583, 1596, and 1610 editions, in all cases without the almanac. The Kalender was specifically attacked by at least one Catholic polemicist, Robert Persons, or Parsons, in *A treatise of three conversions of England from paganisme to Christian religion,* 3 vols., (St. Omer: François Bellet, 1603–4), who made a month-by-month critique of it the principal subject of the third part (volumes II and III) of his work.

12. Eugène Vinaver, *The Rise of Romance* (Oxford: Clarendon Press, 1971), 3, 111.

13. For example, in the enormously influential catechism by the puritan Edward Dering, *A Short catechisme for householders* (London: J. Charlewood, 1580 and various other editions). Once again, compare the attitude of a Counter-Reformation poet such as Tasso, concerned with reconciling ideological (religious) seriousness with romance, as described by Hampton, *Writing from History,* 121. Foxe repudiates "the several types of vices and the grosser shames of the mob" that he associates with Old Comedy in the dedicatory epistle to *Christus Triumphans,* published at Basel in 1556 and translated by Richard Day as *Christ Jesus Triumphant* (London: J. and R. Day, 1598) and republished in *Two Latin Comedies: "Titus and Gesippus" and Christus Triumphans,* trans. and ed. John Hazel Smith (Ithaca, NY, and London: Cornell University Press for the Renaissance Society of America, 1973), 209.

14. Smith, "Introduction," to Foxe, *Two Latin Comedies,* 9. Cf. Judith H. Anderson, "Biographical Truth," in *Biographical Truth: The Representation of Historical Persons in Tudor-Stuart Writing* (New Haven, CT: Yale University Press, 1984), chap. 1; C. S. Lewis, *The Allegory of Love* (Oxford: Clarendon Press, 1936); David Quint, "Renaissance Epic and the Boat of Romance," in Kevin Brownlee and Marina Scordilis Brownlee, eds., *Romance: Generic Transformations from Chrétien de Troyes to Cervantes* (Hanover, NH: University Press of New England, 1988), 178–202.

15. John N. King, "John Foxe," *Sixteenth-Century British Non-Dramatic Writers, First series,* ed. David A. Richardson, *Dictionary of Literary Biography* 132 (New York: Gale Publishing, 1993), 131–40. Smith, "Introduction," in Foxe, *Two Latin Comedies: "Titus and Gesippus" and Christus Triumphans,* trans. and ed. John Hazel Smith (Ithaca, NY, and London: Cornell University Press for the Renaissance Society of America, 1973), 9, points to Sir Thomas Elyot's *The Boke Named the Gouernour* (London: T. Berthelet, 1531), and beyond that to Boccaccio's *Decameron,* as respectively the direct and ultimate sources of *Titus et Gesippus;* cf. John H. Smith, "Sempronia, John Lyly, and John Foxe's Comedy of Titus and Gesippus," *Philological Quarterly* 48 (1969): 554–61, in which Foxe's early experience as a playwright is used to account for the dramatic setup of much of his book, for instance, the examination of John Newman the pewterer (1610 edn., 1769–70). I would disagree, however, with Smith's conclusion, on largely negative evidence, that Foxe was unfamiliar with Boccaccio directly; I would similarly contest his suggestion, meant to contrast the dramas with the *Acts and Monuments,* that the Book of Martyrs "can be called comic only in some specialized sense, if at all" (Smith, "Introduction," 10).

16. A brief foray into the realm of rhetorical theory may be helpful here. In the late Northrop Frye's famous formulation, modified and applied to nineteenth-century historiography by Hayden White some twenty years ago, one can look beyond formal genre to recognize four basic story types or mythoi: romance, tragedy, comedy, and satire: Northrop Frye, *The Anatomy of Criticism* (Princeton, NJ: Princeton University Press, 1957), 131– 239; Hayden White, *Metahistory: The Historical Imagination in Nineteenth-Century Europe* (Baltimore: Johns Hopkins University Press, 1973). One must therefore consider not only whether an author has formally chosen to imitate a particular genre, but whether he or she has actually borrowed from that genre a particular narrative mythos (or, for that matter, any other narrative or stylistic element from character depiction to tropes and images) in an effort to construct a narrative that may itself defy any such generic categorization—that may, indeed, be literally sui generis. Plainly, there are some mythoi that do not in the least fit Foxe's book: there is little about the *Acts and Monuments* that might be called satirical, for instance. There are undoubtedly some wickedly sarcastic passages which hold the medieval clergy and the backsliding Tudor episcopacy up to ridicule, but the

tone of these is earnest, not ironic. If anything, the work is positively naive and unreflective in its chiding, homiletic voice. Nor, in the strict sense, can the Book of Martyrs be seen as a tragedy: it has no single well-defined plot line; complexities of character are not crucial to the development of its narrative; and there is no climactic event involving the fall of a flawed hero.

17. R. W. Southern, *The Making of the Middle Ages* (1953; reprint, London: Hutchinson, 1967), 233.

18. Nancy F. Partner, *Serious Entertainments: The Writing of History in Twelfth-Century England* (Chicago and London: University of Chicago Press, 1977), 200–202. Partner also notes, following Auerbach and William W. Ryding, a paratactical writing strategy in the chroniclers. On the medieval aristocratic chroniclers, for whom the generic connections with romance proper were even more compelling, see William Brandt, *The Shape of Medieval History* (New Haven, CT: Yale University Press, 1966). For a thorough study of the relations between romance and vernacular historiography, that unfortunately appeared too late to be taken fully into account in this chapter, see Gabrielle M. Spiegel, *Romancing the Past: The Rise of Vernacular Prose Historiography in Thirteenth-Century France* (Berkeley and Los Angeles: University of California Press, 1992).

19. Walter J. Ong, S.J., *Ramus, Rhetoric and the Decay of Dialogue* (Cambridge: Cambridge University Press, 1958); idem, *The Presence of the Word: Some Prolegomena for Cultural and Religious History* (New Haven, CT: Yale University Press, 1967), 3, 35, 75; idem, *Rhetoric, Romance and Technology: Studies in the Interaction of Expression and Culture* (Ithaca, NY and London: Cornell University Press, 1971), esp. chap. 2, "Oral Residue in Tudor Prose Style," and chap. 6, "Ramist Classroom Procedure and the Nature of Reality"; idem, *Orality and Literacy: The Technologizing of the Word* (London and New York: Methuen, 1982). Romance structures occur in a socially heterogeneous variety of works ranging from Spenser's *Faerie Queene*—which straddles the border between romance and epic—and the numerous popular ballads and broadsheets of a highly formulaic nature, such as Guy of Warwick. There are obvious parallels between Elizabethan England and twelfth-century society—on a more limited scale—as described by Vinaver, *Rise of Romance*, 4, who refers to the birth of romance as "the birth of a world in which vernacular writings were to share with Latin texts the privilege of addressing the reader through the medium of visible, not audible, symbols."

20. Vinaver, *Rise of Romance*, 7.

21. Patrick Collinson, *The Birthpangs of Protestant England: Religious and Cultural Change in the Sixteenth and Seventeenth Centuries* (New York: St. Martin's Press, 1988), 117; Tessa Watt, *Cheap Print and Popular Piety, 1550–1640* (Cambridge: Cambridge University Press, 1991), 178–216. We know that Foxe himself enjoyed drawing and may have been responsible for the picture of Bonner caning Protestants in his orchard at Fulham: Mozley, *John Foxe and his*

Book, 131. On the printing of various editions of Foxe, see, in addition to the works already cited, Paul S. Dunkin, "Foxe's *Actes and Monuments,* 1570, and Single-Page Imposition," *The Library,* 5th series, 2 (1947): 159–70; Leslie M. Oliver, "The Seventh Edition of John Foxe's *Acts and Monuments," Papers of the Bibliographical Society of America* 37 (1943), 243–60, which is especially good on sizes of edition and on the distribution of the 1570 edition according to the order in Convocation.

22. This table appears also to have been sold separately and was reprinted in 1625 and 1632; see the descriptions in *STC* 2, 496, nos. 11227 to 11228.3. Thomas S. Freeman of Rutgers University, who is completing a dissertation on Foxe, informs me that the Huntington Library copy of the 1583 edition of the *Acts and Monuments* has a dated copy of the table, printed by Day, in contrast to the assertion in *STC* that the table appeared first only in 1610.

23. Foxe had deliberately added comic elements to the story of Titus and Gesippus in his 1545 drama: Smith, "Introduction," 24.

24. On which see the following works: F. Smith Fussner, *The Historical Revolution: English Historical Writing and Thought, 1580–1640* (London: Routledge and Kegan Paul, 1962); F. J. Levy, *Tudor Historical Thought* (San Marino: Huntington Library, 1967); Arthur B. Ferguson, *Clio Unbound: Perception of the Social and Cultural Past in Renaissance England* (Durham, NC: Duke University Press, 1979); D. R. Woolf, *The Idea of History in Early Stuart England: Erudition, Ideology and the "Light of Truth" from the Accession of James I to the Civil War* (Toronto: University of Toronto Press, 1990).

25. Hospitality is another convention commonly to be found in medieval romance and is one of the motifs that connects its heroes with their counterparts in hagiography: Matilda T. Bruckner, *Narrative Invention in Twelfth-Century French Romance* (Lexington, KY: French Forum, 1980).

26. Here, as elsewhere in describing the Henrician Reformation, Foxe leans heavily on Edward Hall's chronicle: but whereas for Hall the base origins of Wolsey flaw him inherently, in Foxe's version they are only a weakness insofar as Wolsey's pretensions and high life are strategies to cloak them.

27. This "climax" does not figure in Foxe's design of his narrative, which did not, in any case, require crises or turning points; the "middle man" thus comes not halfway but nine-tenths of the way through the pages devoted to Mary's reign, and very close to the end of the whole work.

28. On Foxe's female martyrs, see E. Macek, "The Emergence of a Feminine Spirituality in *The Book of Martyrs," Sixteenth Century Journal* 19 (1988): 63–81; Carole Levin, "Women in *The Book of Martyrs* as Models of Behaviour in Tudor England," *International Journal of Women's Studies* 4 (1981): 196–207.

29. The student who commented to me, some years ago, after her class had been shown a series of woodcuts from the Book of Martyrs, that the burnings

were "kind of like our church barbecue" was not merely, as I only later realized, making a humorous remark of questionable taste, but also commenting incisively on the almost festive atmosphere surrounding the illustrations of many of the executions, which contrast sharply in this regard with the dark solemnity in contemporary illustrations of continental *autos-da-fé*.

30. I thank Martha Yeide for drawing this to my attention.

31. Cf. Foxe's account of a related incident at 1103.A.74.

32. Similar fates befall Bishop John Fisher and Sir Thomas More, persecutors both: "they that staine their hands with bloud, seldome doe bring their bodies drie to the grave" (975.B.80). The "horrible deaths of persecutors" theme derives ultimately from Lactantius, *Of the Manner in which the Persecutors Died*, in *The Works of Lactantius*, 2 vols., trans. William Fletcher (Edinburgh: Anti-Nicene Christian Library, vol. XXII, 1871), 164–211. Foxe also explicitly emulates Lactantius's claim, in chapter 52, that "I relate all those things on the authority of well-informed persons; and I thought it proper to commit them to writing exactly as they happened, lest the memory of events so important should perish..." (211). Lactantius tells us how "by the unerring and just judgement of God, all the impious received according to the deeds that they had done" (chap. 50, p. 210). Foxe summarizes the "terrible end of persecutors" at the very conclusion of the 1583 and 1610 editions (1610, pp. 1902–1916).

33. Foxe, *De censura, sive excommunicatione ecclesiastica rectoque eius usu* (London: S. Mierdmann, 1551), discussed by Catherine Davies and Jane Facey, "A Reformation Dilemma: John Foxe and the Problem of Discipline," *Journal of Ecclesiastical History* 39 (1988): 37–65. In Foxe's "Sermon of Christ Crucified," preached in 1570 and cited by Davies and Facey (57), he prayed for the "universal state of Christ's Church, and all other estates and degrees."

34. William Haller, *Foxe's Book of Martyrs and the Elect Nation* (London: Jonathan Cape, 1963); for a critique of this interpretation of Foxe, see K. R. Firth, *The Apocalyptic Tradition in Reformation Britain, 1530–1645* (Oxford: Clarendon Press, 1979).

35. V. Norskov Olsen, *John Foxe and the Elizabethan Church* (Berkeley: University of California Press, 1973), 108–22; John T. McNeill, "John Foxe: Historiographer, Disciplinarian, Tolerationist," *Church History* 43 (1974): 216–29.

36. Foxe subscribed so fervently to this Pauline-Augustinian view of the world as a set of binary opposites that he even included two separate prefaces in the 1563 edition of the work, one to "the persecutors of God's truth, commonly called papists," and another to "the true and faithful congregation of Christ's universal Church."

37. This is the infamous story which the Catholic polemicist Thomas Harding had attacked in earlier editions of *Acts and Monuments* as a fabrication; Foxe defends it, and other seemingly incredible tales, by referring the reader to the

testimony of witnesses still living. The image of the baby cast into the fire in front of its mother was a common one in Reformation and Counter-Reformation propaganda, which would resurface during the Thirty Years' War. Mozley, *John Foxe and his Book,* 223–35, demonstrates that although Foxe may have embellished the tale in many regards, he did not invent it, since records of the women's condemnation are extant. Foxe's earliest critics (first Harding, then Robert Persons) had attacked the martyr status of the women, suggesting that they were in fact accomplices to the theft of a silver cup stolen by one Vincent Gosset, and that Perotine in particular was a prostitute, because her husband is not explicitly mentioned.

38. The choice of "Herodian" as an adjective suggests, again, an appeal to audience familiarity with medieval drama, Herod having been a stock figure of mystery plays. For evidence of the influence of the mysteries on an earlier English humanist historian, see Retha M. Warnicke, "More's *Richard III* and the Mystery Plays," *Historical Journal* 35 (1992): 761–78.

39. The two images are linked. Both are traditional symbols of heat and are tied together in the theory of humors, with which Foxe and his better-educated readers were entirely familiar: a sanguine person is one of warm disposition who is courageous and hopeful, the very qualities that Foxe highlights in his martyrs.

40. For the place of analogy in romance, see Vinaver, *Rise of Romance,* 99–122.

41. Foxe describes Christ being handed over to the secular power of Pontius Pilate, after interrogation by priests, in similar terms (40ff.).

42. For two excellent recent treatments, from different perspectives, of the use of woodcuts in Foxe and other Reformation literature, see John N. King, *Tudor Royal Iconography* (Princeton, NJ: Princeton University Press, 1989), 131–34; and Watt, *Cheap Print and Popular Piety,* 158–59.

43. The Palmer picture underwent several transformations from edition to edition. The 1563 version features the text of the story at p. 1539, without any accompanying woodcut; in the 1570 edition (2124), the martyrdom is accompanied by a woodcut of a single, relatively youthful sufferer, captioned with Palmer's name; the 1576 edition (1840) once again presents a text with no picture. The uncaptioned, two-martyr woodcut first appears in 1583 (1940), and again in 1596 and 1610.

44. I owe this point to Thomas S. Freeman.

45. Frances A. Yates, "Queen Elizabeth as Astraea," in her *Astraea: The Imperial Theme in the Sixteenth Century* (London: Routledge and Kegan Paul, 1975), 29–87, esp. pp. 42–47. Knott, *Discourses of Martyrdom,* 34, makes a similar point.

46. Seymour Byman, "Ritualistic Acts and Compulsive Behaviour: The Pattern of Tudor Martyrdom," *American Historical Review* 83 (1978): 625–43, argues that this is more than Foxe's perception, that in fact his martyrs really

were reenacting the deaths of pre-Nicene martyrs, especially in the manner in which they reassured themselves that they were not simply committing suicide, and in their behavior at the stake: seen in this light, John Bradford's presentation of money to his jailers can be interpreted as a conscious reenactment of St. Cyprian's gift to the headsman in A.D. 258. Byman's argument is open to dispute and probably overrates the learning of many of the real, historical martyrs, but it does clarify the reasons Foxe seems so determined to cast many of them as replicas of their pre-Nicene predecessors.

47. The same impulse to comprehensiveness includes not just martyrs, but also details of church history. Foxe includes a verse he found from a manuscript chronicle on the battle of Brimford between Athelstan and the Danes, "which because they should not be lost, I thought not unworthie heere of rehersall" (134.A.38–71).

48. For the medieval heritage of the *Faerie Queene*, see Lewis, "The Faerie Queene," in *Allegory of Love*, 297–360.

11

Montaigne's *Essais:* The Literary and Literal Digesting of a Life

William E. Engel

"For the *disposition* and *collocation* of that knowledge which we preserve in writing," Francis Bacon remarked, "it consisteth in a good digest of common-places.... I hold the entry of common-places to be a matter of great use and essence in studying, as that which assureth copie of invention, and contracteth judgment to a strength."[1] In the sixteenth century, such a digest, or epitome, of information arranged according to topical headings served as an aid to gain access to knowledge; not only knowledge of ideas and arguments to be called on for future use, but also of the internal and intellectual constitution of the person compiling and arranging that knowledge.[2] It is in this light I will review Montaigne's relation to his book, which he claimed helped him settle and compose his life, even as he penned, published, and revised his essays—his trials—of the Self.[3]

Don Cameron Allen, among others, has argued that "in the case of Montaigne, a commonplace book was father to the essay."[4] Michael Kiernan has pointed out that some would view the first edition of Bacon's *Essayes* (1597) as little more than pages from commonplace books (as collections of practical "sentences" grouped under topical headings). Although perhaps an extreme view, it nonetheless points to a chief characteristic of the earliest versions of Bacon's essays,[5] no less than those of Montaigne. But what exactly were these "sentences" which constituted the loose, although hardly random, structure of the essays to which Bacon and Montaigne turned their attention throughout their lives?

At least a decade before Bacon transformed his series of commonplace notebooks into his collection of ten essays,[6] Montaigne's use of quotations had broken with the traditional practice of compiling *sententiae* in order to gloss or elucidate cruxes in ancient texts.[7] This aspect of Montaigne's *Essais,* more than any other strictly rhetorical feature, characterizes the novel style he pioneered;[8] and, further, a principal component of it was the art of memory.[9] According to the rhetorical tradition in which Montaigne was raised, in which memory was one of the five main divisions,[10] the "artificial memory is a memory strengthened by a kind of training and a system of discipline," while "natural memory is that memory which is embedded in our minds, born simultaneously with thought."[11] Exploring the extent to which Montaigne adopted and transformed an "artificial memory" through his novel approach to composition (of his essays, as of his character) is the aim of this study.

Again Bacon can help us see explicitly what remains implicit in Montaigne regarding the art of memory. In a letter written to Henry Savile about the same time that his *Essayes* were first published, he mentioned various "helps for the intellectual powers" and listed exercises for strengthening the mental abilities for people in different occupations. Then he remarked succinctly: "artificial memory greatly holpen by exercise," by which Bacon meant, "two manners, both with writing and tables, and without" (*Works,* xiii, 301). Bacon further elaborated the practical uses of the art of memory in a section of *The Advancement of Learning* devoted to "the custody of knowledge." He observed: "an art there is extant of it"; but cautioned against applying it for "serious use of business and occasions" (*Works,* vi, 281). Such an art, which involved keeping a digest of memorable passages under designated headings and later transplanting them into the ground of one's own discourse or writing, would seem to be ideally suited to Montaigne's *negotiosum otium,* his busy leisure.

> It is not long since I retired my selfe unto mine owne house, with full purpose, as much as lay in me, not to trouble my self with any businesse, but solitarily and quietly to weare out the remainder of my well-nigh-spent life.... (I.8, 43)

In the course of his setting about to compile his essays, he managed to fashion an "artificial memory" to supplement his self-proclaimed deficient "natural memory," in much the same way commonplace books were used by orators and jurists to store information for later use.[12] Despite his claim to forget authors, places, and words—and even "[A]s much as any thing else I forget mine own writings and compositions"

(II.17, 378)—his essays became for him a way to register his novel thoughts and to record the symptoms of his advancing bodily decay: "For want of naturall memory I frame some of paper. And when some new symptome or accident commeth to my evill [kidney stones], I set it downe in writing" (III.13, 356).[13]

Accordingly, Montaigne drew from Plutarch and Seneca, as the *Danaïdes* drew water: "uncessantly filling, and as fast emptying: some thing whereof I fasten to this paper, but to myselfe nothing at all" (I.25, 149). It is with a sense of genuine modesty, and a touch of irony, that Montaigne implies he has used these authors, and set their words and ideas in his own book, but has not been able to assimilate, or fasten onto himself, the lessons of their words. Further, his recognition of the shortcomings of the commonplace-book method separates his use of earlier texts from those pedants he criticizes.

> Is not that which I doe in the greatest part of this composition, all one and selfe same thing? I am ever heere and there picking and culling, from this and that booke, the sentences that please me, not to keepe them (for I have no store-house to reserve them in) but to transport them into this: where, to say truth, they are no more mine, than in their first place. (I.24, 138)

Although he claims not to retain the words of others, nevertheless they remain a vital part of his project. The numerous citations and *sententiae* mark the collected essays as the "store-house" of his inventions and reading.[14] On the one hand, the mere collecting of *sententiae* and exempla (whether in one's own "table" or by using a printed anthology to supplement and support one's "natural memory") did not lead to the furthering of true knowledge. Montaigne reiterated this commonplace by reaching into his own storehouse of memory to relate a sentence by Cicero, only to demonstrate, although perhaps self-ironically, that he had access to the names of things but not their substance, and that this recognition is the extent of what he knows despite his reading:

> "Assuredly memorie alone, of all other things, compriseth not onely Philosophy, but the use of our whole life, and all the sciences." Memorie is the receptacle and case of knowledge. Mine being so weake, I have no great cause to complaine if I know but little. I know the names of Arts in Generall, and what they treate of, but nothing fur-

ther.... The authours, the place, the words, and other circumstances, I sodainly forget. (II.17, 377–78)

Perhaps he protests too much for us to take him at face value; and yet, it is his deficient memory, he argues, that keeps him from being deceitful toward others—and himself. His essay "Of Lyers" begins with a proclamation: "There is no man living, whom it may lesse beseeme to speake of memorie, than my self, for to say truth, I have none at all: and am fully perswaded that no mans can be so weake and forgetfull as mine" (I.9, 44); and goes on to explain that his daily discourse is the more brief because "the Magazine of Memorie is peradventure more stored with matter, than is the store-house of Inventions" (I.9, 45). Further, as we might expect of a writer fond of juxtaposing divergent points of view through *sententiae,* Montaigne again applied his conversational voice, now to denounce what his use of *sententiae* implied about the basis of his judgment, and therefore about his knowledge more generally.

And it were necessarie they [our souls] should (being yet in the body) remember the said knowledge (as *Plato* said) that what we learn't, was but a new remembering of that which we had knowne before: A thing that any man may by experience maintaine to be false and erronious. (II.12, 259)

Although he takes to task here a literal account of Plato's anamnestic theory of knowledge, we must not lose sight of the centrality of this theme in Montaigne's method of composition. The maxim "knowledge is but remembrance," as it was apprehended and then rewritten into the essays, is the principle of design animating the body of his writing. The author (or rather, some representation of what he aspires to portray) is the matter of the essays.[15] His translation of the Platonic axiom "knowledge is remembrance" into the program of the essays, in both word and in spirit, links Montaigne's use of *sententiae* to the larger epistemological concern of the late sixteenth century regarding how human beings came to know and to view their place in the world.

Among the "background images" regularly used in artificial memory systems was the human body, onto which one imposed a series of mnemonic images so she or he could store and have ready access to whatever was to be recovered—whether arguments for speeches, anecdotes for table talk, or whole sections of scholarly treatises.[16] I am not claiming that Montaigne conceived of his *Essais* as this specific kind of an artificial memory system.[17] Rather, I want to suggest that the idea of the body and the special memories associated with, and his musings on, bodies within that body—within Montaigne's own proper body—were integral to the fabric and composition of his text as a literary self-portrait over time, as a mnemonic body "in motion," as a kind of macabre body in passage.[18]

Montaigne's literary evocation of his body, and of bodies within his body, mirror the way his essays function as a kind of textual body; they supply him with a structure, a treasury to house anecdotes, reflections, citations, and his judgments concerning them. It is here that we can glimpse a folding over, a doubling back, in the fabric of Montaigne's textual patchwork, one that preserves the trace of a remarkable double movement. First, we have his literary movements within the body of his text to examine the movements within his own material body. At the same time, we have also a movement outside the text to explore the body of literature that forms the basis of his literary corpus. By way of interrogating this double movement further, I would call attention to a later addition in the 1588 essay "On Experience." (Citing from three versions, I have terraced the first part of the citation to indicate something of its extraordinary rhythm and rhetorical balance).[19]

> Composer nos meurs est   nostre office,
>   non pas composer des livres,
> et gaigner,   non pas des batailles et provinces,
>   mais   l'ordre et tranquillité   à   nostre conduite.
>   Nostre grand et
>   glorieux chef-d'oeuvre, c'est vivre à propos.
>   Toutes autres
>   choses,
> regner,   thesauriser,   bastir
>   n'en sont qu'appendicules et adminicules pour le plus.

"Have you knowne how to compose your manners? you have done more then he who hath composed bookes." Have you known how to take rest? you have done more than he, who hath taken Empires and Citties. "The glorious master-piece of man, is, to live to the [purpose]": All other things, as to raigne, to governe, to horde up treasure, to thrive and to build, are for the most part but appendixes and supports therunto.

To compose our character is our duty, not to compose books, and to win, not battles and provinces, but order and tranquility of our conduct. Our great and glorious masterpiece is to live appropriately. All other things ruling, hoarding, building are only little appendages and props, at most.

"Ruling, hoarding, building" is how Donald Frame translates Montaigne's "regner, thesauriser, bastir." Florio, using the telltale doublets of his ebullient prose, gives a more complete sense of the semantic field of these terms in the late sixteenth century: "to raigne, to governe," "to hoarde up treasure," and "to thrive and to build." Implied in "thesauriser" is not only the accumulation of wealth,[20] but also the hoarding up of linguistic capital. Furthermore, this catalog of "all other things," whether by accident or by conscious design, provides us with a pattern for scrutinizing the composition of Montaigne's character—in all senses of that term.

These "appendixes" (as Florio translates *appendicules*) are themselves textual and thematic echoes of Montaigne's characterization of his text as grotesque—as so many "monstrous bodies, patched and hudled up together of divers members" (I.29, 195). We would expect no less from a person who, in his retirement from the world, wanted to settle his thoughts but found he had to keep a register of them because if left on their own, they spawned "so many extravagant *Chimeras,* and fantasticall monsters, so orderlesse... one hudled upon the other" (I.8, 44). These monstrous and seemingly alien bodies engendered by and inhabiting his imagination have a very real counterpart in his kidney stones. The curious relation between Montaigne's stones and his melancholy chimeras can best be explained by my remarking on an analogical sequence that emerges from within the body of Montaigne's text. Therefore, in what follows I will elaborate this pattern and demonstrate how it constitutes a kind of macabre mnemonic device integral to Montaigne's program to "endight and enregister these my humours, these my conceits" (III.3, 49). My aim in doing so is to indicate the extent to which Montaigne's attention to *meurs,* which constitutes his "character," is constructed because of, rather than despite, his claim that ruling, hoarding, and building are mere appendices to "the glorious masterpiece of man."[21] His text bears out that these appendices are the most one could hope for, and Montaigne's self-conscious construction of his character within and by virtue of the composition of his essays is unthinkable without the body of his book. "[M]y book and my selfe march together, and keepe one pace. Else-where one may commend or condemne the worke, without the workman; heere not: who toucheth one toucheth the other" (III.2, 24).

Although readers of Montaigne frequently remark on the author's consubstantiality with his book, no one yet has remarked on the place of the author's body both within the text and with respect to the scene of his writing. The author's body (and, by extension, the literary construct that Montaigne refers to as "le moi") is that which would be governed; his reading and reflections, he would hoard and arrange in his essays, which is to say, in the artificial memory he has "framed"; and the building in question is both his text and where it was composed: his ancestral chateau. To obtain a more complete picture of the workman and the work, let us now turn to the site of his busy leisure. Montaigne recorded of Plutarch,

> that he discerned the Latine tongue by things. Here likewise the sense enlightneth and produceth the words: no longer windy or spongy, but flesh and bone.... [Plutarch] can no sooner come into my sight, or if I cast but a glance upon him, but I pull some legge or wing from him. For this is my dissignement, it much fitteth my purpose, that I write in mine own house.... Doe I not lively display my selfe? that sufficeth: I have [my] will: All the world may know me by my booke, and my booke by me: But I am of an Apish and imitating condition.... What I heedily consider, the same I usurpe.... (III.5, 101–4)

Plutarch's words were likely to come within Montaigne's view in his own house, not only because he was surrounded by his books in his library, but also because the *sententiae* of Plutarch and other classical writers decorated the fifty or more beams overhead.[22] Surrounded by these literary and visual mnemonic aids which inspired his inventions, Montaigne wrote as if from within an anthology of his favorite *sententiae*. This special room provided him with a privileged and enhanced view—both materially and metaphorically.

> At home I betake me somewhat the oftner to my library, whence all at once I command and survay all my housholde; It is seated in the chief entrie of my house, thence I behold under me my garden, my base court, my yard, and looke even into most roomes of my house. There without order, without method, and by peece-meales I turne over and ransacke, now one booke and now another. Sometimes I muse and rave; and walking up and downe I endight and enrigester these my humours, these my conceits. It is placed on the third storie of a tower.... It hath three bay-windowes, of a farre-extending, rich and unresisted prospect.... [There I] seclude my selfe from companie, and keepe incrochers from me: There is my seat, there is my throne. I endevour to make my rule therein absolute.... (III.3, 49)

All three "appendages" unite in this site (and cite): building, both his ancestral home and the construction of his text; ruling, of his home, his leisure, and "self"; and hoarding, of his books, his words, and the larger-than-life words of the ancients painted on the beams overhead. But building, ruling, and hoarding can also be seen as corresponding conveniently to three domains of Montaigne's life and text: the domestic, private, and linguistic. Let me elaborate further the ramifications of this interplay of his body and his text as it pertains to the triplex principle of building, ruling, and hoarding. In the domestic realm we have the stones of his ancestral home, to which he retired to "settle his thoughts" and "keepe a register of them" (I.8; II.18); the private, his kidney stones, also which he says he inherited from his father (II.37); and regarding the linguistic realm, the words from the classical fathers quarried from now-ruined civilizations, his select *sententiae* were the building blocks of his essays (I.24). The analogical strata of the domestic, private, and linguistic in the body of Montaigne's essays provide a convenient way to conclude our analysis of the curious relation among patrimony, kidney stones, and writing.

Montaigne describes the interior of his body with the same perspicacity as when he probes and tests his mind and imagination, without sparing the reader his painful recognition that his life is passing away, piece by piece, as he urinates. This is especially poignant when he records that he is prone to sweate with labour, to grow pale and wanne, to waxe red, to quake and tremble, to cast and vomit blood, to endure strange contractions, to brooke convulsions, to trill downe brackish and great teares, to make thicke, muddy, blacke, bloody and fearfull urine, or have it stopt by some sharpe or rugged stone, which pricketh and cruelly wringeth the necke of the yarde [sexual member]:... Consider but how artificially and how mildly she [death] brings thee in distaste with life, and out of liking with the world.... "If thou embrace not death, at least thou shakest her by the hand once a moneth." (III.13, 354–56)[23]

The pain that brings him in touch with his mortality (and, of course, his subsequent joy and relief after passing a stone) also provided an occasion for meditating, not only on his body and his transience, but also on his body with respect to his lineage.

What monster is it, that this teare or drop of seed, wherof we are ingendered brings with it; and in it the impressions, not only of the corporall forme, but even of the very thoughts and inclinations of our fathers?... It may be supposed, that I am indebted to my father for this stonie quality; for he died exceedingly tormented with a great stone in his bladder.... Where was al this while the propension of inclination to this defect, hatched? And when he was so farre from such a disease, that light part of his substance wherewith he composed me, how could it for her part, beare so great an impression of it? And how so closely covered, that fortie five yeares after, I have begunne to have a feeling of it? (II.37, 496)

Where the composition of his character is concerned, in the end—and in the process of his writing—the citations from the classical fathers are, Montaigne claims, "wholly digested" [II.10], even as they are placed in the body of his text; whereas his kidney stones, passed on to him from his father, represent and, indeed, are what is wholly indigestible.

None but fooles will be perswaded, that this hard, gretty and massie body, which is concocted and petrified in our kidneis may be dissolved by drinks [potions]. And therefore after it is stirred, there is no way, but to give it passage; For if you doe not, he will take it himselfe. (III.13, 359)

What emerges from this is a questioning of the place of the body in our being; for, as he continues, "we are nought but ceremonie; ceremonie doth transport us, and wee leave the substance of things; we hold fast by the boughs, and leave the trunke or body.... Wee dare not call our parts by their proper names" (II.17, 355). Montaigne perceived that his (and by extension, that all humanity's) principal duty was to make sense out of the diverse workings of "inheritance," whether in the form of buildings, diseases, or language. In addition to having the stones of his chateau and the stones of his kidneys passed on to him from his father (whose name, Pierre, incidentally means "rock" or "stone"), so, too, the building blocks of his discourse, Latin sentences, were made a part of his experience before he could judge whether he wanted them to become a part of his being. If we believe Montaigne's claim that he was taught Latin before he knew French, then his mother tongue was that of the fathers par excellence (I.26, 185).

These familiar yet seemingly alien bodies within him were precisely what enabled him to feel, and gave him both the means and impetus to depict, his sense of life. The stones reminded him, as they passed out of him, that a little bit of his life had passed away as well. Thus, Montaigne exorcised in his text and sought to give a body to all that had had a role in the forming of his character: namely, the stones making up the tower of his site for writing, the stones backed up within his urinary tract, and the backlog of lapidary words from the books upon which his education was based and which in turn provided the foundation for the composition of his essays.

Montaigne seems to have recognized this lapidary connection metaphorically, if not existentially, for he compared his escalating decrepitude, his bodily decay emblematized through his stones, to the ruin of an old structure.

> Now I entreate my imagination as gently as I can, and were it in my power I would cleane discharge it of all paine and contestation. A man must further, help, flatter and (if he can) cozen and deceive it. My spirit is fit for that office. There is no want of apparences every where. Did he perswade, as he precheth, hee should successfully ayde

me. Shall I give you an example? He tels me, it is for my own good, that I am troubled with the gravell: That the compositions of my age must naturally suffer some leake or flaw. (III.13, 353)

This last—and richly suggestive—phrase is given in the original as: "que les bastimens de mon aage ont naturallement à souffrir quelque goutiere" (1068). Florio's rendering of "bastimens" as "compositions" returns us to the same doubled sense of an artificial construction, both with respect to one's character (those appended accomplishments of one's life) and also an edifice. Thus, in the *Essais,* as in the general usage of the day, these two senses illumine one another; "bastimens" was taken to mean "a building, frame, house, or edifice; also a composition, or compaction of many things together."[24]

Not only is there a parallel between Montaigne's composition of his character and the composition of his book, but the semantic sense implied here can be thought of as the cement that runs throughout and holds together the various building blocks of Montaigne's discourse and life. After all, the chateau was composed out of the stones of the region and owed its construction to the labor of others; his body owed its being to his parents and the labor of his mother; and his book he composed out of the words of others.

The activity of composing his essays, no less than the themes they investigated, enabled Montaigne to compose his character (*meurs*). We recall from "Of Experience" that this is our primary duty; not to rule, hoard, or build, which are mere appendages or members tacked onto the body of our lifework. And in Montaigne's case, this idea applies to his literary lifework no less than to the composition of his character—which brings together and culminates his effort to rule, hoard, and build. With this in mind, we can see in a new light a key passage usually read as the author's most cogent statement of his union with his book:

In framing this pourtraite by my selfe, I have so often been faine to frizle and trimme me, that so I might the better extract my selfe, that the patterne is therby confirmed, and in some sort formed. Drawing my selfe for others, I have drawne my self with purer and better colours, then were my first. I have no more made my booke, then my book hath made me. A booke consubstantiall to his Author: Of a peculiar and fit occupation. A member of my life. (II.18, 392)

It may well imply a union, but one that refers to the constitution of the character created as a result of the essays—seen as they are as a composite element attached to the essayist's being and having a power over it.

In his retirement, his "busy leisure," Montaigne depicted his humors in an effort to purge them. But, just as he was susceptible to the diseases he saw in others, the skittishness of his imagination exacerbated his own condition: "I apprehend the evill which I studie, and place it in me" (1.20, 92). His melancholy enterprise of rendering a self-portrait in the words of those who have long since died makes his essays a mirror in which the author's image comes back to him as an anatomized cadaver. And as we stand just behind him, reading his essays, we can see reflected therein as well the shadow of our own implied future passing.

> I principally set forth my cogitations; a shapeless subject, and which cannot fall within the compasse of a worke-manlike production; with much adoe can I set it downe in this ayrie body of the voice.... Parcels of a particular shew: I wholly set forth and expose myself: It is a *Sceletos;* where at first sight appeare all the vaines, muskles, gristles, sinnewes, and tendons, each severall part in his due place.... I write not my gests, but my selfe and my essence. (II.6, 60)

The essence about which Montaigne writes is but the "character" engendered through the process of his writing about the formation and composition of *meurs;* and it is a character described through the enumeration of his body parts, as members of his life (I.27, 195; II.18, 392; II.37, 490). The resulting image he saw of himself was a fractured body which, like his book, was a pastiche of disparate apothegms and appendages.

> To the end I may in some order and project marshall my fantasie, even to dote, and keepe it from loosing, and straggling in the aire, there is nothing so good, as to give it a body, and register so many idle imaginations as present themselves unto it. I listen to my humors, and harken to my conceits, because I must enroule them.... I never studie to make a booke; Yet have I somewhat studied, because I had already made it (if to nibble or pinch, by the head or feet, now one Author, and then another be in any sort to study) but nothing at all to forme my opinions.... (II.18, 392–93)

Montaigne recognized aspects of himself in the books he read and in the book he spent the last part of life writing and rewriting. He tried to represent all the fragments and divisions, the bones and stones of his being. It is in this sense that knowledge for Montaigne was based on re-collection. And, finally, his literary enterprise to compose his character, "to register so many idle imaginations as present themselves" (II.18, 392), reflected his quest, quite literally, to re-member, and thus to give a body to—which is to say "to digest"—the *membra disjecta* of his experience.

NOTES

A version of this essay, similar in conclusion but different in approach, has appeared as "Cites and Stones: Montaigne's Patrimony," in *Montaigne Studies* 3, (1993): 180–99.

1. *The Works of Francis Bacon,* ed. James Spedding, R. L. Ellis and D. D. Heath, 14 vols. (Boston: Brown & Taggard, 1861–65), 6:280–81.

2. On the commonplace tradition, especially as it pertains to artificial memory schemes as it will be discussed in what follows, see Joan Marie Lechner, *Renaissance Concepts of the Commonplaces* (New York: Pageant Press, 1962), 170; Frances Yates, *The Art of Memory* (London: Routledge, 1966; reprint, Harmondsworth: Penguin Books, 1978), 20–41; Walter J. Ong, *The Presence of the Word* (New Haven, CT: Yale University Press, 1967), 56–66, 79–87; John G. Rechtien, "John Foxe's Comprehensive Collection of Commonplaces: A Renaissance Memory System for Students and Theologians," *Sixteenth Century Journal* 9 (1978): 83–89.

3. Unless otherwise noted, quotations from Montaigne come from *The Essayes or Moral, Politicke, and Militarie Discourses of Lo: Michael de Montaigne,* trans. John Florio (1603; reprint, London: J. M. Dent & Sons, 1965), 3 vols., and appear in parentheses, identified by book, chapter, and page. I would note in passing why I have chosen to use Florio's voice to speak for Montaigne. Although this present essay focuses on the rhetoric of Montaigne's peculiar form of life-writing, my argument can be applied more generally (as I have indicated elsewhere) to English essayists other than Bacon who were conscious of their indebtedness to Montaigne's model (namely Burton and Browne). I would also remark briefly on Florio's obviously idiosyncratic treatment of Montaigne's text. First, I caution the reader unfamiliar with this exuberant translation that chapter numbers differ slightly from Montaigne's, especially in Book One (I.14 through I.40). Second, Florio's tendency to embellish Montaigne's text—to use four

words where one might have sufficed—is precisely what makes his translation the most fertile for recovering the range of meanings available to contemporary readers of the *Essais*. On Florio's usually faithful continuation of Montaigne's text, see Marcel Maistre Welch, "John Florio's Montaigne: From 'Fine French' to 'True English,'" *Style* 12, no. 3 (1978): 286–96; and, on Florio as the "best" translator of Montaigne, see Tom Conley, "Institutionalizing Translation: On Florio's Montaigne," *Glyph Textual Studies*, n.s., 1 (1986): 45–60, esp. 47–48, 56.

4. See his introduction to Francis Meres's *Palladis Tamia* (New York: Scholars' Facsimiles & Reprints, 1938), iv. See also Pierre Villey, *Les sources et l'evolution des "Essais" de Montaigne*, 2d ed., 2 vols. (Paris: Hachette, 1933).

5. *The Essayes or Counsels, Civile and Morall*, ed. Michael Kiernan (Cambridge, MA: Harvard University Press, 1985), xxxi.

6. On the inventory of Bacon's notebooks and their probable times of composition, see *The Life and Letters of Francis Bacon*, 7 vols., ed. James Spedding (London: Longmans, Green and Co., 1862–74), 1:112. On the relevance of these notebooks for Bacon's method, see Jacob Zeitlin, "Commonplaces in Elizabethan Life and Letters," *Journal of English and Germanic Philology* 19, no. (1920): 47–65, at 64.

7. See Hugo Friedrich, *Montaigne*, (Paris: Gallimard, 1968), 42–47; Jean-Yves Pouilloux, *Lire les "Essais" de Montaigne* (Paris: François Maspero, 1969), 20–25; Terence Cave, *The Cornucopian Text: Problems of Writing in the French Renaissance* (Oxford: Clarendon Press, 1979), 275–79; Antoine Compagnon, *La seconde main ou le travail de la citation* (Paris: Seuil, 1979), 288–332.

8. See André Berthiaume, "Pratique de la citation dans les *Essais* de Montaigne," *Renaissance and Reformation/Renaissance et Reforme*, n.s., 8 (1984): 91–105, esp. 94, 97, 101.

9. The connection between the *ars rhetorica* and the *ars memorativa* has been appreciated fully by Daniel Martin in his groundbreaking study "Pour une lecture mnémonique des *Essais:* Une image et un lieu," *Bulletin de la Société des amis de Montaigne*, 5th ser., no. 31–32 (1979): 51–58.

10. Cicero, *De inventione* (I.vii), trans. M. H. Hubbell (1949; reprint, Cambridge, MA: Harvard University Press, 1976), 18–21, discusses the five parts of rhetoric: *inventio, dispositio, elocutio, memoria,* and *pronuntiatio.* See also Floyd Gray, *Le style de Montaigne* (Paris: Nizet, 1958).

11. This distinction between "artificial" and "natural" memory, which remained part of Renaissance rhetorical practice, took its most classic expression from *Rhetorica ad Herennium* III.xvi.28, trans. Harry Caplan (Cambridge, MA: Harvard University Press, 1954), 207.

12. See Yates, *Art of Memory*, chaps. 1 and 6. On Montaigne's conception of *memoria*, with respect to conventional rhetoric and his effort to "re-invent" memory from within the text, see Michel Beaujour, *Miroirs d'encre: Rhétorique*

de l'auto-portrait (Paris: Seuil, 1980), 113–26. On the notion of "le memoire intertextuelle" implicit in my study, see Lawrence D. Kritzman, *Destruction/ Decouverte: Le Fonctionnement de la Rhetorique dans les "Essais" de Montaigne* (Lexington: French Forum Publishers, 1980), 102–5.

13. Cf. *Oeuvres Completes... de Montaigne,* eds. Albert Thibaudet and Maurice Rat (Paris: Gallimard, 1962 [Bibliothèque de la Pleiade, 14]), 1071, and Donald Frame, *The "Essays" of Montaigne* (Stanford, CA: Stanford University Press, 1965), 837: Florio translates as "frame" Montaigne's verb *forger,* which Frame renders as "make."

14. See Mary B. McKinley, *Words in a Corner: Studies in Montaigne's Latin Quotations,* (Lexington: French Forum Publishers, 1981).

15. Cf. *Essais,* I.1, 1, "je suis moy-mesmes la matière de mon livre" and Florio's rendering, "Thus gentle Reader myself am the groundworke of my booke...."

16. Of the many printed works that outline and describe just such a pattern for an artificial memory scheme, see, for example, Filippo Gesualdo, *Plutosophia... nella quale si spiega l'Arte della Memoria* (Vicenza: Heredi di Perin Libraro, 1600), sigs. D2–D3; it sums and rehearses this commonplace device which had appeared in many earlier tracts available to Montaigne's contemporaries, for example, Lodovico Dolce, *Dialogo... nel quale si ragiona del modo di accrescere, & conseruar la Memoria* (Venice: Giouanbattista Sessa & Fratelli, 1586). On the place of the body (and the notion of "body memory") as it relates to "place memory," see Edward S. Casey, *Remembering* (Bloomington and Indianapolis: Indiana University Press, 1987), 146–215.

17. A more likely mnemotechnic paradigm has been suggested by Daniel Martin, "Démonstration mathématique de l'architecture des *Essais* de Montaigne" and "L'Idée du Theâtre de Camillo et les *Essais* de Montaigne" in *Bulletin de la Société des amis de Montaigne,* 6th ser., no. 7–8 (1981): 79–96; and, see especially the crowning achievement to this productive line of inquiry inaugurated by Daniel Martin, *L'architecture des "Essais" de Montaigne: Mémoire Artificielle et Mythologie* (Paris: Nizet, 1992).

18. In what follows I build on these themes developed variously by Jean Starobinski, *Montaigne in Motion,* trans. Arthur Goldhammer (Chicago: University of Chicago Press, 1985), 173–84; and Georges Poulet, *Studies in Human Time,* trans. Elliot Coleman (Baltimore: Johns Hopkins University Press, 1956; reprint, New York: Harper, 1959), 39–49.

19. I cite from three versions because my concern is primarily with the broader semantic implications of the passage. The first is from *Oeuvres Completes,* ed. Thibaudet & Rat, 1088; the second from *The Essayes,* trans. Florio, III.13, 376; and the third from Frame, *The "Essays,"* 851–52.

20. Randle Cotgrave, *A Dictionarie of the French and English Tongues* (London: A. Islip, 1611), sig. 4G6^v.

21. My contention here is that this notion of "man" and "character" is of a different order than the "the self" traditionally spoken of in Montaigne scholarship, as in Donald Frame's exemplary treatment of this theme in "Self-Discovery and Liberation" in his *Montaigne's Discovery of Man: The Humanization of a Humanist* (1955; reprint, New York: Columbia University Press, 1967), 74–95.

22. On the interior design of Montaigne's library, see Donald Frame, *Montaigne: A Biography* (New York: Harcourt, Brace & World, 1965), 120; and John Holyoake, *Montaigne: "Essais"* (London: Grant & Culter, 1983), 58. For a catalog of the *sententiae* in Montaigne's library, see Grace Norton, *Studies in Montaigne* (New York: Macmillan, 1904), 165–88; and Jacques de Feytaud's "Une Visite à Montaigne" in *Le Chateau de Montaigne,* published by *Société des Amis de Montaigne* (1971), 36–43, 53–62.

23. Cf. *Oeuvres Completes,* eds. Thibaudet & Rat, 1069–70, and Frame, *Montaigne,* 836–37.

24. Cotgrave, *Dictionarie,* sig. I3^v.

12

Whose Life Is It, Anyway? Subject and Subjection in Fulke Greville's *Life Of Sidney*

Adriana McCrea

The difference which I have found between times, and consequently the changes of life into which their natural vicissitudes do violently carry men, as they have made deep furrows of impressions into my heart, so the same heavy wheels cause me to retire my thoughts from the free traffic with the world and rather seek comfortable ease or employment in the safe memory of dead men than disquiet in a doubtful conversation among the living; which I ingenuously confess to be one chief motive of dedicating these exercises of my youth to that worthy Sir Philip Sidney, so long since departed: for had I grounded my ends upon active wisdoms of the present, or sought patronage out of hope or fear in the future, who knows not that there are noble friends of mine, and many honourable magistrates yet living, unto whom both my fortune and reputation were, and are, far more subject?

With this long and meandering sentence, Fulke Greville opened the prose exercise known as *The Life of the Renowned Sir Philip Sidney*. First published in 1652 (that is, twenty-odd years after Greville's death in 1628), this *Life* was for three centuries thereafter largely accepted as the authoritative biography of the heroic Sir Philip, recorded, moreover, by one who knew him well.[1] The recent quest for recovering the "real" historical Sidney has begun to put to the question the reliability of Greville's portrait of his friend.[2] In this essay, I will argue that the so-called *Life* scarcely qualifies as a "life" of Sidney at all, and in any case doesn't really purport to be one. Greville called it a "dedication," intending it as a preface to a collected edition of his own writings, which in turn he dedicated to Sidney.³ This dedicatory scheme then provided Greville with a framework within which he expressed his own commitment to politics, and how he went about doing this will be the major focus of my argument. I will demonstrate that the *Life* is a text that is quite obscure when it comes to defining its specific subject as, by the same token, Greville grapples with the problem of being a loyal Elizabethan (and Jacobean) subject. The so-called *Life of Sidney* will thus be seen to speak less of being a biography of "an other" than something of a displaced *auto*biography. Consequently, Greville manifests the fluidity of genre in the late Renaissance. For Greville, however, such fluidity is dictated by the *Life*'s displacement factor—its reluctance to yield a firm and central subject; and this is the crucial literary feature in a work in which textuality and political reality are portrayed as inseparable, although they are ultimately irreconcilable. While arguing, then, about problems fundamentally lodged within the *Life,* I will suggest by way of conclusion that if the original publishers misnamed Greville's composition in 1652, unlike subsequent generations, they seem to have understood full well the various nuances inherent in what might be called its rhetoric of subjection.⁴

As the lines initially quoted indicate, Greville's *Life* opens in a post-Sidney world that immediately sets out to retrieve him. Thirteen of its eighteen chapters are devoted to recreating an image of Sidney, and in these Greville gives vivid testimony to the place Sidney had occupied in his life. They had been friends since 1564, when both, at the age of ten, had entered Shrewsbury School together. Thenceforth they became intimate companions and political colleagues, entering court together under the patronage of the earl of Leicester, Sidney's uncle and the leader of the Elizabethan "Protestant party." Their long-standing friendship abruptly terminated on a fateful October day in 1586, when Sidney fell victim to a wound he had received in a skirmish outside Zutphen. Thereafter, Greville was left to cope with life as best he could.

And cope he did. Greville not only survived his friend, but Queen Elizabeth as well. He even outlasted the reign of James I, to die, albeit as a result of violence, in 1628, at the ripe old age of seventy-four. His career had been a checkered one.⁵ Like Sidney, and during Sidney's lifetime, he had been frustrated in his efforts for employment in the service of a queen who preferred a cautious and frugal foreign policy to the militant anti-Spanish alternative advocated by the Leicester circle. It was only reluctantly, and after the assassination of William of Orange, that Elizabeth dispatched troops under the command of Leicester to shore up the ailing Protestant forces of the Netherlands. Accompanying his uncle was Philip Sidney; left behind from the entire venture was Greville, who explained in the *Life* that it was the queen who recognized that his particular talents lay not in warfare, but in more settled service at the monarch's side (89). Still, it was not until the 1590s that, under the patronage of the gallant earl of Essex, Greville finally gained office. He survived the fiasco of Essex's rebellion and was reputedly on the verge of joining the council when Elizabeth died. But the accession of James I saw the rise to preeminence of Robert Cecil, soon created earl of Salisbury, who had been Essex's great rival, and who remained Greville's archenemy. Greville endured a period of forced political retirement that lasted until 1614, two years after the death of Salisbury. He would owe his return to the court to the powerful pro-Spanish Howard family, the Suffolks, to whom he had first made overtures in 1604. His later career flourished under the auspices of the duke of Buckingham, of whom Greville remained a faithful client until Buckingham's assassination in 1628. In the event, the patron's death was followed within weeks by Greville's own less spectacular demise at the hands of a disgruntled servant.

Greville thus traveled far from many of the ideals he had shared with Sidney—a distance clearly marked by the ideological flexibility he displayed in his quest for patrons.[6] But it was during his singular experience of complete political ostracism that his *Life of Sidney* took on something like its final form; the years, that is, before 1614, while his political career sat on hold and his life was marked by an enforced withdrawal from the active ideal to which, above all else, both he and Sidney had aspired. From this perspective, the *Life* could well purport to be a glorification of times past, a journey made by a former Elizabethan whose day seemed long gone.[7] There are aspects of nostalgia throughout the *Life*, although Greville seems equally concerned to fix not only Sidney, but Essex and Elizabeth as well, into a specific framework of time and space.

For just as Greville's own life had gone on without Sidney, so the *Life* maintains its momentum even after it treats the death of Sidney (Greville doesn't quite deal with it, and this point will be taken up later). Henceforth Sidney becomes invoked only for inspiration, as Greville does in the fourteenth chapter in explaining why he composed his treatises and the tragedies *Mustapha* and *Alaham*. After describing his deliberate destruction of a third play, *Anthony and Cleopatra*, Greville launches into an apologia for the earl of Essex, who was executed for treason in 1601. Then three more chapters follow, acknowledged as a digression, in which Greville portrays the Elizabethan reign as one of bounty and glory. This inclusion is necessary, Greville insists, lest readers misjudge Elizabeth for her "high justice" against that "brave spirit," Essex. In the final chapter, Greville returns to the subject of his tragedies, setting out his purpose in writing them and contrasting his work to Sidney's.

It is, therefore, this contrast between Greville and Sidney that punctuates the narrative scheme of the *Life*. But before discussing the implications of this contrast, it will be useful to establish what the text is not. It is neither quite biography nor history—that is, not quite a "life" of Sidney, much less a "life and times" of either Sidney or the Elizabethan age. In places it certainly threatens to lapse into one or the other, especially when Greville can describe at length the host of personages connected with Sidney, so many of whom he calls, with Sidney, the "active spirits" of the day, and which include William, prince of Orange, the earl of Leicester, and Sir Francis Walsingham. His point in relating these and other instances, however, is to underline the great acumen possessed by Sidney, which these notables all discerned, and to distinguish Sidney as a singular "wakeful" and "good patriot" (51, 75), and as the epitome of virtue. Then an Essex is drawn according to the virtues—not the faults—he manifested as a favorite of the queen. When he comes to describing Elizabeth, Greville paints a picture that telescopes her reign into two issues: she is depicted as the protectress of beleaguered Protestantism abroad and as the upholder of monarchical dignity at home.

Greville knew firsthand that the queen persistently sought to avoid the first of these "honours" while simultaneously having had a lot of trouble convincing some of her subjects as to the verity of the second.[8] Moreover, he had been close enough to both Sidney and Essex to have a keen sense of their weaknesses along with their strengths. His own stated philosophy of history will not suffice for justifying what both he and latter-day historians might call the "liberties" he took in the *Life*, since he recorded his view when discussing his aborted plan to write "a complete history" of Elizabeth. Concerned with both "the truth" of the reign, and, crucially, with his own "defects" as a writer, Greville explains how he approached Cecil for access to the state papers, only to be told that any history he wrote would have to be vetted by the court.

He relates that Cecil suspected he might depict Elizabeth's reign "to the prejudice of this," that is, James's. To this Greville responded by confessing that "an historian was bound to tell the truth, but to tell all truths were both justly to wrong and offend not only princes and states, but to blemish and stir against himself the frailty and tenderness not only of particular men, but of many families" (131). Clearly, the job of a historian could be as much a hassle as a hazard in one's life, which a glance at the tribulations of John Hayward or of those scholars who had had to answer to the council after the Essex rebellion only confirmed.[9]

On the other hand, we shall soon see that Greville's view of worldly truth could differ markedly from what he considered an "absolute truth" discernable only in God (and thus eminently distant and unreachable). Accordingly, this passage becomes something of a puzzle. It declares that the wrongs and offences of princes *should* be exposed, but adds that the historian is apt to suffer for exposing them (and this caution Greville, the man, obviously took to heart, even while he continued to be a patron to historians).[10] Yet it also suggests that any Elizabethan history issuing from the pen of Greville might well have been more critical than commentators have so far thought. The point is moot, however, and we will never know: when faced with Cecil's obstructions, he promptly gave up on the project, contenting himself instead with the departure in the *Life* that became the "short memorial" to Elizabeth.

There is more to be said about Greville's treatment of Elizabeth in the *Life,* but already it transpires that "memory" and "memorial" are key words that distinguish the text as a nonhistory—at least according to Greville.[11] Still, insofar as he is intent to perpetuate a memory of Sidney (and of Essex and Elizabeth), Greville does appear to be conforming to a contemporary concept of history: that proposed by his friend Sir Francis Bacon in his scheme for the "advancement of learning." The *Life* has frequently been set in the context of Bacon's call for more histories and lives of "worthy personages that deserve better than dispersed reports or barren eulogies."[12] There were plenty of what Greville might well have considered "barren eulogies" on Sidney, since quick on his death a veritable avalanche of laments had followed. Thereafter, Sidney's name became a permanent feature in works dedicated to his surviving family members. Mary Sidney, the countess of Pembroke, was by far the most frequent recipient of these, and she cherished *her* memory of her beloved brother. After the publication of the 1590 edition of Sidney's (new) *Arcadia,* prepared by Greville and replete with his emendations, she responded by issuing what she considered the authoritative version—a mixture of the Old and the New. In the interim, the rest of Sidney's poetry began to appear before the public. The net effect of such a "marketing" was that by the early years of the seventeenth century, Sidney was on the way to being remembered less as a courtier devoted to serving the state at home and the Protestant cause abroad than the influential and popular poet he was to become.[13]

This context helps elucidate an important aspect of Greville's construction of Sidney in the *Life*. When discussing Sidney's writings at the beginning of the *Life,* Greville insists that his "end was not in writing, even while he wrote; nor his knowledge moulded for the tables or schools, but both his wit and understanding bent upon his heart to make himself and others, not in words or opinion, but in life and action, good and great" (12). Later, he invokes the *Arcadia,* but the reference is accompanied by the admonition that Sidney's "end," as Greville puts it again, "was not vanishing pleasure alone, but moral images and examples, as directing threads, to guide every man through the confused labyrinth of his own desires and life" (134). Through a catalog of Sidney's deeds, Greville emphatically demonstrates that "his chief ends" were "not friends, wife, children, or himself, but above all things the honour of his maker and service of his prince or country" (25). Moreover, where contemporaries had bewailed the death of "England's Mars and Muse" or, in Sir Walter Ralegh's words, "the Scipio, Cicero, Petrarch of our time," Greville fixes on an image of Mars (albeit a keenly prescient Mars) and repeatedly refers to him as a "patriot."[14] As this portrait of Sidney reaches its crescendo, the epitaph granted is that of "this Briton Scipio" (76)—and Greville conveniently omits the other Raleghean parallels. Greville's Sidney is less an all-encompassing Renaissance man replete with his lighter, playful side (the image cultivated by his sister) than a serious statesman-moralist who, moreover, turned to literature for clear didactic purposes.

Far from signifying Greville's desire to respond to Bacon's call and fill an existing void on the subject of Sidney, then, Greville seems intent instead on clarifying for posterity the priorities in Sidney's life as he believes (or argues) them to have been. And if he is emphatic on the issue of Sidney's literary purposes, Greville is equally at pains to close the door on pastoral poetry, ostensibly because "no man that follows can reach, much less go beyond, that excellent intended pattern of his" (134). Yet while pronouncing upon the end of "imaginative wit," he affirms the value of poetics, particularly his own based on "images of life." Greville wants to eat his cake and have it, too; alternatively, he seems caught between two rival conceptions of didactic theory: those presented by Sidney, on the one hand, and Bacon, on the other.

According to Sidney, poets were society's legislators. They were the guides who, with the aid of imagination, found divine inspiration and taught "what may be and should be." Against poets he set historians, who, "being captivated to the truth of a foolish world, [are] many times a terror from well-doing, and encouragement to unbridled wickedness."[15] Two and a half decades later, Bacon reversed Sidney's dicta. Like Sidney, he categorized poetry as deriving from and pertaining to the imagination; but in the Baconian scheme, imagination was only one of the three faculties of understanding. The others, memory and reason, were addressed by history and philosophy, respectively. While allowing that poetry had a clear area of operation among the means of acquiring knowledge, Bacon nevertheless demoted poets, now dealers in illusion, and their primary role was given over to historians. It was in this context that Bacon also commended Machiavelli, to whom, he wrote, "we are beholden [for showing] what men do, not what they ought."[16]

Greville's verse treatises and tragedies, composed with the vision of a poetics "fixed upon the images of life," or in Baconian terms "what men do," represent a compromise between the competing theories hammered out by his friends. His own deliberate experiments in "images of wit"—clearly the Sidney legacy—lie among the early poems in *Caelica* and cease when Sidney was no longer counted among the living. Thereafter, he develops his own poetic themes that reflect what Jonathan Dollimore calls a "realist mimesis."[17] The relationship between politics and virtue emerges as the main preoccupation—if not a definition—of Greville, the post-Sidneian poet. Throughout the corpus of his work, he tends less to resolve the problematics in that relationship than confess that true virtue cannot really exist. Thus he pronounces in the *Treatise of Religion:*

> Mixe not in functions God, and earth together;
> The wisdome of the world, and his, are two;
> One latitude can well agree to neither;
> In each, men have their beinges, as they doe;
>   The world doth build without, our God within;
> He traffiques goodness, and she traffiques sinne.[18]

Yet this perspective does not lead Greville into passive resignation. His response is to avow that, since we must operate in the world, a duality of virtue must be recognized. The process by which individuals recognize the discrepancy between absolute virtue and the dictates of duty, and consequently the need to "compromise" virtue and adopt the ways of the world, is the key component of Greville's mimetic realism.

While these issues permeate his tragedies, in the *Life* they do not emerge—except by innuendo and implication, and then only in regard to the narrator. He burns one of his plays rather than have to answer to the authorities for any suspected resemblance to contemporary politics; he desists from writing a history when threatened with censorship; and, in spite of his clear admiration for the active life of war and diplomacy, he is at first made into a stay-at-home advisor of the queen, then becomes a withdrawn spectator who eschews the company of the living to find solace among the heroic dead, long since and lamentably past. On the face of it, he could easily be taken for a spineless coward. But this same narrator, so candid in displaying his caution and "defects," is far from silent on how readers should interpret his work. He expressly denies that they are entertainment. Rather, he calls for clear parallels to be made "on that stage whereon [the reader] himself is an actor, even the state he lives in." And he proposes that "for every part [in the tragedies, the reader] may perchance find a player, and for every line (it may be) an instance of life..." (135). Such instructions mirror Greville's explanation of Sidney's "end" in his poetics; this time it is clear that the writing practice he describes is his own.

On these terms, the *Life* represents less an expression of Greville's realist mimesis than an articulation of the correspondence between living and writing—something he applies to Sidney as well. Accordingly, if occupied in writing, inaction—withdrawal or lack of employment—is a state that ceases to have meaning, for writing is participation by other means, hence the danger of what might follow should a text be read by an enemy and a critic. Hence, as well, the possibility that through the *Life* (with its glorification of Sidney's, Essex's, and Elizabeth's warrior ways), Greville provides a not-so-subtle commentary on the contemporary peace policy toward Spain. The narrative technique, while not consistent throughout the text, is crucial here, contributing to this sense of the *Life* as a critical portrait of Jacobean (and Cecilean) England. For, when Greville describes various episodes involving Sidney but witnessed by him—like the disagreement with the earl of Oxford or the attempt to join Drake, both of which incurred Elizabeth's displeasure—the drama of those moments is captured, the past comes alive, and Greville actually seems to be reexperiencing not only Sidney's company, but his own desire for political action as well; then, in the long descriptions of Sidney's ideas and foresight about foreign affairs, the narrator dissolves into the narration, and it is only by parenthetical reminders that such were Sidney's words and views that a sense of separation between Greville the companion of Sidney and Greville the narrator of events past (not to mention Greville the political analyst) is restored. The narrating "I," which usually anchors the text, provides Greville with a base from which to enter the past, pass firm judgments on the intentions of the dead, and occasionally assess his present in terms of his past. Publication of the work in a different political climate, or even reading it in an environment in which military valor and anti-Spanish sentiment were cultivated (such as the court of Prince Henry, before his death in 1612, or in other circles during the early 1620s when anti-Spanish themes became quite à la mode), could well render it a critique of peaceful policies and, indeed, a call to arms.[19] The *Life* could thus become Greville's way of salvaging his conscience for abandoning (publicly, at least) the principle of militant Protestantism he had shared with Sidney; his means of atonement for having sought office through the favor of the Hispanophile and pacific Howards.

But to be categorical about interpreting the *Life* in this way would be folly. Its detached tone, its melancholic mood, its meandering structure, all operate to undermine its several didactic passages. The subjective aspect of the *Life* is in many ways its most curious feature, both in terms of its place among Greville's entire oeuvre and in regard to its effect on the *Life* itself. As a rule, Greville preferred to be abstract and unobtrusive. In his verse treatises and tragedies he is an outsider, the observer of and commentator on the subjects he treats. This posture enables him to discuss questions of knowledge, virtue, and power from various perspectives; as he discourses upon their worldly functions, he always distinguishes these from their eternal and immutable values, which find little application on earth. Thus the dark, pessimistic, Calvinist poet with whom we are most familiar.[20] It is only in the poems of *Caelica* and the *Life* itself that an indomitable "I" surfaces. But whereas the poems are short and, in a sense, exploratory of their "I," the *Life* seeks rather to explain. First on the agenda is the meaning of Sidney's writings and his own. This in turn provides the meaning of Sidney's life and, implicitly,

Greville's own.[21] Writing and living (or acting) are inseparable in Greville's perspective. In attempting to convey his message of political commitment, however, he cannot avoid the most daunting problem in his life/*Life:* the fact that Sidney dies while he lives on. This haunting reality informs the mood of the text even as it dictates its continuation after the description of Sidney's end at Zutphen. The magnitude of the problem is suggested by Greville's recourse to convention.

The *Life* is in fact the most conventional of Greville's compositions. As John Gouws has noted, the classical rhetorical structure of the panegyric as defined by Quintilian—with its clear chronology, its praise of the subject from birth to death, its record of words and deeds—informs Greville's task right from the start. The Plutarchan model of the portrait of an exemplary life is also evident, ensuring that any "realism" in depicting Sidney is kept under control. Significantly, the rhetorical aspect of the portrait of Sidney in the *Life* enables Greville to provide the only instance in his oeuvre of the perfect compatibility between the principles and actions of an individual.[22] Elsewhere, characters who represent unblemished virtue are never quite seen in "action," and, moreover, tend to get murdered because of their virtue (for example, the prince in *Mustapha*). Still, the perfection represented by Sidney does lead to his death: too magnanimous to be at an advantage over others, he throws off his leg armor because he sees another soldier without his. Thereby he incurs the wound that claims his life.

Although contemporaries disagreed over whether Sidney's neglect in wearing his cuisses had more to do with his haste in getting to the battlefield or his adherence to the new fashion of riding lighter so as to not impede horsemanship, Greville does not stoop to consider such practical possibilities.[23] The *Life* has been constructed to climax at the point of Sidney's death, has been written in light of Sidney's death, and up to that point there have been frequent references to Greville's desire "to keep company with him even after death, esteeming his actions, words and conversation the daintiest treasure my mind could then lay up, or can at this day impart with our posterity" (71). Unsurprisingly, then, Sidney's death is a model one, and in Greville's discussion of it the explanatory power falls entirely to God. "Thus you see," writes Greville in lamenting the close of Sidney's "too short life," "how it pleased God to show forth, and then suddenly withdraw, this precious light from our sky" (83). But for all that Greville renders a description of a death in keeping with the *ars moriendi,* the death scene jumps rather awkwardly, almost by way of escape, into describing Sidney's relevance for the Dutch, whose trading patterns, Greville readily notes, have more to teach the English than they have so far cared to learn.

Literary conventions notwithstanding, Greville has trouble in actually closing off the life of one who seems to have been *the* love of his life. When news of Sidney's death reached Greville, he wrote that he did not know "whether weeping sorrow or speaking sorrow may most honour his memory that I think death itself is sorry for."[24] Seventeenth-century writers from Sir Robert Naunton to John Aubrey remarked that Greville "would often professe" that he had been "a friend to Sir Philip Sidney."[25] These very same words formed part of the brief epitaph by which Greville sought to be remembered when death claimed him. Spartan and to the point, the epitaph on his tomb at Warwick reads: "Fulke Greville, servant to Queen Elizabeth, councillor to King James, and friend to Sir Philip Sidney." The *Life,* with its difficulty in closing off Sidney's life, its ability to do so only rhetorically, is not only a token of the friendship Greville shared with Sidney: it is an expression of ongoing loss. Of "the true affection" between them, Greville asserts, "death hath no power" (86).

It is precisely on this point, however, that the *Life* confronts one of its key dilemmas. Sidney's death is the key component of the *Life,* but the tension between Greville's desire that Sidney's worth "not fatally be buried with him" and his relief that, through his early death, Sidney is "divided and not incorporated with our corruptions" (23) is almost overwhelming. Moreover, Greville is intent to present an authoritative image of Sidney for posterity, one by which he will be accorded the honors that were passed over him in life, but this is a unique portrait representing a standard of virtue that cannot be replicated or duplicated by others. This is established in at least two ways. In the first, adamant that none should attempt to replicate Sidney's example in composing pastoral verse, Greville, as we have seen, insists that he wishes "that [the *Arcadia*] may be the last in this kind, presuming that no man that follows can ever reach, much less go beyond, that excellent intended pattern of his": if writing is tantamount to action, how, according to Greville, could any other mortal attempt to emulate "that excellent pattern" Sidney set in living? Second, Greville may lament the coming of "effeminate times," lacking lustre and glorious activity; but he goes on to portray an Essex who precipitates his doom by not recognizing "the unequal balance between humours and times, nature and place" (93). Sidney himself, Greville strongly implies, would have had problems had he survived the Netherlands campaign to witness "the difference between times" and "the changes of life into which their natural vicissitudes do violently carry men" (3).

The *Life* thus turns on Greville's concern with the instability of temporal affairs—the theme that underlies and actuates (if it does not dictate) the practice of "realist mimesis" in his verse tragedies and treatises. In this light, it is worth bearing in mind that the *Life* is the sole prose work completed by Greville—completed not without difficulty, perhaps, but in contrast to the only other extant prose piece, the *Letter to an Honourable Lady,* complete, nevertheless. That work, too, discusses the flux brought about by time, in this case, the passage from happy marriage to living with infidelity, containing advice on how to persist in such "unhopinge times."[26] The message of passive acquiescence should perhaps have come easily there, since Greville presents marriage, as did most of his contemporaries, as a partnership between unequals. But the complaints raised in the *Letter* find no ready resolutions: the tensions are too large, and the work suddenly halts amid the author's attempt to guide the lady in ways of the inner virtue that go unseen in the world.

Evidently, the commonplace ways of discussing politics during the Renaissance had become unsatisfactory for Greville, concerned as he was with finding a means of properly articulating a Baconian-type interest in "what men do." Bacon, himself keen to apply his own theories, experimented with a number of forms, not least of which was the "essay." Montaigne had developed the form, and his subjective perspective, which makes his literary perambulations appear impervious to time, was the key strategy that enabled him to take new departures and contest to such effect prevailing conventions, whether literary, political, or moral. Bacon's experiments in the genre were objective and abstract in tone. They could be equally provocative, however, although he masked any potential for reading dissidence into politically sensitive subjects by denying that the genre was a recent innovation and pointing out its kinship with the Senecan epistle. He called the letters to Lucilius nothing other than "*Essays,* that is, dispersed meditations, though conveyed in the form of epistles."[27] Greville's *Letter* belongs to this same category, but it was an unsuccessful experiment in adapting the epistle or essay to convey a message of compromise and subservience. Whether prose itself was too close to life as it was lived is an interesting question to ponder in relation to Greville. Politics, the *raison d'être* of his life, was a prosaic world from which he was frequently excluded. Entering and becoming a vital part of it posed him the greatest difficulties.

Equally problematic was the issue of how to discuss it. On the one hand, he became attached to a different Senecan form, the closet drama, but realized that that was hardly the stuff by which to show his ability in politics, having to burn one of his plays because it might be considered too critical of contemporary events and power-brokers. On the other, he preferred the ambiguity that poetry could lend to any discussion of politics, especially in light of his fervent commitment to Sidney's concept of poets as the legislators of humankind. Still, he admitted in the *Life* the difficulties he faced when it came to genre, noting that he subjected his *Treatise of Monarchy* to revision upon revision. The *Treatise* emerged from the choruses of his plays, but looking too dangerously critical of monarchy, in revision Greville first tried to give it a courtly style, then, not content with the result, recast it as a satire. That, too, was unsatisfactory for such a "grave subject which should draw reverence and attention" (92). Finally, in David Norbrook's words, "he left the treatise in such a state that his descriptions of the artifices of power could be applied equally to kings or tyrants, leaving it to the reader to decide what conclusions to draw."[28] Equally important, however, was his decision not to publish it, for he left it to "sleep out" his own time. For all his trouble, at least one of his protégés, Sir William Davenant, failed to read the *Treatise* in terms that Greville might have wished. Davenant later complained to John Aubrey that the revisions succeeded only in destroying what was at one time "a delicate thing."[29]

Davenant, of course, was a young Royalist and Cavalier poet in the making. He was a poet who, moreover, seems to have been untroubled by the problems confronting Greville, veteran of the Elizabethan age and witness to the cultural shift that took place, from manly displays at the tilt to the masques and tourneys now preferred by royalty.[30] Courtliness itself, Greville might have said, was in decay (although in practice he could perform the courtesies demanded first by Elizabeth, then by the Stuarts and their "grandees"). And having abandoned the "courtly" style he himself had practiced, he goes to great length in the *Life* to demonstrate that Sidney had been no mere courtly poet.[31] Turning to prose might have seemed an important means of establishing the point.[32] But completing a prose discussion provided problems for a Greville who was only marginally more comfortable as a poet.

One model may well have informed his task in the *Life:* that provided by the Flemish classicist, Justus Lipsius, who in applying his expertise reinvented closure. Through the dialogue *De constantia,* humanist openness and debate met an end as the Lipsian individual learned to subsume his argumentative skills for the sake of public peace. Lipsius mobilized the Stoic concept of "right reason" as the mechanism by which to distinguish the conflicting duties owed to God and the state; in an age of religious warfare, he became the prophet of "constancy," advocating outward conformity and obedience to the state, despite the private beliefs an individual might harbor, and indeed as the means by which diversity of belief need not intrude upon the duty of obedience required of all subjects. Lipsian constancy, moreover, was constructed on the basis of the equality of reason but the inequality of wisdom in a world governed by flux. Stoicism gave way to neostoicism as Lipsius insisted on a new type of self-discipline as essential to post-Reformation Europe. To this purpose, he depicted a sage wise in the ways of the world—a survivor—who passes on his knowledge and wisdom through a process of "contubernium," a Roman military term signifying the friendship that resulted from the deference shown by the young and inexperienced in heeding the sage. Individuality was swallowed up in this trope, as the pursuit of wisdom became the goal common to all neostoics. And acknowledgement of change—of the differences that arise in the temporal world—and, as a result, coming to terms with the need for obedience to governors, were the vital components of the Lipsian lesson on survival.[33]

The great attraction of Lipsius among contemporaries was not just his message, but also the vehicle by which it was conveyed. Composing his texts almost entirely out of classical quotations—from a host of poets, philosophers and historians, and by running the gamut of antiquity—he literally affirmed the ontological status of language by demonstrating the ongoing relevance of the wisdom of the past.[34] For Greville, such a standard is not quite valid. The meaning of Sidney's writings needs to be set forth by him: this is an essential part of the task he has set himself in the *Life*. Moreover, in discussing his own work, he draws attention to its language to avow that: "it is rich or poor, according to the estate and ability of the writer, so the value of it shall be enhanced or cried down according to the grace and capacity of the reader, from which common fortune of books I look for no exemption" (135). Greville frequently reiterated his own suspicions about "the craft of words," avowing rather the instability of language—the "doubtful conversation," which he maintained was a key feature of the age in which he was living. Meaning, for Greville, was as impermanent as Sidney's life had been.

Yet despite such disclaimers, a crucial paradox is immediately apparent, emerging from the very conception of the *Life*. Greville is out to immortalize Sidney, but must do so through a text. This text, moreover, asserts that it was "not in words or opinion, but in life and action" that he was "good and great," although Greville cannot deny that life and action brought Sidney little reward, and that his goodness and greatness procured his death. In the end, it is his words and opinions that are themselves set forth as of enduring value—according to Greville's words and opinions. Consequently, Sidney is himself textualized. Whether he likes it or not, Greville implicitly avows an adherence to the ontology of the word.

If the Lipsian dialogue on "constancy" informed Greville's task in the *Life*, it was therefore with typical Grevillean ambivalence. Still, there are other clues in the *Life* that strongly suggest that it helped Greville to formulate his work; notably, for all the familiarity with which Sidney is portrayed, Greville is at pains to insist on both his own "inferiority" to Sidney and Sidney's "unequal" status to his contemporaries. And for all that Greville and Sidney were exact contemporaries and the most intimate of friends, the Sidney portrayed in the *Life* is a composite model which stands larger than life. Loving him really, Greville can only depict him rhetorically; moreover, in order to do so, he must adjust the terms of their relationship. The topos of friendship that underlies Greville's praise gives way, throughout the body of the text, to a relationship discussed more in terms of "contubernium."

But who is the sage and who is the student? The unifying theme in the discussion of Sidney consists of Greville's (indeed everyone else's) inferiority to Sidney, but the burden in the *Life* is to demonstrate Greville's inability to emulate him, to "sail by his compass" (89). The readiest explanation is the passage of time. The *Life* is almost an indictment of the unceasing march of time, of the mutability inherent in it, the corruption it inevitably brings, as Greville bows to the explanatory power of "the difference between times," the "unequal balance between humours and times, nature and place" (93). The uniqueness of Greville's treatment of time in the *Life*, however, is that it comes across as less a matter of convention than totally wrapped in the passing of Sidney.[35] And by portraying a Sidney of "unequal" talents—that is, one without peer whether in fighting, diplomacy, or writing poetry—Greville can also account for his own less-than-heroic activities.

The one constant in the so-called *Life of Sidney*, therefore, is the survivor, Greville, who is himself "constant" (in a Lipsian sense) by recognizing the changes brought by time. On the one hand, he is the sage who can look back to the Sidney days with longing, acknowledging, however reluctantly, that they are past. On the other, he is something of a "grammatical fiction" (to borrow Arthur Koestler's term), a figure who lives first in the shadow, then in the memory, of Sidney. Claiming to be writing in memory and in the shadow of Sidney, Greville's text actually shapes a Sidney in Greville's image, even while it avows the reverse. The *Life* and the Sidney of it are less a reflection of who Sir Philip may have been than the Greville who is struggling to discover who and what he might be in a world without Sidney.

In effect, the *Life* expresses a rite of passage undergone by Greville, and it is a testament as well to his ability (or desire, or need) to adapt to changing circumstances (he will soon become the "councillor to King James," as his tomb records). But here a second key dilemma faced in the text must be noted. The *Life* consistently defines Greville in terms of others. Not least of these is an awe-inspiring, not to say absolutist, sovereign.[36] For, even in affirming the value of Sidney's life in shaping his own, in the final analysis, Greville is impelled to go on to write "in honour of her to whom I owe myself," that is, Queen Elizabeth (97). In view of the various difficulties inherent in the text of the *Life*—the problem of closure, of dealing with the death of Sidney, of the inability to define Sidney without recourse to textuality—the issue at the heart of this text emerges as less the problem of subject in terms of identity. It is the question of subjection, or lack of autonomy—both literary and political.

Greville's literary autonomy is effectively curtailed in that his narrative progressively requires further elaboration and clarification. He is first "enforced to bring in pregnant evidence" of Sidney's "true worth" (13). Thereafter, he is driven to elaborate or clarify Sidney's role in England (and abroad), to spell out Essex's virtue while avoiding a discussion of his "precipitate fortune" (93), and finally to grant his "short memorial" to Elizabeth. Less than elaboration and clarification for their own sake, however, these additions are required in light of the conditions under which Greville writes. Which is to say: had Sidney been free to express his inestimable virtue, there would have been no need for his portrait in a "life"; had Greville been free to follow his goals, he would be expressing his virtue (however tainted) in action, not writing. Wanting to be an actor, he can only be a writer. Wanting to record the truth, he is faced with the promise of supervision and censorship. Wanting to be a loyal servant, he becomes a critic.

For as Elizabeth gave Sidney little of what was his due, Greville's intervention was required to set the record straight. She, too, disapproved of her servants taking upon themselves the direction of policies, punishing those who tried, as she did Essex, while advancing those who toed the line (Cecil's rise began under Elizabeth). The queen makes and unmakes her subjects; she is an "absolute princess" (88), ruling by her "legal and royal wisdoms" (97). But in absolute monarchies, as every political author (courtly or otherwise) knows, standards, whether of politics or of literature, descend from and revolve around monarchs.[37] Rarely can subjects, least of all one as impotent and underused as Greville, be subjects of a text. Worse, through most of his text, Greville has implicitly criticized the queen, which he turns to correct by lavishing praise on her. It is entirely open to question whether admiration of Elizabeth and not caution (in one who believed in God yet knew the world) led Greville to set down his memorial to the queen, since, curiously, the *Life* now drops its subjective voice. Was this Greville's way of providing the substitute for the history of her reign upon which he could not freely work? More likely, it signaled Greville's response to the politics and literature of absolutist England. As Greville becomes the perfectly loyal and devout (political) subject of the queen, what we discern is the total displacement of Greville as (literary) subject of the *Life*. The subject vanishes amid his subjection.

Greville's oft-mentioned caution in the *Life* suggests, as does the narrative structure, his ultimate discomfort with such subjection: he must continually remind himself of it. Yet, while not free to write precisely what he wanted, and even less free to act as he might have wished, he is free to suppress all consideration of publishing the *Life*—the ultimate act of subjection, and tellingly another aspect of his adaptability and willingness to serve. As David Norbrook has suggested in discussing the resemblance of the *Life* to Etienne de la Boétie's *De la servitude volontaire*, Greville becomes a voluntary slave to the present, leaving his "pamphlets," including the *Life,* to sleep "out [his] own time."[38] Then, Greville warns, "if they happen to be seen hereafter, shall at their own peril rise upon the stage when I am not" (132). In 1652, when the *Life* was released for public consumption, there was less peril to be had than he could have foreseen.

He might even have been aghast, as were many contemporaries, that England had undergone a civil war that climaxed in regicide. But what was called for by the new Commonwealth government was the voluntary involvement of all would-be servants of England. A new age had been inaugurated, which, replete with a new military precocity, repudiated absolutism and the effeminacy of a Stuart court, subsequently abolished. Greville's laconic, apologetic text fitted the Commonwealth's agenda very well. For one thing, its "anti-courtliness" was a natural foil to Cavalier lamentations for Charles I. For another, it attested to a once and future heroic age for England. Through its rhetoric of subjection, it also spoke of the difficulties but necessity of compromise in order to meet the requirements of the day. In all its ambiguities, this "*Life of Sidney*" prefigured the themes raised by Marchamont Nedham and Andrew Marvell, as in their very different ways they wrote to win converts for the infant republic.[39] How far it might have helped them articulate their work cannot truly be said. What is clear is that in 1652 the Commonwealth of England had need of heroic Sidney types; above all, it demanded flexible, adaptable Greville types.

NOTES

I wish to acknowledge the financial support provided by the Social Sciences and Humanities Research Council of Canada, which enabled me, as a post-doctoral fellow at Dalhousie University, to take time to pursue and complete this study. An earlier version of this paper was presented to the History Department at Simon Fraser University, and I profited from comments made there, as well as from a close critical reading by Daniel Woolf.

1. Donald A. Stauffer, *English Biography Before 1700* (Cambridge, MA: Harvard University Press, 1930), 140 ff. More recently, Greville's *Life of Sidney* has been considered a biography by Stephen L. Collins in his *From Divine Cosmos to Sovereign State: An Intellectual History of Consciousness and the Idea of Order in Renaissance England* (New York and Oxford: Oxford University Press, 1989), 140–42. The quoted passage comes from *A Dedication to Sir Philip Sidney*, in *The Prose Works of Fulke Greville*, ed. John Gouws (Oxford: Clarendon Press, 1986), 3. Henceforth, all page numbers noted in parentheses within the text refer to this edition.

2. Greville's depiction of Sidney is questioned in various essays of the commemorative volume, Jan van Dorsten, Dominic Baker-Smith, and Arthur F. Kinney, eds., *Sir Philip Sidney: 1586 and the Creation of a Legend* (Leiden: Publications of the Sir Thomas Browne Institute, 1986); see also Katherine Duncan-Jones, *Sir Philip Sidney: Courtier Poet* (New Haven, CT and London: Yale University Press, 1991).

3. See John Gouws, "Introduction," in *A Dedication to Sir Philip Sidney*, in *The Prose Works of Fulke Greville*, ed. John Gouws (Oxford: Clarendon Press, 1986), 3.

4. My own approach to Greville's "rhetoric of subjection," and to the "subject/subjection" of my title, offers less ambivalence than might be argued. I have nevertheless profited from Michel Foucault, "The Subject and Power," *Critical Inquiry* 8 (1982): 777–95; the works of Stephen Greenblatt, especially *Renaissance Self-Fashioning: More to Shakespeare* (Chicago: University of Chicago Press, 1980); Richard Helgerson, *Self-Crowned Laureates: Spenser, Jonson, Milton and the Literary System* (Berkeley and Los Angeles: University of California Press, 1983); and Louis Adrian Montrose, "The Elizabethan Subject and the Spenserian Text," in Patricia Parker and David Quint, eds., *Literary Theory/Renaissance Texts* (Baltimore: Johns Hopkins University Press, 1986), 303–40.

5. For Greville's life and career, see Ronald Rebholz, *The Life of Fulke Greville, First Lord Brooke* (Oxford: Clarendon Press, 1971).

6. Greville's ideological flexibility is noted by F. J. Levy, "The Courtier as Philosophic Poet," *Modern Language Quarterly* 33 (1972): 433–48.

7. A nostalgic interpretation of the *Life* is given by Rebholz, *Life of Greville*, 205–13; cf. Joan Rees, *Fulke Greville, Lord Brooke, 1554–1628: A Critical Interpretation* (Berkeley and Los Angeles: University of California Press, 1971), 65–75.

8. Compare Greville's description of Elizabeth in *Life*, chaps. 15–17, with that offered earlier, when he notes the queen's reluctance to involve England in the Wars of Religion. I shall argue that Greville's awareness of his implicit criticisms of the monarch prompts the final chapters; for an analysis of the means by which Elizabeth maintained her authority, see Christopher Haigh, *Elizabeth I* (London: Longmans, 1988). More recently, part of the reign has been examined by Wallace T. MacCaffrey, *Elizabeth I: War and Politics, 1588–1603* (Princeton, NJ: Princeton University Press, 1992).

9. Greville's remarks here bear on the problem of counsel as well as the dangers of writing history, the two being neither mutually exclusive nor separately conceived. For an incisive study of the literature of counsel and its inherent dangers, see Daniel Javitch, *Poetry and Courtliness in Renaissance England* (Princeton, NJ: Princeton University Press, 1978). For Hayward and others, see F. J. Levy, "Hayward, Daniel, and the Beginnings of Politic History in England," *Huntington Library Quarterly* 50 (1987): 1–34; and for the control of history

by the authorities, see D. R. Woolf, "The Power of the Past: History, Ritual and Political Authority in Renaissance England," in Paul A. Fideler and T. F. Mayer, eds., *Political Thought and the Tudor Commonwealth: Deep Structure, Discourse and Disguise* (London and New York: Routledge, 1992), 19–49.

10. See Kevin Sharpe, "The Foundations of the Chairs of History at Oxford and Cambridge: An Episode in Jacobean Politics," in his *Politics and Ideas in Early Stuart England: Essays and Studies* (London: Pinter Press, 1989), 207–29.

11. Greville's deliberate use of such terms points up the problem of taxonomy in the Renaissance, for which see the editors' introduction in this volume. See also Nancy S. Struever, *The Language of History in the Renaissance* (Princeton, NJ: Princeton University Press, 1970); D. R. Woolf, *The Idea of History in Early Stuart England* (Toronto: University of Toronto Press, 1990); and Donald R. Kelley, "The Theory of History," in Charles B. Schmitt and Quentin Skinner, eds., *Cambridge History of Renaissance Philosophy* (Cambridge: Cambridge University Press, 1988), 746–61.

12. Francis Bacon, *The Advancement of Learning,* in *Works of Francis Bacon,* 7 vols., ed. James Spedding, R. L. Ellis, and D. D. Heath (London: Longmans, Green and Co., 1857–59), 3:337–38.

13. See Michael Brennan, *Literary Patronage in the Renaissance: The Pembroke Family* (London: Croom Helm, 1988), chap. 4; Rees, *Fulke Greville,* 55; and W. A. Ringler, "Sir Philip Sidney: The Myth and the Man," in Jan van Dorsten, Dominic Baker-Smith, and Arthur F. Kinney, eds., *Sir Philip Sidney: 1586 and the Creation of a Legend* (Leiden: Publications of the Sir Thomas Browne Institute, 1986), 11–13.

14. Charles Fitzgeffrey, *Sir Francis Drake* (London: J. Broome, 1596), sig. B4^v; Sir Walter Ralegh, "An Epitaph Upon . . . Sir Philip Sidney Knight," in R. S., ed., *Phoenix Nest* (London: I. Jackson, 1593), sig. C1^v.

15. Sidney, *A Defence of Poetry,* ed. Jan van Dorsten (Oxford: Clarendon Press, 1966), 26, 37–38.

16. Bacon, *Works,* 3:343ff., 430.

17. Jonathan Dollimore, *Radical Tragedy: Religion, Ideology and Power in the Drama of Shakespeare and his Contemporaries* (Chicago: University of Chicago Press, 1984), 78–81, 120–33.

18. *Fulke Greville: The Remains, Being Poems of Monarchy and Religion,* ed. G. A. Wilkes (Oxford: Oxford University Press, 1965), 227, stanza 98.

19. The political contexts of these periods are discussed by J. W. Williamson, *The Myth of the Conqueror, Prince Henry Stuart* (New York: AMS Press, 1978); Roy Strong, *Henry, Prince of Wales and England's Lost Renaissance* (New York: Thames and Hudson, 1986); Graham Parry, *The Golden Age Restor'd* (Manchester: Manchester University Press, 1981), esp. 64–94; and Thomas Cogswell, *The Blessed Revolution: English Politics and the Coming of War* (Cambridge: Cambridge University Press, 1990).

20. Cf. Richard Waswo, *The Fatal Mirror: Themes and Techniques in the Poetry of Fulke Greville* (Charlottesville: University Press of Virginia, 1972). Greville could with profit be subjected to an analysis such as Greenblatt's "Psychoanalysis and Renaissance Culture," in Patricia Parker and David Quint, eds., *Literary Theory/Renaissance Texts* (Baltimore: Johns Hopkins University Press, 1986), 210–24.

21. I have profited from the theories of autobiography discussed by William L. Howarth, "Some Principles of Autobiography," in James Olney, ed., *Autobiography: Essays Theoretical and Critical* (Princeton, NJ: Princeton University Press, 1980), 84–114; and by James Olney, "The Ontology of Autobiography," ibid., 236–67, esp. 239.

22. See the general introduction in *Prose,* ed. Gouws; and John Gouws, "Fact and Anecdote in Fulke Greville's Account of Sidney's Last Days," in Jan van Dorsten, Dominic Baker-Smith, and Arthur F. Kinney, eds., *Sir Philip Sidney: 1586 and the Creation of a Legend* (Leiden: Publications of the Sir Thomas Browne Institute, 1986), 62–82.

23. Gouws, "Fact and Anecdote," 68–69.

24. Greville to Archibald Douglas, 1586, as quoted in Rebholz, *Life of Greville,* 68.

25. Naunton, *Fragmenta Regalia,* quoted in *Poems and Dramas of Fulke Greville,* ed. Geoffrey Bullough, 2 vols. (Edinburgh: Oliver and Boyd, 1939), 1:7; *Aubrey's Brief Lives,* ed. Oliver Lawson Dick (London: Secker and Warburg, 1949), 8.

26. *Letter to an Honourable Lady,* in *Prose,* ed. Gouws, p. 158.

27. For Montaigne, see David Lewis Schaefer, *The Political Philosophy of Montaigne* (Ithaca, NY: Cornell University Press, 1990); for Bacon, *Life and Letters of Francis Bacon,* 7 vols., ed. James Spedding (London: Longmans, Green and Co., 1862–74), 4:340, and F. J. Levy, "Francis Bacon and the Style of Politics," *English Literary Renaissance* 16 (1986): 101–22.

28. David Norbrook, *Poetry and Politics in the English Renaissance* (London: Routledge and Kegan Paul, 1984), 170.

29. *Aubrey's Brief Lives,* ed. Dick, 86.

30. On Davenant, see Martin Butler, "Early Stuart Court Culture: Compliment or Criticism?" *Historical Journal* 32 (1989): 425–35, and idem, "Politics and the Masque: *Salmacida Spolia,*" in Thomas Healey and Jonathan Sawday, eds., *Literature and the English Civil War* (Cambridge: Cambridge University Press, 1990), 59–74. For courtly entertainment under the Tudors and Stuarts, see Sydney Anglo, *Spectacle, Pageantry and Early Tudor Policy* (Oxford: Clarendon Press, 1969); Alan Young, *Tudor and Jacobean Tournaments* (London: George Philip and Son, 1987); Steven Orgel, *The Illusion of Power* (Berkeley and Los Angeles: University of California Press, 1975); Parry, *Golden Age Restor'd;*

and R. Malcolm Smuts, *Court Culture and the Origins of a Royalist Tradition in Early Stuart England* (Philadelphia: University of Pennsylvania Press, 1987).

31. Greville's style is discussed by Norbrook, *Poetry and Politics,* 171–73; but see also Lauro Martines, *Society and History in English Renaissance Verse* (Oxford: Basil Blackwell, 1985), 86–92.

32. Cf. Samuel Daniel's retreat to prose, discussed in D. R. Woolf, "Community, Law and State: Samuel Daniel's Historical Thought Revisited," *Journal of the History of Ideas* 49 (1988): 61–83.

33. Lipsius's role in the emergence of a new order in the early modern period is the subject of Gerhard Oestreich's *Neostoicism and the Early Modern State,* ed. B. Oestreich and H. G. Koenigsberger, trans. David McLintock (Cambridge: Cambridge University Press, 1982); Mark Morford, *Stoics and Neostoics: Rubens and the Circle of Lipsius* (Princeton, NJ: Princeton University Press, 1991), 14–30, focuses on Lipsius and his appropriation of the Roman concept of "contubernium." The rest of the following is developed in my book-in-progress, tentatively entitled *Constant Minds: Political Virtue and the Lipsian Paradigm in England, 1584–1650* (Toronto: University of Toronto Press, forthcoming).

34. Cf. Anthony Grafton, "Portrait of Justus Lipsius," *American Scholar* 56 (1986/76): 382–90.

35. Cf. the direction of Donne's *Anniversary* poems, where lamentations for Elizabeth Drury lead to considerations on time but end in consolation. Cf. John L. Mahoney, "Donne and Greville: Two Christian Attitudes Toward the Renaissance Idea of Mutability and Decay," *College Language Association Journal* 5 (1962): 203–12.

36. Orthodoxy now has it that absolutism—in England, at least—was perceived as not necessarily a bad thing: see J. W. Daly, "The Idea of Absolute Monarchy in Seventeenth-Century England," *Historical Journal* 21 (1978): 227–50.

37. See Jonathan Goldberg, "Authorities," in *James I and the Politics of Literature: Jonson, Shakespeare, Donne, and Their Contemporaries* (Baltimore: Johns Hopkins University Press, 1983), chap. 1; and for some of the ways by which authors subtly circumvented such "politics of literature," see Annabel Patterson, *Censorship and Interpretation: Conditions of Writing and Reading in Early Modern England* (Madison: University of Wisconsin Press, 1984).

38. Norbrook, *Poetry and Politics,* 160–66.

39. See my "Reason's Muse: Andrew Marvell, R. Fletcher, and the Politics of Poetry in the Engagement Debate," *Albion* 23 (1991): 655–80.

13

Exemplarity and Gender: Three Lives of Queen Catherine de' Medici

Sheila ffolliott

in memoriam Nancy Lyman Roelker

Increasingly over the past decade, scholarly discussion has investigated early modern commentators on woman and women, in the various genres in which they wrote, such as defenses, dialogues, or conduct books. Analysis of these texts' rhetorical strategies, in particular, demonstrates how women, while praised, are ultimately contained by most arguments.[1] One of the questions this volume considers has been somewhat ignored in larger discussion: are there distinctive issues regarding the rhetoric employed by the writers of early modern lives of women?[2]

The conventions that governed what comprised history—of which life-writing was a part—largely excluded women from a practice devoted to chronicling exemplary deeds and demonstrations of civic virtue.[3] Thus, in chapter 7 of this book, Diana Robin treats a woman's attempt to record her own autobiography through an alternative form: the *epistolae*. But because of their public positions and potential exemplarity, two classes of women—saints and queens—had been and would continue to be the subject of life-writing in forms resembling those used for their male counterparts.[4] From the early Middle Ages when the genre rose, the writing of queens' biographies—which will be my concern here—assumed a didactic exemplary purpose transcending the recording of individual lives. For the most part, exemplary life-writing occurred only after the subject's death, and concerned itself with locating the subject in the narrative continuum of history, a moral enterprise that at the same time reflected particular—and polemical—positions.

Employing rhetoric appropriate to their desired ends, medieval authors fit individuals into one of two polarized versions of queenship, in both of which gender was always at the fore.[5] The praiseworthy model of queenship illustrated what such exemplary biographies continued to reproduce as the best that could be expected from the acknowledged inferior sex. Such a representation largely conflated queenship with female sainthood, for it de-emphasized the queen's public—what might be called political—role in favor of what was advocated as more appropriate female conduct. Demonstrations of piety or charity, qualities also associated with sainthood, were exemplified by someone like Clotilde, queen consort of Clovis, who, in fact, became a saint. The negative queenly exemplar, on the other hand, was she who involved herself, inappropriately for her gender, in politics. Biographers of queens such as Fredegonde, Brunhild, or Bathild used their lives to present early examples of the consequences of what was represented as their "wicked" behavior.[6] This constantly reinscribed blameworthy model of queenship came, in the aggregate, to exemplify the evils of female rule generally.

But unlike "king," the category "queen" is unstable, describing different states.[7] Most commonly the term denotes the king's spouse, the nonruling queen consort: for example, Claude, wife of Francis I of France; or Isabella of Portugal, wife of Charles V. In countries that did not prohibit women from succeeding to the throne, the term also applied to a female monarch. Thus, the modifier *regnant* distinguished queens, such as Elizabeth I, who ruled in their own right. In the sixteenth and seventeenth centuries, however, queen consorts frequently served temporarily as regents for their absent husbands or minor sons, even in countries that prohibited women themselves from succeeding to the throne. It is the biographical representation of this hybrid, the queen regent, that I shall examine in this chapter.

Catherine de' Medici, one such queen regent, was the subject of three different independent examples of what can be called life-writing. The first, chronologically, was Nicolas Houel's *Histoire de la Royne Arthémise* (Paris, 1562); the second, attributed to Henri Estienne, *Discours merveilleux de la vie, actions, & deportemens de Catherine de Médicis, Royne Mère...* (Paris, 1575; many other editions and translations); and the third, her funeral oration by Renaud de Beaune, Archbishop of Bourges (Blois, 1589). During this period, as Robert Kolb has shown in chapter 3 of this volume, the funeral oration often provided the first occasion for the composition of a life narrative.[8] In the case of Catherine de' Medici, significantly—and unusually—the other two "lives" appeared while the queen still lived.[9] Although each biography originated in a different set of circumstances, the three share a common organizing principle relating to the medieval tradition: the queen is at the center of the narrative and her agency determines everything that is good or bad. While sixteenth-century French historiography began a transformation, in which historical writing moved away from personal to impersonal explanations, these writings, significantly, retained their personal locations. This chapter, focusing on Houel's *Histoire,* but making references to the other two lives, will examine the rationale for these authors' choice of—and rhetorical strategies within—the genre of life-writing. It will also briefly touch upon similar rhetoric in the visual arts in the depiction of individual queenship.

Through a sequence of unlikely events (and despite her being the first of her family to be nobly born), in 1560 Catherine de' Medici found herself queen regent of France for her young son Charles IX.[10] While civil war threatened, the widowed queen mother attempted to hold together both the institution of the monarchy and the realm itself. Like many rulers before her, to help her gain authority, the new regent needed a symbolic system to cement, in the terms of Norbert Elias, her particular *person* to the regent's *position.*[11] This imperative prompted the writing of the first of the "lives."

An amateur and probable autodidact in historiography, Nicolas Houel, aided the queen in her quest for symbolic assistance.[12] This bourgeois Parisian, trained as an apothecary and doubtless seeking patronage at court, presented her in 1562 with a life of a model ancient queen who, appropriate to the current situation, had ruled her kingdom after her husband's death. He composed a manuscript *Histoire,* in over one hundred folios, of Artemisia, the fourth-century B.C. queen of Caria, in Asia Minor.[13] But, significantly for the concerns of this volume, in dedicating his text, Houel informed Queen Catherine that she would see her own life reflected in that of the ancient queen. Thus, he provided her with an exemplary biography in the humanist tradition with the intent that the principal reader would recognize herself encoded within an ancient model.[14]

Although sharing some rhetorical strategies, as will be demonstrated, Houel's work departed from earlier treatments of women's lives—whether in written or illustrated form, or a combination of the two—in three significant ways. First, it is an extensive biography of one woman, neither one in a collected "lives" of famous women like Boccaccio's *De mulieribus claris* (in which the sum total of individual lives serves also to reinforce a concept of ideal womanhood), nor a brief mention contained within a biography of her husband or male relative, as happens in the collection of lives by Paolo Giovio.[15] Second, unlike such collections—in which illustrations were frequently limited to a single generalized portrait per exemplar—Houel arranged for artists, primarily Antoine Caron (1521–99), to make accompanying illustrations chronicling diverse episodes in the subject's life.[16] Furthermore, what makes this example of "life-writing" particularly unusual in form is that Houel's concept extended beyond the confines of a bound volume. He suggested that the almost seventy highly finished drawings (17" x 24") illustrating episodes from Artemisia's life, preserved separately from his text, should serve also as models for tapestries, the Northern European medium of choice for large-scale decorative art.[17] Thus, in addition to the tradition of the illustrated manuscript or printed book, these images also participate in the related discourse surrounding the rhetoric of monumental decorative complexes exhibiting the feats of famous individuals, one example of which is the contemporary Hall of Deeds at the Farnese Villa at Caprarola.[18] Significantly in the history of representation, among female subjects, only the life of the Virgin (both saint and queen of heaven) was imagined in similar narrative scope.

When such an exemplary biography is presented to a living patron, the dynamics of courtly patronage interpose themselves upon the pedagogical process. This necessitated the biographer's consideration of his relationship to the living subject, a problem common to the genre, as Erasmus had long before realized.[19] In examining Houel's ensemble in the context of life-writing, it is important to see it not simply as representative of the way Houel imagines that the queen—his primary reader—might wish to figure her own authority, given the circumstances, but—inter alia—as he wishes to figure his own. His manuscript text could itself circulate at court, as had Guillaume Budé's *Institution du Prince*, written in 1519, but published only in 1547.[20] Houel viewed the entire ensemble, text and tapestry, as serving both a primary reader and a larger interpretive community.[21]

Donald R. Kelley's remark about the conditions that give rise to the invention of "history" is significant in considering what bound this interpretive community together. "In general, history is not something which, like poetry, is recollected in tranquility. On the contrary, it is precisely in times of crisis, in times of self-doubt and self-searching, that men begin most intensely to question their antecedents and to seek the reasons for their plight."²² Houel wrote precisely during such a time of crisis—mid-sixteenth-century France—when religious wars threatened stability and it was necessary first to accept a female regent, then even more important to reinscribe the masculine terms of monarchy in the person of a small boy. To this end, Houel chose life-writing as a genre through which he could prescribe an exemplary path for the queen regent, in an attempt to stabilize the queen's conduct. Recognizing herself in the ancient queen, she would accordingly direct her own life in such a way as to permit its subsequent narration in a mode consonant with what Houel assumes to be the prevalent desires of those around her. As will be seen, when compared with a life written directly about the queen a decade later, Houel's purpose would not have been served by simply writing and having illustrated a life of Queen Catherine as herself. Because of her gender and national origin, under no circumstance would the interpretive communities of late Valois France have regarded this queen in positive terms.²³ Although, as Timothy Hampton has demonstrated, the rhetoric of exemplarity was losing its force at the end of the sixteenth century, Houel, unlike his contemporary revisionist historians, chose life-writing deliberately because of its focus on personal agency.²⁴ As a participant in a patronage system, his own life could change as a result of individual action. Not surprisingly, therefore, he sought to allay the generalized communal fears and effect a return to normalcy through the powerful medium of life-writing. Why did life-writing hold such power?

Houel himself stated outright that it was his intention in the *Histoire d'Arthémise* to imitate one of the most famous ancient models of life-writing: Xenophon's *Cyropaedia* (The Education of Cyrus). Scholars have seen intertwined in the *Cyropaedia* a number of literary genres that would later grow more distinct from one another.²⁵ Renaissance notions of life-writing, like ancient rhetoric, permitted, within a single text, the embellishment of what might now be called the historical with the fictive to forge the exemplary.²⁶ Since writers usually composed lives to praise or blame persons whom they considered virtuous or malicious, they derived a method from epideictic oratory whose purpose was similar.²⁷ Both the *Cyropaedia* and Houel's imitation narrate the life of an individual by detailing that person's exemplary qualities, demonstrated by good deeds. To pen a lengthy "life" based on the very small number of extant sources regarding the historical Artemisia, Houel expanded the narrative with thinly veiled references to contemporary France and to Catherine de' Medici herself, reflected back on to an antique setting. To the contemporary reader, this strategy increased considerably the legitimacy of her deeds. The authority to be gained by invoking antiquity was especially necessary in this case since this exemplum was a woman.

In adapting the *Cyropaedia* model for a life of Artemisia/Catherine, Houel never problematized one particular dilemma: doesn't exemplary rule require a *male* exemplar? When making a rhetorical proof (the *paradigma*), Quintilian advocated the desirability of comparing like with like, especially with regard to historical parallels.[28] Gender was an important point of distinction: male and female were not like. At the outset of his text, however, Houel boldly claimed that Artemisia's life, that is the life of Artemisia as he narrated it, would be every bit as valuable as those of men (specifically Julius or Augustus Caesar), her exploits having been as exemplary as theirs.[29] Here he also made a personal claim, contending that his text—that is, his own creation—was as valuable as the lives of men narrated by other men.

Following Quintilian, Houel's narrative exemplification of the queen's model qualities took place within a gendered system, as did those of the other two lives discussed here. Thus these writings, following prescriptions for rhetoric, conformed as well to social practice that placed men and women on different tracks. Notably, in detailing the qualities that Artemisia possessed, Houel called "virtues" (from *vir*: a male)—and provided male exemplars for—those qualities associated with good rule: e.g., "the diligence of Pyrrus, the mind of Alexander...." What, in contradistinction, he calls the queen's female "graces" include "the fidelity of Polyxena, the beauty of Helen..."[30] These female-associated attributes, however, especially as figured in their exemplars, do not relate primarily to royal duties. As Constance Jordan has demonstrated persuasively with regard to other humanist writings on women, they reflect instead the qualities that the period considered ideal in a *woman*.[31]

But at one point Houel allowed that in certain circumstances Artemisia might seem exemplary both to men and to women. Quintilian recommended this approach as being most useful in exhortation: "Courage is more remarkable in a woman than in a man. Therefore, if we wish to kindle someone's ambition to the performance of heroic deeds, we shall find that parallels drawn from the cases of Horatius and Torquatus will carry less weight than that of the woman by whose hand Pyrrus was slain and if we wish to urge on a man to meet his death, the cases of Cato and Scipio will carry less weight than that of Lucretia."[32] Toward the end of the *Histoire,* Houel creates a particularly self-conscious bit of life-writing–within–life-writing to contain this exhortation. He gives the queen's son a funeral oration to deliver and the young king eulogizes the queen's life as having been, "exemplary to women on account of her *modesty* and to men on account of her *courage* and *valor.*"[33] This follows Quintilian's advice precisely because for men her courage and valor would seem all the more exemplary. At the same time, however, the referents for the qualities clearly retain their gendered associations: even when practiced by a woman, modesty is exemplary to women as courage is to men. Moreover, Houel gives the male orator the authority to make these assertions.

In such a system (like:like), exemplarity is gender specific, and exemplary characteristics cannot simply be gender neutral. It is clear Houel conceptualized his ideal *woman ruler* in that order, first conforming to a constantly reinscribed definition of the ideal *woman,* who, in addition—and exceptionally—possessed all the male-associated virtues desirable in an ideal *ruler.* Thus, Houel did not directly challenge the gendered notion of exemplarity with regard to rule; he just typically claimed Artemisia as another "great exception." As Romeo DeMaio characterized the problem in his study of Renaissance biographies of women, what the humanists considered *excellent* women simply corresponded with social expectations of normal males; her excellence consisted in demonstrations of her having overcome what was presumed to be her sex's normal inferiority.[34] In the case of rule this required, therefore, her assimilation of male-associated qualities.

While Houel defines qualities as gender specific, other writers on queen regency followed Quintilian's precepts of comparing like with like even more closely and contained the discourse by comparing women exclusively with other women. To shore up her own power base, in 1520 the previous French female regent, Louise de Savoie, had herself directly commissioned a life of the thirteenth-century Blanche of Castile, perhaps the most famous queen regent in France to that time.[35] Etienne le Blanc, author of this manuscript exemplary life, *Les Gestes de Blanche de Castille,* narrated significant episodes from the life of Blanche, mother of Louis IX (St. Louis).[36] Of interest to us here, LeBlanc cites historic precedents for her regal actions, finding these primarily among Old Testament heroines and queens, such as Judith and Esther.

The famed orator Renaud de Beaune, archbishop of Bourges, adopted a similar strategy at Catherine de' Medici's death in his funeral oration for the queen, one of the "lives" being considered here.[37] To establish her proper female credentials first, he promoted her exemplarity both as mother herself and as advocate of mothers.[38] To move from there to an observation more appropriate to a queen mother, Beaune noted that like Semiramis, Catherine de' Medici had preserved the realm for her children. Considering the polarized positive-negative versions of queenship generally produced, invoking female exemplars required a filter that let through what were presented as positive qualities while blocking those that—in the context of gender—would be considered bad. The problem with exemplarity is that it is two-edged: another writer might just as well have invoked Semiramis to make a negative exemplary point.

Beaune saved his strongest rhetoric to declare that not only were there female exemplars with whom Catherine de' Medici could compare, but also whom she can be said to have surpassed. He called her *more* chaste than Susanna, *more* mighty than Judith, *more* patient than Sarah, *more* affectionate in marriage than Penelope.[39] This rhetorical strategy, in which the subject outshines not just one other exemplar, but an entire series with whom she is compared, also supplies the structure of a painting depicting a queen regnant, Elizabeth I: *Queen Elizabeth and the Three Goddesses* of 1569 (fig. 1). On the right are the three Roman goddesses—Juno, Athena, and Venus—frequently compared individually with Renaissance women in art, literature, ceremony, and theater, depending upon the specific context desired in the allusion. An iconic Elizabeth I, carrying the orb, appears in a portico at the left, and displaces Juno, who moves to the right to join the other two goddesses, now all positioned beneath her. In addition to much other symbolism, the rhetoric here illustrates how the singular Elizabeth overshadows not just other mortals, but three goddesses.[40]

Constance Jordan and Pamela Benson have asserted that the sixteenth-century English writer Sir Thomas Elyot, in *The Defence of Good Women,* first published in 1540, challenged the more prevalent Aristotelian notion of gendered characteristics prevalent in discourse surrounding the practice of virtue, seen in both Houel's and Beaune's lives.[41] Elyot argued, drawing on Plato, that one system of virtues exists for both sexes, and that proper education would permit some women to rule. To illustrate the truth of his assertions, he drew upon the tradition of exemplarity, using the life of another famous ancient queen, Zenobia of

Fig. 1. Monagrammist HE: *Queen Elizabeth and the Three Goddesses*, 1569. (The Royal Collection © 1994 Her Majesty Queen Elizabeth II.)

Palmyra.[42] But his treatise demonstrates its argumentative function in part by taking the form of a dialogue rather than a narrative "life." It is not an example of life-writing. Jordan has argued, moreover, that Elyot's work served as a call to action for Catherine of Aragon to serve as regent, in case circumstances warranted.[43] For Elyot, then, narrative exemplarity served to make a regency situation concrete for a would-be regent. Houel's exemplary biography of Artemisia served a similar goal, narrating an exemplary life for Catherine de' Medici to follow: his purpose, to create the portrait of what a queen regent ought to be; his hope, that this would lead back to the political and social normality of a king.[44] Both authors (Houel and Elyot) used ancient prototypes to authorize their assertions, but also to distance them somewhat from contemporary polemic.

Houel's avoidance of a head-on challenge to gendered exemplarity finds its analogue in his textual strategy. Writing a sort of roman à clef allowed him to sidestep some of the conventions of biography that would have proved awkward in presenting his subject in a positive light.

Biography per se (and even strict adherence to the *Cyropaedia* model) would have required him to begin with his subject's lineage and birth and attach great significance to how they determined her good character, which in turn accounted for her benevolent deeds.[45] These genre constraints would have failed miserably in a France that (because of the Salic law) was suspicious not just of women in authority, but also Italians in general, and what they considered Catherine de' Medici's inferior birth, ideas that received constant reinscription in sixteenth-century discourse.

It is instructive in this regard to compare Houel's approach in his *Histoire,* written while Catherine was regent for Charles IX in 1562, with what—by its title—purports to be the first deliberate biography of Catherine herself. This was the anonymously published *Discours merveilleux de la vie, actions, & deportemens de Catherine de Médicis, Royne Mère* (Marvellous discourse on the life, actions and misconduct of Catherine de' Medici, Queen Mother) that appeared in 1575, while she was regent once again.[46] The pamphlet has been attributed to Henri Estienne (c. 1528–98), born in Geneva and part of a distinguished family of Huguenot writers and printers. His own specialty was Greek texts, and he would shortly write about the pernicious influence of Italy on France's language and culture.[47] His educational background, religion, and published views on Italians make him a likely candidate for authorship of the diatribe. Significantly, too, in this context, the Latin translation of the pamphlet bears the title *Leggenda S. Catharinae Mediceae vita, actorum et consiliorum,* doubtless a conscious attempt to align the work with hagiography, an important traditional locus for the written lives of women. The reference here is a deliberately ironic inversion of the genre, for his Catherine is anything but a conventional saint.[48]

Houel's *Histoire* not only displaced persons and events in time and place; its author also avoided potential minefields by beginning the life of his protagonist queen only with her husband's death and making no mention of Artemisia's origins or family. The *Discours,* on the other hand, written in the heat of Huguenot fervor against the queen mother precipitated by the St. Bartholomew's Day Massacre, opens forcefully with a strong inward-moving invective directly about its subject. "Catherine de' Medici, in the first place, is Florentine. Among nations, Italy takes the prize for *finesse* and *subtilité,* and within Italy, Tuscany, and within Tuscany, Florence."[49] These French words connote artifice and cunning much more negatively than do their English cognates. Then, again following biographical convention that placed a premium on lineage, the author went on to describe her family, the Medici, as deriving from humble origins, not really esteemed, and above all *parvenu* because mentioned only in very recent history.[50] At the same time, he buttresses his accounts of the Medici with materials from two Italian historians, Giovio and Guicciardini. Furthermore, he insists, the Medici are not a family known for virtuous acts. Against so strong an initial condemnation, such a protagonist hardly stands a chance.[51] Houel's strategy of displacement and omission avoided the absurdity of arguing otherwise in the context of presenting his main subject—Catherine herself as regent of France—in the most favorable light possible. At the same time, however, his narrative strategy severely limited what qualified as the relevant portions of her life, which "began" only at her husband's death.

Even Renaud de Beaune—who owed his prominent position to his close association with the queen—used a similar nationalist discourse against her in 1588, the year before her death.[52] He called the Italians, after the heretics, "the greatest plague in the realm. The Italian foreigner, that is, Catherine de' Medici, has cruelly plundered all France. It is this foreigner who has thrown the apple of discord among the French . . . and who impedes peace."[53] Here he cranked up the rhetorical volume by resorting to a punning and gendered mythic prototype. The apple of discord is not the edible Edenic fruit, but rather a mythical golden apple that Eris, goddess of strife, threw into the banquet of the gods celebrating the marriage of Peleus and Thetis. Intended as a prize for the fairest goddess, her gift resulted ultimately in the Trojan War.[54] Eris sounds like Iris, goddess personification of the rainbow, associated with peace and identified with Catherine de' Medici when she came to France as the bride of the Duc d'Orléans. Thus, with the shift of a single letter, Beaune transformed the Iris of peace into the Eris of strife, solely responsible for the French religious wars. But the following year—and to a different audience—he sang a different tune, arguing that Catherine was, in fact, more French than the French. He challenged those hearing (or later reading) her funeral oration: "You who are truly French, recognize that you have lost the greatest queen that has ever reigned in France."[55] The lawyer Etienne Pasquier negotiated the extremes of these two rhetorical positions and supplied a corrective on both accounts. He criticized the

Fig. 2. Antoine Caron, *The Riding Lesson*. Pencil, pen, and wash. Bibliothèque Nationale, Paris. Print no. AD 105, folio 31. (© cliché Bibliothèque Nationale Paris.)

author of the *Discours* for having unfairly written a "satyre la plus mordante," but he also allowed that Renaud de Beaune's funeral oration represented the queen mother as a "princesse sans tache."[56]

Houel's use of the Artemisia prototype to figure an idealized Catherine de' Medici in his *Histoire,* a kind of roman à clef, finds its counterpart in the accompanying pictorial materials. Figuring a contemporary person in a saint, goddess, or acknowledged past heroine to make a point follows a long-standing tradition in the visual arts. Although Houel stated that Catherine would see herself reflected in his life of Artemisia, the Artemisia depicted by Caron in the accompanying drawings does not bear the physical traits of Catherine de' Medici. Conventions of Renaissance court portraiture, however, did not require exact physical likeness for references to be apparent to viewers. The term *portrait* is used to describe both visual representations and biographical texts; the appro-

Fig. 3. *The Riding Lesson.* (Courtesy of Minneapolis Institute of Arts.)

priateness of the term in proportion to likeness based on observed similarity is a problem more for the modern than for the Renaissance eye.[57]

In his autobiography, the Florentine sculptor Benvenuto Cellini reported that when he described his proposed *Mars Fountain* to King Francis I (Catherine's father-in-law), he informed his patron the king that the colossal Mars "is designed after" (*è figurate per*) him, not that it "portrayed" him.[58] Cellini, like Houel, may have been negotiating issues of decorum, a living subject, and a changeable interpretive community, and hedging his bets with his sign system. As "reference" Mars can refer specifically to François I, then to François-identified-with-Mars as ideal exemplar, and thence to all past and future kings. Like the rhetoric of exemplarity, the reference provides a point of comparison. The illustrations accompanying Houel's Artemisia *Histoire* permit reading the protagonist simply as Artemisia, an exemplary ancient queen. A different system of signification, placed outside the narratives in the decorative frames, locates the specific reference for this particular queen. The changing exemplary narratives inhabit the central field, while the borders or margins defining the specificity of the connection inhabit another.

Comparison of Antoine Caron's preparatory drawing (*modello*) for "The Riding Lesson" (fig. 2), with the tapestry made from it in the seventeenth century (fig. 3) make clear how the specifics of the border imagery could and did change. The *modello* border contains Catherine de' Medici's initials, coat-of-arms, and Latin motto *Ardorem testantur extincta vivere flamma* [the glow lingers though the flame is gone], glossed by emblems—scythes, broken mirrors—referring to her widowhood and concomitant grief. The tapestry, on the other hand, features the royal French arms at the top center, while an emblem based on an *L* for Louis XIII, whose mother, Marie de' Medici, was another widowed queen regent, appears at the bottom center.[59] While the individual queen regent might differ, the concept of model queenship (as well as the desire of the interpretive community viewing them to return to the norm of kingship) is assumed to remain constant. Both text and tapestry employed strategies to contain the exemplary possibilities of contemporary queenship. While some sort of model queen regent might exist, to the viewer, now or in the future, she is not exemplified by Catherine de' Medici herself but, rather, by some long dead and safe ancient prototype.

NOTES

I would like to thank David Harris Sacks, Georgianna Ziegler, the anonymous press reviewers, and especially the late Nancy Roelker, all of whom commented on versions of this chapter.

1. Foremost among them is Constance Jordan. See her "Boccaccio's Infamous Women: Gender and Civic Virtue in the *De Mulieribus Claris*," in Carole Levin and Jeanie Watson, eds., *Ambiguous Realities: Women in the Middle Ages and Renaissance* (Detroit: Wayne State University Press, 1987), 25–47; "Feminism and the Humanists: The Case of Sir Thomas Elyot's Defence of Good Women," *Renaissance Quarterly* 36 (1983):181–201; and *Renaissance Feminism* (Ithaca and London: Cornell University Press, 1991). A recent contributor with a more diverse view is Pamela Joseph Benson, *The Invention of the Renaissance Woman: The Challenge of Female Independence in the Literature and Thought of Italy and England* (University Park: The Pennsylvania State University Press, 1992).

2. For additional insights into the problem of women's biography, see Anne Jacobson Schutte, "Irene di Spilimbergo: The Image of a Creative Woman in Late Renaissance Italy," *Renaissance Quarterly* 44 (1991): 42–61.

3. See Phyllis Rackin, "Patriarchal History and Female Subversion," in her *Stages of History* (Ithaca: Cornell University Press, 1990), 146–200.

4. See Brigitte Cazelles, *The Lady as Saint: A Collection of French Hagiographic Romances of the Thirteenth Century* (Philadelphia: University of Pennsylvania Press, 1991).

5. On the polarity in subject positions allocated to women, see Glenda McLeod, *Virtue and Venom: Catalogs of Women from Antiquity to the Renaissance* (Ann Arbor: University of Michigan Press, 1991).

6. Pauline Stafford, *Queens, Concubines, and Dowagers: The King's Wife in the Early Middle Ages* (Athens, GA: University of Georgia Press, 1983), 30. See also Janet L. Nelson, "Queens as Jezebels: Brunhild and Balthild in Merovingian History," in *Politics and Ritual in Early Medieval Europe* (London and Ronceverte: Hambledon Press, 1986), 1–46.

7. A recent popular book, Lisa Hopkins, *Women Who Would Be Kings: Female Rulers in the Sixteenth Century* (New York: St. Martin's Press, 1991), takes up this subject; but see the review by Charmarie Blaisdell in *Sixteenth-Century Journal* 13 (1992): 807–8.

8. With regard to gender and the funeral oration, see Sharon T. Strocchia, "Funerals and the Politics of Gender in Early Renaissance Florence," in Marilyn Migiel and Juliana Schiesari, eds., *Refiguring Woman: Perspectives on Gender and the Italian Renaissance* (Ithaca, NY, and London: Cornell University Press, 1991), 155–68.

9. Vasari, in his *Lives of the Artists* (1568), calls each artist's biography a "life," except when they were still alive at the time—for example, Titian, who merits instead a "Description of the Works."

10. These events included the death of her husband's elder brother that made her dauphine in 1545, the accidental death of her husband, Henry II, in 1559, and the premature death of their eldest son, Francis II, late in 1560.

11. Norbert Elias, *The Court Society,* trans. Edmund Jephcott (New York: Pantheon Books, 1983), 24.

12. For information on Houel (born in Paris, c. 1524), who sought royal patronage for his charitable enterprise intended to teach orphans the apothecary arts, see Jules Guiffrey, "Nicolas Houel, Apothicaire Parisien, Fondateur de la Maison de la Charité Chrétienne et Premier Autheur de la Ténture d'Arthémise," *Mémoires de la Societé de l'Histoire de Paris et de l'Ile-de-France* 32 (1898): 179–220; and Antoine de Laborde, *Nicolas Houel, Fondateur de la Maison de la Charité Chrétienne* (Paris: Societé des Bibliophiles Françaises, 1937).

13. *Histoire de la Royne Arthémise contenant quatre livres, recueillié de plusiers autheurs. En laquelle sont contenues plusiers singularitez dignes de remarque, touchant l'antiquité. Ensemble un petit discours de l'excellence de la plate peinture,* par Nicolas Houel, Parisien, 1562. Paris, Bibliothèque Nationale, Manuscrits, fr. 306. See also my preliminary analysis, "Catherine de' Medici as Artemisia: Figuring the Powerful Widow," in Margaret Ferguson, Maureen Quilligan, and Nancy Vickers, eds., *Rewriting the Renaissance: The Discourses*

of Sexual Difference in Early Modern Europe (Chicago: University of Chicago Press, 1986), 227–41.

14. For a nuanced discussion of the relationship of reader(s) to text, see Timothy Hampton, *Writing from History: The Rhetoric of Exemplarity in Renaissance Literature* (Ithaca, NY, and London: Cornell University Press, 1990), 3–13.

15. Paolo Giovio, *Elogia Virorum Illustrium*, in *Opera*, vol. 8, ed. Renzo Meregazzi (Rome: Istituto Poligrafico dello Stato, 1972), 482/323 for Henry II of France, her husband, and 368/170 for Piero de' Medici, her grandfather.

16. The most complete accounts of the illustrations can be found in Maurice Fenaille, *Etat general de la Manufacture des Gobelins depuis son origine jusqu'à nos jours, 1600–1900* (Paris: Hachette, 1923), 1, 109–60; and Ulrika von Haumeder, "Antoine Caron: Studien zu Seiner 'Histoire d'Arthémise,'" Ph.D. diss., Heidelberg University, 1976.

17. Houel, *Histoire*, fol. 7^r. These drawings are currently split between the collections of the Bibliothèque Nationale and the Musée du Louvre, Paris. Those in the Bibliothèque Nationale are contained in an eighteenth-century binding. Those in the Louvre are unbound.

18. For Caprarola, see Clare Robertson, *"Il gran cardinale": Alessandro Farnese, Patron of the Arts* (New Haven, CT: Yale University Press, 1992), 95–100; and Loren Partridge, "The Sala dei Fasti Farnesiane," *Art Bulletin* 38 (1972): 238ff. The larger subject is also taken up by Jonathan Brown and J. H. Elliott in *A Palace for a King: The Buen Retiro and the Court of Philip IV* (New Haven, CT and London: Yale University Press, 1980), 147ff.; and Randolph Starn and Loren Partridge, *Arts of Power: Three Halls of State in Italy* (Berkeley and Los Angeles: The University of California Press, 1992).

19. Desiderius Erasmus, "Apologia pro panegyricis," *The Education of a Christian Prince*, ed. and trans. Lester K. Born (New York: W. W. Norton, 1968), 144–45.

20. David A. McNeil, *Guillaume Budé and Humanism in the Reign of Francis I* (Geneva: Droz, 1975), 7.

21. Hampton, *Writing from History*, 11–13; Hampton's application of Habermas's term *interpretive community* is useful here in considering the range of meanings of exemplarity for different audiences at different times.

22. Donald R. Kelley, *Foundations of Modern Historical Scholarship: Language, Law, and History in the French Renaissance* (New York and London: Columbia University Press, 1970), 11; Hampton, *Writing from History*, 18, also mentions this same period as a time in which "communities are in disarray."

23. Her mother was a French princess with royal blood; nevertheless the French regarded her as a foreigner.

24. Hampton, *Writing from History*, 299.

25. James Tatum, *Xenophon's Imperial Fiction: On The Education of Cyrus* (Princeton, NJ: Princeton University Press, 1989), xv: the *Cyropaedia* has represented "a pedagogical novel, a historical novel, a romanticized biography, a mirror for princes, an ideal romance, a novel before the novel, or a contribution to Greek constitutional theory." Lester K. Born, ed., *Education,* 49, called the *Cyropaedia* "biographico-romantic." Leslie C. Warren, "Humanistic Doctrines of the Prince from Petrarch to Sir Thomas Elyot: A Study of the Principal Analogues and Sources of *The Boke Named the Gouvernour*," Ph.D. diss., University of Chicago, 1937, 32, used the term "historical romance," and O. B. Hardison, *The Enduring Monument: A Study of the Idea of Praise in Renaissance Literary Theory and Practice* (Chapel Hill: University of North Carolina Press, 1962), 72, called the *Cyropaedia* the "prime specimen of exemplary biography" in his classic discussion of that genre.

26. The assumption was, as Judith H. Anderson noted, that "fiction and history, creative invention and objective truth, are presumed to be inseparable rather than opposed": Judith H. Anderson, *Biographical Truth: The Representation of Historical Persons in Tudor-Stuart Writing* (New Haven, CT and London: Yale University Press, 1984), 69. See also Arnaldo D. Momigliano, "Ancient History and the Antiquarian," *Journal of the Warburg and Courtauld Institutes* 13 (1950): 285–315; Albert H. Buford, "History and Biography, the Renaissance Distinction," in Arnold Williams, ed., *A Tribute to George Coffin Taylor* (Chapel Hill: University of North Carolina Press, 1953); Myron P. Gilmore, "The Renaissance Conception of the Lessons of History," in W. H. Werkmeister, ed., *Facets of the Renaissance* (Los Angeles: University of Southern California Press, 1959); George Huppert, *The Idea of Perfect History* (Urbana, Chicago, and London: University of Illinois Press, 1970); Kelley, *Foundations of Modern Historical Scholarship;* Orest Ranum, *Artisans of Glory* (Chapel Hill: University of North Carolina Press, 1980).

27. For a discussion of epideictic oratory in the Renaissance, see John W. O'Malley, *Praise and Blame in Renaissance Rome: Rhetoric, Doctrine and Reform in the Sacred Orators of the Papal Court ca. 1450–1521* (Durham, NC: Duke University Press, 1979). Seeking to persuade an audience, the orator, rather than argue in some abstract fashion about goodness, organized his exemplary subject's virtuous or evil deeds into a narrative.

28. Quintilian, *Institutio Oratoria,* trans H. E. Butler (Cambridge, MA, and London: Harvard University Press and William Heinemann, 1980), V.xi.1.

29. Houel, *Histoire,* fol. 8^r.

30. Houel, *Histoire,* fol. 13^v.

31. Jordan, "Feminism and the Humanists," 181.

32. Quintilian, *Institutio Oratoria,* V.xi.10.

33. Houel, *Histoire,* fol. 82^r, "la vie d'Arthémise exemplaire aux femmes en pudicité et aux hommes en vaillance et vertu."

34. Romeo De Maio, "La donna della biografia," in his *Donna e Rinascimento* (Milan: Mondadori, 1987).

35. I would like to thank Myra Orth for her insights into Louise de Savoie and this work in particular.

36. Bibliothèque Nationale (Paris), MS fr. 5715.

37. Regnault (Renaud) de Beaune, "Oraison Funebre faicte aux obseques de la royne mère du roy," 4 February 1589. A Bloys, pour Jamet Mettayer, imprimeur du Roy, et P. L'Huillier, libere jure, 1589, reprinted in *Lettres de Catherine de Médicis,* Hector de la Ferrière and Gustave Baguenault de Puchesse, eds. (Paris, 1880–1905), 9, 498ff. See also Frederic J. Baumgartner, "Renaud de Beaune, Politique Prelate," *Sixteenth Century Journal* 9 (1978): 99. Beaune's reputation for eloquence brought him many commissions for funeral orations, including those for Catherine de' Medici, Mary Stuart, and the Duc d'Anjou. Additionally, the *politique* Renaud was "one of the first French bishops to recognize the Protestant king of Navarre, Henry of Bourbon, as French king in 1589."

38. Beaune, "Oraison Funebre," 499: "par l'exemple de sa vie... mère et advocate des mères, des veuves, et orphelins." LeBlanc, too, argued for the appropriateness of the mother as regent.

39. Beaune, "Oraison Funebre," 508: "Elle a surpassé toutes les vertueuses femmes que l'Escriture saincte nous peut suppediter, hors la sacrée vierge Mère de Dieu, qui ne reçoit aucune comparaison. Elle a esté plus chaste que ceste renommée Suzanne, car elle n'a oncques donné ny apparence ny soupçon de calomnie sur sa personne; plus forte et magnanime que Judith, car elle a donné tesmoignage de sa valleur plusiers fois. Elle a surpassé en patience ceste Sara, car sa vie a esté en continuel exercise de patience. Elle a vaincu en affection maritale ceste chaste Penelope et ceste tant renommée Dido, et autres semblables Heroides. Ornée de toutes les graces de Dieu et dons de nature, forte et saine en sa constitution, le corps beau, de belle taille et habitude, le visage doux, modeste, accompagné toutefois d'une gravité digne d'une roye, mais surtout saincte at accomplie en toutes vertus: bref, ce sera en la posterité l'exemplaire de ceste vertueuse femme recherchée jusqu'aux extremitez de la terre."

40. The essential study of her portraits is that by Roy Strong, *The Portraits of Queen Elizabeth I* (Oxford: Clarendon Press, 1963).

41. There is no reason to think that Houel drew upon this English work, from the more general "defenses of women" genre, although they doubtless drew upon the same ancient sources: Benson, *Invention of the Renaissance Woman,* 183; and Jordan, "Feminism and the Humanists," 242, have also raised this issue.

42. The most thorough discussion of Zenobia as exemplar, raising many of these same issues, is that provided by Valerie Wayne in "Zenobia in Medieval and Renaissance Literature," in Carole Levin and Jeanie Watson, eds., *Ambiguous Realities: Women in the Middle Ages and Renaissance* (Detroit: Wayne State University Press, 1987), 48–65.

43. Jordan, "Feminism and the Humanists," 191.

44. Houel, *Histoire*, fol. 12ʳ.

45. Eric Cochrane, *Historians and Historiography in the Italian Renaissance* (Chicago and London: University of Chicago Press, 1981), 399, discusses the biographical imperative to go back in time to the birth of the subject. According to Hardison, *Monument*, 75, the genre of which the *Cyropaedia* is the prime example followed a standard biographical formula. It began with praise for the subject's good nature, familial origins, personal appearance, and education; the principal emphasis, however, was placed on the person's noble deeds.

46. The complete title is: *Discours merveilleux de la vie, actions, & deportemens de Catherine de Médicis Royne mère, auquel sont recitez les moyens qu'elle a tenu pour usurper le gouvernement du royaume de France, & ruiner l'estat d'iceluy.* D.D. LXXV. Robert M. Kingdon, *Myths about the St. Bartholomew's Day Massacres, 1571–1576* (Cambridge, MA, and London: Harvard University Press, 1988), 201, states: "Probably no single piece ... was as quickly and as widely distributed ... [in] no less than ten separate editions in 1575–76, in Latin, French, German, and English."

47. Kingdon, *Myths*, 202.

48. Henri Hauser, *Les sources de l'histoire de France, XVIe siècle (1494–1610)* (Paris: Librairie Alphonse Picard et Fils; Kraus Reprint, Neudeln, Liechtenstein, 1967), III, 271 (item #2240). I would like to thank Mack Holt for locating this reference for me.

49. *Discours Merveilleux*, 5; translations mine.

50. *Discours Merveilleux*, 7. Beaune's funeral oration, on the other hand, evoked her grand ascendance on both sides: he noted the "grande maison de Médicis."

51. As Nicola M. Sutherland demonstrated, the origins of the legend that made a "wicked queen" of Catherine de' Medici are to be found in Estienne's *Discours;* its polemic was readily absorbed into later French history, right up to fairly recent biographies; see her "Catherine de' Medici: The Legend of the Wicked Italian Queen," *Sixteenth Century Journal* 9 (1978): 45.

52. Baumgartner, "Renaud de Beaune," 99, notes that he rose to a position of influence owing to his sister, who was among Catherine de Medici's favorites.

53. Ibid., 103; quoting from *La harangue et proposition faicte au Roy* (Paris: n.p., 1588), 21.

54. The *Discours Merveilleux,* moreover, made a further link of Catherine with the apple, attributing to her an ingenious attempt to poison Condé by sending him a decorated apple full of poisonous vapors, which his suspicious doctor fed to a dog with predictable results.

55. Beaune, "Oraison Funebre," 501: "Vous qui estes vray Francoys, recognoissez que vous avez perdu la plus grande Royne en vertus, la plus noble en race et generation, la plus excellente en honneur, la plus chaste entre toutes les

femmes, la plus prudente en son administration, la plus douce en sa conversation, la plus affable et benigne a tous ceuz que l'ont voulu aborder, la plus humble et charitable envers ses enfans, la plus obeyssante a son mary, mais surtout, la plus devote envers Dieu, la plus affectionnée envers les pauvres que Royne qui oncques regna en France."

56. Etienne Pasquier, *Lettres historiques pour les annees 1556–1594,* ed. D. Thickett (Geneva: Droz, 1966), Lettre VIII "La Mort de Catherine de' Médicis," 386–88.

57. Lorne Campbell, *The Renaissance Portrait* (New Haven, CT: Yale University Press, 1990), introduction; and Erica Harth, *Ideology and Culture in Seventeenth-Century France* (Ithaca, NY, and London: Cornell University Press, 1983), 68–96.

58. Benvenuto Cellini, *Vita,* ed. Ettore Camesaca (Milan: Rizzoli, 1968 and 1985), 459 (II.xxi).

59. Candace Adelson, *European Tapestries in the Minneapolis Institute of Arts* (Minneapolis: Minneapolis Institute of Arts, 1993).

14

The Politics and Poetics of the Mancini Romance: Visions and Revisions of the Life of Louis XIV

Elizabeth C. Goldsmith and Abby E. Zanger

In late July 1658, a young and eminently marriageable Louis XIV fell in love with Marie Mancini, one of the three nieces the king's minister Jules Mazarin had brought to court from his native Italy. A more inappropriate and suspect liaison could not have been imagined, for Mazarin was a controversial figure in France, even after returning from exile imposed between 1651 and 1653; the powerful minister was considered suspect by the French nobility, who wondered if he was not angling to put his own flesh and blood on the Bourbon throne.[1] Given Mazarin's shaky, albeit powerful, position in the Bourbon dynasty (not to mention the importance of marriage to dynastic politics in early modern Europe), the liaison between the king and his minister's niece was politically explosive; it perpetuated Mazarin's image as the Italian (and bourgeois) invader-corrupter of the Bourbon dynasty, bringing back memories of the Fronde.

That the Mancini affair did not explode may be simply due to the fact that it was, ultimately, inconsequential, one in a series of amorous alliances expected of the king, marking the return to France of the virile monarchy in the style of Henry IV. But while the event may have made the king seem virile, it did not make him seem powerful: if some commentators credited the resolution of the crisis to the political wiles of the minister, and others to the influence of the regent Anne of Austria in her desire for a marriage with her brother's child, the infanta María Teresa, no one credited the king's own resolve. Indeed, it may be for its very highlighting of the king's power and powerlessness in the face of the multiple pulls of Louis's sexual desire, Mazarin's dynastic ambitions, and the queen's sentimentality for her own Hapsburg origins that the event was so compelling. For, if the Mancini debacle seemed resolved by the prospect of Louis XIV's marriage to the infanta of Spain, the romance continued to capture the imagination of the French populace, even as their monarch journeyed to his wedding in the spring of 1660. Decades later, after the king's desires had publicly settled on other women, the story still maintained its interest for memorialists, who reworked it in their biographical accounts of Louis XIV's "formation" as absolute ruler.

In the following pages, we explore Louis XIV's affair with Marie Mancini both as a political event and as the product of narrative manipulation. More precisely, we analyze a series of accounts of the king's love for Marie in order to highlight the role of this particular form of life-writing in the creation of Louis's image as absolutist monarch.[2] While the serious issues of rulership may seem far removed from the kind of gossip that kept the court buzzing and fueled the "novels" of libertines such as Bussy-Rabutin and Courtilz de Sandras, it is our thesis that fictions about the king's sexuality played a role in the constitution of his absolutist rule. At their inception, for example, such stories may have allowed Mazarin to manipulate—indeed, accelerate—political events by utilizing the king's attachment to his niece to play a (perhaps dangerous) game of dynastic roulette, shuffling Marie, the princess of Savoie, and the Spanish infanta on and off the list of marriage prospects to achieve the most politically advantageous alliance for the Bourbons. Years later, the Mancini story would become a kind of founding myth of the mature king's authority (or lack thereof), persisting as a point of interest, particularly among female memorialists. We refer to the second round of this mythmaking as rescripting or revision to account for the activity of reworking the original script.

In accounting for this process of mythologizing and revising the story of the king's life, this chapter focuses on three different narrative stages. We look first at medical journals and news accounts, which do not directly discuss the Mancini affair but which we believe are nonetheless fundamental to understanding the romance's role in images of the king being formulated in 1659. We then examine the correspondence of Jules Mazarin as he wrote to the young king, to the king's mother, the regent Anne of Austria, to his niece's governess, Madame de Venal, and to various other courtiers and diplomats in an apparent attempt to end the romance and seal the accord with Hapsburg Spain that would give

France not only a new queen, but also a new position in the arena of international political affairs.[3] We turn last to accounts written by three eyewitnesses to the events—the novelist Madame de Lafayette; Anne of Austria's lady-in-waiting Madame de Motteville; and the king's first cousin, the duchess of Montpensier—who all featured the romance prominently in their memoirs of court life.[4] In analyzing these three discursive domains, we show how, in a court climate where stories spread quickly and in which private letters, even those of a minister, were rarely kept secret, stories did not evolve in a linear or teleological fashion but emerged as variants on already existing narratives. Indeed, it may be this highly unstable quality that kept the myth functioning as a kind of low-level murmur about the king, just loud enough to keep interest alive, but not so loud as to impeach the dignity of the monarchy. This idea is borne out by the story's enduring popularity, most particularly in writings of the late nineteenth and early twentieth centuries, which treated the Mancini episode not as History with a capital *H,* but as what the French call "la petite histoire," a decidedly secondary category considered as curiosity or titillating anecdote.

Constructing a Romance: The Political Script

We begin our exploration of the Mancini affair not in Mazarin's letters nor in the memorialists' writings, but *avant la lettre,* in the latter years of Louis XIV's adolescence, when his mortal body was first exposed to the dangers of his divine task, that is, at the moment of his first military campaigns in Flanders in 1658. It was a crucial moment for setting the stage of Louis XIV's adult life. For, although at twenty the monarch had come into his majority seven years earlier, advisors, most notably his mother and Jules Mazarin, were still making most, if not all, important political decisions. The government of this triumvirate, however, was far from stable. Just six years earlier, the rebel nobility had forced the minister into exile; during that period, Louis XIV and his mother had also been forced to flee Paris. Although by 1652 this episode of civil war commonly referred to as the Fronde had more or less ended in Paris, unrest continued in the provinces. In 1658, when Louis XIV departed for the Low Countries to "participate" in campaigns there against the Spanish, his general, Turenne, was battling the prince of Condé, a former Frondeur, one of the rebel nobility who, not having come to terms with the royal family, was in exile in Spain and fighting against the French.

Thus, when the young Louis XIV departed for his first military campaigns in the Low Countries in the late 1650s, he was not only displaying his military capacities to his country, he was proving the ongoing stability of his rule[5]—rather, his potential rule, because he had not yet formally acceded to the throne. He would do so only in 1661, nearly a year after his marriage, upon the death of the minister Mazarin.

It was during this staged display of the young king's prowess—staged because Louis XIV was not really leading the troops in Flanders or fighting the battles—that the young king was forced into a very real battle for his life, a battle that threatened dire consequences for the continuation of the dynasty, as can be seen in contemporary accounts of the king's failing health. While the officially sanctioned *Gazette* assured the populace of the king's imminent recovery, his own physicians kept a journal of the events that is more telling.[6] In reading the physician Vallot's account, one notices immediately the narrative's insistence on the fact that Louis was displaying a youthful valor by exposing himself to illness in the first place. The king fell ill, it is suggested, because he was excessively brave on the battlefield: "the corruption of the air, of the infected waters, of the large number of sick people, of the many cadavers on the field, and of many other circumstances" caused the king to contract "a hidden poison which, after having infected his humours and troubled his temperament, caused him to fall into a state that forewarned me of the misfortune that eventually did befall him, on account of his great impatience and his eagerness to be present in the case of need, with no regard for his own life and health" (52).[7] It was his own excessive courage that had exposed the king to illness; he had not contracted the disease because of any constitutional weakness in himself, but because of external and unavoidable factors, the horrible conditions of the battlefield that he so courageously sought out.

While the doctors were loathe to suggest that his illness implied that the king was in any way a weak physical specimen, their notes leave no doubt that Louis XIV was truly gravely ill. Among other symptoms mentioned, the monarch was purple and swollen, feverish, and convulsive, and, at one moment of crisis, even unable to breathe (54–57). Indeed, the king almost did die. According to Madame de Montpensier, he was given last rites.[8]

Such serious illness could only weaken the image of a strong and virile young king that was regularly presented to the public. In fact, the illness threatened to aggravate the political uncertainties of battlefield and court. While courtiers scrambled to secure favorable positions in the event of the king's demise, his doctors quarreled over the proper strategy of treatment, over how to win the medical war.[9] The tensions among Louis XIV's doctors thus could be said to reproduce or echo what was occurring at the court as it waited for news about the king's condition.[10] The king's illness, like the battle against the Hapsburgs in Flanders, had ramifications for the body politic as well as for the body of the king.[11] The *Gazette,* in announcing the king's convalescence, acknowledged that the illness had been an "illness that seemed to threaten France with the most devastating loss that she could have suffered."[12]

In this sense, the king's recovery was a sign of the state's recovery. The news that the king was past his crisis was quickly disseminated.[13] The physician's report of the illness focused as extensively on the convalescence as on the crisis.[14] Reasons given for the recovery varied, but in all accounts it seemed important to contrast the king's temporarily weakened state with his new and vigorous constitution. Even when Madame de Motteville credited a higher authority (than medical science) for the king's convalescence—"God, who did not want to deprive France of this prince endowed with so many eminent qualities that were to make him a king worthy of the name, in his mercy, gave him a new life"—she was underlining the king's ability to regenerate.[15] What Motteville called "a new life" was a kind of resurrection, as much a sign of biological vitality as one of eternal sovereignty by divine intervention. It is in this sense that the physician's journal and reports in the *Gazette* underscored the fact that once the king was feeling better, it was hard to restrict his activity.

If the king's recovery meant a vigorous mortal body, and such a body were necessary for the health of the body politic, what better way to demonstrate the first body's constitution than by a romance? For while one might report about the king from the battlefield, a romance could occur on the spot, at the court. In a milieu where conversation and the spreading of gossip were among the founding rules of sociability, news of the king's exploits could spread quickly. Erotic urges would also be a useful advertisement at a moment when the Bourbon family was forced to realize the importance of producing heirs: with no offspring, the death of Louis XIV would have placed his brother on the throne. It was commonly accepted that the younger Bourbon had neither the constitution nor the inclination for ruling, not to mention for producing offspring to further the dynasty.[16]

It is thus not surprising that the romantic episode followed so closely upon the medical one. That one event was linked to the other was indeed part of the liaison's founding myth: it was said that when the king was deathly ill and the court was buzzing with rumors and intrigue, Marie Mancini seemed genuinely stricken with grief. The story continues that when the king recovered and heard of Marie's anxiety about his condition (as well as some of the other business that went on at court during his "absence"), he fell madly in love with the young girl who had been his childhood playmate.[17] While we shall explore variations in the myth in the third section of our chapter, it does seem clear at this point that as the story was handed down, the romance's origin was linked to deathwatch politics and the ongoing stability or instability of the throne. The new romance, then, had obvious possibilities as a propaganda device: it could serve as a pleasant diversion from the anxieties about the king's health, appealing to the French imagination and reminding the onlookers that the continuation of the Bourbon line depended on the king's physical health and his ability (and desire) to procreate.

Epistolary Negotiations

If the romance served to divert the French populace from more weighty concerns in 1658, it has continued to divert or rather confuse its "readers" into the twentieth century. Biographers have often expressed exasperation over the conflicting narratives of the story where the relative guilt and guile of each protagonist shifts with every account.[18] The most consistent chronology of events is as follows: In late July 1658, Louis XIV and Marie Mancini became publicly enamored of each other. The romance evidently intensified over the ensuing months such that by late spring of the following year, it was apparently considered an impediment to a more suitable marriage. In June the pair was separated, although the next few months saw them writing each other voraciously, and several "last" audiences were granted the young couple. In August 1659, the two were definitively separated, Louis being sent to Chantilly, while Marie was "exiled" to the coastal fortress of Brouage with her governess. It is not surprising that there are different shadings given to the intensity of feelings during these events, as well as to the motivations of the various characters, since the very first source we have reflecting upon the romance (or rather, its dissolution), a series of letters written by Mazarin, already evokes conflicting interpretations of the romance.

The letters in question date from the six-month period between July and December 1659. They are part of a large and ongoing correspondence written by Mazarin to various officials and to members of the royal family in Paris while he was in the midst of the negotiations of the Peace of the Pyrenees, the treaty whose articles included Louis XIV's marriage to the infanta of Spain. Read as part of the larger corpus, the letters on the Mancini affair seem like incidental forays into the sentimental life of the king. Considered on their own, they appear more forcefully engaged in psychological and political maneuvering to convince the young monarch to terminate the affair with Marie.[19] In the year following the king's illness, a romance that had initially seemed like an image-building diversion had become a political liability, necessitating a simultaneous negotiation by Mazarin of the treaty *and* the romance (enacting the first and dissolving the second). The letters concerning the romance are not just asides, nor do they represent an independent obsession on the part of Mazarin. They are as much part of the process of negotiating the treaty as they are a "private" negotiation between the minister and his young royal charge.[20]

To see how the negotiation to end the romance fits into the larger political scenario, it is important to understand what points Mazarin covers in those letters and then to consider how the means he uses—epistolary communication—affects what he seemed to be saying. What immediately strikes the reader is the rhetoric of disease used by Mazarin to persuade Louis to abandon Marie. Mazarin does not describe the romance as an adolescent whim, a last (although also more-or-less first public) fling before taking on the responsibilities of kingship. Rather, he refers to it as an illness which, as he writes Louis in July of 1659, threatens to "blacken your honor and expose your person and your State" (356) and which, if not remedied quickly, "will become incurable" (360).[21] For Mazarin in 1659, the romantic inclinations of the king toward Marie Mancini were characterized as similar to the Calais illness, that malady which, as we previously noted, also darkened the king's persona (blackening his body if not his honor!).

As in the case of the Calais illness, Louis XIV's love disease was not a secret or invisible malady. This fact troubled the minister, and he noted at many points in his correspondence that the romance was too public. For example, in a letter written on 29 July, Mazarin warned the king that:

all Europe is talking about your passion and everyone talks about it with a freedom that is prejudicial to you. Even in Madrid the business has exploded, for it is being written about from Flanders and Paris with the intention of causing confusion and of ruining the marriage project that is on the table, thus preventing a peace agreement as well. When I have the honor to see you I will show you papers that will enlighten you on much more than I have written you on this matter. And, if you do not remedy it without delay, the situation will worsen daily and will become incurable (360).

This admonition echoed the more subtle reprimand Mazarin had written two weeks earlier in witnessing that he knew the king was still involved with his niece: "It is said (and this is confirmed by letters from court to persons in my entourage), . . . that you are constantly off alone writing to the person you love. . . ." (351). If initially the king's interest in Marie had been publicized as a sign of the young king's physical recovery, his prolonged sentimental attachment to her was now seen as a sign of royal weakness. While the visible Calais illness was, ultimately, not the young monarch's fault, or perhaps was the fault only of his overzealousness, the too-visible love sickness did indeed cast doubt on the king himself, affecting his reputation.

And what precisely did the world see and write about, what was in those papers that could be so damaging that the minister refused to summarize it? What was so visible as to provoke such anxiety in the minister that he felt he must generate a barrage of letters on the subject? On one level, the problem seems obvious. Mazarin was negotiating a treaty of which one part was the king's marriage to the infanta. In that context, Louis's exploits could be harmful to the outcome of those negotiations. Louis's ardor for Marie was known in Madrid, placing Mazarin in a difficult position. On 23 July, he wrote the king that he was glad his own health had delayed meetings with the Spanish minister "for to confer with Don Louis, all the while knowing that I would deceive him in what I would be telling him of your intentions concerning your desire to accomplish the marriage, this I cannot resolve to do" (362). If Mazarin's lip service to openness in negotiations seems ironic considering the byzantine quality of the treaty he did finally negotiate, perhaps there were more practical political issues at stake.[22] For, if the alliance was important to the French for their own political ends, it was repugnant to their adversaries poised on the French border, waiting for an excuse (ostensibly an attempted royal marriage with Marie Mancini) to invade:

> And I can assure you on good authority that the Prince of Condé and plenty of others are alert to all that will come of this, hoping, if things happen as they would like, to profit from the plausible pretext that you would give them. In such an event the prince has no doubt that he would have the support of all the parliaments, the lords and the nobility of the kingdom, indeed of all your subjects. And the opportunity would not be missed to proclaim loudly that I was the advisor and the instigator of all your conduct. (354)

Note here that the adversaries were not just those of the king, but also those of Mazarin, most notably the prince of Condé, former Frondeur and adversary of the minister.

In reading through Mazarin's protestations to the king, it becomes clear that the minister was not only concerned with the state of French affairs, but with his own situation as well. The king's visible actions will affect not only the king's happiness and that of all Christianity (354), but also the reputation of the minister himself. Thus, Mazarin counseled the king to control his passion so that he would have a happy marriage, even as he threatened the king with God's wrath: "How can I keep from telling you that you are prejudicing the outcome of your affairs, that you are drawing the reproaches of everyone, and that you are exposing yourself to the wrath of God, if you go to your marriage hating the princess you are marrying and intending to live badly with her" (380–81). Just as he moralized more generally about monarchical duties: "God has established kings . . . to safeguard the wealth, security and repose of their subjects, and not to sacrifice this wealth and repose to their own private passions and when there have been kings unfortunate enough to have obliged divine Providence to abandon them on account of their conduct, history is full of revolutions and disasters that they have brought upon themselves and their States" (353). But in so doing, the minister also seemed to be reflecting on what the king's actions suggested about Mazarin, that is, that he was promoting the liaison with his niece to serve his own interests over those of the state.

Even in his earliest letters on the subject, Mazarin did not hide that worry but, rather, summarized the innuendos against himself: "They add that I am in agreement and that I am secretly plotting with you, pushing you to this behavior to satisfy my own ambition and to prevent the peace" (352). Indeed, one could read the entire sequence of letters as an extended self-justification insofar as Mazarin stages himself as ready to sacrifice everything for the king. He threatens, for example, to return to Italy and take his family with him: "to go away to a corner of Italy to spend the rest of my days, praying to God that this remedy, that I have applied to your illness, should produce the cure that I wish for more than anything in the world..." (356).

What becomes evident in reading through the correspondence is that if there is a disease to purge from the king's body, it comes from Mazarin himself, or rather, from his niece, who, despite their apparently stormy relations, was intimately and inextricably linked to the minister in the eyes of the public. In Mazarin's view, Louis's obsession with Marie "cannot exist without scandal, and I would say without damaging the person's reputation and my own" (352).[23] If Mazarin was attempting to absolve himself from guilt when he wrote to the king that "the letters from Paris, Flanders and other places say that you are no longer recognizable since my departure, and not because of me, but because of something that belongs to me" (352), he nonetheless seemed to have trouble extricating himself completely when he added later that "nothing is capable of preventing me from dying of displeasure if I see that a person who so closely belongs to me is causing you more misfortunes and prejudice..." (385). The Mancini contagion, like the Calais disease, had come from without even as it reflected on the king's own strength. Mazarin's assault on Louis's "love sickness" was also an effort to cleanse his tarnished reputation. To make it absolutely clear that he was in no way provoking Louis's new sentimental illness, Mazarin cast himself in the role of a physician. Writing the queen mother on 16 July, he evoked a "guérison," or cure, he would effect.

One might ask, however, if this display of selfless loyalty to the crown did not in some sense add to the publicity surrounding the Mancini affair. In fact, Mazarin was acutely sensitive to any sign from the Spanish that they were taking for granted his desire to effect a combined marriage and peace treaty. It was not prudent to let the Spanish think that the French saw no impediments to the marriage. As Mazarin indicated in a letter to the queen mother on 29 July, the Spanish were far too confident, and he was "despairing at the phlegmatic conduct of Don Louis; the atmosphere in his country must be obliging him to do this, and possibly also his belief that he thus will take advantage of the impatience of the French" (367).²⁴ What the Spanish think the French are impatient about becomes clearer in a self-congratulatory letter written to the queen on 3 September. In it, Mazarin remarked:

> ...I can tell you that things are finishing rather well, and that I am upholding as I should all that is due to the dignity and service of the *confident,* and I hope that soon Don Louis will come around. At least I will give him no peace until this happens, and the most advantageously to you as possible. He thinks that his best card, to oblige us to do the things he wants, and particularly in regard to the prince of Condé, is the marriage. I pity him, and you will too, since you know as well if he is taking the correct steps in this (387).²⁵

If the Spanish thought that the French were obsessed with the marriage between their monarch and the infanta, and that was their trump card for manipulating the French, they were sorely mistaken; Mazarin had his own trump card, the niece over whom he protested so much!

For is it not possible that the same Marie, the germ born of her uncle, whose romance with the king so handily demonstrated his vigor, also could serve the political script? Could not the Mancini debacle have served to distract the Spanish from the real issues of the negotiation, the status of Condé (who was to be rehabilitated), the fixing of borders and territories, and, most important, that of determining the infanta's dowry and its relation to her renunciation of the Hapsburg throne, just as it continues to distract us today from the practices of state building it facilitated? Thus, all the moral and political reasonings for ending the king's liaison with Marie, even all the remarks concerning Mazarin's reputation, may have been part and parcel of encouraging a large "scandal."²⁶

There is, in fact, ample evidence to suggest that Mazarin was quite aware that his letters would not just be read by their addressees. The letters themselves use cipher (Mazarin does not refer to Louis, his mother, or Marie by name even when writing to them about themselves) and repeatedly allude to postal spying.²⁷ We know that Mazarin usually used a secretary to correct his Italianisms when writing in French, so we might assume much of his writing was not totally secret. We also know that Mazarin's correspondence from the negotiations circulated in a manuscript form before their first official publication in 1690, although it is impossible to assign a precise date to extant manuscript copies.[28] The eventual publication of the correspondence does indicate that copies of it were preserved.[29] We know as well that Mazarin was capable of using letters to create what we would refer to today as media leaks. He was no newcomer to this kind of publicity: during the Fronde, one of the most popular modes of attacking the minister had been in the form of pamphlets purporting to be secret epistolary exchanges between Mazarin and Anne of Austria.[30] Indeed, the minister could not erase the public curiosity about his epistolary output. While he had learned his lesson about the power of such publications and had clamped down on the periodical press after his return to power, it is not unrealistic to assume that he was still capable of exploiting those methods to his own ends.

One final curious detail to note is the absence of any other remaining published allusion to the romance dating from the late 1650s; except for the Mazarin correspondence, it is not until the 1670s, after the minister's death and well into Louis XIV's reign, that the episode is mentioned in print.[31] While it is possible that any publications were confiscated and eradicated, copies of enough other confiscated material have survived from that period to show that Mazarin may have been able totally to stop information about the king and his niece from being produced. One aspect of this suppression was that Mazarin himself, by writing letters about the publicity the romance was getting, was in fact adding to and shaping that publicity.

It is important to underline that the story the minister was supplementing or creating was narrated in such a way as to suggest multiple interpretations of the origins of the affair and the motivations of its principal players. Mazarin's letters simultaneously suggest and purge his own culpability, dissuade Louis from the affair and draw attention to it, worry over alienating the infanta (and the Spanish) and overtly threaten her (them), and so on. In sum, Mazarin's letters offer a story that may be purposefully unstable precisely to suit a series of interlocutors, legitimate and illegitimate, and to enact a multifaceted agenda. In so doing, however, these plurivocal letters take our attention away from the characters, Louis and Marie, and highlight the craft and skill of the minister in manipulating—indeed, in scripting and exploiting—their relationship. Nonetheless, if Mazarin's portrayal of the romance served his own political agenda and his own self-creation, as well as the larger political interests of the Bourbon dynasty, it ultimately laid the foundation for a larger debate over motivations because of its very protean or unstable quality.

This debate would be taken up after the fact by the memorialists Lafayette, Montpensier, and Motteville.[32]

Rescripting a Romance

Thus, what first appeared to be a romance, in the sense of a love affair, begins to develop as a romance adventure or story; like all narratives or "fictions," this biographical romance offers the possibility of debate. In turning to a second stage of passion's metamorphosis into a more conventional form of life-writing, therefore, we shall discuss how a political script, utilized for a multifaceted negotiation, also served the varied agenda of three memorialists, Lafayette, Motteville, and Montpensier, eyewitnesses to the event, perhaps readers of Mazarin's letters, certainly listeners to gossip, but above all, creators in their own right of (the life story of) the king and his court.[33]

The most complex of the three contemporary accounts of the Mancini affair is the one written by Madame de Lafayette. Lafayette tells the story in the opening pages of her *Histoire de Madame Henriette d'Angleterre*, a supposed memoir of the life and death of the young wife of Monsieur, the king's brother. Written between 1665 and 1669, the work bears many similarities to Lafayette's later novel *La Princesse de Clèves*, most notably in its profoundly cynical view of erotic love.[34] Through Lafayette's eyes, the Mancini episode becomes a lesson in infidelity, in the fragility of all human attachments based on passion and ambition. Her narration of Mancini's story functions in the *Histoire* in much the same way as the historical preamble about the loves of Henry IV functions in *La Princesse de Clèves:* as a cautionary tale framing and foreshadowing the events in the heroine's story.[35]

Lafayette begins her narrative of the romance in a manner common to all the memoirs, focusing on Mazarin and his role in the affair. For Lafayette, what is of principal interest is the distorted image of the minister's heroic role in the Fronde transmitted by the queen to her young son:

> The troubles that had been excited by the poor conduct of this cardinal were presented to (the young king) as an effect of the hatred of princes for a minister who had wanted to limit their ambition; he was taught to consider the minister as a man who alone had held the tiller steady while a storm rocked the ship of state, a man whose good conduct had perhaps prevented its loss. (22)

According to the novelist, Mazarin's all-encompassing power further extended to matters of love. Louis's mother, whom Lafayette terms "naturally lazy," was totally dominated by her minister, and her son in his youth inherited this "submission suckled with milk" (23). She continues:

> The star that gave him [Mazarin] such total authority extended even into the realm of love. The king was unable to take his heart outside the family of this fortunate minister: he gave it, in his tender youth, to the third of the Mancini nieces; and if he withdrew it later at a more advanced age, it was only to give it even more entirely to a fourth niece of the same name Mancini, to whom he submitted himself so totally that one might say she was the mistress of a prince who we have since seen to be master of his mistresses and his love. (23)

All the elements of Lafayette's interpretation of this episode in the king's life are packed into this sentence, beginning with the fundamental link between political and affective authority in both Mazarin and Louis. Marie is presented as simply one in a series of nieces (they are not even distinguished by name). And the king's passion is presented as an exercise in submission that he will later reverse to display an absolute mastery, not only of his next mistress, but of his "love," that is, of the entire emotional side of his character.[36]

Lafayette focuses on the king's love for Marie as a crucial turning point in the development of the king's character and does not get bound up with analyses of the young girl, whom she entirely depersonalizes. Thus, the end of the affair and the king's marriage is not an event filled with pathos, but marks the moment when Louis moves from being human to being superhuman. Lafayette stresses that the king's passion originated in a moment of extreme weakness, when he was seriously ill. Marie's display of emotion at this time has a violent effect on the king, whose reciprocal passion thus becomes a kind of last phase of his illness:

> During a dangerous illness that the king had contracted at Calais, she demonstrated such a violent affliction over his misfortune, and she hid her feelings so little, that as soon as he started to feel better everyone told him about the unhappiness of Mademoiselle de Mancini; perhaps later she herself told him about it. Finally she showed him such pas-

sion, and so thoroughly freed him from the constraints placed upon him by the queen mother and the Cardinal, that one might say that she constrained the king to love her. (29)

The king's love for the "Mancini niece" (i.e., her "mastery" of him) is here described as the first step in his transformation into the legendary king whose most salient trait was to be his stupefying degree of self-control. Louis's moment of extreme weakness paves the way for his subsequent assertion of power. Furthermore, the king, like Lafayette's fictional heroine Madame de Clèves, breaks free of his mother (and by extension Mazarin) as he falls into the thrall of a romance.

In Lafayette's version, finally, the affair ends as it had begun: in a display of weakness. Louis simply drops Marie (as does Lafayette) once the cardinal removes her from his sight: "the king saw mademoiselle de Mancini at Saint-Jean-d'Angély; he seemed more in love than ever in the few moments that he had to be with her, and promised her his eternal fidelity. Time, absence, and reason in the end made him break his promise..." (30).

It is interesting to note here that while for Lafayette the king's experience of intense passion is a necessary preliminary to his later ability to repress emotion, his new persona does not become visible to others until after the death of Mazarin. Even for a short time after Mazarin's death, his ghost seems to retain control of the court: "his shadow was still the mistress of all things" (24), and courtiers react as though the king had not changed. At the cardinal's death, the men scramble to replace him, assuming that the king "would abandon himself to the guidance of a minister," and the women rush to replace Mancini, who "had seemed to have over him the most absolute power that a mistress had ever had over the heart of her lover..." (24). The king's surprise announcement that he will govern his ministers is thus linked to his new ability to govern his mistresses. As if to stress this final point, Lafayette suggests that Marie's ultimate departure from France was motivated by her unwillingness to accept the king as her master: "In the end she continued on her way and went to Italy, with the consolation of no longer being the subject of a king whose wife she had thought she would be." The controlling specter of Mazarin that had emerged victorious from the Fronde is thus displaced onto this final image of Marie, exiled to her Italian homeland, with her illusion of domination shattered. In Lafayette's account at least, the story of the king's romance that begins with Mazarin seems to serve as well to reject his influence, albeit in the guise of Marie, through a gesture of displacement.

While Lafayette casts the Mancini affair in the mold of a historical novel with its focus on a struggle for power, Mademoiselle de Montpensier in her memoirs sees the affair as a family drama with tragic overtones. Its political implications are, as elsewhere in Montpensier's memoirs, more implied than explicitly stated. Herself a member of the royal family, Montpensier always describes politics as naturally emanating from the personal lives of the elite, with the erotic misadventures of royal personages, like those of the gods of antiquity, having heavy consequences for the world below. In her description of the Mancini romance, her disdain for Mazarin and his family is felt in the exaggerated silence to which she confines them, though the heavy hand of Mazarin is present behind every step in the events. She remarks cryptically that when Louis fell ill, he started to spend all his time with Marie and stopped seeing her older sister Olympe, the countess of Soissons. The relationship seems to have two effects on the king. First, he becomes more sociable, more civilized in the Italian tradition of courtliness much admired by Montpensier and her contemporaries. She remarks: "The king was in a much better mood since he had fallen in love with Mademoiselle de Mancini. He was gay; he chatted with everyone. I think that she had advised him to read novels and verse; for he had a number of them, and collections of poetry and plays, and he seemed to take pleasure in them..." (101). Second, he becomes more defiant: at Marie's urging, Montpensier tells us, the king challenged his mother's conservative insistence that there be no balls during Lent. The regent, described by Montpensier as anxious and ineffective, appeals to Mazarin, who seems to be waiting in the wings and who mysteriously resolves their quarrel, a familiar role for the minister whom we have already seen as adjudicator of wars between physicians, countries, and other members of the royal family.

In the end, Montpensier has difficulty reconciling her aristocratic sensibility with her writer's urge to tell a juicy story. Writing in 1677, she seems clearly aware that she is recounting an episode in the amorous life of her cousin that already had been freely circulated via gossip and print.[37] Her response to this is, on the one hand, to refuse to descend to the rhetorical level of the *nouvellistes* and, on the other, to acknowledge their power. In her closing comments on the affair, she alludes to what she views as this invasion of a narrative space that belongs only to the elite:

> I forgot to say that before leaving Paris, M. le Cardinal had made his three nieces leave; that he had sent them to Brouage, and this departure caused much commotion. The king was very angry about it; it was even said that he had got on his knees before the queen and M. le Cardinal to ask to marry Mlle de Mancini. As I only know what I have heard rumored about this, I will say no more; it is not for me nor for anyone else to discuss what our masters do, nor even what others say about it. (113)

Montpensier may well have been thinking of a recently printed *libelle* claiming to describe in detail "the loves of Madame de La Vallière and others."[38] Its anonymous author had described two moments in the Mancini affair destined to be repeated inevitably in any published account of the story. The first depicts the king, on his knees before Mazarin, tearfully begging to be allowed to marry Marie, and the second describes the king again in tears, this time as Marie prepares to leave the court: "This mistress who was so unhappy, hurrying to leave and climbing into her carriage turned and said quite wittily to her lover, who was more dead than alive from his great sorrow: 'You are weeping, you are king, and yet I am unhappy and am really leaving!'" (*Palais Royal,* 260).[39]

Montpensier objects to this popular debasement of what she prefers to see in more elevated terms. In 1670, Racine's play *Bérénice* had provided the public with just such a framework for reconsidering the Mancini romance. The play's subject, as Racine describes it in the opening sentence of his preface, is the emperor Titus's decision to sacrifice Bérénice, whom he loves, for the good of the state: "Titus, who passionately loved Bérénice, and who, it was believed, had promised to marry her, sent her back to Rome, despite himself and despite her, in the first days of his empire." Although the plot of *Bérénice* differs in most of its details from the story of Louis's romance, the allusion was obvious to the tragedy's first spectators, and Racine rendered Marie's famous parting words into alexandrine form in Bérénice's line: "Vous êtes empereur, Seigneur, et vous pleurez!" (v.1154).[40]

Thus Montpensier narrates the king's first love affair as high, even tragic, drama. Our third memoir writer, Madame de Motteville, narrates it as a melodramatic episode in the epic romance of the king's life. While Montpensier tries to dismiss Mazarin or to put him in his proper place as mere servant to the royal family, Motteville portrays him as a sly, villainous figure whose influence over the queen seems darkly magical. His greatest desire, she writes, was to achieve dominance by somehow drawing into himself all the authority vested in the king and the regent ("the great passion that he had to dominate and to enclose in himself the authority of both mother and son..." [151]). He offers his nieces like so many sacrificial victims to the king, until finally, against her dying mother's wishes, he takes Marie from a convent to place her "on the stage of the court":

> The cardinal, after the marriage of madame la comtesse de Soissons, despite the prayers of his dying sister, placed the third of the Mancini sisters on the stage of the court, taking her out of the convent of Sainte-Marie where she had been for a time. He wanted to give her and her sister Hortense, who was perfectly beautiful, to the king for agreeable company. (82)[41]

Motteville lays much emphasis on the point that Marie, unlike Hortense, was not pretty ("one could call her... quite ugly"), a point that seems to enhance her perception that Marie had a sinister power over Louis, comparable to the influence Mazarin exerted over the regent. The king was bewitched, his character was transformed, he began reading novels and mooning about under trees, evoking in the inevitable troupe of onlookers the image of a character from one of the pastoral romances that Marie's Italian tastes had encouraged him to discover.[42] Indeed, to account for the story, Motteville, ironically, has recourse neither to historical fiction nor tragedy, but to Italian romance, Tasso's *Gerusalemme Liberata*. She writes this episode in the king's life with allusions to an epic voyage to and siege of Jerusalem by medieval French crusaders. For Motteville, Marie's role is comparable to that of Tasso's enchantress Armida, who seduces the warrior hero Rinaldo away from his glorious mission. Motteville's allusion is not without pertinence since, in the epic, Armida is the niece of Hydraotes, "a famous and noble sorcerer," who dispatches her to the enemy French camp. There she uses her powers to divert the warriors from their purpose.[43] Although in Tasso's romance, Armida is seduced by her own powers and falls in love with Rinaldo, making off with him to her enchanted garden where he becomes her willing slave, the message is not lost. For Motteville, Marie/Armida is the arm of her uncle Hydraotes/Mazarin. The sorcerer is no friend of the French in this script of a political romance.

In Motteville's version of the Mancini story, the king is able to throw off the niece's enchantment because of the presence of a third figure, his mother. Anne plays an active role in facilitating her son's "escape" from the dangerous Marie, a role comparable to the role played by Rinaldo's comrades who force him to look at his glistening shield and see his emasculated image reflected there.[44] Motteville describes Anne's decision to force her son out of his obsession:

> ... she told the cardinal, who was preparing to leave, what she felt; she made him see her wish to separate the king her son from this object that kept him attached to chains that she found shameful: she wanted to show the king the mirror that was presented to Rinaldo not just to pull him from Armida's enchantments, but to oblige him also to flee such an ugly prison. She counted on the loyalty owed her by the cardinal to carry out this plan; it was from him that she requested a remedy for this ailment, though he had seemed on this subject to have criminal temptations, he had already failed her on many occasions, he had usurped all of her power, and he had taken pleasure in destroying her. (150–51)[45]

For Motteville, Mazarin had not only played the villain in this romance, but he also played the villain who was tamed, who in the end submitted to the will of the good queen and used his powers to remedy the damage he himself had caused. In Motteville's account, Mazarin had actually initially suggested to the queen the possibility of a marriage between Louis and Marie and had received a withering reply that had discouraged him from further pursuing his own ambitions.[46]

Seeing that there is no chance of a royal marriage with his own family, Mazarin takes the lead in opposing it, and he tells Louis that he will do nothing to stop the inevitable revolt against the king if he attempts to marry Marie Mancini.[47] In Motteville's version, he goes as far as to threaten to kill Marie rather than see her marry the king, thus displacing onto his niece any responsibility for bearing the consequences of his family's inappropriate ambition. Mazarin and the regent join forces to drive out the evil influence of Marie, and the king's romance becomes an occasion for both the queen and Mazarin to resume their proper roles.

As in *Jerusalem Delivered,* the episode is a brief but dangerous threat to the historical mission of the French crown. Motteville follows her description of Marie's disappearing carriage with a reflection on the political imbalance that Mazarin's ambition had created, and which is now redressed.[48]

In having Mazarin reject Marie, the hostile Motteville redeems him somewhat and, more important, permits both Mazarin and Anne to ally themselves in the project of "curing" the king, or rather, of enabling the king to cure himself. In the same way that Rinaldo, who after leaving Armida's enchanted prison is made to contemplate images of his ancestors and reflect on his duty to family and nation, so Louis must undergo this last stage of disenchantment. Motteville's final pages on this episode describe how Anne and Mazarin slowly persuaded the king of the wisdom of Marie's exile, through the queen's conversations and the minister's letters.[49] In the end, Louis thanks them for a lesson in both love and statecraft:

> The king, letting himself be brought to reason, understood, despite what he felt for mademoiselle de Mancini, that those who ingratiated themselves to him by encouraging his passion, or rather his amusement, did not love his glory, and that the queen and the minister, who were telling him the truth, were the only people he should believe. (164)

And later, after his marriage to Marie-Thérèse, Louis thanks his mother for having exiled the unworthy Marie to give him the infanta:

> The Queen Mother, who knew her son to be a bit cold and serious, admitted to us that she had been afraid that her son's soul would be damaging to the niece that she had so longed for him to marry... Immediately after the wedding, she did us the honor of telling us... speaking of the king's satisfaction and contentment, that he had thanked her for having saved him from the heart of mademoiselle de Mancini (whom he admitted never having esteemed in a rational way) to give him the infanta, who would in all likelihood make him happy through her virtue, her pleasing manner, and the affection that she bore him. (218)

It is not surprising that Motteville, of Spanish origin like the regent Anne of Austria and the infanta, glorifies the Hapsburg-Bourbon alliance. Nonetheless, with the king's marriage, what has been achieved is a substitution of one niece (Anne of Austria's) for another (Mazarin's), Anne's influence for Mazarin's, peace for instability, legitimate authority for foreign domination. The infanta is described as everything Marie was not: beautiful, virtuous, deferential, affectionate (as opposed to Marie: ugly, ambitious, jealous, passionate).[50] Interestingly, what is implied in Motteville's description of Louis's transformation is that the affair with Marie was necessary to assure the king's virility. The qualities that his mother had been concerned about ("indifference," "coldness") were precisely the qualities that Marie had made disappear and thus helped occasion the king's real marriage on the world stage.[51]

In concluding this section, it is important to note a few historical facts about this corpus of memorial literature that characterize not only its production, but also its status. Most particularly, we should note that these accounts or reworkings of the Mancini affair occurred during a more stable moment of the king's career than the events of the romance itself; they were written in the fifteen to twenty years after his formal accession to the throne, while he was producing the real and symbolic monuments of his reign (Versailles, military victories in Flanders, architectural projects, historiography, heirs, and so forth). These memoirs, written in private and circulated in the quasi-public sphere of salon society, were finally published and disseminated long after their writing. Written by figures whose lineages made them suspect to the monarchy, but who managed to recuperate their positions vis-à-vis the court at least on some level, these writings may not be classed as either entirely antagonistic toward, nor supportive of, the absolutist regime.[52] Finally, written in France, yet published in Amsterdam, these texts inscribe themselves within a sphere of illegitimacy, all the while participating in the late-seventeenth-century and early-eighteenth-century vogue for private memoirs of *"les grands."*[53]

As such, the memoir narratives constitute both a public body of life-writing and a corpus that is not necessarily legitimate. It is interesting that the images of the king that they produce, while used as sources by later historians of the romance, are considered less reliable sources than Mazarin's letters. This may be due not only to the ambiguous status of these texts, but also to the fact that such narratives are more obviously engaged in image making. These are not texts that present themselves as letters written for public service, meant to achieve political goals. Rather, they are inscribed from the outset as personal reworkings, reconsiderations, memories, and thus subject to distortion and personal bias. Although the same characteristics may be applied to Mazarin's letters, they are not read as such.[54]

Visions and Revisions of the King's Life

We began our essay by positing that the romance of Louis XIV and Marie Mancini was part of an epistolary strategy of envisioning the king that proposed different images to readers at various points in the political and familial network. We then explored how that vision began to take on a life of its own as versions of the story were multiplied when memoir writers offered their own interpretive frames. It is worth noting at this point that modern-day historical narratives of the Mancini affair inevitably have been constituted by a kind of patchwork of these earlier "eye-witness" interpretations. Yet if all who study this story inevitably must recognize its dialogical construction, its status as the result of an interweaving and interacting of voices, it is nonetheless true that historians and biographers traditionally have opted for the relative veracity of one account over the others.[55] It seems as if there is an impulse, all the stronger perhaps because of the notable absence in this story of the voices of its principal players, to retrieve from the multiplicity of perspectives a single, privileged viewpoint.[56]

Perspectives that favor a single viewpoint have long been the hallmark, not only of a certain kind of history writing, but also of studies of Louis XIV. Even scholarship that has recognized and explored the narrative and performative strategies at work in the texts that scripted Louis XIV's life as he was living it has tended to privilege such a monolithic viewpoint; work that focuses solely on the king or on one well-known representer of him reproduces the symbolic processes of the absolutist project it is deconstructing.[57] Our study has attempted to shift that focus by concentrating on the interworkings of multiple perspectives and by placing the representation of the king within that of a larger cast of characters. In examining the king within a grid of relations and perspectives, we argue that the creation of Louis XIV's political image was essentially an interactive and pluralistic project. Focusing away from the dynastic or monumental (monolithic) side of the king's image also highlights the symbolics of his private body.[58] For despite their aura of intimacy, epistolary and memorial genres (not to mention medical reports) may be as symbolic as their monumental, and more formal, counterparts. And yet, both their status as "private" and the object on which they focus—details of the king's private, mortal life—may divert our attention from these texts' participation in, and commentary on, affairs of state which we are apt to categorize apart from affairs of the heart.

NOTES

We wish to thank Caroline Ford of Harvard University for her helpful comments and criticism for the revision of this chapter.

1. Indeed, Marie was not the first Mancini in whom Louis XIV had displayed an interest; Marie's older sister Olympe had also captured the young monarch's fancy in the intimacy of the royal circle inhabited by the Mancini nieces. For details of the lives of the various family members Mazarin brought to France and the court, see Georges Mongrédien, *Une aventurière au grand siècle: la duchesse Mazarin* (Paris: Amiot-Dumont, 1952); Amédée Renée, *Les Nièces de Mazarin* (Paris: Didier, 1857); R. Chantelauze, *Louis XIV et Marie Mancini* (Paris: Didier, 1881); Pierre Goubert, *Mazarin* (Paris: Fayard, 1990); and Claude Dulong, *Marie Mancini: La Première Passion de Louis XIV* (Paris: Perrin, 1993). All translations from the French in this chapter are our own.

2. On the public construction of the king's image, see Jean-Marie Apostolidès, *Le Roi-machine* (Paris: Minuit, 1981), and *Le Prince sacrifié* (Paris: Minuit, 1985); Peter Burke, *The Fabrication of Louis XIV* (New Haven, CT: Yale University Press, 1992), Louis Marin, *Le Portrait du roi* (Paris: Minuit, 1981), and Orest Ranum, *Artisans of Glory: Writers and Historical Thought in Seventeenth-Century France* (Chapel Hill: University of North Carolina Press, 1980).

3. Ultimately the marriage provided the French with the Spanish Hapsburg throne when, in the early eighteenth century, one of Louis XIV and Marie-Thérèse's grandchildren acceded to it. Today, ironically, the only "reigning" Bourbon is the current titular monarch of Spain. For a brief overview of the Treaty of Pyrenees, see the first chapter of Peter Sahlins's *Boundaries, The Making of France and Spain in the Pyrenees* (Berkeley: University of California Press, 1989), 25–60. For a more detailed discussion, see François Mignet's introduction to his collection of previously unedited texts, *Négotiations relatives à la succession d'Espagne sous Louis XIV ou correspondances, mémoires, et actes diplomatiques concernant les prétentions et l'avènement de la maison de Bour-*

bon au throne d'Espagne..., 4 vols. (Paris: Imprimerie Royale, 1835–42). Abby Zanger is currently completing a study of symbols of the marriage and treaty in a book entitled *Exploding Symbols: Imagining the Queen in the Marriage of Louis XIV*.

4. There is one more memoir in which the Mancini-Louis XIV liaison figures prominently, L'Abbé de Choisy's *Memoires pour servir à l'histoire de Louis XIV*. We have excluded this text from our discussion, however, because the writer was quite young at the time of the events and so his discussion, based on his mother's accounts, probably also owed a great deal to Lafayette, Motteville, and Montpensier. We would include him in the next wave of treatments of the affair.

5. In so doing, he was also establishing that France would not once again lapse into the kind of unrest witnessed during the wars of religion.

6. The physicians kept notes organized by year, recording and commenting on the king's health and illnesses and the ensuing treatments. The manuscript of these notes remained in the family of the last of the three physicians to make entries, Guy-Crescent Fagon. When Fagon's son died in 1744, the pages were passed on to what was then the Bibliothèque Impériale. The text is currently accessible under the title *Journal de la Santé du Roi Louis XIV de l'année 1647 à l'année 1711 écrit par Vallot, D'Aquin et Fagon* (Paris: Auguste Durand, Libraire-Editeur, 1862), edited by J.-A. Le Roi from a copy of the original manuscript located in the Bibliothèque de la ville de Versailles, a copy the editor asserts is identical to the original manuscript. The section describing the 1658 illness was written by Antoine Vallot. Other sources that mention the illness include the memoirs of Motteville and Montpensier, the *Gazette* (the officially sanctioned news journal edited by Renaudot), and Loret's *La muse historique,* as well as letters written by the physician Guy Patin, who derided Vallot's methods of treatment. These latter sources essentially echo what one finds in the *Journal,* while also documenting the disputes among the king's physicians as to how the illness should be treated.

7. In another description of the illness, Vallot links the king's valor and neglect for his person to the illness more directly when he notes, "It is thus quite certain that the king, because of his extraordinary passion for glory, having neglected his person and his health in order to achieve his generous goals, was in the end made vulnerable to a kind of popular contagion by his diminished strength and the impurity of his body that had developed over time..." (65).

8. Mademoiselle de Montpensier, *Mémoires*, vol. 2 (Paris: Librairie Fontaine, 1985), 53.

9. The king's condition puzzled his doctor, who sensed that it was important quickly to apply the appropriate remedy, although, as he notes at least indirectly, what the remedy would be was as uncertain as the disease, hence his proposal of at least two courses of action. It is not surprising that this uncertainty and the

pressure it would have created provoked contention among the various doctors, a discord that is noted several times in the journal and is noted elsewhere as well, most notably in the letters of the Sorbonne doctor Guy Patin.

10. In ridiculing the treatment in a letter to Falconnet, Guy Patin placed the physician of the Duc d'Anjou (who was next in line for the throne) in the role of arguing for Vallot's desire to use a "vin émétique" in front of Mazarin. Mazarin is depicted in the journal as well as in other sources as being the mediator of the physicians' disputes. Patin has a very ironic comment about this (imagined?) scene which sums up the level of political tensions during the illness: " . . . (such are the ways of our century), the doctor of the heir to the Crown, and the immediate successor, *adhibetur in consilium pro rege, et venenatum stibium audet praescribere*. If he had believed, and if the king had died, he would have been a royal doctor. *Non sic grat in principio*, in other times doctors of princes of the blood were never called to treat an ailing king, for very good political reasons (but which today are ignored)." This text is found in the appendix of the *Journal*, 375.

11. On the notion that the two "bodies" of kingship are united, see Ernst Kantorowicz, *The King's Two Bodies: A Study in Medieval Political Theology* (Princeton, NJ: Princeton University Press, 1981), 446–49. While the common assumption is that the mortal body of a king that could get ill was separate from his divine body, and thus from the body politic, we argue here for their interconnection. Indeed, Kantorowicz underscores that his model applies more to England than to France and even less to the monarchy of Louis XIV. Roger Chartier also underlines how the cult of kingship established by Louis XIV's reign involved not the separation of the "King's two bodies," but, rather, what he calls the absorption of the political body of state by the natural body of the monarch, the melding of the person of Louis XIV with the concept of the state, in *Les Origines Culturelles de la Révolution Française* (Paris: Editions du Seuil, 1990), 159. Chapter 6, entitled "Le Roi désacralisé?" includes an excellent overview of the state of current scholarship on the king's body.

12. Note the past tense. It may have been impossible to speak of the illness in these terms during its course.

13. News of the king's recovery was circulated in the *Gazette* as well as in engravings. See the *Journal*'s "pièces justificatives," 373. There was also a *Te Deum* held to celebrate the recovery as indicated in the occasional pamphlet, *Lettre du roi, envoyée à monseigneur le chancelier de France, contenant la parfaite guérison de Sa Majesté, avec ordre de faire chanter et d'assister au Te Deum* (Paris: P. Ricolet, n.d.). For a discussion of the role of the *Te Deum* in what he calls the desacrilization of the king, see Chartier, *Les Origines*, chap. 6.

14. The physician's focus on recovery may be explained in part by the fact that the success of the treatment was a credit to the doctor, Vallot, who used a controversial remedy, the *vin émétique*, as both the *Journal* and the *Gazette* note.

15. Madame de Motteville, *Mémoires pour servir à l'histoire de la vie d'Anne d'Autriche* (Paris: Didier, 1866), 91.

16. The physician of Louis XIII, Héroard also kept journals in which he witnessed, among other things, the king's general indifference to women. That Anne of Austria took twenty-two years to produce an heir was commonly thought to be linked to Louis XIII's lack of interest in women, a characteristic his second son, Philip d'Anjou (later D'Orléans) was said to have inherited. France evidently yearned for a virile (and politically powerful) king such as it had not had since Henry IV. It would be interesting to trace discursive structures associating heterosexual virility with political force across that period, an era that also corresponds to the reign of the Bourbon dynasty.

17. See, for example, the description of this moment by Claude Dulong in *Le Mariage du Roi-Soleil* (Paris: Albin Michel, 1986), 29.

18. In his biography of Mazarin, Pierre Goubert expresses his initial exasperation with the conflicting versions of the Mancini story: "the author of these lines wondered for a time if this whole story were not a likeable fabulation concocted by the eternal inventors of what they call history": *Mazarin* (Paris: Fayard, 1990), 415.

19. Excerpts from this correspondence are available in several places, including the biographical studies cited in note 1. Chantelauze reproduces the most complete range of the letters. Mazarin's correspondence from the period of the treaty negotiation was first published in Amsterdam in the 1690 *Lettres du cardinal Mazarin où l'on voit le secret de la négotiation de la paix des Pyrénées, et la relation des conférences qu'il a eues pour ce sujet avec D. Louis de Haro, ... avec d'autres lettres très curieuses écrites au roi et à la reine par le même cardinal, pendant son voyage* (Amsterdam: A. Pierrot, 1690). It was republished in 1692, 1693, 1694, and 1745 by other publishers within the same city. All these publications appear to be based on circulating manuscript editions of the letters. For more information on this source, see note 29.

20. In fact, Mazarin was Louis XIV's godfather, and the tone of the letters often does seem quite fatherly.

21. We are citing from the letters in Chantelauze because the volume is readily available in most libraries and because the editions of the letters concerning the treaty vary widely in contents and pagination.

22. As previously noted, it is commonly accepted that for the French, the treaty was a means to usurp the Hapsburg throne. Their agreement, that the infanta would renounce her rights of succession in exchange for a sum the French knew was too large for the depleted Spanish treasury to pay out, allowed the French to claim Marie-Thérèse's inheritance at various opportune moments beginning in 1667 and continuing over the next three decades until 1700, when Louis XIV's grandson, the duke of Anjou, second son of the dauphin, acceded to the Spanish throne as Philip V. For a brief overview of the history of France's

role in the Spanish succession, see Lucien Bély et al., *Guerre et Paix dans l'Europe du XVIIe Siècle,* vol. 2 (Paris: SEDES, 1991), 58–76.

23. The term *person* here refers to Marie.

24. Don Louis would be Haro, the Spanish minister, who was Mazarin's counterpart in the negotiations.

25. The term *things* in line one refers to the conference or negotiation. *Confident* in line three refers to Louis XIV.

26. It would not be the first time Mazarin used romance as bait to catch the Spanish. It is commonly accepted that the French court's trip to Lyon to meet with the duchess of Savoy and her daughter was bait set to convince the Spanish to act on the marriage-treaty offer. Indeed, Philip IV sent Pimentel to Lyon as a secret envoy toward that end, rising to the bait. On this subject, see, for example, E. Ducéré, *Le mariage de Louis XIV d'après les contemporains et des documents inédits* (Bayonne: A. Lamaignère, 1908), 7–24.

27. The categories of public and private as we understand them today in relation to the written word have been shown to be vastly different for the early modern period. On this difference, see volume 3 of Georges Duby and Roger Chartier, eds., *The History of Private Life* (Cambridge, MA: Harvard University Press, 1987), especially the articles by Roger Chartier, Madeleine Foisil, and Jean-Marie Goulemot.

28. Correspondences and memoirs of the time allude to Mazarin's epistolary discussions with the king and his mother about the Mancini affair. The memoirs of Madame de Motteville, for example, contain references to these as yet unpublished letters (Motteville died in 1689).

29. Published between 1690 and 1745, these editions vary as to the number of letters they include. There are also at least two circulating manuscript copies of the correspondence, one at Versailles, mentioned by Claude Dulong in her *Le Mariage du roi soleil,* and one at the Houghton Library at Harvard. Many original letters are available in manuscript form in various archives, as listed in Dulong's bibliography. While it is not possible to date accurately the manuscript versions of the letters in question, some attempts at dating the volume in Houghton using watermarks, for instance, do not rule out the possibility that the text could indeed have been produced on or close to the period of their original writing. For help with dating the manuscripts, we wish to thank the staff members of the Houghton Library at Harvard.

30. To understand the power of the Fronde pamphlets, see Christian Jouhaud, *Mazarinades: la Fronde des mots* (Paris: Editions Aubier Montaigne, 1985).

31. The most significant absence is probably the letters between Marie and the king, a commerce Mazarin alludes to as too public and thus scandalous. Interestingly, no other contemporary observer remarks on this correspondence. The nineteenth-century historian Amédée Renée first noted these letters in his book *Les Nièces de Mazarin.* He included some quotations from a copy of the

correspondence that had been preserved in the Louvre library. A fire subsequently destroyed much of the collections in this library, and historians have assumed that the letters disappeared in the fire. Nearly a century ago, Lucien Perey (a pseudonym for Clara Herpin) published a book on the Mancini affair entitled *Le Roman du grand roi: Louis XIV et Marie Mancini d'après des lettres et documents inédits* (Paris: Calmann Lévy, 1899). Perey relied heavily on a copy of the Mancini–Louis XIV correspondence that she had found in the private archives of a descendant of Marie's brother, the Duc d'Havrincourt. No one else has ever seen this copy, although attempts have been made to view it, most recently by Claude Dulong in researching *Le Mariage du roi-soleil*. She notes in her book that her letters to the Havrincourt family were not answered. In our view, the letters as quoted by Perey do not seem authentic. Nonetheless, one wonders what did happen to those love letters if they actually existed.

32. In Madame de Lafayette, *Histoire de Madame Henriette d'Angleterre* (1720; Paris: Mercure de France, 1988); Mademoiselle de Montpensier, *Mémoires* (1728; Paris: Fontaine, 1985), and Madame de Motteville, *Mémoires pour servir à l'histoire de la vie d'Anne d'Autriche* (1723; Paris: Didier, 1866).

33. While other memorialists have written on this event, we limit our discussion to those writers who were adult eyewitnesses in part because they are the other major source for later interpretations and analyses of the romance by such varied commentators as Voltaire in the eighteenth century and John Wolf in the twentieth. Thus, we do not discuss the description of l'Abbé de Choisy, as mentioned earlier. Other possible sources—for example, the diplomats Loménie de Brienne and the Duc de Grammont, who actually participated in the negotiations of the marriage—do not mention the romance in their memoirs. Later writers such as Saint-Simon and Voltaire do discuss the romance, but they probably knew of it largely from the earlier sources and so must be considered along with the nineteenth- and twentieth-century biographers of Marie and Louis.

34. The book was published posthumously in 1720, after the death of Louis XIV. In her preface, Lafayette recounts how she began to write the "memoirs" of Henriette's life at her subject's request, then continued the story in a lengthy description of her death (20–21).

35. For a discussion of *Histoire de Madame Henriette d'Angleterre* in the larger context of women's historiography in the seventeenth century, see Faith Beasley, *Revising Memory: Women's Fiction and Memoirs in Seventeenth-Century France* (New Brunswick: Rutgers University Press, 1990).

36. Louise de la Vallière, Louis's first mistress after his marriage, is always portrayed as adoring and submissive. Her portrait can be neatly contrasted in many respects with the legend of Marie: Marie was plain, Louise beautiful; Marie aggressive, Louise kind; Marie ambitious, Louise self-sacrificing. Marie was repeatedly escaping from convents, Louise chose to enter one for the rest of her life as soon as the king began to lose interest in her.

37. Extant versions of the story printed during Louis XIV's reign are rare, although in the ones that do survive it is clear that the writers assume a readership already familiar with the story. Two early anonymous pamphlets recounting the Mancini affair are: *Les Agrémens de la jeunesse de Louis XIV ou son amour pour Mademoiselle de Mancini* and *Le Palais Royal*, both in D. Boiteau and C. L. Livet, eds., *L'Histoire amoureuse des gaules suivie des Romans historico-satiriques du 17e siècle*... (Paris: Jannet, 1857). They were originally published in 1670 and 1667, respectively. The latter, *Palais Royal*, was apparently widely circulated and popular enough to elicit an attack in Pierre Bayle's *Réponses aux questions d'un provincial*, published in 1701. Bayle systematically attempted to disprove, based on factual errors in the texts in question, the accounts of the king in tears before Mazarin and later before Marie as she leaves Paris.

38. This is actually the subtitle of *Le Palais Royal*.

39. For a longer analysis of shifts in representations of the king's "tearful" moments, see Elizabeth Goldsmith, "Louis XIV, Marie Mancini et la politique de l'intimité royale," in Roger Duchêne and Pierre Ronzeaud, eds., *Ordre et contestation au temps des classiques* (Tubingen: Biblio 17, 1992), 235–43.

40. The king's sister-in-law, for example, writes that she was told that "the king and Madame Colonne furnished the subject." Cited in Raymond Picard, *Nouveau Corpus Racinianum* (Paris: CNRS, 1976), 494. The abbé de Villars, who wrote a negative critique of the play, reports that this line drew laughter from the spectators. See his *Critique de Bérénice*, reprinted in G. Michaut, *La Bérénice de Racine* (Paris: Société française d'imprimerie et de librairie, 1907). The literary quarrel over Bérénice prefigures in many respects the debates, later in Louis XIV's reign, over how to interpret the Mancini romance in the official history of the king's life. The central issue in the "querelle de Bérénice" was whether an emperor who behaved as Titus did—displaying great uncertainty and vainly struggling to overcome his passion—could be taken seriously as a heroic figure. Officially approved accounts of the lives of Louis XIV and Mazarin produced later in the reign either erased the Mancini episode altogether or took pains to debunk the popular image of the king's tearful displays of passion. See, for example, Aubery, *Histoire du Cardinal Mazarin* (Paris: D. Thierry, 1688), and Bayle, *Réponses*.

41. Motteville describes the reactions of the eldest to this exploitation: "She had perceived that the friendship of the King was only an amusement, and she was not pleased to see that her uncle the Cardinal Mazarin... was using her only to preserve his credit with the King, and to enclose him within his own family" (81).

42. Chantelauze, *Louis XIV et Marie Mancini*, 27.

43. Tasso describes Armida as disguising her uncle's wisdom with her feminine charms: "He calls her to him, and shares with her his plan, and desires that she should take charge of it. He says: 'Oh my dear, who under golden hair and

outward beauties do so delicate keep concealed a manly heart and gray-haired wisdom, and in my arts already outstrip myself, I am revolving a great plan. And, if you lend it your aid, the results will answer to our hopes. Weave the web that I show you all laid out, a bold-hearted agent for a cautious old man.'" *Jerusalem Delivered,* trans. Ralph Nash (Detroit, 1987), canto 4, p. 74.

44. One of the recurrent arguments underlying Motteville's descriptions of political and social events is that Anne of Austria was an authoritative leader, an argument that opposed the view of many historians and polemicists who saw the regent as fundamentally, almost congenitally, submissive, first to Mazarin, then to her son.

45. The method of "curing" the king here involves two steps, as in Tasso. It is important that the love-struck warrior first be humiliated by the sight of what he has become, then willingly flee the prison that he now sees in its true ugliness. See *Jerusalem Delivered,* canto 16, verses 30–41, pp. 345–47.

46. Motteville records the following response from Anne: "I do not believe, monsieur le Cardinal, that the King would be capable of this cowardice; but if it were possible that he has thought of it, I warn you that all of France would revolt against you and him, and that I myself would be leading the rebels, and that I would enlist my son" (144).

47. "... he would see his entire kingdom rise up against him to prevent him from dishonoring himself by such an unworthy marriage" (Motteville, *Mémoires pour servir à l'histoire,* 152–53).

48. "In all that I have written one can see that for several years the extreme authority that the minister had usurped in this kingdom had greatly absorbed the legitimate (authority) ...": Motteville, *Mémoires pour servir à l'histoire,* 156.

49. Motteville refers repeatedly to Mazarin's letters to Louis on this subject, although she stresses that they were written at the queen's request, which is not what is suggested by the letters themselves. Since Madame de Motteville died in 1689, before the first printed edition of Mazarin's letters was published, her detailed knowledge of the contents of the minister's letters to the king confirms that this material was circulated in some form before its publication.

50. Motteville's description of Louis's gratitude for the "happiness" that his marriage will bring him is also reminiscent of the gratitude expressed by the contrite Rinaldo when he is told, after he leaves Armida, that he is destined to father a great race of men (canto 17, verses 90–94). As we have noted, foremost in the minds of all those observing Louis's health at this time was the concern for his ability to produce heirs.

51. As we noted previously, these were precisely the qualities attributed to Louis's father, Louis XIII, in relation to women.

52. All three writers, Lafayette, Motteville, and Montpensier, were of aristocratic background and were either directly opposed to Mazarin during the Fronde or were associated with his opponents. We know, for example, that

Montpensier, Louis XIV's cousin, led the aristocratic opposition to Mazarin; that Motteville, of part Spanish origin, was sent away from the court and her association with Anne of Austria by Richelieu, who wished to separate the queen from Motteville's mother; and that Lafayette, the youngest of the three, came from a family close to Retz, a noble at the center of the aristocratic uprising. Nonetheless, they all functioned in Paris in the years of Louis XIV's reign. None was exiled from Paris or the court, even if Montpensier's relations with her cousin remained strained. Motteville, in fact, regained access to Anne of Austria in 1643 after Richelieu's death.

53. While we have evidence that they were all writing their memoirs in the decades following the Mancini debacle—Lafayette in the years between 1665 and 1669, Montpensier in 1677, and Motteville at some point prior to 1689, the year of her death—it is interesting to note that these writings, which portray the king's early vulnerability, were written during the decades of his political entrenchment and the consolidation of his power (during the years of the production of the great monuments of his rule—Versailles, the historiography of Racine, the rise of court spectacle, continued military triumphs). It is not surprising, however, that the texts were not published until after the king's death; Lafayette's were published in 1720, Montpensier's in 1728, and Motteville's in 1723. Nor is it surprising that they were not published in France, but in Amsterdam, traditional site for unapproved publications. For information about publishing practices in early modern France, see Henri-Jean Martin's study of publishing, *Livre Pouvoirs et Société à Paris au XVIIe Siècle (1598–1701)*, 2 vols. (Geneva: Librairie Droz, 1969), and Roger Chartier and Henri-Jean Martin's recently reedited *Histoire de l'édition française*, vols. 1 and 2 (Paris: Fayard, 1989–90).

54. The memoir writers picked up on the details of what they perceived as Louis XIV's private affective life, not only because they may have had access to Mazarin's letters circulating in manuscript form in the salons, but also because their writings are marked by a particular attention to the details of everyday life. Faith Beasley has argued in *Revising Memory* that the "particularities," or details, that interested memorial writers such as Lafayette and Montpensier constituted a unique kind of history writing engaged in by women in the classical period. Yet, as we read them, Mazarin's letters might also be placed in the same (female?) category of history writing!

55. See, for example, Voltaire, *Le Siècle de Louis XIV* (Paris: Flammarion, 1966), 99–100; John Wolf, *Louis XIV* (New York: Norton, 1968), 98–113; Georges Bordenove, *Louis XIV, roi-soleil* (Paris: Pygmalion, 1982), 80–88; and the study by Claude Dulong cited in note 17.

56. As we noted previously, the correspondence between Louis XIV and Marie has been lost, and even in her own memoirs, Marie Mancini relegates the love affair to a small (and uninformative) chapter, fewer than ten pages in a text

over two hundred pages long. There is an interesting publishing history for Marie's memoirs. After the appearance of a counterfeited version of them, Marie wrote and published her own version. For further discussion of this text, see René Démoris, *Le Roman à la première personne* (Paris: Armand Colin, 1975), 116–22, and Elizabeth C. Goldsmith, "Publishing the Lives of Hortense and Marie Mancini," in Elizabeth C. Goldsmith and Dena Goodman, eds., *Going Public: Women and Publishing in Early Modern France* (Ithaca, NY: Cornell University Press, forthcoming).

57. See the work of Apostolidès and Marin, which has firmly established that the image of Louis XIV was largely a symbolic construct and that his personal and institutional force was a result of representational and performative strategies.

58. As Kantorowicz has shown, in European political theology in the early modern period, kings were considered to have two bodies, one private and mortal, the other public and dynastic. The first was given to mortal appetites and frailties while the second was considered sacred and eternal (see *The King's Two Bodies*). More recently, Alain Boureau has criticized Kantorowicz's thesis in *Le simple corps du roi* (Paris: Les Editions de Paris, 1988). While both Marin and Apostolidès focus on the king as monumental body, Marin has discussed the representation of the king's sexuality in two essays, "Le corps glorieux du Roi et son portrait" and "Le corps pathétique et son médecin: Sur le *Journal de Santé de Louis XIV*," both in *La parole mangée et autres essais théologico-politiques* (Paris: Klincksieck, 1986). Claude Reichler has also considered the private, sexual side of the king in "La Jambe du Roi," in *L'age Libertin* (Paris: Minuit, 1987). These essays do not take into consideration issues of gender in the representation of the king, nor do they consider that the king's sexual, mortal body might be constitutive of, and not detrimental to, monarchical power. Abby Zanger offers a reading of the representation of gender and sexuality in the constitution of the absolutist state in "Making Sweat: Gender and the Sexuality of National Reproduction in the Marriage of Louis XIV," *Yale French Studies* 86 (1994): 187–205.

Contributors

F. W. Conrad received his doctorate from Johns Hopkins University, where he studied under the supervision of J. G. A. Pocock. He has taught at Augustana College and at Washington University, St. Louis, where he is now associate research fellow. He is at work on a book-length study of the political thought and career of Sir Thomas Elyot.

William E. Engel is assistant professor of English at Vanderbilt University. He has published articles in such journals as *Montaigne Studies* and is at work on a book.

Sheila ffolliott is associate professor of art and art history at George Mason University, Fairfax, Virginia. She has published numerous articles and a book, *Civic Sculpture in the Renaissance* (1984). She is completing a full-length study of representations of Catherine de' Medici.

Elizabeth C. Goldsmith is associate professor of French at Boston University. She is the author or editor of several books and articles, including *Exclusive Conversations: The Art of Interaction in Seventeenth-Century France* (1988) and *Writing the Female Voice: Essays on Epistolary Literature* (1989). She has just completed work on an edited volume entitled *Going Public: Women and Publishing in Early Modern France*.

Robert Kolb taught for many years at Concordia College in St. Paul, Minnesota, before assuming the directorship of the Institute for Mission Studies at Concordia Seminary in St. Louis, where he is also Missions Professor of systematic theology. He is the author of numerous books and articles and is editor of the *Sixteenth Century Journal*.

Thomas F. Mayer is associate professor of history at Augustana College, Rock Island, Illinois. He is the author of *Thomas Starkey and the Commonweal: Humanist Politics and Religion in the Reign of Henry VIII* (1989) and has also edited Starkey's *Dialogue between Pole and Lupset* for the Camden Society. His articles have appeared in such journals as the *English Historical Review, Historical Journal, Archiv für Reformationsgeschichte,* and *Journal of the History of Ideas.* Most recently he is the coeditor of *Political Thought and the Tudor Commonwealth: Deep Structure, Discourse and Disguise* (1992). He is at present working on a number of projects connected to Cardinal Pole, especially a new biography.

Adriana McCrea received her doctorate from Queen's University, Ontario, and has been SSHRCC postdoctoral fellow at Dalhousie University, where she has taught for several years. She has written articles in journals including *Albion* and the *Dalhousie Review.* She is completing a book on early seventeenth-century English neostoicism. She lives in Pleasantville, Nova Scotia.

James V. Mehl is professor of humanities at Missouri Western State College in St. Joseph, Missouri. He received his doctorate from the University of Missouri, Columbia, where he worked under the direction of Charles G. Nauert, Jr. He is the editor of *Humanismus in Köln* (1991) and author of numerous articles on the later history of conciliarism and Ortwin Gratius.

Catharine Randall is assistant professor of French at Barnard College and adjunct professor of Religion at Columbia University. She is the author of two interdisciplinary studies on Calvinism: *Subverting the System: d'Aubigné and Calvinism* (1990), and *(Em)bodying the Word: Textual Resurrections in the Martyrological Narratives of Foxe, Crespin, de Bèze and d'Aubigné* (1992). She has published articles in such journals as *Renaissance Quarterly, Journal of Medieval and Renaissance Studies, French Forum,* and *Renaissance and Reformation/Renaissance et Réforme.* She is currently at work on a book-length manuscript entitled *The (Dis)ordering of Power: Calvinist Structures and the Catholic State.*

Diana Robin is professor of classics and chair of the Department of Foreign Languages and Literatures, and director of Comparative Literature at the University of New Mexico. She has written *Filelfo in Milan* (1991) and many articles. Her translations of the complete letters and orations of Cassandra Fedele and Laura Cereta are forthcoming in two separate volumes with the University of Chicago Press.

Barbara J. Watts is assistant professor of visual arts at Florida International University and is at work on a study of Vasari's *Lives*.

Timothy J. Wengert is associate professor of divinity at Lutheran Theological Seminary, Philadelphia. He has written *Philip Melanchthon's Annotationes in Johannem in Relation to its Predecessors and Contemporaries* (1987).

D. R. Woolf is professor of history at Dalhousie University. He is the author of *The Idea of History in Early Stuart England* (1990) and of essays in *Renaissance Quarterly, Journal of the History of Ideas, Past and Present,* and other journals. He has most recently coedited a volume of essays, *Public Duty and Private Conscience in Seventeenth-Century England* (1993). He is at work on a study of perceptions and representations of the past in England between 1550 and 1730.

Abby E. Zanger teaches in the Department of Romance Languages and Literatures at Harvard University, where she is also a member of the Committee on Degrees in Women's Studies. She has published widely on French classical theater and is currently completing a book, *Exploding Symbols: Imagining the Queen in the Marriage of Louis XIV*, which concerns the representation of the Spanish infanta at the moment of her marriage to Louis XIV.

T. C. Price Zimmermann has taught at Reed College and at Davidson College, where he is Charles A. Dana professor of history. He has written on Renaissance autobiography and is currently completing a biography of Paolo Giovio.

Index

Aaron, 108
"Ana" (published table talk), 17
Absolutism, 315, 320
Adrian IV, pope, 41
Alberti, Leon Battista, 64
Albertists, 175
Alcionio, Pietro, 49
Allegory, 108, 229, 261
Allen, Don Cameron, 283
Allen, William, 212
Altoviti, Bindo, 86
Amicitia, 20
Anabaptists, 104
Anachronism, and exemplarity, 55
Analogy, 261, 281
Ancestors and ancestry, 41
Anderson, Judith H., 8, 21, 134, 146, 337
André, Bernard, 137
Andreae, Jakob, 102, 105, 107, 108
Anecdotes, 62, 65, 119, 233, 255, 287, 343
Angst, Wolfgang, 166, 179
Anne of Austria, queen regent of France, 341, 342, 350, 352, 366
  See also Lafayette, Madame de; Montpensier, duchess of
Anne, Queen of Navarre, 188
Apelles, story of the three disciples (Polygnotus, Scopa, and Diocles) of, 43–44
Aphthonius, the *progymnastica* of, 119
Apostolidès, Jean-Marie, 25, 372

Ariosto, Ludovico, 18, 247
Aristippus, 150
Art history, 2
Art of dying (*ars moriendi*), 107, 308
Artemisia, queen of Caria, 18, 25, 323, 324, 325
  Catherine de' Medici represented as, 24, 326, 327, 329
Arthur cycle, the, 249
Asclepiades of Myrlea, 135
Astraea, Elizabeth I represented as, 25
Aubrey, John, 311
Auerbach, Erich, 252
Augustine, St., 16, 53, 258
Aurifaber, Johannes, 110
Ausonius, Decimus Magnus, 43
Authorship, collective, 21, 169, 176–77, 181
Autobiography, 16–17, 36, 207, 223, 300, 319, 321
  autobiographical representation, 4
  autobiographical voice, 68
  Calvinist meditational writing as a form of, 227–28, 229
  collaborative, 8
  confessions as a form of, 16
  table talk as a form of, 17
  See also Biography; Life-writing
Azor, Juan, 213

Bacon, Francis, 1, 7, 15, 283, 284, 296, 303, 305
Badby, John, 261
Baglione, Giovanni, 14
Bale, John, 249

Baptistery of Florence, 89
Barbarigo, Marco, doge of Venice, 189
Barbaro, Daniele, 61
Barbaro, Francesco, 191, 197
Barbarolexis, 174
Barolsky, Paul, 14, 20, 65
Barzizza, Gasperino, 167
Bathild, queen, 322
Bayle, Pierre, 14, 369
Beasley, Faith, 371
Beatrice, queen of Hungary, 195
Beaune, Renaud de, Archbishop of Bourges, 322, 328, 331, 338
Beccadelli, Antonio ("Il Panormita"), 7
Beccadelli, Ludovico, 205, 206, 208, 209, 211, 212, 213, 217
Becker, Reinhart, 21, 172, 173
Bede, 11, 244, 246, 272
Benson, Pamela, 29, 328
Benstock, Shari, 187
Bertano, Pietro, 210
Berthault, R., 155
Bertoldo di Giovanni, 69, 73, 75, 77, 98
Bèze, Théodore de, 18, 22, 227, 228, 229, 230, 234
    emblem book of Christian martyrs, 233
    meditational writings of, 230–31
Bible or Scripture, 100, 104, 225, 226, 227, 229
    as allegory, 229
    Chaldean, 105
    Hebrew, 105
    reading of, 107
Bietenholz, Peter G., 33
Bilney, Thomas, 261
Binardi, Giovanni Battista, 209, 210, 219
Biography, 1, 2, 4, 7, 11–16, 19, 26, 39, 115
    and autobiography, 8, 12, 300
    biographical narratives, 133
    biographical representation, 4

biographical romance, 353
"biographical truth," 21
    exemplary, 324–25
    and fiction, 58, 135, 136
    Greek, 10–12, 49
    and history, 24
    humanist, 13–15, 26, 42–43
    queens' biographies, 321
    quest for holiness in, 16
    Roman, 11
    sacred (*see also* Hagiography), 11
    See also Life-writing
Blanche of Castile, queen regent of France, 327
Bland, John, 259, 260
Boase, T.S.R., 61
Boccaccio, Giovanni, 13, 197, 323
    De casibus virorum illustrium, 13
    De mulieribus claris, 13, 29, 47, 323–24
Body and text, 232, 233–34, 235, 289–92
Bollandists, 12, 15
Bonelli, Giuseppe, 216
Bonner, Edmund, Bishop, 265, 278
Borghini, Vincenzo, 90
Borgia, Cesare, 45
Bornkamm, Heinrich, 108
Boucquin, Peter, 121
Bourbon, House of, 341, 342, 345, 346, 363
Boureau, Alain, 372
Braccio da Montone, 39
Bracciolini, Poggio, 167, 190, 198
Braden, Gordon, 7
Bradford, John, 258
Bramante, Donato, 96
Brant, Sebastian, 184
Brunelleschi, Filippo, 94
Brunhild, queen, 322
Bruni, Leonardo, 13, 53, 137, 167, 190, 191, 197, 198
Budé, Guillaume, 324
Buondelmonti, Zanobi, 153
Burckhardt, Jacob, 6, 46

Burke, Kenneth, 3, 9, 10, 258
Burnet, Gilbert, bishop, 213, 214
Busche, Hermann von dem, 21, 164, 170, 171, 172, 176, 183

Caccamo, Domenico, 210
Caesar, Augustus, 326
Caesar, Caius Julius, 16, 326
Caesarius, Johannes, 163, 164
Caesaropapism, 103
Calvin, John, 16, 224, 253
Calvinism, 223, 224
Camden, William, 15
Camerarius, Joachim, 12, 20, 22, 24, 115–27
   Elementa Rhetoricae, 117
   ethical categories in his biography of Melanchthon, 118
   "friendship" of Melanchthon and Luther, 124, 125
   influence of his representation of Melanchthon, 125–26
   Melanchthon as a Stoic hero, 123
   Melanchthon's rhetorical skills, opinion of, 122
Camermeister, Jerome, 118
Campano, Giovanni Antonio, 39, 167
Caraffa, Gianpietro, 216
Carion, Johann, 97, 244
Caritas, 86
Caron, Antoine, 324, 332
Cassirer, Ernst, 6
Castagno, Andrea del, 51
Castelvetro, Ludovico, 209, 210, 219
Castiglione, Baldesar, 190, 191, 192, 193, 196, 197, 198
Castracani, Castruccio, 31, 152
Catechetical manuals, Calvinist, 224
Catherine of Aragon, 149, 205, 209, 329
Catullus, 191, 193
Cecil, Robert, earl of Salisbury, 301, 302, 303, 315
Cellini, Benvenuto, 333
Celtis, Conrad, 167
Censorship, 306

Cereta, Laura, 17, 189, 190, 198
Cervini, Marcello
   See Marcellus II, Pope
Chantelauze, R., 366
Character, as a component of personality, 45, 47, 49, 60–61, 294
Charles I, king of England, 316
Charles IX, king of France, 323, 330
Charles V, emperor, 21, 52, 139–45, 152, 322
Chartier, Roger, 371
Chorographies, 15–16
Chrétien de Troyes, 249, 250
Chria, 119
   See also Anecdotes
Christian values, 97
Christine de Pizan, 13
Chronicles or annals, 1, 97
Church, William, 25
Cicero, Marcus Tullius, 42, 117, 136, 166–67
Ciceronian moral philosophy, 45
Cimabue, 72
Clement, John, 148
Clement VIII, Pope, 213
Clotilde, queen consort of Clovis, 322
Clough, Cecil, 166, 167
Clovis, king of the Franks, 322
Cochlaeus, Johann, 107
Cochrane, Eric, 4, 7, 14, 221–22
Coelius, Michael, 110
Collins, Stephen L., 316
Cologne, 166
   bursa Cucana, 172
   bursa Laurentiana, 171
   University of, 166, 171
Columbus, Christopher, 48
Comedy, 6, 23, 255–57
   comic tone, 193
   Old, 247
Commonplace books, 283
Commynes, Philippe de, 16
Condé, Prince de (Louis de Bourbon), 343, 349, 351
Condivi, Ascanio, 68
Confession of sins, 107

Contarini, Gasparo, 206
Contubernium, 312, 313, 320
Corinna, 192
Cornelius Nepos, 11, 47
Counter-Reformation, 10, 26
Cox, Patricia, 11
Coxe, Leonard, 137, 145–46
Cranmer, Thomas, archbishop of Canterbury, 143, 246, 254, 259, 265, 268
Crespin, Jean, 17, 231, 234–35, 238
Crewe, Jonathan, 8, 134
Crivelli, Lodrisio, 39, 40
Crocus, Richard, 116
Cromwell, Thomas, earl of Essex, 148, 149, 151, 152, 253
Crotus Rubeanus, 21, 164, 170, 173, 174, 175, 176, 181
Cyprian, St., 282

d'Aubigné, Théodore Agrippa, 22–23, 223–25, 226–37
Dante Alighieri, 16, 66
  Dante's *Comedia* as a model for Giorgio Vasari's *Lives,* 66
Davanzati, Bernardo, 213, 221
Davenant, William, Sir, 311
David, Old Testament king, 229–31
Davis, Natalie Zemon, 3
Day, John, 251
de Man, Paul, 187, 198
De Thou, Jacques-Auguste, 16
Déboublement, 226
Decembrio, Pier Candido, 39, 190, 198
Decio, Filippo, 50
Delgado, Francisco, 210
DeMaio, Romeo, 327
Democritus, 256
Denley, John, 259
Devereux, Robert, earl of Essex, 301, 302, 306, 309, 314, 315, 398
  the Essex rebellion, 303
Dialogue, 7, 138
Digression, 255, 270
Dilthey, Wilhelm, 30

Diogenes, 46
Diogenes Laertius, 12, 47, 64, 139, 152
Dionysius of Halicarnassus, 55
Dionysius of Syracuse, 14, 43, 150, 152
Dollimore, Jonathan, 305
Donatello, 20, 69
  compared to Michelangelo in Vasari's *Lives,* 20, 69–90
  generosity of, 86
Doni, Angelo, 80, 82
Donne, John, 225, 320
Donner, H.W., 149, 150
Drake, Francis, Sir, 307
Drury, Elizabeth, 320
du Bellay, Martin, 16
du Bourg, Anne, 232
Dudic, Andras, 206, 207, 208–11, 213
  conversion to Calvinism, 210
  influence of his biography of Pole, 210–11
  printing of his biography of Pole, 211
Dudley, Robert, earl of Leicester, 300, 302
Dulong, Claude, 367
Dürer, Albrecht, 17

Eadmer, 11, 246
Eakin, Paul John, 187
Edgar, king of England, 263, 271
Edward VI, king of England, 206, 208, 217, 267
Einhard, 11
Einhorn, Paul, 122
Eisleben, 108
Eleanora of Aragon, duchess of Ferrara, 192, 195
Elias, Norbert, 323
Elizabeth I, queen of England, 25, 301, 302, 303, 307, 309, 314, 315, 317
Eloquence, 191, 199
Elton, Geoffrey, Sir, 134

Elyot, Thomas, Sir, 21, 139–45, 147–53
  The Defence of Good Women, 148, 328
Emblems and emblem books, 52, 233
Emulation, 67, 93, 275
Encomium, 5, 17, 42–43, 67, 119
Enlightenment, 2
Epic poetry, 7
Epistles
  See Letter collections, humanistic; Letters, Renaissance
  manuals on the writing of
Epistolae obscurorum virorum
  See *Letters of Obscure Men*
Epistolario
  See Letter books
Erasmus, Desiderius, 12, 139, 163, 164, 166, 167, 169, 324
  De copia verborum ac rerum, 137–39
Erfurt, circle of humanists, 175
  University of, 116, 170
Essay as a genre, 23–24, 169
  relation to commonplace books, 283
Este, Alfonso d', 41, 44
  See also Este of Ferrara, House of
Este, Beatrice d', 190, 195
Este, Isabella d', 190
Este of Ferrara, House of, 41, 44, 188
Esther, 327
Estienne, Henri, 322, 330
Eucharist, 259–60
  See also Lord's Supper
Eusebius, 244, 245–46, 272
  Eusebian model, 245
Exegesis, 224, 237
Exempla and exemplarity, 1, 3, 20, 24, 26–27, 41, 42, 45, 50, 53, 55, 105, 224, 285, 321–22, 324–26, 327, 333–34, 336
  gender-specific exemplarity, 327–28
  moral examples, 118, 321
Ezzelino da Romano, 14, 45

Facio, Bartolomeo, 7, 42, 47
Faita, Marcantonio, 216
Fagon, Guy-Crescent, 364
Fanlo, Jean-Raymond, 226
Farnese, Alessandro, Cardinal, 50
Farnese Villa, 18, 324
Fedele, Angelo, father of Cassandra, 188
Fedele, Cassandra, 17, 22, 187–99
  associated with Camilla, 197
  hermaphroditic themes in the writing of, 197–98
  letters of, 189–99
  life of, 187–89
  sexuality, 191, 197
  use of diminutive language by, 193–96
  virtus and gravitas (male attributes) of, 191, 198
Federigo da Montefeltro, 43
Ficino, Marsilio, 167, 190
Figura, 224
Filelfo, Francesco, 190, 198
Filelfo, Giovanni Maria, 167
Finke, Laurie A., 187
Fischart, Johann, 176
Fisher, John, bishop of Rochester, 142, 149, 209
Flacius Illyricus, Matthias, 102, 103, 108, 119, 123
Florio, John, 288, 293, 295
Fortune, 45, 118, 140
Foucault, Michel, 8, 317
Fox, Alistair, 134
Foxe, John, 17, 23, 27, 140, 231, 235, 238, 243–82
  Acts and Monuments ("Book of Martyrs"), 243–82
  availability of, 252
  Catholic atrocities recounted in, 260–61
  chronological problems in, 269, 270
  fragmentation and unity of the text, 245–46
  influence of comedy in, 251–53

Foxe, John (*continued*)
  Acts and Monuments (*continued*)
    influence of hagiography on, 246–47
    influence of history on, 244–46
    "Kalender" of martyrs, 246
    mimesis in, 252
    persecution punished in, 257, 261, 262
    printing various editions of, 278–79
    romance elements in, 247–49
    use of running headers in, 245–46
    use of woodcuts in, 251, 260–61, 265–67
  conflicting authorial purposes in the writings of, 23
  dramatic works by, 247, 248
  narrative strategies of, 243, 248
  readership/audience, 244, 250, 251, 272
  theme of division in the writings of, 260–61
  theme of unity in the writings of, 257–60
  use of comparison by, 267–69
  use of metaphor by, 260, 261
  use of oral evidence by, 251, 271
Fragnito, Gigliola, 210
Frame, Donald, 288, 298
Francesco da Carrara, 9
Francis I, king of France, 322, 333
Francis II, king of France, 335
Franco, Veronica, 17
Franklin, Julian, 4
Fredegonde, queen, 322
Frederick, elector of the Palatinate, 120
Frederick, John, 118
Frederick the Wise, elector of Saxony, 99
Frey, Winfried, 174
Frith, John, 151
Fronde, the, 341, 343, 352, 355, 370
Frye, Northrop, 23, 277
Fueter, Eduard, 7

Fulvio, Andrea, 47
Funeral orations and sermons, 7, 20, 97–109, 322, 328, 331, 335
  biographical detail in, 100
  family background in, 102
  "Hauskreuz" ("the cross of family life") in, 20, 103
  See also *Leichenpredigten*

Gadamer, Hans-Georg, 3
Gaguin, Robert, 167
Galahad, 248, 249
Gallus, Nikolaus or Nicholas, 104, 106, 121, 123
Gardiner, Stephen, bishop of Winchester, 257
Garraty, John, 10
Gender, 197, 322, 326
Genre, 1–2, 4, 6, 7, 14, 243–44, 245, 321, 330
  generic distinctions, 8, 187
  imitation of genres, 244
  inversion of genre, 330
Georg, prince of Anhalt, 102, 105, 106
George of Trebizond, 137
Gerbelius, Nicolaus, 183
Gerschmann, Karl-Heinz, 175
Gesta, 11
Gherio, Filippo, 216
Ghiberti, Lorenzo, 64
Ghirlandaio, Domenico, 69, 72, 76
Giles of Viterbo, 46
Gillow, Joseph, 212
Gilmore, Myron, 137
Ginzburg, Carlo, 3
Giotto, 72
Giovio, Paolo, 5, 9, 15, 18, 19, 20, 39–53, 63, 324, 331
  biographies, 39–45
  impresa, 52–53
Glover, Robert, 271
Gnesio-Lutherans, 119, 125, 126
God, 97, 99, 101, 103, 118, 226, 227, 228, 231, 232, 234
  See also Word of God; Providence

Golden Age of art, 64
Golden Legend, 12, 65, 246
    See also Voragine, Jacobus de
Gonzaga, Gianfrancesco, lord of Mantua, 193, 194
Gonzaga of Mantua, House of, 189
Goubert, Pierre, 366
Gouws, John, 308
Gran, Heinrich, 164
Gratius, Ortwin, 21, 170–73, 176
Gravina, Pietro, 42
Greenblatt, Stephen, 3, 317
Gregorovius, Ferdinand, 46
Greville, Fulke, Lord Brooke, 24, 299–316
    construction of Sidney, 306, 309
    at the court of Elizabeth I, 299–300
    depiction of Elizabeth I, 302
    difficulties with genre, 310–12
    motives for writing *Life* of Sidney, 306–7
    relationship with Sidney, 306–7, 309–10
Grimani, Antonio, 45
Guevara, Antonio de, 139
Guicciardini, Francesco, 41, 48, 331
Guillén, Claudio, 169
Guy, John, 134, 146
Guy of Warwick, 278

Habermas, Jürgen, 336
Hackett, John, 149
Hagiography, 11–12, 15, 23, 98, 99, 209, 244, 246–47, 249, 272
Hahn, Reinhard, 174
Hall, Edward, 255, 279
Haller, William, 258
Hammer, Wilhelm, 115
Hampton, Timothy, 20, 41, 49, 325, 336
Hapsburg, House of, 342
Harding, Thomas, 280
Harold II, king of England, 271
Harpsfield, Nicholas, 134, 140, 141, 144, 206–9, 211, 259
Hayward, John, 15, 303

Hebrew scholarship, 105
Heerbrand, Jakob, 105, 107
Heffernan, Thomas, 2, 3, 11
Heidelberg, 120
Heldelin, Caspar, 102, 103, 104
Heller, Agnes, 6
Helmolt, Karl von, 125
Helt von Forchheim, Georg, 116, 118
Henderson, Judith, 128
Henry II, king of France, 335
Henry IV, king of England, 261
Henry IV, king of France, 341, 353, 366
Henry IV, Emperor, 245, 250
Henry VIII, king of England, 22, 45, 140, 146, 150, 152, 205–6, 207, 211, 267
Henry, Prince of Wales, 307
Herbert of Cherbury, Edward, Lord, 15
Hermaphrodism, 191, 197
Herodotus, 10
Heshusius (or Hesshus), Tileman, 106, 120–23, 125
Hessus, Eoban, 116, 117
Heywood, John, 140, 148, 151
Higden, Ranulf, 246
Historiography, 4
    Counter-reformation, 205
    French, sixteenth-century, 323
    humanist, 205
    positivist, 21, 22
    and romance, 250
History, 7, 9, 39, 40, 41, 43, 321, 323, 362
    ancient categories of, 135
    ecclesiastical, 244–47, 272
    historical scholarship, early modern, 4
    imaginary dialogue and speeches in, 135
    Renaissance understanding of, 175
    rhetoric in, 5, 56, 270
    "scientific" or "empirical," 5
Hitchcock, E.V., 143–44
Hochstraten, Jacob, 170, 171
Holy Spirit, the, 104, 108

Homer, 46, 105, 107
Homiletical theory, 100, 110
Hooper, John, Bishop, 253, 257, 268
Horace, 182
Horányi, Alexius, 206
Hosius, Stanislaus, cardinal, 211, 216–17
Hospitality, 279
Houel, Nicolas, 18, 25, 322–27, 329–33
Howard family, 301, 307
Humanistic-scholastic debates, 166
Humfrey, duke of Gloucester, 268
Humor, 176, 255–56, 273
Humors, theory of, 281, 294
Huppert, George, 4
Hutten, Ulrich von, 21, 164, 166, 170, 171, 173, 174, 175, 177
Hymn singing, 107

Ianziti, Gary, 16
Identity, 3
Imitation, artistic, 93, 244
Impresa, 52–53
Individualism, 6
Interpretive communities, 324
Intertextuality, 223, 224, 236, 238
Ion of Chios, 10
Irony, 4, 193, 256, 330
Isabella of Portugal, 322
Isabella of Spain, 190

James I, king of England, 300, 309, 314
Jameson, Fredric, 30
Jena, University of, 103
Jerome, St., 12
Jews, 105, 107, 171
John, elector of Saxony, 99
Jonas, Justus, 110
Jordan, Constance, 328, 329, 334
Judith, 327
Julius II, Pope, 71, 89

Kahn, Victoria, 41, 47
Kantorowicz, Ernst, 365, 372

Kaplan, Caren, 187
Karben, Victor von, 171
Kelley, Donald R., 4, 324
Kempe, Margery, 188
Kerrigan, William, 7
Kiernan, Michael, 283
King, John N., 265
Klebitz, Wilhelm, 120–21
Klinger, Linda, 50
Koestler, Arthur, 314
Könneker, Barbara, 164
Küchenlatein (kitchen Latin), 174

La Vallière, Louise de, 357, 368
LaCapra, Dominick, 3, 4, 5, 6, 115
Lafayette, Madame de, 343, 353–56
Lampridius, Aelius, 56
Lampson, Dominic, 34
Landino, Cristoforo, 64
Lanham, Richard, 5
Latimer, Hugh, Bishop, 253, 257, 264
Laudatio, 17
Laudatio funebris, 11
    See also Funeral orations and sermons
Laurence, St., 268
Law, T.G., 211
Le Blanc, Etienne, 327
Le Grand, Joachim, 213
Leichenpredigten, 20, 98
    See also Funeral orations and sermons
Leipzig Interim, the, 119
Leipzig, University of, 116
Lejeune, Philippe, 8
Leo X, Pope, 41, 44, 52
Leonardo da Vinci, 72, 77
Leoni of Arezzo, 86
Leto, Pomponio, 46
Letter books
    See Letter collections, humanist
Letter collections, humanist, 17, 21, 163–64, 167–69, 188, 189–91, 321

authorship and authenticity, difficulty in ascertaining, 169, 176
autobiographical tendencies of, 169, 177, 201
collections of fictional letters, 168
as forerunner to the essay and novel, 169
Letters, Renaissance manuals on the writing of, 167, 180
Letters of Obscure Men, 8, 21, 163–67
Liberal arts, 118
Life-writing, 1, 2, 6, 7, 10–19, 23, 42, 52, 67, 97, 187, 223, 321, 322, 323–24, 325, 353, 361
  ancient models of, 7
  Calvinist, 237
  correspondence of, and "real life," 3–4, 10, 125–26, 187
  exemplary, 321
  humanist, 13–15
  meditational writing as, 227–29
  moral/didactic function of, 1
  nonliterary forms of, 17–18
  Reformation, 224–25, 236–37
  Renaissance, 117, 323–24
  See also Autobiography; Biography; Lives
Lippincott, Kristin, 53
Lipsius, Justus, 24, 312, 313
  Lipsian constancy, 312–13
Lives, 1
  of artists, 2
  collections of, 13–15
  of emperors, 11
  life of the Virgin, 324
  of saints, 15, 246
  of scholars, 14
  of women, 321, 323, 330
Livy, 138
Lollards, 250, 261
Lord's Supper, 107, 120–22, 259
  koinonia, 121
  transubstantiation, 121, 259
Lot, 108

Louis IX, king of France, 327
Louis XIII, king of France, 334
Louis XIV, king of France, 25, 341–63
  as an absolute monarch, 342
  illness of, 344–46
Louise de Savoie, queen regent of France, 327
Lucian, 136
Lucretia, 327
Lupset, Thomas, 148
Luther, Martin, 15, 17, 97, 98, 99, 104, 106, 107, 108, 109, 117, 120, 124, 125, 126, 253
Lutherans and Lutheranism, 100–101, 102, 104, 105, 115, 119, 125
Lydgate, John, 13
Lyons, John, 50

Macaulay, Thomas Babington, 46
MacDonald, Michael, 27–28
Machiavelli, Niccolò, 26–27, 31, 139, 152, 305
  on Cosimo de' Medici, 8
  Istorie fiorentine, 8
  La vita di Castruccio Castracani, 13, 139
Maffei, Bernardino, cardinal, 209
Magdeburg Centuries, 97, 98, 244, 271
Maguire, John, 134
Major, Georg, 105, 106, 120
Malory, Thomas, 250
Man, Thomas, 263
Mancini, Marie, 25, 341–63
Mander, Karel van, 34
Manichaeanism, 108
Manlius, Johannes, 120
Mantegna, Andrea, 72
Manuzio, Paolo, 210
Mapelli, Gian-Maria, husband of Cassandra Fedele, 189
Marcellus II, Pope, 211
Mariá Teresa, infanta (Queen Marie-Thérèse), 341, 360
Marin, Louis, 25, 372

Marius, Richard, 134
Martelli, Ruberto, 70
Martin, Alfred von, 6
Martin, Daniel, 296, 297
Martin, Henri-Jean, 371
Martyrology, 7, 22, 23, 26, 98, 103, 227, 234
Martyrs, 26, 231, 232, 233, 235–37, 281–82
Marvell, Andrew, 316
Mary I, queen of England, 243
Mathesius, Lorenz, 97, 103, 108
Maucroix, François, 213
Maurice of Saxony, 118
Maurists, 12
Mazarin, Jules, cardinal, 25, 341–63, 366
   correspondence of, 342, 346–53
   rhetoric of disease in the Mancini affair, 347–48, 350
Medici, Alessandro de', 49
Medici, Catherine de', queen-regent of France, 24–25, 321–34
Medici, Cosimo "Il Vecchio" de', 8, 71, 78
Medici, Cosimo I de', duke of Florence, 39, 52, 71, 213
Medici family, 78
Medici, Lorenzo "Il Magnifico" de', 8, 71, 73, 74, 144, 190
Medici, Marie de', 334
Melanchthon, Philip, 12, 20, 22, 97, 98, 100, 101, 106, 109, 115–26, 145
   Loci communes, 118
   relationship with Luther, 124, 125
   See also Camerarius, Joachim
Memorial verses, 146
Memory, 303, 305
   artificial and natural, 284–87, 297
Mencel, Hieronymus, 101, 104, 106, 108
Merula, Giorgio, 40
Mesnard, Pierre, 164
Metaphor, 4, 104, 175, 258, 260
Metonymy, 4, 9

Michelangelo Buonarroti, 20
   artistic autonomy of, 69
   compared to Donatello in Vasari's *Lives*, 69–90
Microcosm, Renaissance representations of, 23
Microstoria, 3
Mimesis
   in Foxe, 252, 264
   "realist mimesis," 305, 306
Mini, Antonio, assistant to Michelangelo, 87
Miracles, 246, 247
Modernity, 23
Momigliano, Arnaldo, 4, 54
Monluc, Blaise de, 16
Montaigne, Michel Eyquem de, 23, 24, 283–95
   consubstantiality of essays and self, 287, 289, 293
   distinction between body and self, 292
Montpensier, duchess of, 343, 353, 356–58
Morandi, G.B., 210
More, Cresacre, 141–42
More, Thomas, Sir, 8, 21, 133–53, 166, 209
Morice, Ralph, 253
Mörlin, Joachim, 122
Morlin, Maximillian, 129
Morone, Cardinal, 211
Mossellanus, Peter, 116
Motteville, Madame de, 343, 345, 353, 357–61
Mozley, J. F., 274
Musaeus, Simon, 101, 108
Mutianus Rufus, Conrad, 170
Mylius, Georg, 105

Nadel, Ira, 4
Narrationes, 117
Naunton, Robert, 309
Nausea, Frederick, 151
Navagero, Bernardo, Cardinal, 210
Nedham, Marchamont, 316

Neostoicism, 23, 312
  See also Stoics
Nestor, 105
Netherlandish art, and life-writing, 14
Neuenahr, Hermann von, count, 113, 164
Neuss, Heinrich von, 183
New communitarians, 6
Newman, John, of Maidstone, 259
Nifo, Agostino, 48
Nogarola, Isotta, 191
Nominalists, 175
Norbrook, David, 311, 315
North, Thomas, 155
Novel, 169, 273
Novick, Peter, 5, 10
Nuremberg, 116
Nussbaum, Felicity, 187

Oestreich, Gerhard, 320
Oldcastle, John, Sir, 250, 265
Olney, James, 187
Ong, Walter J., 250
Opitz, Josua, 104, 106
Oral/textual relationship, 225
Oration, 169
Origen, 271
Orsini, Vicino, 18
Osiander, Lukas, 102, 105, 108
Otto of Freising, 244
Overfield, James H., 163, 164

Paden, William, 237
Palmer, Julius, 265–66
Panvinio, Onofrio, 15
Pasquier, Estienne, 331
Pate, Richard, 143, 147
Patin, Guy, French physician, 364, 365
Patronage, 20, 79–82, 324
Patterson, Annabel, 275, 320
Paul III, Pope, 189
Paul, St., 108
Pauline-Augustinian world view, 280
Pellegrino, Gaspare, 30
Penelope, 328

Percival, 248
Perey, Lucien, 368
Periodization, problems of, 9–10, 23, 224
Personality, 49, 51
  distinguished from character, 60
Persons, Robert, 212, 280
Perugino, Pietro, 76
Peter of Ravenna, 171, 172
Petrarch (Francesco Petrarca), 9, 13, 16, 47, 166, 168
Pfefferkorn, Johannes, 170, 171, 172
Pfeffinger, Johann, 97, 103, 108
Philip of Hesse, landgrave, 120
Philippists, 125
Phillips, Thomas, 214
Philophilippus, Timotheus, 121, 122
Philoxenus of Cythera, 43–44
Piccolomini, Enea Silvio (Pope Pius II), 14, 47, 167, 190
Pico della Mirandola, Giovanni, 167
Piero della Francesca, 43
Piety, 100, 108
Pigman, G. W. III, 275
Pilgrimage of Grace, 148
Pio, Battista, 50
Pius II, Pope
  See Piccolomini, Enea Silvio
Plato, 150–51, 192, 286, 328
Pliny the Elder, 64
Pliny the Younger, 43, 167
Plutarch, 11, 19, 39, 40, 45, 47, 136, 285, 289
  Plutarchan exemplary life, 13, 308
  "Plutarchan" models for writing, 25, 39, 49, 51
Poach, Andreas, 105, 106, 107
Poetics, 6
Poetry, 305
Pole, Reginald, Cardinal, 8, 22, 205–15
  encounter with Henry VIII at Westminster, 206–9
  manuscripts of, 210
Polemic, 21, 119, 209, 223
  confessional polemics, 100

388   Index

Politian
  See Poliziano, Angelo
Poliziano, Angelo, 74, 145, 167, 190, 192, 197, 198
Pollen, J. H., 212
Polley, Margery, 260
Pollini, Girolamo, 212, 213
Polybius, 135
Polycarp, St., 245, 268
Pontano, Giovanni, 42, 49
Pope-Henessey, John, 73, 75
Porta, Conrad, 106, 108, 109
Positivism, 4
  See also Historiography, positivist
Predestination, 223
Print and printing press, 17, 167, 211, 250–51
Priuli, Alvise, 210
Progress, artistic, 64, 69, 90
Propaganda, 166, 346
Prosopopeia, 187, 198
Providence, 99, 109, 245, 255
Puritans, 237
Pye, Benjamin, 214–15

Quentell press, 171, 172
Querini, Angelo Maria, 206
Quintilian, 46, 47–48, 117, 119, 308, 326–27
  importance of historical parallels, 326
  precepts for praise and blame, 47–48

Rabelais, François, 176
Racine, Jean, 357, 371
Ralegh, Walter, Sir, 27, 304
Ranum, Orest, 25
Raphael, 65, 76
Rastell, William, 151
Ratzeburger, Matthaeus, 107
Reader response to texts, 127, 244
Realists, 175
Redemption, Protestant idea of, 235
Reed, A. W., 151
Reformation, 10, 12, 23, 26, 98, 176

Reformation Parliament, 151
Rembrandt, 18
Renaissance, 3, 6, 7, 9, 10, 11, 19, 20, 21, 23, 24, 51, 310
Renée, Amédée, 367
Resurrection, 226, 233
Reuchlin, Johannes, 163–64, 166, 170, 172, 176
Rey, Eusebio, 212
Rhenanus, Beatus, 166
Rhetoric, 3, 5, 6, 12, 16, 20, 21, 46, 50, 97, 100, 115, 117, 119, 135, 284, 321, 324, 325
  autobiographical, 228
  classical tradition of, 135–37
  demonstrativum, 100
  dialogismos, 138
  epideictic, 5
  humanist tradition of, 98, 137–38
  progymnastica, tradition of, 20, 119
  Reformation, 227
  rhetorical invention and distortions, 138–39
  sophismata, 123
Ribadeneira, Pedro de, 212
Richelieu, Armand Jean du Plessis, Cardinal, 371
Ridley, Gloucester, 214
Ridley, Nicholas, Bishop, 140, 253, 257, 264, 268
Rilievo schiacciato, 74
Ro: Ba:, biographer of Sir Thomas More, 140–41
Rogers, John, 265
Romance, 23, 154, 247–50, 252, 272, 353
Rood of Dovercourt, the, 267
Roper, William, 21, 28, 133–34, 139–53
Roscoe, William, 57
Roth, Heinrich, 104
Rubel, Veré, 146
Rummel, Erika, 166

Sabellico, Marcantonio, 190
Sadoleto, Jacopo, 47

St. Bartholomew's Day Massacre, 330
St. German, Christopher, 149, 151
St. Peter's Basilica, 87–88
Saint-Simon, Claude de, 368
Saints, 88, 102, 107, 109, 246, 247, 321, 322
Sallust, 138
Salutati, Coluccio, 33, 167
Samuel, prophet, 108
Samuel, Robert, 261
Sander, Nicholas, 211, 213, 217, 221
Sansovino, Francesco, 188
Santucci, Agostino, 180
Sappho, 192
Sarah, 328
Sarcerius, Erasmus, 105, 121
Sartre, Jean-Paul, 30
Sarto, Andrea del, 65
Satire, 21, 166, 169, 173, 176
Saunders or Sanders, Laurence, 268
Savile, Henry, Sir, 284
Sawtrey, William, 261
Scaliger, Joseph Justus, 17
Scaliger, Julius Caesar, 22, 197
Scannapeco, Girolamo, 42
Scheible, Heinz, 126
Schellhorn, Johann Georg, 216
Schiffman, Zachary Sayre, 28
Schlüsselburg, Conrad, 103, 106
Scholasticism, 21, 170, 173
Schongauer, Martin, 73
Selden, John, 17
Self, sense of, 4, 9, 22, 228, 236, 237
Selnecker, Nikolaus, 105
Semiramis, queen, 328
Seneca, 167, 285, 311
  Senecan epistle, 310
  Senecan moral philosophy, 45
Sententiae, 283, 285, 289, 298
Sermons, 98
  See also Funeral sermons
Sextus Empiricus, 135
Seymour, Edward, duke of Somerset, 206, 268
Sforza, Francesco, 39, 40

Sforza, Lodovico ("Il Moro"), 195, 198
Sforza, Muzio Attendolo, 39, 40
Sforza family, 189
Shakespeare, William, 248
Sherry, Richard, 147
Sidney, Mary, countess of Pembroke, 303
Sidney, Philip, Sir, 24, 299–316
  contrasting of poets and historians, 305
Silberschlag, Georg, 104, 106
Simoncelli, Paolo, 37, 205
Simonetta, Giovanni, 40
Simons, Joseph, 212
Sin, 99, 102, 227
  Seven Deadly Sins, 172
Singleton, Charles S., 66
Sleidan, Johannes, 213, 222, 244
Smalcald War, 117
Smith, Sidonie, 187
Soderini, Piero, 82, 95
Southern, Richard, Sir, 249
Spartianus, Aelius, 56
Spenser, Edmund, 273
Spiegel, Gabrielle M., 278
Sponde, Jean de, 22, 227, 228, 237
Squarcione, 72
Stähelin, Friedrich, 118, 120
Staphylus, Friedrich, 120
Stapleton, Thomas, 141–42
Starn, Randolph, 32
Stauffer, Richard, 224
Stella, Gianfrancesco, 216
Stoics, 118
  friendship, Stoic concept of, 118
  Stoicism, 20, 24, 118, 312
  See also Neostoicism
Stossel, John, 129
Strobel, Theodore, 127
Strozzi, Ruberto, 87
Subjection, 24
  "rhetoric of subjection," 300, 317
Subjectivity, 24
Suetonius, 11, 19, 40, 47
  Suetonian tradition, 13, 65

Sulpicia, 192
Summers, David, 95
Supernatural, in hagiography, 12
Susanna, 328
Sutherland, Nicola M., 339
Symonds, John Addington, 46
Synecdoche, 4, 9, 53
Szczucki, Lech, 210

Tasso, Torquato, 247, 358, 369
Taylor, Charles, 49, 225
Taylor, Rowland, 259
Tegrimi, Niccolò, 13
Tertullian, 260
Tham, Augustin, 101
Theology, 223
Theon, 135
Thomists, 175
Thucydides, 11, 138
Time, literary distortions of, 154
Timothy, St., 108
Tomasini, Jacopo Filippo, 188, 197
Tomasso de' Cavalieri, 86
Tongern, Arnold von, 170, 171
Tottel's Miscellany, 146
Tragedy, 6–7
Tragicomedy, 7
Transubstantiation
  See Lord's Supper
Tropes, 4, 196, 248, 258
Truber, Primus, 108
Truchsess, Otto, 217
Truth and fiction, 135
  See also Biography; Rhetoric
Tübingen, University of, 116, 124
Tudor interlude, the, 249
Tyms, William, 260
Tyndale, William, 143, 268
Typology, 78, 108, 264–65

Valerius Maximus, 7
Valla, Lorenzo, 56, 167
Vallot, Antoine, physician to Louis XIV, 344, 364
Varchi, Benedetto, 213

Vasari, Giorgio, 14, 19–20, 34, 50–51, 63–90
  comparison of Michelangelo and Donatello, 66–90
Veneziano, Domenico, 51
Vergerio, Pier Paolo, 41, 217
Verrocchio, Andrea del, 72
Vespasiano da Bisticci, 14
Villani, Filippo, 14
Villiers, George, duke of Buckingham, 301
Virgil, 197
Virginity, 191
Virtue and virtues, 106, 109, 198–99, 306, 326
Viruli (or Virulus), Carolus, 167
Visconti, Filippo Maria, 39
Vives, Juan Luis, 148
Vocation, 109
Voltaire, 368
Voragine, Jacobus de, 12, 65
  See also Golden Legend

Wallace, William E., 28
Walsingham, Francis, Sir, 302
Wars of Religion, 317, 325
Webbe, Rowland and Richard, 272
Wendorf, Richard, 8
White, Hayden, 3, 4, 5, 277
White, Rawlins, 261
Whittle, Thomas, 254
Wigand, Johann, 103, 105, 107
William I (the Conqueror), king of England, 271
William of Malmesbury, 12
William of Orange, 302
Wilson, Thomas, 146
Winsheim, Veit, 106
Wittenberg, 104, 105, 109, 116
Wolsey, Thomas, Cardinal and archbishop of York, 253, 279
Women, 6
  and autobiography, 17, 198, 201, 321
  education of, 148
  female martyrs, 279

as humanists, 189, 200
metaphor of garden for, 192
perceived feebleness of the female body, 196
social perceptions of educated, 191, 197
tropes regarding, 196
women's work, 197
Woodcuts, 17, 23, 251, 281
Word of God, 100, 101, 228, 230, 233

Writing
as action, 308
and sex, 191, 197, 231

Xenophon, 7, 11, 325–26

Yates, Frances A., 267

Zenobia of Palmyra, 148, 328–29, 338
Zwingli, Ulrich, 246